Luminos is the Open Access monograph publishing program from UC Press. Luminos provides a framework for preserving and reinvigorating monograph publishing for the future and increases the reach and visibility of important scholarly work. Titles published in the UC Press Luminos model are published with the same high standards for selection, peer review, production, and marketing as those in our traditional program. www.luminosoa.org

A

BOOK

The Philip E. Lilienthal imprint
honors special books
in commemoration of a man whose work
at University of California Press from 1954 to 1979
was marked by dedication to young authors
and to high standards in the field of Asian Studies.
Friends, family, authors, and foundations have together
endowed the Lilienthal Fund, which enables UC Press
to publish under this imprint selected books
in a way that reflects the taste and judgment
of a great and beloved editor.

The publisher and the University of California Press Foundation
gratefully acknowledge the generous support of the
Philip E. Lilienthal Imprint in Asian Studies, established
by a major gift from Sally Lilienthal.

Bridging Two Worlds

Bridging Two Worlds

Comparing Classical Political Thought and Statecraft in India and China

---

Edited by

Amitav Acharya, Daniel A. Bell, Rajeev Bhargava, and Yan Xuetong

UNIVERSITY OF CALIFORNIA PRESS

B Berggruen
Institute

University of California Press
Oakland, California

Suggested citation: Acharya, A., Bell, D. A., Bhargava, R. and
Xuetong, Y. (eds.) *Bridging Two Worlds: Comparing Classical Political
Thought and Statecraft in India and China*. Oakland: University
of California Press, 2023.
DOI: https://doi.org/10.1525/luminos.135

Library of Congress Cataloging-in-Publication Data
Names: Acharya, Amitav, editor. | Bell, Daniel (Daniel A.), 1964– editor. |
    Bhargava, Rajeev, editor. | Yan, Xuetong, editor.
Title: Bridging two worlds : comparing classical political thought and
    statecraft in India and China / edited by Amitav Acharya,
    Daniel A. Bell, Rajeev Bhargava, and Yan Xuetong.
Other titles: Great transformations ; 4.
Description: Oakland, California : University of California Press, [2023] |
    Series: Great transformations ; 4 | Includes bibliographical references
    and index.
Identifiers: LCCN 2022014516 (print) | LCCN 2022014517 (ebook) |
    ISBN 9780520390980 (paperback) | ISBN 9780520390997 (ebook)
Subjects: LCSH: India—Foreign relations—21st century. | China—Foreign
    relations—21st century. | India—Politics and government—21st century. |
    China—Politics and government—21st century.
Classification: LCC DS446.3 .B65 2023 (print) | LCC DS446.3 (ebook) |
    DDC 327.54051—dc23/eng/20220628
LC record available at https://lccn.loc.gov/2022014516
LC ebook record available at https://lccn.loc.gov/2022014517

32   31   30   29   28   27   26   25   24   23
10   9   8   7   6   5   4   3   2   1

CONTENTS

ACKNOWLEDGMENTS

We are most grateful to the Berggruen Institute, which provided generous funding and support for the whole multiyear project. We are also grateful to Shandong University's School of Political Science and Public Administration, which hosted the first workshop, and to the Kaifeng Foundation, which cofunded that workshop. Thanks also to Tsinghua University's Department of International Relations, which hosted and cofunded the second workshop. We are also grateful to the Parekh Institute of Indian Thought, CSDA in Delhi, which was due to host the third workshop that had to be moved from India to Thailand due to international tensions at the time. The Berggruen Institute's center at Peking University was particularly helpful: we would like to thank Song Bing, Li Xiaojiao, Shelley Hu, Sun Xinwei and Jennifer Bourne. Liu Yuhan helped with the workshop in Qingdao and Chang Jie with the workshop in Beijing. We are also very grateful to Craig Calhoun and Nils Gilman, the two editors of the Great Transformations series with the University of California Press, to Naomi Schneider, our editor at the University of California Press, to Summer Farah and Francisco Reinking, who helped with the production process, and to Paul Tyler for copyediting. Finally, we would like to thank all the scholars who participated in our three workshops with excellent papers and comments that helped to shape the contributions to this book: Julian Baggini, Navnita Behera, Li Li, Siddharth Mallavarapu, Sun Xuefeng, Wang Binfan, Wang Rihua, Zhang Shulan, and Zhao Tingyang. We are particularly grateful to three anonymous referees who wrote long and constructive comments on an earlier draft of the manuscript.

Setting the Stage, Part I

Overview of the Project

Daniel A. Bell

In June 2020, Indian and Chinese troops fought each other in harsh mountain conditions along the Sino-Indian border, resulting in the deaths of dozens of soldiers. Such skirmishes have flared up since the bloody war between China and India in 1962 that left unresolved border conflicts (in contrast, China has peacefully resolved territorial conflicts with eleven of its other neighbors). Notwithstanding economic ties—today China is India's second largest trading partner—the risk of another full-blown war is ever-present. In February 2021, India and China agreed to pull back troops from the Pangong Lake border hotspot, but tensions remain high, and political and military leaders in the two countries seem to regard each other as natural enemies. There are few cultural and academic exchanges between the two great Asian powers and even economic ties seem to be worsening, with India imposing bans on TikTok, WeChat, and other Chinese apps.

It wasn't always the case. India and China were both members of the nonaligned movement in the 1950s, and Indian prime minister Jawaharlal Nehru went so far as to say that India's foreign policy with China should be based on "brotherhood." In the more distant past, Nehru's ideal may have been closer to the reality. The two countries lived in peaceful coexistence and cultural ties were deep. Buddhism spread peacefully from India to China, to the point that it has become far more influential in China. In the 1920s, the poet Tagore deeply marked Chinese intellectual culture when he visited China. The great Chinese intellectual Liang Shuming regarded Indian culture as the apex of human moral growth. And the learning was mutual: India benefited from China's paper, gunpowder, and silk. Perhaps China's greatest gift to India was the preservation of Buddhist texts, accomplished by Chinese and Indian translators living and working in China. After Buddhism disappeared in India and original texts were lost or destroyed by invaders, these Chinese translations preserved Buddhist *sutras*, which could then be retranslated for Indians. As Amitav Acharya notes, Buddhism would have been lost to Indians without Chinese help, just as Arabs preserved Greek texts in science and philosophy that would otherwise have been lost.

Our project aims to recover the deep respect and mutual learning between the two great Asian powers with thousands of years of history and such dynamic and diverse cultures. Such respect can improve political ties between India and China. But our aims are primarily academic. The current debates about international political thought and statecraft are based mainly on theories in international relations derived from the Western experience(s). What's missing in these debates are the contributions from ancient Chinese and Indian thinkers. Both India and China had profound political thinkers who developed innovative thoughts and theories of interstate relations that may still have lessons for today. Such political thoughts are not well known outside of China and India. And there is hardly any engagement between intellectuals from India and China.

We should state at the outset that it is controversial to use the terms "India" and "China" to refer to the distant past. As Benjamin Elman and Sheldon Pollock put it, "The countries, nations, regions, or civilizations—depending on how we define these apparently simple but actually quite complex terms—that we now identify by the names China and India have long and complicated histories."[1] The histories of "India" and "China" do indeed have sharp discontinuities, but they also have surprising, millennia-long continuities. Given the complexities, we do not attempt to survey the whole of political thought in both countries/civilizations/political spaces. We limited our focus to "classical" ideas about political thought and statecraft, meaning that (1) they emerged in ancient political spaces that we now call China and India and (2) set the terms for much political debate in subsequent Chinese and Indian history. In China, the "hundred schools of thought" emerged in the Spring and Autumn (770–476 BCE) and Warring States (475–221 BCE) periods, before the country was unified by Qin Shi Huangdi, the self-proclaimed "First Emperor" of China. This period produced complex and profound thoughts and theories about interstate relations, including Confucianism and Legalism, the two most influential schools of political thought in subsequent Chinese political history (Legalism influenced political practices but it was buried as an official ideology for about two thousand years, until it was revived by Chairman Mao in the twentieth century). The two most prominent thinkers of the Confucian school in this period were Confucius (Kongzi) and Mencius (Mengzi), who tended to defend what we would call "rule by soft power" (moral example, education, ritual, persuasion, concern for the people, etc.). Han Feizi synthesized the Legalist tradition that emphasized what we would refer to as "hard power" (building up a strong state, military might, harsh laws, rule by fear, etc.). Xunzi was influential in both traditions. All these thinkers are discussed in depth in our book. In ancient India, two influential schools of political thought—Brahmanical Vedic (subsumed later by the term "Hindu") thought with its emphasis on rule by eternal law and morality (*Dharma*) and Kautilya's emphasis on hard-nosed political realism and self-interested foreign policy—similarly emerged in a period of turmoil and interstate warfare, although Ashoka temporarily led a unified "empire" and defended values of respect for diverse communities and forms of life, broadly influenced by Buddha's teachings. These three traditions set the terms for much political thought and action in subsequent Indian history, although Kautilya's *Arthasastra* disappeared from official discourse for about fourteen hundred years until it was (literally) rediscovered in the early twentieth century. All these political traditions from ancient India are discussed in depth in our book.

Why bother recovering political traditions from the distant past? The most obvious reason is that these ancient schools of thought offer rich and profound ways of thinking about politics and statecraft and explicitly or implicitly shape much political debate in India and China, similar to the way rich and profound ancient Greek and Judeo-Christian schools of thought set the terms for much political debate in subsequent "Western" history. Just as, say, Augustine's ideas about just war influenced "universal" Christian thinking about just war, so Mencius's ideas about morally justified warfare influenced Confucian thinking about morally justified warfare, and it is worth asking in both cases to what extent the theories have universal value, to what extent the ideals influenced government policies in history, and to what extent they ought to influence policies in the future. In the same vein, the Thucydides Trap is one way of thinking about conflict between states, but Kautilya's insights on forging alliances with the enemy of my enemy may also have lasting value, perhaps more so. At the very least, we should be open to the possibility that hitherto-neglected ancient Indian and Chinese ideas can enrich contemporary thinking about political theory and international relations.

Needless to say, we do not mean to draw direct implications from the past to the present. Many factors other than ancient ideas shape foreign policy thinking and decision-making in modern societies. Capitalism, nationalism, and new technologies set new problems and agendas that could not have been anticipated by ancient thinkers. Still, there may be lessons for today. We discuss thoughts and theories about politics that emerged mainly in what Karl Jaspers famously called the "Axial Age" (ca. eighth to third century BCE): whether in Greece, China, India, and Persia, old traditions and communal ties broke down, leading to social transformations and political chaos, with the consequence that brilliant thinkers from around the globe developed new theories and ways of thinking meant to address new challenges and ways of life. At the same time, proto-modern institutions, such as a complex and meritocratic bureaucratic system, emerged in political contexts such as China. Today, arguably, we are undergoing another period of great social and political transformations, and some of the ideas and institutions that emerged from the "Axial Age" may offer solutions for today's challenges as well (hence we appreciate the opportunity to be published in the "Great Transformations" series by the University of California Press).

Why bring classical Chinese and Indian thoughts and theories about politics and statecraft into dialogue with each other? Here, too, there are compelling reasons. It is striking that Indian and Chinese ideas about politics, no matter how diverse and influenced by the rest of the world and no matter how much interaction between China and India for two or more millennia in other domains, emerged and developed in what appears to be relative isolation from each other, with the possible exception of Buddhism. The rich and diverse Confucian tradition(s) had almost zero impact in India, and the rich and diverse Hindu tradition(s) had almost zero impact in China until the twentieth century. But it is not too late for mutual learning. The gaps and problems in Chinese political traditions can be enriched by engaging with and learning from thoughts and theories in the Indian traditions, and vice versa. We encouraged our contributors to think about what can be learned from the political thoughts of the other country's traditions that discuss similar themes and topics. There is a more practical/political reason for mutual engagement. As we will see, ancient Chinese and Indian ideas continue to be influential in contemporary political debates in China and India and inform diplomatic thinking and policy-making. So Chinese thinkers can learn about what influences thinking about political thought and statecraft in contemporary India, and Indian thinkers can learn about what influences thinking about political thought and statecraft in contemporary China. Cooperation and competition between two great Asian powers will inevitably impact international relations and political futures in Asia and the rest of the world. Deeper mutual understanding can form the basis for mutual appreciation and friendship, or at least help to avoid clashes based on misunderstandings.

In short, there is a dire need to bring the thoughts and theories of profound political thinkers from ancient India and China into dialogue with each other, as well as to think about implications for today's world. This multiyear project aims to remedy this gap. In 2017, the four editors of this book met at Schwarzman College (Tsinghua University, Beijing), and we realized that there was a need for a project that systematically compares classical international political thought from India and China. We are pleased that recent books compare China and India in different ways: the Sheldon Pollock and Benjamin Elman edited volume, *What China and India Once Were*, compares histories of different domains in India and China from the early modern period (ca. 1500–1800) and the Rajiv Ranjan and Guo Changgang edited volume, *China and South Asia*, looks at the changing dynamics and regional powers plays between contemporary China and South Asia.[2] Other books explore classic works from the two great and diverse Asian civilizations, and they are sometimes compared with classic texts in international political thinking from the West, but no book-length manuscript systematically compares classic works in political thought from India and China with each other. So we launched and conceptualized this project with generous support from the Berggruen Institute. From 2017 to 2019, we brought together leading political theorists of international thought for workshops held in China, India, and Thailand. We asked experts in Chinese political theory and international relations to write about the contributions of ancient Chinese theorists, and we asked experts in Indian political theory and international relations to write about the contributions of ancient Indian theorists. We also invited our contributors to engage with insights from the "other" philosophical tradition and to draw implications for political thinking and international relations theory as well as some policy implications for the modern world.

We held three workshops that resulted in this book. The dialogues coalesced along seven leading themes in international relations theory and global political thought: methodology of studying history and philosophy of interstate relations; moral leadership; amoral realism; empire; just war; diplomacy; and balancing, hegemony, and mandalas. These themes informed classical political thinking in India and China help us to make sense of the present, and they serve to structure our book. Each of the seven sections has an essay by a specialist on ancient Indian political thinking paired with an essay by a specialist on ancient Chinese political thinking. The essays are the product of a multiyear engagement and dialogue. The essays on ancient Chinese political thinking were presented at the Shandong University workshop in 2017, with comments by specialists in ancient Indian political thinking. The essays on ancient Indian political thinkers were presented in Bangkok in 2018 (we had to move the workshop from India to Thailand due to international tensions between India and China at the time), with comments by specialists in ancient Chinese political thinking. The final workshop at Tsinghua University in 2019 involved presentations by experts in both ancient Chinese and Indian political thinking, and we asked presenters to discuss what they had learned from the other "side" over the course of the multiyear exchanges and to draw implications for the theory and practice of contemporary international relations. The essays were further refined over the next year. This overview draws links and implications that are not always explicit in the essays themselves.

METHODOLOGY

The first section focuses on methodological issues. How should we study ancient ideas of interstate relations from ancient India and China? How can the two ancient civilizations be compared? Is it possible to draw implications for the contemporary world from ideas developed in a radically different time and context? The section leads off with Patrick Olivelle's essay. Olivelle—professor of Sanskrit and Indian religions at the University of Texas at Austin—warns against the dangers of "essentialism." There is no "essential" and unchanging Indian (or Chinese) thinking. Ancient Indian thinkers were extremely diverse and each thinker must be discussed in his specific context: who was he or she addressing and why. The terms need to be translated in ways that avoid misunderstanding generated by modern concepts. For example, the terms usually translated as "state" in ancient India refer to small political communities led by a king in a constant state of warfare (the empire of Ashoka is an exception), in contrast to imperial China where the political community was usually a huge territory governed by a complex bureaucracy. Nor does it make much sense to refer to an "Indian" tradition since the thinkers held such radically different ideas over time and space. Olivelle illustrates his argument by contrasting the ideas of Ashoka, the idealist monarch in the third century BCE; Kautilya, the "realist" political advisor in the first century CE; and Manu, the defender of Brahminism in the second century CE who attempted to defend an international order based on *dharma* (often translated as "moral law") that transcends any particular polity. Olivelle cautiously and tentatively draws implications for the modern world, noting Ashoka's idea that moral foreign policy involves the provision of medical knowledge and medicinal plants abroad (the ancient equivalent, perhaps, of sharing vaccines with other states) and Manu's idea of punishments for planetary ecological crimes and harm to animals.

Olivelle's dialogue partner is Roger Ames, humanities chair professor at Peking University in Beijing. Ames has often been criticized for "essentializing" Chinese philosophy in his efforts to show what is unique about Chinese philosophy and how it differs from thinking generated in other contexts. But Ames criticizes the language of "essentialism" itself as inappropriate to understand Chinese philosophy: the different Chinese thinkers, no matter what their orientations, did not adhere to a worldview of "essences" that stands apart and above the ever-changing empirical world. Such Platonic and Christian notions—which may be inherited from earlier Indian metaphysics—are absent from ancient Chinese thinking that assumed a world of constant change. Nor is there anything wrong with generalizing from particular ideas and concepts in Chinese history if the aim is to show contrasts with influential concepts in other traditions, so long as the cultural "translator" is self-conscious about the risks of losing sight of internal diversity in the particular culture. Moreover, historical accuracy matters. The pure normative philosopher might draw implications for the modern world even if it distorts history. But Ames tries to be as accurate as possible in his analysis (and translation) of what thinkers said in the past, while recognizing that the "translator" can never completely transcend his or her own context and field of interpretation. At the end of his essay, Ames invokes the ancient Chinese idea of *tianxia* (often translated as "All-under-heaven") to make sense of the ideal informing China's Belt and Road Initiative (BRI). *Tianxia* is respectful of diversity and assumes an interdependence of "heaven" and people. In practice, it means a "win-win" scenario with economic benefits for all participants and cultural learning and improvement in ever-changing mutual relations, in contrast to the universal and self-sufficient idea of a "*dharma*" that never changes in time and space. Ames recognizes that there is a large gap between the ideal of *tianxia* and the reality of BRI, but the ideal can and should be employed as a standard to judge success and failure in reality.

What is clear from the dialogue between Olivelle and Ames is that they have converged to a certain extent from radically different starting methodological viewpoints. Olivelle defends the method of the political historian, similar to the

Quentin Skinner school in contextual political theory: it is most important to place thinkers in their context, and to trace in great detail who said what to whom and why. Particularity matters more than generality. Ames defends the method of the normative philosopher who looks at thinkers from ancient China to show the contrast with other civilizations and to draw lessons for today. But they are both cultural pluralists committed to better appreciation and respect for the world's diverse cultures. Both recognize that there are continuities and commonalities (and priorities) that may be distinctive to particular traditions. They both converge on the point that generalizations can be appropriate if they are done self-consciously and in ways that do not flatten the contours of history or marginalize dissident viewpoints in particular traditions. And both thinkers draw thought-provoking implications for the behaviors of states in relation to each other in the contemporary world.

POLITICAL LEADERSHIP

The next theme discusses the role of political leadership in international relations. International relations theorists in the West tend to fall into two "camps": one emphasizes economic and military power in explaining outcomes in international relations and the other emphasizes the role of ideas and ideals. Missing, however, is the role of political leadership: To what extent do different kinds of political leaders affect change in international relations? Yan Xuetong, dean of the Institute of International Relations at Tsinghua University in Beijing, has formulated a theory arguing that political leadership is the key "independent variable" that can help explain the rise and fall of great powers (see his works *Ancient Chinese Thought, Modern Chinese Power* and *Leadership and the Rise of Great Powers*).[3] Yan argues for a rigorous scientific theory, "moral realism," that would be appropriate for the modern world and is directly inspired by ancient Chinese political thinkers, especially the ancient Confucian thinker Xunzi (313–238 BCE).

Yan's essay compares Xunzi's thought on interstate politics with that of Kautilya (370–283 BCE). Both thinkers lived in an era of incessant interstate warfare and both wrote the most systematic political theory treatises of their time (Kautilya's thought is more commonly compared with that of Han Feizi—see Xu's chapter in our book—but Yan argues that Han Feizi did not say much about interstate political thought, unlike Xunzi). Their theories, however, are substantially different. As a method, Xunzi draws on history to support his points, while Kautilya's *Arthasastra* uses deductive logic. Xunzi argues for an ideal humane authority who rules with compassion and unifies the political world primarily by means of moral power, whereas Kautilya argues for the need to expand one's territory by means of aggressive warfare and such "Machiavellian" tactics as extensive spying networks that plant lies and sow dissension in enemy states. What they have in common, however, is that both offer proposals for dealing with the nonideal political world.

In Xunzi's case, he has good things to say about the imperfect "hegemon" who can form alliances with other states and is strategically reliable in the sense that he keeps his promises to friends. Kautilya is more cynical: "peace" alliances with other states can and should be broken once they are no longer in the interests of the state with more power. More importantly, from Yan's point of view, both Xunzi and Kautilya argue for the importance of political leadership: a leader, working with capable ministers, can literally make or break a state in an international system characterized by deadly dog-eat-dog competition. Yan concludes that Xunzi's thought hasn't had much impact on contemporary Chinese foreign policy, whereas Kautilya's thought has influenced Indian foreign policy and his theory can provide rich resources for scholars to develop new IR theories.

Rajeev Bhargava, former director of the Centre for the Study of Developing Societies in Delhi, argues that Xunzi's thought shares more affinity with the ideals of Emperor Ashoka, who lived in the third century BCE in India (Kautilya's ideas are more commonly compared with those of Han Feizi, the ultra-realist "Legalist" thinker who was Xunzi's student). Bhargava's essay discusses Ashoka's political ideals and argues that they are meant for both intra- and interstate relations. Ashoka is a rare counterexample to the dictum that power corrupts and absolute power corrupts absolutely: he became "good" after a history of immorality. Ashoka expanded his state via brutal warfare, including a war on Kalinga that left at least a hundred thousand dead, but then he had a Buddhist-inspired moral conversion. He advocated rule by moral power rather than the brute force of domination, similar to Xunzi's ideal of humane authority. But Ashoka shared the doubts and regrets expressed by Roman emperor Marcus Aurelius in his *Meditations* and Chinese emperor Kangxi in his Final Valedictory: his inscriptions often express self-criticism and regret at the harm he has caused to humans and animals.[4] We know Ashoka's political thinking because his edicts, scattered in more than thirty places throughout India, Nepal, Bangladesh, Pakistan, and Afghanistan, have survived across the centuries and can still be seen today on rocks, cave walls, and stone pillars.

Ashoka's political morality seems relatively modern because it is designed for a political community characterized by what we would today call moral pluralism. Ashoka's empire was indeed composed of highly diverse religious and social groupings and he argued for a political ethic that binds the various groups, not just in peace but in a kind of harmony that respects, if not celebrates, diversity (a parallel might also be drawn with the Confucian ideal of "diversity in harmony" (和) as opposed to uniformity and sameness (同)). Most original, Ashoka argues not only for a personal ethic characterized by such Buddhist values as compassion and truthfulness but also for an intergroup morality that allows for peaceful coexistence and moral progress. In contrast to, say, Christian missionaries who tried to spread the moral truth and (implicitly or explicitly) downgraded other moral systems, Ashoka's envoys aimed for mutual learning that requires restrained and respectful speech. If envoys refrain from excessive self-glorification and immoderate criticism of other groups, they can maintain the peace and avoid humiliating people who think differently. And they must also strive to transform their own views via actions, similar to Xunzi's idea of rituals involving members of different social hierarchies that have the effect of lifting participants out of their selfish orbits and generating a sense of common concern. As Bhargava explains, "Ashoka says that those seeking improvement in their ethical views should not only communicate with others with different perspectives in order to learn from them but even follow their precepts, 'obey' them. Thinking as if you were in someone else's shoes may not on occasion be sufficient; you have to act with their shoes on. This practical ethical engagement brings an experiential dimension that could be ethically transformative." Bhargava notes that Ashoka's ideals of tolerance, respect, and mutual learning influenced the thought of India's first prime minister, Jawaharlal Nehru (although Yan notes that Nehru also referenced the arch-realist Kautilya). Instead of the physical and verbal violence that so often poison international relations today, Ashoka's ideals can promote mutually enriching relations with other states in a multipolar and multicultural world.

AMORAL REALISM

The next section focuses on the theme of "amoral realism" in international relations. Nearly two millennia before Machiavelli penned the (in)famous line in *The Prince* that rulers must "learn how not to be good," Chinese and India thinkers defended hard-nosed realist approaches to interstate relations that emphasized commitment to maximizing the power of the state and allowed for, if not encouraged, amoral methods such as aggressive warfare and fraud. In the Chinese tradition, the third-century BCE thinker Han Feizi systematized the "Legalist" tradition with its emphasis on rule by fear and harsh punishment. Han Feizi inspired the self-proclaimed First Emperor of China, Qin Shi Huang, who unified China after centuries of constant warfare, but Emperor Qin's dynasty was short-lived and he went down in history as a brutal dictator. In ancient India, Kautilya was not so straightforwardly amoral, but he too was committed to amoral methods as necessary to secure and expand state power in the context of "anarchical" international relations with no higher authority than the individual state. Both ancient thinkers—especially Han Feizi—were more consistently "Machiavellian" than Machiavelli himself, who softened his political theory in *The Discourses*.

Xu Jin of the Chinese Academy of Social Sciences in Beijing systematically compares the international political thought of Han Feizi and Kautilya. His main conclusion is that Han Feizi is a more thoroughgoing "amoral realist." Both thinkers lived in an era of brutal warfare, which led them to develop theories that prioritized material interests and state power above moral considerations. Han Feizi argues that Confucian-style morality may have been appropriate in an earlier era of peace and material abundance, but such means would lead to disaster in the Warring States period. In chaotic times, stabilization and unification can only be achieved by aggressive warfare abroad and the use of harsh punishment and fear at home. Both thinkers held a pessimistic view of human nature as evil, selfish, materialistic, and untrustworthy, but Kautilya's thought did have a religious foundation with commitment to some sort of ethics. Han Feizi argued for the ruthless pursuit of victory by any means in interstate relations, although he did say that a sovereign who implements an impartial legal system is more likely to succeed. Kautilya similarly allowed for force and fraud in interstate relations, while placing more emphasis on diplomacy than war. He was concerned with the well-being of people and seemed to have more faith in the idea that a wise and moral ruler could be good for his country. In his conclusion, Xu suggests that since states often prioritize national interests in the global arena, both thinkers can help states to develop realistic policies in contemporary times, although he sides with Kautilya's view that the well-being of people should be the moral foundation of any foreign policy.

Deepshikha Shahi of O.P. Jindal Global University even more forcefully argues that we need to look beyond the seemingly immoral (or amoral) methods advocated by political realists. She argues that the hard distinction between morality and realism is the product of Eurocentric international relations and cannot do justice to the thinking of ancient theorists from radically different contexts. Kautilya did defend immoral methods such as targeted assassination, but such methods were meant to preempt worse means such as warfare. Similar to modern theories of just war, organized violence should be a last resort. Moreover, immoral methods were meant to serve moral goals in international relations. At home, the ruler should be driven by the ideal that "in the happiness of his subjects lies his happiness" and abroad the conqueror state should respect the value systems of the subjects of the enemy state to the point that the distinction between self and other becomes blurred. Han Feizi prioritized warfare and showed less obvious concern for the well-being of people at home and abroad. But his theory of the successful ruler may have been underpinned by an underlying moral concern. Unlike Kautilya's counsel that the ruler's source of power comes from moral-energetic action, Han Feizi argued that the ruler's power is increased by nonaction (*wu wei*). Once the ruler sets the law in place, he should withdraw to a mysterious and inaccessible realm, and show his face only when absolutely necessary. Such nonaction is necessary both to maintain a sense of awe and to ensure that the ruler refrains from showing his desires and thus be open to manipulation by his ministers. The effect, however, is to ensure that subjects are not frequently the targets of arbitrary power from the top and to ensure that mediocre rulers do not do too much damage to the polity. The exchange between Xu and Shahi is striking because both thinkers charitably construe the thoughts of the political theorists from the less familiar tradition.

EMPIRE

The next theme is empire, and both interlocutors compare ancient Chinese and Indian ideas of empire that differ from Eurocentric notions of empire. Such "defamiliarization" opens new normative possibilities for future international relations inspired by ideas and practices from the past. Zhou Fangyin, dean of the School of International Relations at Guangdong University of Foreign Studies, asks the question, was ancient China an empire, and if so, in what sense? If empire is defined in a broad sense as a great power that establishes a hierarchical order with some degree of control over less powerful political entities composed of different nationalities and cultures, then China did establish and maintain an empire in East Asia. But the Chinese empire had distinctive features that differ from its Western counterparts. At the heart of the Chinese empire was the ideal of political unification, so that there was always a pressure to reunify when the empire was broken into smaller parts.[5] The assumption was that the well-being of the people could only be secured via a stable and unified political entity rather than through a separatist regime. Another contrast with empires in the Western world is that the ideal of political unity did not translate into a highly expansionary foreign policy. More often than not, the rulers of Chinese empires relied on "soft power"—rule by example, ritual propriety, and moral education—to expand beyond the core area of Chinese civilization: "China usually does not exercise effective administrative control over its neighboring countries, does not collect taxes, does not control their armed forces, and has limited impact on their foreign relations." Such institutions as the civil examination system were spread to tributary states such as Korea and Vietnam largely through peaceful means. Zhou recognizes the counterarguments of "realists" who point to occasional violent conflicts launched by Chinese rulers, but he argues that the East Asian regional order established by various kinds of "tributary systems" relied less on coercion and forceable imposition of rulers, institutions, and unequal treaties compared to European empires. Even when the Chinese empire had the capacity to expand militarily, it often refrained from doing so.

What's lacking, perhaps, is a knockdown argument against the realist school: that the Chinese empire did not use military force against peripheral regions even when it was in its long-term interest to do so. Still, it is worth investigating the hypothesis that Chinese empires relied less on violence and coercion compared to European empires; and even if it is not always historically accurate, the myth about China's past may play a role in restraining Chinese foreign policy in the future. In his conclusion, Zhou argues that the ancient Indian empires similarly had a clear opposition to war and did not pursue systematic colonization of foreign countries. But there are important differences between the Indian and Chinese empires; most notably, Zhou argues that the ideal of "grand unification" was not so prevalent in India's past. Such differences in political culture help to explain why the Indian empires were more often characterized by periods of division compared to China's empires: Zhou points out that the grand unification in India was often founded by foreign nationalities such as the Sultanate of Delhi and the Mughal empire (it is possible to overstate this difference: the Maurya empire was not founded by a foreign nationality and Chinese empires were sometimes reunified by foreign nationalities such as the Mongolians and the Manchus).

Upinder Singh, professor of history at Ashoka University, concurs with Zhou that both China and India had hierarchically ordered empires, not only because they had a degree of control over peripheral regions but also in the sense that thinkers from the core areas expressed the idea of a morally superior civilization opposed to the culture of "barbarians" (foreigners and tribals) in surrounding areas (as we will see in Pardesi's essay, such an outlook was more common in Chinese history). Unlike the Chinese empires, the Indian ideal of empires explicitly distinguished between emperors and kings. The emperor was supposed to rule over other kings: "What is emphasized in India is political paramountcy among a hierarchy of rulers rather than political unification. An ancient Indian emperor did not have to eliminate other kings; he had to get them to acknowledge his paramountcy." Arguably, a parallel can be drawn with tributary rulers in Korea and Vietnam who paid symbolic obeisance to Chinese emperors in exchange for security and economic benefits. But the Indian emperors more explicitly allowed for a multistate order, and the idea of empire coexisted with the idea of expansionist regional kingdoms, which was rare in the Chinese case.

In Indian thought, there is a strong tension between the extremes of nonviolence and idealization of a violent warrior ethic. On the one hand, there was a strong commitment to nonviolence. In the Indian context, "the symbol that emerged fairly early as a symbol of empire is the wheel (*cakra*). The *cakravartin* is an emperor, a great paramount king, universal victor, whose chariot wheels roll everywhere unimpeded, and who is victorious over the four quarters of the earth" (ancient Chinese thinkers also thought of the earth as a place with four quarters). Singh shows that the ideal is important in Jaina, Buddhist, and Brahmanical texts. In the Jain tradition, the *cakravartin* is a great emperor who follows the wheel and brings the whole world under his sway without indulging in any violence. In the Buddhist tradition, Ashoka deployed the symbol of the wheel to represent the ideal of *dhamma*, meaning nonviolence toward all living human beings, including humans and animals. The Sanskrit epics, however, allowed for, and sometimes glorified, martial virtues. In the *Mahabharata* and *Ramayana*, the ideal of the paramount king has moral qualities that are explicitly combined with exceptional warrior qualities, although in the *Mahabharata* the old-world warrior ethic of the *Ksatriya* who blindly fights unto death is replaced with a new-age warrior who is assailed with questioning and doubt. Kautilya's *Arthasastra* puts forward the goal of a great king who should aim to enjoy the earth without sharing it with any other ruler, and Kautilya allows for carefully planned war as a means to accomplish his aim. Indian monarchs, with the exception of Ashoka, advertised and celebrated their martial victories, even though "the violence of war is aestheticized through the use of poetic language."

Indian emperors were supposed to be highly energetic and vigorous rulers, followed (according to the poet Kalidasa) by its opposite in the form of renunciation: the sage-king was supposed to give up power and go off to the forest to live out the rest of his live performing yoga and meditation. In contrast, the Chinese ideal *wu wei* (rule by nonaction) was meant to be a long-lasting strategy, and renunciation is not celebrated in classic Chinese texts. What is common in both Chinese and Indian empires was the emphasis on rule by culture and economic benefits with lots of room for local autonomy, even if the empires expanded by means of war. Of course, the practice often deviated from the ideal, but neither Indian nor Chinese empires expanded beyond neighboring regions (Indian empires were land-based polities) and they largely refrained from naked economic exploitation and annexation of territory, in contrast to European colonialism. In a contemporary context, of course, China and India would need to drop the myth of moral superiority and allow for learning from the cultures of other states, no matter how small. But it may not be a bad outcome if the world's two most populous countries, inspired by ancient ideals and practices, aim to (re)establish establishing hierarchical orders within their regions by leading with moral example at home and providing security, health, and economic benefits to surrounding weaker powers.

JUST WAR

The next section turns directly to the theme of just war: When is it morally justified to launch a war against another country? What are the morally justified rules of combat (if any)? What are the obligations of "conquering powers" after a war is fought and won? Ancient Indian and Chinese thinking about just war may help to enrich contemporary debates, if not positively influence the actions of states in the future. In ancient India, the text that engages most closely with these questions is the *Mahabharata*, one of the two major Sanskrit epics of ancient India (the other is the *Ramayana*). The text, probably compiled between 500 BCE and 500 CE, narrates stories that took place much earlier. The text revolves around a family feud turning into a bloody catastrophic war, known as the Bharata War / Kuruksetra War, traditionally described as a *dharmayuddha*, or just war. Kanad Sinha, professor of ancient Indian and world history at the University of Kolkata, discusses the notion of *dharmayuddha*, or just war, as well as the intense debates about war and peace that preceded the war. The debates revolved around the extreme ideologies of martial heroism (of the *ksatriya* caste) and nonviolence. The protagonists debated difficult and agonizing questions: Should a wrong be avenged or forgiven? Is violence justified to obtain a rightful end? Even if a war is justified, what are the rules to conduct it? Even if a side proves to be morally superior, what if it takes the wrong steps? Sinha argues that the *Mahabharata* ideal of *Anrishamsya* (noncruelty) should be central to modern thinking about just war in the contemporary world as well. Ancient Chinese thinkers did not make the value of noncruelty central to their debates, but arguably it's similar to the Confucian value of 仁 (*ren*, humaneness), except that the value of noncruelty in ancient India developed into a form of moral consciousness that applied equally to humans and animals. Still, there are clear differences with ancient Chinese debates about just war. In terms of form, female protagonists were active participants in ancient Indian debates, whereas female voices were largely silent in ancient China (or at least, they do not show up in written recorded history). In terms of substance, the ancient Indian debates revolved around the polar opposites of pacifism and martial heroism, whereas neither of these extremes were parts of debates in ancient China. On the one hand, Chinese thinkers were not pacifist advocates of nonviolence (even Mozi allowed for the possibility of defensive war); on the other hand, they never celebrated martial virtues (even advocates of aggressive war such as Han Feizi recognized that war is, at best, a necessary evil and they did not valorize militant aggression and war as a manly effort).

Daniel A. Bell, dean of the School of Political Science and Public Administration at Shandong University, turns to the thought of Mencius (372–289 BCE), arguably the most influential thinker in the Confucian tradition after Confucius himself. Bell asserts that Western debates on just and unjust war have largely ignored Chinese contributions and he attempts to formulate a Confucian perspective inspired mainly by the philosophy of Mencius. Mencius is famously criticized for being too idealistic. He does uphold an ideal theory of sage-kings who govern the world by means of rites and virtues rather than coercion that seems far removed from the real world. However, Mencius also puts forward principles designed to provide practical, morally informed guidance for the nonideal world of competing states (Mencius was writing in the Warring States period), particularly when rulers must decide whether or not to go to war. He is severely critical of rulers who launched ruthless wars of conquest simply to increase their territory. But states can defend themselves if their rulers are supported by the people. Mencius also argues that wars of conquest can be justified if the aim is to bring peace to foreign lands, so long as particular conditions are in place: the conquerors must try to liberate the people who are being oppressed by tyrants; the people must welcome their conquerors and the welcome must be long-lasting; and the wars of conquest must be led by virtuous rulers who can make a plausible claim to have the world's support. Bell argues that such conditions can inform modern debates about humanitarian intervention to liberate people who are being oppressed by their own rulers.

Sinha endorses Mencius's view that the forceful liberation of people from unjust rule is justified when the people welcome the force (and the welcome is long-lasting), and he draws implications for the modern world: "India's military intervention in liberating Bangladesh would have been justified according to Mencius. But the same cannot be said about the presence of American forces in Iraq. Mencius would raise controversial but relevant questions about Chinese control over Tibet or India's handling of Kashmir." Bell, however, argues that Mencius would restrict invasion of another country only to circumstances when foreign rulers engage in systematic and purposeful killing similar to what we could call today genocide. War involves killing and it is only justified to prevent more killing. Bell and Sinha do agree that Mencius is handicapped by his view that human nature tends to be good, along with the implication that it is just a matter of getting people to follow their naturally good instincts. Mencius doesn't allow for the possibility that some people can be born bad and cannot be changed. Nor does he think the people as a whole can be misguided and in favor of war, to the point of being bloodthirsty and fundamentally immoral. In the *Mahabharata*, by contrast, the people themselves can be wrong and immoral, so moral rulers sometimes need to go against the people. There is also a glaring contrast with respect to views about just conduct in war. The more tragic view of human nature in the *Mahabharata* informed detailed prescriptions of *jus in bello*, such as the rule against killing noncombatants. Mencius, however, preferred to bury his head in the sand: perhaps the thought that violence in war is so incompatible with his view of human nature left him unwilling to think through in detail the implications of going to war. Not surprisingly, Xunzi, who argued that human nature tends to be bad, specified rules of combat that more closely approximate both those in the *Mahabharata* and modern Western views of justice in war.

DIPLOMACY

The next theme is diplomacy in international relations. Diplomacy involves managing relations with other states, typically by a country's representatives abroad. Similar to arguments about just war, arguments about diplomacy flourished in ancient China and ancient India, especially when states coexisted and competed in the equivalent of a multistate system. In the case of India, the views about diplomacy inherited from the *Mahabharata* continue to have great influence. Drawing on extensive fieldwork with India's Ministry of External Affairs, Deep K. Datta-Ray shows that modern-day diplomats in India's foreign service often think in terms of categories set by the *Mahabharata* and that such ideas continue to influence policy. If we want to understand India's foreign policy, Eurocentric categories are not always helpful. In this essay, Datta-Ray, senior visiting fellow at the S. Rajaratnam School of International Studies, argues in a more normative vein that Mahatma Gandhi drew inspiration from the *Mahabharata* and solved an unsettled paradox from that text: the question of how to defend without offense. Gandhi's answer was to extend the idea of nonviolence. Far from the sort of passivity condemned by *ksatriya* adherents of martial heroism in the *Mahabharata*, the ideal of nonviolence is an *active* commitment to disinterested action: "Its success is contingent on its practitioner entirely giving up any interest in themselves, laying themselves open to offense, and in absorbing it, converting it." The practitioner of nonviolence aims to convert the aggressor via the spectacle of the effects of aggression, for example by making the British realize the true evil of the opium trade. Arguably, Gandhi's active nonviolence cannot work with perpetrators of violence who lack any moral conscience (Hitler comes to mind). But Datta-Ray shows that the ideal had direct and positive impact on the foreign policy of India's first prime minister, Jawaharlal Nehru. Inspired by Gandhi's ideal of nonviolence as a global vision, Nehru committed to peaceful use of nuclear energy and proposed a ban on nuclear testing. More recently, however, India's foreign policy seems to have traded disinterested diplomacy in favor of a more "modern" commitment to purely self-interested tit-for-tat aggression. Datta-Ray criticizes India's airstrike against Jaish-e-Mohammed inside Pakistan by nuclear-capable fighter-bombers in February 2019. India described the airstrike as a "nonmilitary preemptive action," but it could have escalated into a nuclear exchange had Islamabad not exercised self-restraint.

Zhao Yujia, who teaches international relations at Shandong University, similarly argues in a normative vein: ideals inspired by ancient political thought can help to deal with the challenges of modern-day diplomacy. She notes that China has not been very successful in promoting its vision of "win-win" Belt and Road Initiative (BRI) projects. According to public opinion to date in English-speaking countries, a majority of respondents accept China's win-win economic rationale for the projects, but less than five percent accept China's ideal of "military conservativeness," meaning that China aims at peaceful development rather than seeking to leverage BRI projects for military gains (there may be more support for China's view in developing, non-English-speaking countries). Such findings suggest that China has failed to gain the trust of other countries via its diplomacy. In response, Zhao suggests looking to both history and philosophy. The historical case is China's success at gaining the trust of the Wu Sun independent federacy during the "ancient silk road" with Central Asia in 139–114 BCE. The Han dynasty rulers succeeded by informing the Wu Sun about the Han's economic and military capabilities. The Wu Sun were able to form a good understanding of the Han's strategic interests, thus allowing for trust-building. Zhao argues that the ancient Confucian ideal of "brightness" (明) helps to makes sense of the process of trust-building. "Brightness" is a virtue of exemplary persons (君子), but it also underpins the kind of trust-building that characterizes successful diplomacy. If rulers and diplomats are honest and transparent about their intentions and act in accordance with clear and transparent rules, they can gain the trust of friends and allies and thus rule the world as a "good hegemon" (in Xunzi's sense of the hegemon who gains friends and allies through strategic reliability). Conversely, it is difficult to trust a state that is opaque or deceitful about its military capabilities.

Datta-Ray also endorses the virtue of brightness in diplomacy and emphasizes that it goes beyond ties bound merely by self-interest. The *Zuo Zhuan*, an ancient Chinese commentary on the *Spring and Autumn Annals*, recorded a story that the King of Zhou and the Lord of Zheng exchanged their sons as hostages to enhance their bilateral relation. However, the Lord of Zheng still secretly sent troops to seize Zhou's grain, thus undermining the possibility of trust between states. A ruler may stop loving his son after a long separation and his son can be sacrificed for the national interest. In other words, this weak sense of reciprocity, with states striking deals that are mutually advantageous, is fragile. The deals may have been transparent and honest at one point in time, but once the situation changes and the deal is no longer advantageous to one of the states, that state can simply opt out of the deal. A more modern example might be the Trump administration's decision to renegotiate or scrap free trade accords with allies and friends on the grounds that those deals no longer benefit the United States. What's lacking in these cases is a deeper sense of reciprocity and trust that comes from shared values and attachment to a common good. For Xunzi, shared rituals over time generate a sense of community. The rituals themselves need to embody other-regarding actions that prove one's sincerity. Ashoka-style self-restrained speech can also contribute to a stronger sense of reciprocity that survives changing fortunes and power relations. What might this mean for China's BRI projects? Zhao is not explicit, but win-win economic relations that materially benefit both states, even if they are transparent and honest, are not sufficient to build lasting trust. Deeper ties with surrounding countries can only be built by such means as Xunzi-style ritualized cultural exchanges and Ashoka-style restrained and respectful speech.[6] Of course, foreign policy is not entirely independent of domestic policy. The Chinese government will find it difficult to gain the trust of neighbors and trading partners if it doesn't treat its own citizens with humanity and compassion.

BALANCING, HEGEMONY, AND MANDALAS

The final section of our book is titled "Balancing, Hegemony, and Mandalas." Both of these essays—historical in nature—argue that balancing theories in mainstream (i.e., Westcentric) international relations theory cannot explain the maintenance and change of international order in ancient China and India. Qi Haixia, professor in the Department of International Relations at Tsinghua University in Beijing, asks, why did China's Spring and Autumn and Warring States (SAWS) period end with the unification of the Qin dynasty? Qi explains that the Spring and Autumn period was relatively stable, with limited warfare, because states were bound by a patriarchal feudal order with *Zhou Tianzi* at its core. Different kinship states competed within this order, but warfare was limited by "just war" norms such as courtesy in the process of war and the obligation to stop fighting once the goal had been achieved. "Good" hegemons in Xunzi's sense emerged from this global order—stronger powers gained the trust of weaker powers and provided security against invading "barbarians." This order, however, gradually declined. Hegemons grew in power and paid only lip service to *Zhou Tianzi*, and warfare became a more straightforward affair of brutal conquest and annexation; as Qi puts it, "In order to win, ignoring rules became the 'only rule.'" Patriarchal clans ties broke down and rulers sought out political talent, regardless of family background. Confucius, Mencius, Xunzi, and Han Feizi roamed from state to state offering different kinds of political advice, but they converged on the need for some form of political meritocracy and helped to break down rule by patriarchal clans. Qi concludes that the "balance of threat" theory can explain the emergence of balancing behavior but cannot account for its success or failure. As the Qin's state power grew, the Wei and Qi states did attempt balancing efforts. But the Qin managed to thwart their efforts by "allying with faraway states while attacking those nearby, reducing the readiness of the relatively distant states of Qi and Chu, and making its eventual unification of the six kingdoms a foregone conclusion."

The Qin's strategy may not have been directly inspired by Kautilya's theory of the mandala, but Kautilyas's theory can, arguably, better explain Qin's success compared to theories about balance derived from the Western historical experience. Kautilya imagined an international order similar to the Warring States period, with states using amoral means, including war if necessary, to expand their power relative to other states. In this situation, neighboring states should be treated as natural enemies, but faraway states—the enemy of my enemy—could potentially serve as (temporary) friends. A relatively small state such as Qin, if it intelligently forges alliances with faraway states for the purpose of attacking those nearby, can eventually grow in size and influence, if not become a self-declared empire.

Manjeet S. Pardesi, senior lecturer in international relations at Victoria University of Wellington, invokes Kautilya's theory to explain the international order of ancient India. The Mauryas did establish a hegemonic international order dominated by a single policy for five and half decades (ca. 260–205 BCE). But Mauryan domination was exceptional and relatively fleeting and ancient India was not typically characterized by a balance-of-power system. In the nine centuries from the emergence of territorial states in ancient India (ca. 600 BCE) until the second phase of hegemony under the Gupta empire (post-320 BCE), the interstate order of ancient India typically consisted of a de-centered mandalas, with five "circles" of states characterized by relations of amity (in the case of faraway states) and enmity (in the case of contiguous states). Power relations often shifted within the mandala order that was informed by a "deep structure" of political and cultural heterogeneity. Pardesi draws contrasts with ancient China. Even if the Qin achieved victory in the Warring States period by means of Kautilya-like strategies, other factors help to explain the transformation of an ancient Chinese multi-polity system into a relatively *long-lasting* empire (though the Qin dynasty itself lasted only fifteen years). First, the quest for political peace is absent in the Indian textual tradition (with the exception of Ashoka). The default assumption was that small states were constantly competing with each other for territorial gain. In contrast, China's multiple philosophical traditions agreed on the ideal of a unified polity that provided peace to *tianxia* (all-under-heaven) long before the emergence of an all-encompassing empire. Second, the Mauryan empire was short-lived because the mode of empire-building was informed by the norm of *dharma* that left vanquished rulers, states, and their traditions intact, and hence was prone to fragmentation. In contrast, empire-building in China was characterized by bureaucratic incorporation of the vanquished kingdoms and empire-wide standardization of the "soft technologies" of governance such as a unified script and advanced transportation and communication system. Third, ancient India was an "open" region of South-Western Eurasia that had close contact with other large and culturally sophisticated empires. Triumphant rulers such as Ashoka could pronounce themselves as heads of the civilized world, but they knew there were serious competitors out there. In contrast, Rome and Greece (and India) were far away from China, so ancient Chinese rulers could more consistently view themselves as heads of the civilized world surrounded by "barbarians."

Pardesi argues provocatively that a de-centered mandala regional order also characterizes relations between states in the Indo-Pacific. Rather than apply contemporary IR theories that emerged from the Western historical experience to the Asian region (the "Thucydides trap" is only the latest example), it makes more sense to view the Indo-Pacific "as four (partially) overlapping *mandalas* (or sub-regions): South Asia, Southeast Asia, Northeast Asia, and Oceania." The mandala framework has several key features that contrast with the Thucydidean power transition theory. First, the Indo-Pacific is a relatively open region that includes external powers such as the United States. Second, it is a de-centered region, both in the political sense that there are multiple power centers and in the "ideational" sense that there are several competing political and economic models. Third, the secondary smaller states try to maintain autonomy in their strategic decision-making. Fourth, the Indo-Pacific region has multiple domination seekers that are neither hegemonic nor practice systemic balance-of-power politics. Pardesi suggests that the de-centered mandala order should also serve as an ideal for Asia's future, but arguably Kautilya's theory would need to be updated. If proposals for global peace and interstate collaboration to deal with pandemics and climate change are to make any headway, for example, it may be necessary to reject

Kautilya's view that rulers are motivated first and foremost by self-interest and states should always try to expand their territory.

MOVING FORWARD

In the next introductory essay, Amitav Acharya discusses why it is important to compare classical political thought in India and China from the perspective of an international relations theorist. Such a comparison would counter Eurocentrism and what he calls the "Greco-Romanocentrism" that is rampant in all branches of the social sciences and humanities. In international relations, theoretical debates tend to center on the West, even when they are comparative. Han Feizi is compared to Machiavelli and Kautilya is compared to Machiavelli, but Han Feizi and Kautilya are rarely compared to each other. So the first benefit of systematic comparison between ancient Chinese and Indian political thought is that each "side" can learn from the "other": experts in classical Chinese thought can learn about classical Indian thought, and vice versa. Our book is the first work that systematically compares ancient thoughts and theories about international politics between the two great Asian civilizations. In that sense, it is an original and important work, but we realize it's only a beginning, and we hope to generate more intellectual engagement of this sort. It's not just that India and China can learn *about* the other; they can also learn *from* the other. Political thoughts and theories from ancient India can help address the issues and problems that thoughts and theories from ancient China may not have been able to answer adequately, and vice versa. For example, Kautilya's mandala theory can help to explain Qin's success in the Warring States period, and Mencius's theory of just war may add some nuance to ancient Indian views on warfare that oscillated between the extremes of nonviolence and idealization of martial heroics.

That said, Acharya cautions about the limitations and dangers of comparison, including the belief about history repeating itself and essentializations of concepts and countries (see also Olivelle's chapter). Another risk is cultural arrogance, as when leaders and regime intellectuals in China and India glorify their cultures to justify present-day foreign policies and downgrade the contributions of other powers. Our contributors do their best to avoid crude nationalist narratives that downgrade other cultures and trace a direct line between past glory and present-day politics. This volume's purpose is primarily educational: to identify and debate political ideas and institutions from ancient India and China on their own terms, in their own time and context, without standards and concepts set by "Greco-Romanocentrism." We cannot entirely avoid using concepts and ideas from Western histories (not to mention that we are writing in the English language), but our contributors do their best to gain a relatively undistorted view of ancient Indian and Chinese ideas and thoughts about politics and statecraft.

Beyond the intellectual benefits, there are also compelling political reasons to care about theories from ancient China and ancient India. The theories formulated by thinkers in long-dead civilizations founded on assumptions that seem empirically wrong or morally obtuse from modern perspectives are primarily of historical interest, without implications for decision-making in the modern world. But India and China are very much "live" civilizations with a deep sense of history. Thinkers and leaders in India and China seek inspiration from ancient ideals in their history, just as American thinkers and leaders seek inspiration from the (much more recent) ideals of the Founding Fathers. Since we are rapidly moving toward a multipolar age with China and India as leading economic and military powers, it is important to understand classical political thought about statecraft in India and China. If categories and values that inform foreign policies in India and China can be explained, at least partly, by categories and values inspired from ancient theories and thinkers, then those seeking to understand the contemporary foreign policies of India and China need to understand those intellectual foundations. The parochial universalism of theories derived entirely from ancient Greek, Roman, or Christian sources won't be sufficient. That said, good understanding *per se* is not sufficient. Knowledge about intellectual foundations can be used for good or bad purposes. A state can use knowledge about another state to more effectively destroy it. A better outcome is that China and India, with deeper mutual understanding, can (re)establish peaceful, economically beneficial, and culturally enriching ties.

NOTES

1.   Sheldon Pollock and Benjamin Elman, eds., *What China and India Once Were: The Pasts That May Shape the Global Future* (New York: Columbia University Press, 2018), 4.

2.   Pollock and Elman, *What China and India Once Were*; and Rajiv Ranjan and Guo Changgang, eds., *China and South Asia: Changing Regional Dynamics, Development and Power Play* (Delhi: Routledge India, 2021).

3.   Yan Xuetong, *Ancient Chinese Thought, Modern Chinese Power*, ed. Daniel A. Bell and Sun Zhe, trans. Edmund Ryden (Princeton, NJ: Princeton University Press, 2011); and Yan Xuetong, *Leadership and the Rise of Great Powers* (Princeton, NJ: Princeton University Press, 2019).

4.   See Jonathan D. Spence, *Emperor of China: Self-Portrait of K'ang-hsi* (New York: Vintage Books, 1988).

5.   See Yuri Pines, *The Everlasting Empire: The Political Culture of Ancient China and Its Imperial Legacy* (Princeton, NJ: Princeton University Press, 2012).

6.   See Daniel A. Bell and Wang Pei, *Just Hierarchy: Why Social Hierarchies Matter in China and the Rest of the World* (Princeton, NJ: Princeton University Press, 2020), chap. 3.

Setting the Stage, Part II

Why Compare the Classical Political Thought of China and India?

Amitav Acharya

The aim of this book is to compare classical Chinese and Indian political thought, especially as it relates to "global" or "world" order-building.[1] What is the rationale for such a comparison? What insights might one derive from such an exercise that are not presently available from the literatures on political science, international relations, and political philosophy? And what are the key referent objects or questions that would make such an exercise useful and meaningful? In this essay, I offer some thoughts on these and related questions from the perspective of an international relations (IR) scholar (albeit one who takes a very broad view of that discipline), although much of my argument can be extended to other fields in the social sciences and humanities.

GREECE AND ROME, CHINA AND INDIA

Western scholarship often holds up Greece and Rome as the definitive sources of concepts and approaches to political science, history, philosophy, and IR. In IR, for example, there is a common tendency to go back to the Greco-Roman period when tracing the origins of democracy, diplomacy, anarchy, and empire. As Daniel Deudney writes:

> Action and words from classical Greece and republican Rome stand enshrined as foundational in the modern conception of the West as a distinct civilization, and ancient writers and events have exercised a startlingly powerful presence in all aspects of Western thought, particularly about politics . . . For two millennia Western thinking about politics and history has been a long dialogue with the ancient figures of Herodotus, Hippocrates, Socrates, Plato, Thucydides, Aristotle, Livy, Polybius, Cicero, Tacitus, and others. The works of major modern political theorists such as Machiavelli, Montesquieu, and Rousseau are as much about ancient writers and experiences as modern ones.[2]

This Greco-Roman centrism is the forerunner and foundation of modern Eurocentrism. Thus, the idea of anarchy is traced back to the Greek city-states system, democracy to the Greek *Polis*, and rationalism to Greek philosophers like Thales and Aristotle. Herodotus is the "father" of history, Thucydides of realism, and so on. Although Deudney stresses republican and not imperial Rome, it is the Roman Empire (not the Persian Empire, which predated it and was as extensive) that is held up in the West as the ideal type and even a model for all great empires. Indeed, the Victorian and Edwardian apologists of the British Empire often invoked the Roman Empire to legitimize British colonialism in India. And after the US invasion of Iraq in 2003, both critics and supporters of the invasion likened America to a new Rome. In the vocabulary of international relations or political thought, Greco-Roman dominance is commonplace because its ideas and contributions are approximations to the contemporary institutions and practices of world order.

Yet the history of world politics and order-building did not begin with Greece and Rome. The Sumerians, along with the Egyptians, invented the institution of universal divine kingship (which was adored and adopted by Aristotle, pupil of Plato, the philosopher of the *Polis*). The city-states system was Sumerian in origin (between the fourth and third millennia BC).[3] It was a system of internally independent city-states, with a shifting leadership (or collective hegemony). The "great kingship" over all the city-states was not hereditary, and its main function was to arbitrate among fellow rulers. The earliest recorded diplomatic system was what scholars now call "Amarna Diplomacy" (early to mid-fourteenth century BC), and the great powers of the period were Egypt, Hatti, the Kassite kingdom of Babylon, Assyria, and Mittani. This was a "Brotherhood of Kings," or a "club" of powers, based on a fairly equal status for all of them.[4] This club utilized diplomacy, communications (through a common Akkadian language), gift exchanges, and marriages to maintain stability and order. The ancient Middle East also gave rise to the idea of universal empire (hegemony), well before the rise of the Roman Empire.

The Indian and Chinese civilizations, the subject of this project, emerged earlier than, but overlapped with, the Greco-Roman civilizations and contributed much to the political, strategic, and economic interactions of the pre-modern period. After the seventh century, Islam served as a bridge between the classical and modern eras, between the East and the West, and between ancient Greek (as well as Indian and Chinese) knowledge and the Renaissance. Yet mainstream Western narratives have ignored or marginalized the contributions of these and other non-Western civilizations. In explaining the Renaissance, European artists, scientists and scholars are given all the credit for the revival of classical Greco-Roman ideas, while the contribution of the prior ideas and practices of the Egyptians, Sumerians, and Persians to the rise of the Greek civilization, and that of the Muslims to the preservation of Greek knowledge after the collapse of the Roman Empire, are forgotten. The Renaissance and the Enlightenment are contrasted with the East's backwardness, its lack of scientific rationality, or otherworldliness, while the massive intellectual debt of Renaissance Europe to the ideas and innovations of China,

India, and Islam are sidelined. The Greco-Roman heritage is seen as more progressive, scientific, advanced, and democratic and its practices and ideas as universal and applicable to all. Such assumptions serve as the bedrock for modern social sciences and humanities.

These disciplines often stress the attractive sides of Greco-Roman civilizations, while ignoring their shortcomings and dark sides. The Roman Republic is presented as the antecedent of republican government, even though Rome degenerated into one of the most brutally tyrannical empires in history. Athenian democracy is privileged over Athenian tyranny. Greek democracy is adored as an approximation of the modern democratic system and taken as the universal standard or model to which all societies must aspire. But Greek democracy had a very limited scope and span as a political system and degenerated into periods of tyranny and dictatorship. A clear majority of people in Athens were not part of the citizenry, including women, children, and slaves. The Greek idea of liberty often meant liberty for the *polis* rather than for the individual person, since only a small number of the Greeks qualified to be citizens; these included the propertied classes and other elites. Life in the *polis* could be stifling due to the stringent system of social discipline, fear of ostracization, and martial training. And while Greek civilization prized liberty for the city-states, it could not prevent warfare among them. It had a poor record in conflict management or maintaining peace and order. Also, Greek democracy does not come across as a very successful and exportable model.[5] Its longevity, or that of democracy in general, pales in comparison to that of the Eastern model, invented by the Sumerians and Egyptians, then perfected by the Persians, of universal monarchy or empire. Even after the Peace of Westphalia and the advent of the nation-state, Europe continued to feature monarchies and empires. Even in the case of scientific rationality, although the Greeks are credited with the invention of natural philosophy, they borrowed heavily from the Sumerians, the Mesopotamians, and the Egyptians. The Greeks, however, continued to assign causality to divinities and oracles in preparing for conflict and colonization. Plato, like Pythagoras, had much in common with Hinduism, which then and now believes in the existence of the soul. Thus, as it is increasingly being realized, the Greco-Roman age is not as enlightened or sanguine as is often depicted in the Western classics literature. Yet, its dominance in modern Western imagination persists.

At the same time, the non-West continues to suffer from epistemic prejudice, injustice, and neglect, without due regard for its rich intellectual heritage and practical contributions. Romila Thapar has pointed to the intellectual "inferiority complex" produced by Hellenocentrism:

> The superiority of Greek civilization has been so over-emphasized, as to produce an unfortunate inferiority complex among members of certain other civilizations. This has quite naturally resulted in an effort to prove that non-Greek cultures have identical values as those of the Greek-dominated ones. But progressive research shows

that every culture and every civilization has its own "miracle," and it is the purpose of historical investigation to reveal it. This cannot be achieved by seeking to discover identical values in every civilization, but rather by pointing out the significant values of each culture within its own context.[6]

Against this backdrop, a comparative study of classical Chinese and Indian political thought introduces a much-needed non-Western corrective to traditional approaches to political science, philosophy, international relations, and the related fields of social sciences and humanities. Speaking from an IR perspective, whereas Greece and Rome are considered in the West to be the classical foundations of modern statecraft, the discipline of IR as presented in the West privileges the advent of the nation-state with the Peace of Westphalia of 1648 as its modern foundation (hence the "international" in international relations). But if one studies IR with the nation-state as its core unit of analysis, one has less than four hundred years of history to play with. This is also the period of the rise and dominance of the West. If, however, one studies IR from the perspective of civilizations, one has over five thousand years of human history to reflect on and analyze. During the last five thousand years, civilizations have risen, fallen, survived, and failed. From this long-term historical perspective, no civilization can claim a monopoly over ideas or approaches to politics, justice, morality, and security. Many civilizations have contributed to the substance of philosophy, political science, and IR, including ideas about domestic political organization, interstate relations, and world order-building.

Taking into consideration the ideas and practices of other societies through history such as that of China and India[7] helps IR, political science, and philosophy to draw from the broad canvas of human interactions. The benefits of such an approach can hardly be overemphasized. Mindful of the dangers of historicism, and without assuming that the past may repeat itself, a historical analysis such as that available from a comparative study of Chinese and Indian political thought offers us a range of possible ways of organizing world order that either supplement or challenge existing concepts that are derived mainly from European history. Here, one might accept Wang Gungwu's argument: "History never really repeats itself and every event when closely examined is different." But "history can teach us about an important kind of reality." "When enough of the historical is knowable, that might go some way in preparing ourselves for what individuals and societies might do in the future."[8]

We are acutely mindful that the application of the comparative method in general and to history in particular has been controversial, because of its association with colonial-era comparative studies that looked at non-Western societies as inferior or deviant. As Benjamin Elman and Sheldon Pollock point out, comparative studies emerging during the European colonial period took Europe as the "standard" or "ideal type," or gave it "the defining status" (or "secundum comparatum"); "everything compared with it ... was not just different, but deviant and even deficient."[9]

Such Eurocentrism has hardly disappeared. A good example in Western comparative writings on civilizations is Henry Kissinger's 2014 book, *World Order*, which begins with early modern Europe (in two chapters), before turning to China, India, and Islam, sometimes rather disapprovingly (his chapter on Islam is subtitled "A World in Disorder"), and ends by presenting the United States as "Acting for All Mankind," and discussing President Woodrow Wilson—a confirmed racist—under the heading "America as the World's Conscience."[10] Kissinger thus not only reverses history, he also leaves no one in doubt that Europe represents the ideal-type of world order. Eurocentrism, with its strong racist framing and bias, was foundational to the emergence of international relations as a discipline about a century ago and this has significantly not abated to this day; and "EU-centrism" has been a central feature of the comparative study of regions and regionalism.[11] While there is a body of non-Eurocentric literature on the comparative history of civilizations,[12] the balance between Eurocentric and non-Eurocentric comparisons, we submit, remains overwhelmingly in favor of the former, not the least because it is embedded within more general histories of civilizations, and more importantly, in school and university curricula and in the more general popular discourses. In the words of Chinese international relations scholar Qin Yaqin, whose work draws heavily on classical Chinese history and philosophy, "no matter what you theorize about, its soul is Western."[13] While there have been attempts to diversify and "decolonize" the curriculum of disciplines like history and international relations, Canadian philosopher Justin Smith concludes: "The goal of reflecting the diversity of our own society by expanding the curriculum to include non-European traditions has so far been a tremendous failure." Speaking especially of philosophy, but in words that are applicable to all social sciences and humanities, he finds that "Western philosophy is always the unmarked category, the standard in relation to which non-Western philosophy provides a useful contrast. Non-Western philosophy is not approached on its own terms, and thus philosophy remains, implicitly and by default, Western."[14]

My highlighting of Greco-Roman centrism in the earlier part of this chapter does not, however, mean that Greece and Rome have not influenced the approaches of India and China to modernity. Neither do I assume India and China are approaching "modernity" in their own distinctive ways. Or that they are simply deploying a colonial modernity. These are extreme positions. Rather, the point is that the Greek and Roman civilizations have such an overwhelming influence in shaping the evaluation of what is considered modernity that alternative pathways have been ignored and marginalized. As the quotes from Deudney and Thapar suggest, there is a growing awareness that ancient Greece and Rome have dominated and shaped our thinking about history, politics, philosophy, etc. To redress this is one of the key objectives of this book. To this end, drawing from classical Indian and Chinese history could be an important step, as would be similar exercises involving other civilizations such as Islam and Africa.[15] Instead of using Eurocentric standards, we acknowledge the notion of "multiple modernities" proposed by Eisenstadt,[16] which gives space to the ideas and worldviews of China and India to articulate their own approach to modernity. This is not a mutually exclusive situation. We do not assume or project that China and India will simply revert to their precolonial classical past, because of the enormous constraints and costs of such a move. At the same time, both are likely to take great account of their pasts as a way of not only challenging the dominance of the West but also finding ways to build and articulate and strengthen domestic politics and foreign policy.

In this volume, we do not avoid Western categories entirely, but at the same time we make no assumption about, in fact we challenge, Europe as a model and Western categories as superior. We are sympathetic to the "cosmopolitan comparison" approach proposed by Elman and Pollock, but we also do not want to convey the impression that a comparative approach can avoid engagement with European categories entirely. To have a dialogue between Western and non-Western scholarship (which we do not take as entirely homogenous; our contributors are drawn from both), one also has to deploy and target certain concepts that are part of the standard literature on humanities and social sciences (as with natural sciences) all over the world. Otherwise, the result would be a monologue, and can degenerate into parochialism.[17]

This volume also does not engage in "connected history,"[18] at least not in the sense of tracing how ideas from one civilization influenced the other, although we keep in mind examples of classical Buddhist ideas that traveled between the two civilizations (it was more of a two-way street than commonly presented).[19] Neither is this book a relational study—i.e., a study of China-India relations through the ages, as Tansen Sen has so masterfully done.[20] We do hope, however, that this book will be useful to policymakers and academics in thinking about China-India relations, and in being better informed and avoiding prejudices as the two countries become increasingly important forces in shaping world order.

Our major concern in this volume is to present the main elements of the classical political thought of China and India, especially to those who may not be familiar with them. The book is comparative mainly in the sense that it helps scholars and readers from China and India, who are already familiar (at least to some degree) with the classical traditions of his/her own country, to be better informed about the political ideas and institutions of the other. Such an exercise would hopefully engender a comparative sense of both civilizations, and engage in mutual learning, without presenting either as superior. In this respect, we are very encouraged that during the course of this project, a considerable amount of mutual understanding and learning has been accomplished. When the project started in 2017, few of the contributors had much of a sense of the other civilization's political and philosophical ideas; when the project ended, they were considerably more familiar with those of the other civilization. This is the kind of cognitive shift that the book seeks to stimulate in the minds of its readers, following in the footsteps of Elman and

Pollock (although our volumes focus more specifically and in depth on politics and philosophy).

With the above in mind, let me make the following points about the insights and benefits of a comparative study of the classical political thought of China and India.

CIVILIZATIONAL COMPLEXITY AND DYNAMISM

Despite their differences, China and India make up for a plausible exercise in the comparative study of political thought and practice. They are two of the largest and oldest continuous civilizations of the world.[21] Moreover, both have extended well beyond their original cultural core, whether through material (including conquest and trade) or ideational (cultural diffusion) means. Moreover, neither China nor India is a singular or monolithic entity. They are testimony to the fact that civilizations exist in the plural. Every civilization combines different, even opposite, characteristics and values: realist and idealist, spiritual and rational, just and unjust, humane and coercive. Stereotyping civilizations as benign or aggressive, materialistic or spiritual, is a very flawed way of looking at these entities. In addition, every civilization is influenced by other civilizations. It is a process of mutual influencing that defines the relationship among civilizations. This is as true of China and India as of other civilizations. India and China offer striking examples of this simplified rendering of non-Western civilizations in the West. While stereotyped as "otherworldly," with their politics seen as shaped by a deference to the divine or the Heaven (in the Chinese case), classical Chinese and Indian thought were much more complex and diverse. Some schools within Hindu philosophy (like the Samkhya and Charvaka schools) rejected the idea of a creator God. Buddhism, a reaction against Hindu orthodoxy, rebelled against Hindu notions of divine origin. In China, where before the advent of Buddhism spiritual concerns might have mattered less than in India, ideas such as the mandate of heaven and *Tianxia* were about managing very practical and secular concerns about political legitimacy and compromise. They coexisted with sacrifices and other rituals of purification. Eastern civilizations are not the singular, homogenous entities often depicted in the Western imagination.

What is also striking is that within a relatively short historical period, China and India each developed within themselves widely divergent, even opposing, ideas about domestic governance and interstate relations. Thus, while China during the Spring and Autumn and Warring States periods witnessed the rise of the extremes of Legalism on the one hand and Confucianism and Daoism on the other, India within the relatively short span of the Maurya dynasty exhibited Kautilyan realism prescribing conquest and expansion, as well as Ashokan idealism urging abstinence from force and governance through morality and righteousness. The modern orientalist view of ancient India and China as the antithesis of

Greece/the West—that is, as despotic, mystical, imperial, and otherworldly—is misleading. The classical Indian and Chinese civilizations were fundamentally eclectic, combining rationalism and spiritualism, realism and idealism, republicanism and monarchy, and anarchic and hierarchic orders.

It also emerges from a study of China and India that civilizations are not passive or static entities but highly dynamic ones; the same civilization can generate different types of world orders through time. Thus, the Chinese civilization had an anarchic phase (the warring states) as well as a hierarchic phase (after the unification under Qin and under the tributary system). Similarly, the classical Indian civilization was anarchic before the Mauryas and hierarchic thereafter. The Islamic civilization has had many centers, thus displaying both anarchic and hierarchic tendencies and structures in different stages of its evolution.

THE PROMISE OF COMPARISON

It is against this backdrop that this project compares the classical political thought of China and India. Such a comparative study yields a number of benefits for scholars of international relations, political science, and political philosophy, although I will limit myself to IR here. First, the history of classical political thought in China and India helps us to test the validity of supposedly universal concepts and models of statecraft and international relations that we take for granted in contemporary political theory or philosophy. In other words, the comparative classical political thoughts of two of the longest and largest civilizations can go a long way toward redressing the problem of "tempo-centrism" or "presentism"—assuming the present to be eternal and universal through time, which pervades the social sciences and humanities today. Is the Westphalian notion of "international system" a truly universal category or is it a historically specific form? As noted, the term international system is associated with modern nation-states. The tributary system challenges the universality or timelessness of both the Westphalian system and the balance of power theory, which Western scholars generally trace to the time of the Greek city-state system and the Roman Republic. Does the balance of power logic really apply itself to different cultures across time? While some scholars equate Kautilya's ideas to a balance of power theory, this is misleading, since the ultimate objective of Kautilya's doctrine was to help the ruler achieve hegemony. As Roger Boesche argues,

> Kautilya, in fact, was not offering a modern balance of power argument . . . One does find this argument occasionally in Kautilya: "In case the gains [of two allies of equal strength] are equal, there should be peace; if unequal, fight," or, "the conqueror should march if superior in strength, otherwise stay quiet." Whereas these balance of power theorists suggest that a nation arm itself so that it can ensure peace, Kautilya wanted his king to arm the nation in order to find or create a weakness in the enemy and conquer, even to conquer the world, or at least the subcontinent of India.[22]

Related to the above, a study of the classical Indian and Chinese civilizations suggests that the anarchy-hierarchy dichotomy considered to be a central element of international relations theory is an inadequate way of viewing interstate systems through history. This dichotomy focuses on material structure while bracketing the ideational elements of the system, or its moral purpose. Another way to analyze international systems would be along the realpolitik-normative spectrum and the intersection of the two. India and China offer powerful examples of how the classical world combined and reconciled the moral purpose of the state with realpolitik. In this sense, comparing classical Chinese and Indian thought might offer further support for Yan Xuetong's "moral realism."[23]

Second, comparing the classical thought of China and India helps in appreciating the multiple and global origins of current global norms, institutions, and practices that are now often solely credited to the West. One can offer a number of examples, including the origins of republican and anarchical systems in ancient China and India (as well as Sumer, as discussed earlier), which are overwhelmingly presented as a legacy of the Greco-Roman world. Another important example of this is the Just War tradition, whose roots in ancient China and India are analyzed in this project. The essays on diplomacy also serve a similar purpose. Another area that can benefit from a comparative study of China and India is the origins of human rights norms, which some writers claim as having had no place in classical non-Western thought.[24] But as Amartya Sen argues:

> The idea of human rights as an entitlement of every human being, with an unqualified universal scope and highly articulated structure, is really a recent development; in this demanding form it is not an ancient idea either in the West or elsewhere. However, there are limited and qualified defences of freedom and tolerance, and general arguments against censorship, that can be found both in ancient traditions in the West and in cultures of non-Western societies.[25]

These claims can be seriously tested by analyzing the doctrines of Confucius, Mencius, Ashoka, Kautilya, and the Code of Manu.

Third, a comparison between Chinese and Indian classical political thought might help to uncover ways of statecraft and order-building that have been absent in the European Western tradition and interstate systems, and/or received little attention from them. It may be possible to discover entirely new ways of promoting peace or extending hegemony that scholarship drawing only from Western history have missed or obscured. The *Tianxia* model is a leading example from China,[26] while Pollock's idea of "Sanskrit Cosmopolis"[27] also bears examination as a novel form of world order-building through the pacific diffusion of language, ideas, and political culture. The Indian *mandala* system (theorized by O. W. Wolters,[28] not to be confused with the *mandala* of Kautilya) in classical South and Southeast Asia offers another example of relatively distinctive approaches to politics and interstate relations that are not captured in the existing political science, philosophy, or IR literatures. The classical *mandala* states of South and Southeast Asia represent "indigenous, culturally oriented" models of state that ought to be differentiated from "the Marxian and Weberian notions of the state with fixed boundaries and the rule of law over a given territory."[29]

Exploring and theorizing such patterns could considerably enrich the social sciences and humanities and offer policy prescriptions for managing order and securing peace that remains elusive in the current Westphalian global order. Sometimes, comparisons can lead to a more productive hybridization of different cultural and political concepts, including Western and non-Western ones, as has been done in the case of Western and Chinese concepts by scholars such as Yan Xuetong (especially his aforementioned "moral realism"). His and Qin Yaqing's "relational theory of world politics,"[30] which challenges Western IR to come to terms with classical Chinese approaches to statecraft, could provide inspirations for similar Indian efforts to develop new or hybrid theoretical approaches. Such an effort could benefit immensely from a comparative study of Chinese and Indian approaches to world order.

Fourth, the comparative study of Chinese and Indian classical political thought helps to answer some of the most important puzzles and questions facing history, political science, and IR. One such question is when and why an anarchic system becomes a universal empire. Or why some anarchic systems stay as such, as with Europe after Westphalia, while others transform into hierarchical systems, as with classical India and China. As noted, in the first millennium BC, both China and India had very well-developed "anarchic" systems—the republics of India and the warring states of China—before each established their first empires: the Maurya for India and Qin for China. What are the factors and modalities which contributed to the transition from anarchy to hierarchy and empire? Was it ruthless force and discipline imposed by the legalists for China and the Kautilyan realpolitik for Mauryan India? What was the role of ideas relative to material forces and organizational innovation? One can get a broader answer to this question by comparing China and India rather than limiting oneself to the Greek city-states or Rome's march from republic to empire.

Fifth, as suggested above, comparing Chinese and Indian classical thought helps to analyze the peaceful circulation of ideas in world politics. Political science and IR are not just about relationships based on power and wealth. They are also a relationship of different ideas. The "clash of civilizations" thesis proposed by the late Samuel Huntington ignores the varieties of ways, including pacific ways, in which civilizations have borrowed and exchanged ideas and engaged in mutual learning. If one takes the long-term view, the nearly two thousand years of recorded interaction between Chinese and Indian civilizations has been overwhelmingly pacific.[31] The history of civilizations may thus be told not in terms of blood, treasure, and conflict, but of the convergence of ideas, identity, and mutual benefit.

The classical intercivilizational interactions between China and India reached its peak when a humble Buddhist pilgrim from the imperial Tang Dynasty took a long and hazardous journey to India where he spent sixteen years of travel, study, and document collection. But what is sometimes forgotten is that Xuanzang was by no means the only Chinese pilgrim to visit India in search of knowledge. He had been preceded by Faxian (who came through the desert and returned to China by sea), and followed by Yijing (who made both legs of his journey to India by the sea route). Nor was the "Nirvana traffic" (my term) a one-way flow of Chinese monks visiting India. A possibly greater number of Indian monks traveled to China, to preach, teach, translate, and advise. During the fifth and sixth centuries, a parade of Indian monks with names such as Gunarahhata, Gunavarman, Gunabhadra, Shanghbhadra, and so on, spread out in China founding monasteries and temples, translating Buddhist sutras (some of these Indian monks were fluent enough in Chinese to write books in Chinese). One prominent monk was Paramartha (Zhendi in Chinese), who, after arriving in China in 546 AD, spent twelve years in the area now called Guangzhou, playing a key role in the introduction of Mahayana Buddhism to China. Another monk named Bodhidharma, who had arrived a couple of decades earlier, crossed the Yangtze River and moved further northwest. Settling in the Shaolin temple already established by yet another Indian monk, Bodhidharma founded the sect of *Chan* Buddhism, which the Japanese borrowed, developed, and made famous worldwide as *Zen*.

The Nirvana traffic between India and China suggests that no civilization is an island. They are often interconnected with other civilizations. Civilizations exist in relation to others within a complex and influence each other. Moreover, civilizations respect and learn from each other. And they often do so peacefully. The Buddhist diffusion between India and China, or for that matter between India and Southeast Asia, which was through the maritime route via Southeast Asia, was overwhelmingly peaceful.[32]

CONCLUSION

Much has been written about the contribution of Greece and Rome in shaping Western civilization and modernity, and thus to contemporary theories and concepts of political science, philosophy, and international relations. This has led to an undue neglect of the role of the ideas and practices of other civilizations, such as India, China, and Islam. As a result, the so-called West versus the Rest debate or the idea of the "great divergence," which underpins a good deal of the conceptualization of world or global order today, rests on a remarkably narrow or one-sided narrative. A comparative study of the characteristics and contributions of other civilizations, especially those that preceded the rise of the West, is therefore important in developing a more balanced picture of the evolution of global order.

TABLE, PART 2.1   Classical Indian worldview and political order

- Transition from republics to empire (the Mauryas, established around 321 BC, before the Roman empire and the first Chinese empire).
- Main Realist Thought: Kautilya's *Arthaśāstra*, which advises a ruler to achieve hegemony through war, spying, alliances, and conquest. Kautilya also gave first detailed descriptions of the elements of a state.
- Main Idealist Thought: Ashoka's Law of Righteousness, abstinence from war, and humanism (protection of the people from cruel and unjust rule).
- Epistemology: rationalism blended with spiritualism.
- "World ordering": (1) "Chakravartin": the ideal universal king who represents the highest principles expected of a ruler (King Ashoka). (2) "Sanskrit Cosmopolis" (coined by Sheldon Pollock) through peaceful export of ideas and institutions abroad, such as Buddhism, Hinduism, and associated institutions to Asia and China, compared to spread of Greek ideas or "Hellenization" before and after Alexander through physical conquest.

TABLE, PART 2.2   The classical Chinese worldview and political order

- Transition from "anarchy" to empire of Qin established in 221 BC.
- Main Idealist Thought: Confucianism assumes the essential goodness of human nature and rule by virtue and example, with the belief that social hierarchy based on merit would inspire trust and confidence in the ruler. But ruler's legitimacy is conditional upon just and wise exercise of authority that served people's welfare and happiness. Elitist, but not an absolute justification for authoritarian rule.
- Main Realist Thought: Legalism, which assumes human nature to be inherently wicked, rejects Confucianism's idea of ruler's obligation to people and ruling by virtue and benevolence, emphasizing instead rule by a code of law strictly enforced by force and harsh punishment and the need for power and order above everything else. Underpinning the transition from the Warring States period to the Qin Dynasty in 221 BC, Legalism offers insights into how an anarchic system becomes an empire. Challenges balance of power theory. Balancing can fail, leading to hegemony.
- Epistemology: rationalism and ritualism.
- "World ordering": (1) Mandate of Heaven: if the ruler was not wise and just, the Heaven would withdraw its mandate and his right to rule; (2) *Tianxia* ("all under heaven"): idealized conception of interstate relations where highest unit is the "world" not the state (hence, the opposite of the Westphalian system); (3) Tributary system, a hierarchical system in which a leading power (China) enjoys deference by offering the benefits of trade, recognition, and protection.

Such an exercise is also critical to building truly global disciplines of philosophy, history, political science, and international relations, all of which suffer acutely from Greco-Roman centrism and Eurocentrism. For example, the global IR approach argues that this substance and practice of "international relations" was not invented in the West, nor did it begin with the Peace of Westphalia in 1648. Other and older civilizations—e.g., India, China, Islam—pioneered different modes of governance, interstate systems, and world orders (how they viewed the world, and organized their own foreign relations to achieve stability and progress), and hence their contribution should be integral to the study of IR. Such a broadening of what IR means, and its scope, can easily be applied to other fields such as history and philosophy. With the rise of the rest, e.g., China and India, it is even more necessary to pay attention to these "other" civilizations and their contributions. In IR as in philosophy, history, and related disciplines, a "global turn" would require drawing from the broad canvas of interactions among all civilizations, even as some have been more powerful than others at different stages in history. Insights from the classical political thought of China and India can help the imagining of such an inclusive "global order" (rather than a narrow world order in the manner of the "liberal world order") and contribute to building such an order at a time of profound turmoil and transition.

NOTES

1. "Order," as used in this project, refers to a situation of relative stability, or the absence of major conflict, through rule-governed behavior. Change is evolutionary, not revolutionary, and is mediated by norms and institutions that help to mitigate conflict. The distinction between "world order" and "international order" is not always clear, but world order does away with the assumption of nation-states as its unit. John K. Fairbank used the term "Chinese World Order" rather than "international system" to analyze the Chinese tributary relations (especially during the Qing dynasty), because it did not feature the principles of Westphalian sovereignty. A world order can thus be based on civilizations rather than states as its main unit. A world order can be less than global; arguing that a true "global order" has never existed, Henry Kissinger defines a "world order" as a "concept held by a region or civilization about the nature of just arrangements and the distribution of power thought to be applicable to the entire world." Kissinger, *World Order* (New York: Penguin Press, 2014), 2, 9.

Going by Kissinger's definition, the ancient civilizations of India and China (or Islam), despite having not yet been nation-states, and not having encompassed the entire globe, could still qualify as world orders. "Global order" is geographically and conceptually a broader category than "world order" or "international order." It is a recent or futuristic notion, a product of globalization, including both state and nonstate actors, unlike the narrow state-centric idea of international order or some conceptions of world order. Amitav Acharya, *Constructing Global Order: Agency and Change in World Politics* (Cambridge: Cambridge University Press, 2018).

2. Daniel H. Deudney, *Bounding Power: Republican Security Theory from the Polis to the Global Village* (Princeton, NJ: Princeton University Press, 2007), 91.

3. Adam Watson, *The Evolution of International Society: A Comparative Historical Analysis* (New York: Routledge, 1992).

4. Amanda H. Podany, *Brotherhood of Kings: How International Relations Shaped the Ancient Near East* (New York: Oxford University Press, 2010). Here, there are some echoes of the European Concert of Powers in the nineteenth century.

5. Responding to criticism that Kautilya's *Arthasastra* was vastly inferior to the work of Plato and Aristotle, the Indian historian D. D. Kosambi writes: "Aristotle's royal pupil Alexander [the Great] did not put the learned Stagirite master's political ideas into action. Athenian democracy failed after a singularly brief span, for all the supposed wisdom of its constitution . . . disciples and admirers of Socrates . . . did less than nothing to bring the Sokratic ideal *Republic* into existence. In contrast, the Indian state . . . grew without a setback from small and primitive beginnings to its intended final size." Hence, Kosambi concludes: "'The Greeks make excellent reading; the Indian treatise [*Arthasastra*] worked infinitely better in practice for its own time and place." D. D. Kosambi, *The Culture and Civilisation of Ancient India*, reprint (New Delhi: Vikas, 2001; original publication 1964), 141.

6. Romila Thapar, *Ashoka and the Decline of the Mauryas*, 3rd ed. (New Delhi: Oxford University Press, 2012), 268.

7. Amitav Acharya, "Global International Relations (IR) and Regional Worlds: A New Agenda for International Studies," *International Studies Quarterly* 58, no. 4 (2014): 1–13, at 9.

8. Wang Gungwu, "The Universal and the Historical: My Faith in History," Fourth Daisaku Ikeda Annual Lecture (Singapore: Singapore Soka Association, 2005), 6.

9. Benjamin Elman and Sheldon Pollock, "Introduction," in *What China and India Once Were: The Pasts That May Shape the Global Future*, ed. Sheldon Pollock and Benjamin Elman (New York: Columbia University Press, 2018), Kindle, https://www.amazon.com/What-China-India-Once-Were-ebook /dp/B07CX6ZB4L?asin = B07CX6ZB4L&revisionId = &format = 2&depth = 1.

10. Henry Kissinger, *World Order* (New York: Penguin Press, 2014). For another heavily Eurocentric account, see Niall Ferguson, *Civilization: The West and the Rest* (New York: Penguin Books, 2011).

11. On Eurocentrism in IR, see Amitav Acharya and Barry Buzan, *The Making of Global International Relations* (Cambridge: Cambridge University Press, 2019). On "EU-centrism" in comparative regionalism, see Amitav Acharya, "Regionalism beyond EU Centrism," in *Oxford Handbook of Comparative Regionalism*, ed. Tanja A. Börzel and Thomas Risse (Oxford: Oxford University Press, 2016), 109–30.

12. A leading example here is John Hobson, *The Eastern Origins of Western Civilization* (Cambridge: Cambridge University Press 2006).

13. Qin Yaqin, "Why Is There No Chinese International Relations Theory," *International Relations of the Asia-Pacific* 7 (2007): 325.

14. Justin Smith, "Philosophy's Western Bias," *New York Times*, June 3, 2012, https://opinionator .blogs.nytimes.com/2012/06/03/philosophys-western-bias/.

15. For an important recent contribution covering China, Southeast Asia, and Islam, see Hendrik Spruyt, *The World Imagined: Collective Belief and Political Order in the Sinocentric, Islamic and Southeast Asian International Societies* (Cambridge: Cambridge University Press, 2020).

16. S. N. Eisenstadt, "Multiple Modernities," *Dædalus* 129, no. 1 (2000): 1–29.

17. I have discussed elsewhere the dangers of civilizationalist arrogance and exceptionalism and some ways of avoiding it. Amitav Acharya, "From Heaven to Earth: 'Cultural Idealism' and 'Moral Realism' as Chinese Contributions to Global International Relations," *Chinese Journal of International Politics* 12, no. 4 (Winter 2019): 467–94.

18. One of the best articulations of connected history is Sanjay Subrahmanyam, *Explorations in Connected History: From the Tagus to the Ganges* (Oxford: Oxford University Press, 2004); Sanjay Subrahmanyam, *Connected History: Essays and Arguments* (London: Verso Books, 2022).

19. See Tansen Sen, *Buddhism, Diplomacy and Trade: The Realignment of Sino-Indian Relations, 600–1400* (Honolulu: University of Hawai'i Press, 2003). In the modern era, India's thinking on "nonalignment" and opposition to great power military pacts influenced Chinese foreign policy in the 1950s, especially at the 1955 Asia-Africa conference in Bandung. Amitav Acharya, *East of India, South of China: Sino-Indian Encounters in Southeast Asia* (New Delhi: Oxford University Press, 2017).

20. Sen, *Buddhism, Diplomacy and Trade*.

21. The view that Indian civilization is discontinuous, unlike China's, ignores the fact that the ideas and rituals of the Vedic India (mid-second millennium BC, contemporary of China's Shang and Zhou) are still extant today in the daily lives of a majority of Indians. And as Deep Datta-Ray has shown, the Indian epic *Mahabharata* continues to cast a long shadow over contemporary Indian ideas and practices of diplomacy and statecraft. Deep K. Datta-Ray, *The Making of Indian Diplomacy: A Critique of Eurocentrism* (Oxford: Oxford University Press, 2015); Amrita Narlikar and Aruna Narlikar, *Bargaining with a Rising India: Lessons from the Mahabharata* (Oxford: Oxford University Press, 2014). Both Chinese and Indian civilizations suffered frequent foreign invasions and extended periods of foreign rule, but both absorbed and were enriched by these external influences, and key elements of India's classical civilization have persisted to no lesser extent than China's.

22. Roger Boesche, "Kautilya's 'Arthasastra' on War and Diplomacy in Ancient India," *Journal of Military History* 67, no. 1 (January 2003): 19–20.

23. Yan Xuetong, *Leadership and the Rise of Great Powers* (Princeton, NJ: Princeton University Press, 2018).

24. Jack Donnelly, "The Relative Universality of Human Rights," *Human Rights Quarterly* 29, no. 2 (2007): 281–306. Donnelly seems to associates human rights with capitalism or property rights, rather than culture or politics *per se*.

25. Amartya Sen, "Universal Truths: Human Rights and the Westernizing Illusion," *Harvard International Review* 20, no. 3 (Summer 1998): 42.

26. Zhao Tingyang, "Redefining the Concept of Politics via 'Tianxia': The Problems, Conditions and Methodology," trans. Lu Guobin and ed. Sun Lan, *World Economics and Politics* 6 (2015): 4, 22; Zhang Feng, "The *Tianxia* System: World Order in a Chinese Utopia," http://www.chinaheritagequarterly.org/tien-hsia.php?searchterm = 021_utopia.inc&issue = 021.

27. Sheldon Pollock, *The Language of the Gods in the World of Men: Sanskrit, Culture and Power in Premodern India* (Chicago: University of Chicago Press, 2006).

28. O. W. Wolters, *History, Culture and Region in Southeast Asian Perspectives* (Singapore: Institute of Southeast Asian Studies, 1982).

29. Craig Reynolds, "A New Look at Old Southeast Asia," *Journal of Asian Studies* 54, no. 2 (1995): 426.

30. Qin Yaqing, *A Relational Theory of World Politics* (Cambridge: Cambridge University Press, 2018).

31. There are minor exceptions to the absence of military conflict between an classical Indian polity and a Chinese-backed one. This occurred in the mid-seventh century between Chinese forces of Tang envoy Wang Xuance and minor Indian king Arunasa, around the time of King Harsa's death. Sen, *Buddhism, Diplomacy and Trade*, 22–23.

32. Amitav Acharya, *Civilizations in Embrace: The Spread of Ideas and the Transformation of Power* (Singapore: Institute of Southeast Asian Studies, 2012).

Methodology

Mining the Past to Construct the Present

Some Methodological Considerations from India

Patrick Olivelle

In this volume, and in the three workshops leading up to it spanning three years, a group of scholars working on India and China have been engaged in searching for ways in which Asian classics can be mined to develop a new Asia-focused international relations theory. In this chapter I attempt to explore some methodological problems facing such an enterprise, problems to which, I feel, our group has not always paid adequate attention. In this regard, I address two interrelated issues: (1) methodology: how can we use responsibly the systems of political science and philosophy developed by ancient Indian and Chinese scholars in constructing theories of international relations for contemporary times? (2) case studies: I present three examples of political theory from ancient India as case studies in the practical application of the methodology I have enunciated.

PART ONE

Methodological Considerations

I will organize my comments on methodology around five topics: (1) dangers of essentializing; (2) multiple voices; (3) problems of translation and definition; (4) importance of context; and (5) gleaning from the past for contemporary global order.

1. Dangers of Essentializing. Current historians of the religions and culture of ancient India are keenly aware of the danger of essentializing—that is, assuming there is and searching to discover the essence of a culture or a religion. Such assumptions—sometimes explicit, but often implicit—were common among an earlier generation of scholars, of both India and China. I cringe when people begin sentences with "Hindus believe," "Buddhism is," or "Indian philosophy posits"—and their Chinese counterparts. As a young student, I was told that we—the students of religion, the historians—should learn from the social scientists in this regard. There are no essences to be discovered but only dynamic and ever-changing social, cultural, and religious institutions, practices, and beliefs. Today, however, I am astounded how easily these very scientists—be they anthropologists, sociologists, or political scientists—sink into essentialism when they speak about pre-modern or ancient societies. They seem to have absorbed the old British colonial image of "an unchanging India." Let us recognize that all societies and cultures, both modern and ancient, are historically dynamic, geographically diverse, and ever changing. Let us give back agency to the people we are studying: these changes do not simply happen; they are brought about by the work of individuals and groups.

Let me be blunt here at the risk of giving offense. In our past meetings, as I have had occasion to observe, I was dismayed when people talked about "Chinese thought" or "Chinese philosophy" as if it were one and singular, as if it has an unchanging essential core. I would never dare to make such blanket statements about India—ancient, medieval, or modern; India was and is diverse, vibrant, dynamic, and ever changing. So, when we talk about ancient Indian theories of statecraft and international relations, we must recognize that they were as diverse as such theories are in modern Europe or America. We would not ever speak about an American political science as a singular and essential entity. Let us be clear. There is no ancient Indian political philosophy. For sure, there are continuities and commonalities within the traditions, given that the past cultural and religious ideas and institutions influenced thinkers of later times. But such influences provoked not just acceptance or incremental change but also outright rejection. Continuities, however, do not constitute an essence. Speaking metaphorically, it is best for us to leave Aristotle and his essences behind and follow the Buddha, who insisted on the absence of any substance, any soul, behind the composite and every changing entities we encounter, including ourselves. A culture, the Buddha would have said, is like a river; there is an illusion of substance but the water is never the same.

My friend and colleague Roger Ames, who has partnered with me in writing the chapters on method, has argued strongly for what he terms "thick generalizations," which he distinguishes from essentializing. I can readily agree that generalization—moving from the particular to the general—is essential to all scholarly and scientific endeavors. Theory, after all, is a generalization that attempts to explain the atomistic and particular phenomena. But for a cultural historian, I still feel, such generalizations, unless done self-consciously, as Roger urges us to do, can flatten the contours of history that often contain rejections of the accepted views that often form the basis for those generalizations. For the cultural historian it is much more important to identify and understand the rich internal contours of Chinese or Indian cultural history than to see how these cultures or philosophies differ from their "Western" counterparts. The multiple voices of the tradition should not be flattened to fit a preconceived notion of what "Chinese" or "Indian" culture or philosophy is. Even when we opt to choose a particular voice from that tradition, as we will do in the process of creating a new IR theory, we must be cognizant that it does not represent *all* of that tradition and that the very selection may distort our perception of that rich and diverse tradition.

2. *Multiple Voices.* A direct corollary of a nonessentialist and dynamic view of a culture is the recognition of multiple voices in any given period of time and, a fortiori, across history. This seems like an obvious point, but even when scholars speak of multiple authors, there is a tendency to distill their voices into a singular position. In the ancient Indian legal tradition (Dharmaśāstra), this position is presented as an exegetical principle: all the authoritative texts, both the Vedas and the authoritative legal texts called *smṛti*, present the same truth; any differences we detect in them must be eliminated using various hermeneutical strategies. So, the tradition itself presents the illusion of a seamless and uniform doctrine and law. Modern scholars often seem to be quite content to follow that lead.

Often the very terms and categories we use entice us to think this way. So we speak of Hinduism, Buddhism, Indian Philosophy, and the like, giving at least the impression that there are essences, substances, behind these terms, that they are in some sense univocal. There aren't. We must force ourselves to listen to the multiple voices in ancient India. Ashoka's views on state, religion, and morality were singular and, as we will see, vastly different from those of Kautilya and Manu, or the authors of the *Mahābhārata*. We cannot and should not put them all into a blender to obtain a consistent and bland cocktail.

3. *Problems of Translation and Definition.* Ancient Chinese wrote in classical Chinese and ancient Indians wrote in several languages, but principally in Sanskrit. This is an obvious point, but it is often overlooked. Philosophical and scientific works use technical terms in both languages. We must be attentive to this problem, even as we use translated texts to understand those works and to draw inspiration from them in order to construct theoretical frameworks suitable for the contemporary world. Much is, indeed, lost in translation. When we use a translated English term, we frequently miss the old connotations and implicitly import modern meanings associated with the English term. Take, for example, the term "state," which is central to the work entailed in this volume. There are several Sanskrit terms translated as state, but the principal ones are *rāṣṭra* and *rājya*, both connected to a king, the *rāja*. In ancient India, except for the period of Ashoka's rule, a *rāṣṭra* meant a rather small territory ruled by a king, a polity that was always jostling for space and power with its neighbors. Inhabitants of such a state did not necessarily identify themselves as citizens of that state. Simply moving to a different polity was always

a possibility for subjects, and such large-scale migrations proved to be a danger that a king was advised to guard against. These states did not base their identity on ethnic, religious, or linguistic grounds. In contrast, for most of Chinese history, except for the period of the warring states, China was a singular empire with a central administration.

So, in these contexts how do we define "state"? Can we extrapolate from theories based on these ancient "states" to the modern nation-states? There are significant differences between ancient Indian and ancient Chinese political dispensations that militate against using their respective political philosophies to build IR theories without taking these differences into account. These issues need to be addressed if we are to use ancient sources responsibly.

4. *Importance of Context*. The three points I have already raised bring us to the centrality of context in understanding political theories formulated by ancient Indian or Chinese thinkers. The context includes, among others factors, the political, social, economic, and religious conditions of the time and the place. The context also includes the life circumstances of the author. Thus, we need to take into account whether the author was working for a king or state, whether he (it is invariably a "he") was a bureaucrat or military officer, whether he was from the rich elite or a common person—that is, if such information is available.

In the Indian context, the three authors I deal with were from different historical periods and from different sociopolitical backgrounds. Ashoka was a powerful emperor living in the middle of the third century BCE, who, however, repented his violent past and became a devout Buddhist committed to the end of killing and violence. Kautilya, who wrote three centuries later in the middle of the first century CE, was probably a bureaucrat and was within a specialized intellectual tradition that dealt with governance, law, and war. His work was addressed to kings and high government and military officials. Manu, who lived probably a century or so after Kautilya, came from a conservative Brahmanical background, intent on fostering Brahmanical privilege and exceptionalism. He also probably wrote for the classroom where Brahmanical education took place. During both Kautilya's and Manu's time, northern India was subjected to military invasions from northwestern regions, especially central Asia. They established large polities—first the Śakas and then the Kuśānas, in northcentral India. Manu, in a special way, reflects some of the social disruptions of these times.

5. *Gleaning from the Past*. Before application must come understanding. And understanding must be historically grounded. That is the reason for the four foregoing points I have presented. We can understand what an author is saying only if we understand his or her language and the socio-politico-religious context of his or her life. Contextual understanding is the only reliable and legitimate form of understanding. Humility is a virtue here. We can never be sure that we have

truly understood what an ancient thinker intends to communicate. And we must be humble enough to acknowledge it, knowing that our understanding is subject to correction and improvement as new data and new methods of interpretation open themselves to us. Just think of what the discovery of bamboo-strip writing from ancient China has done to our understanding of major Chinese texts. And in India the pivotal *Arthaśāstra* came to light only in 1905.

Once such an understanding is acquired, we can cautiously and tentatively— and let me emphasize *cautiously* and *tentatively*—move to the next phase: applying that understanding to contemporary issues. This is true in the areas of religion and philosophy. It is doubly true for the case at hand: attempting to glean inspiration and ideas to create a blueprint for a new global order.

PART TWO

Ancient India and International Relations Theory

So, with that methodological backdrop and with all the caveats that it engenders, I think it may be useful to present some test cases of using ancient theories to generate new knowledge for the contemporary world. The best way to undertake such an enterprise, I think, is to ask a series of questions from the ancient sources. Although not an expert on world order or international relations, I suggest that a theory must present ideas which seek to transcend the interests of individual polities and to provide a legal and moral framework for relations among such polities. We have several such frameworks, imperfect and subjected to criticism though they may be: for example, the UN Declaration of Human Rights, the UN Convention on the Law of the Sea, the Chemical Weapons Convention, Crimes against Humanity, International Court of Justice, and so on.

Here are some ways we may want to interrogate our sources. In what ways do ancient theories attempt to rise above and beyond the specific polities within which they are embedded or on whose behalf the authors may have been working? How do they envisage law/moral code as transcending individual polities? Is there a transcendent source of law/morality that must be respected by each polity? Can one polity intervene in another when that transcendent law is violated by the authorities of that polity? In other words, does an ancient theory provide the basic ingredients to make it suitable as a source for creating a modern IR theory?

Ashoka. Ashoka (reigned ca. 268–232 BCE) consolidated the empire he inherited from his grandfather, Candragupta,[1] the founder of the Maurya empire, extending it to much of India, from Afghanistan to Bengal and south into what is today Karnataka. He left numerous inscriptions on stones and pillars containing the emperor's instructions and advice to his officials and subjects. Two features of Ashoka's corpus of writings stand out. First, we have them *in situ* exactly as they were written at the emperor's command. Second, we know exactly when they were written down. In ancient Indian history, these two features of texts are unique.

Ashoka, however, does not explicitly articulate a foreign policy. His inscriptions are addressed to his officials and subjects, and his mention of foreign kings and his relations with them are given tangentially. Thus, we have to tease out what his thinking with regard to foreign states and rulers would have been.

The centrality of social and personal morality encapsulated in the term *dharma* in Ashoka's political philosophy is well known. He used his state bureaucracy and his inscriptional activities in his efforts to lead his people to cultivate moral virtues and to build moral character. I have previously described this as Ashoka's "civil religion," using *mutatis mutandi* the expression popularized by Robert Bellah (1970) within the context of the United States.

Taking a step back, it is clear that Ashoka, following in the footsteps of his father and grandfather, continued an aggressive program of territorial expansion, waging war against independent states bordering his growing empire. The most notorious of these was the war against the Kalingas, what is today's Orissa, which he annexed eight years after his royal consecration, that is, in the year 260 BCE. This was a particularly brutal war, and in his 13th Rock Edict, Ashoka expresses remorse at the death and destruction he caused, with 100,000 killed and 150,000 taken away as captives. It is significant that the most common term Ashoka uses for kingdom, state, or empire is *vijita*, literally "conquered" and from the same verbal root as the Kautilyan term for king, *vijigīṣu*, which we will soon encounter.

All this changed with Ashoka's conversion to Buddhism, probably two years after the end of the Kalinga war. It was after this pivotal event that Ashoka became fixated on his mission to propagate *dharma*. A cornerstone of Ashoka's definition of *dharma* is the abstention from killing extended to both humans and animals. His abhorrence of war comes out loud and clear. After his horrific military adventure in Kalinga, Ashoka says in his Rock Edict 13 that the greatest victory for him now is the victory of *dharma* (*dharmavijaya*). But this victory of *dharma*, in Ashoka's mind, is not restricted to his own empire. It is a victory he seeks in every territory and kingdom known to him:

> But this is for the Beloved of Gods [i.e., Ashoka] the foremost conquest, namely, the conquest through dharma. This again has been won by the Beloved of Gods here and among all the neighbors, as far as 600 Yojanas where the Yona king named Antiyoka resides; and, beyond that Antiyoka, the four kings named Tulamaya, Antekina, Maka, and Alikasundale; and, in the south, the Codas, the Pandyas, and as far as Tamraparni. Likewise, here in the king's domain, among the Yonas and Kambojas, the Nabhakas and Nabhapaṃtis, the Bhojas and Pitinikas, the Andhras and Paladas—everywhere they follow the dharma instruction of the Beloved of Gods.

> Even where envoys of the Beloved of Gods do not go, after hearing about the dharma discourses, the ordinances, and dharma instruction of the Beloved of Gods, they conform to dharma and they will conform to it in the future. In this manner, this conquest has been won everywhere. In all cases, however, the conquest is a source of joy. And joy has been obtained in the conquest through dharma.
>
> This joy, however, is truly insignificant. Only what is done for the hereafter, the Beloved of Gods thinks, bears great fruit.

The intention of Ashoka in sending these missions to faraway countries is clear: it was a missionary effort to spread his *dharma* philosophy, to get rulers of these countries, as also their subjects, to adopt Ashoka's moral philosophy in their personal lives, internal administration, and external affairs. How successful these missions were is hard to gauge, but Romila Thapar (1997: 126) thinks that at least in the west the missions did not amount to much. Thus, in Pillar Edict 7, the last of his inscriptions written in the twenty-seventh regnal year and consisting of a retrospect of his activities on behalf of *dharma*, Ashoka does not speak about his foreign activities but only of his domestic successes.

Yet, whatever the outcome, Ashoka's guiding principle in his foreign relations—as also his domestic policy—is clear: it is the moral philosophy rooted in *dharma* and fostering peaceful coexistence. In Rock Edict 2, however, Ashoka provides some details about what activities his *dharma* missions entailed. They included, significantly, the provision of medical knowledge and medicinal plants:

> Everywhere in the territory of the Beloved of Gods, King Piyadasi, as well as in those at the frontiers, namely, Codas, Pandyas, Satiyaputras, Keralaputras, Tamraparnis, the Greek king named Antioch, and other kings who are that Antioch's neighbors—everywhere the Beloved of Gods, King Piyadasi, has established two kinds of medical services: medical services for humans and medical services for domestic animals. In whichever place medicinal herbs beneficial for humans and domestic animals were not found, he had them brought in and planted everywhere. Likewise, in whichever place root vegetables and fruit trees were not found, he had them brought in and planted everywhere. Along roads he had trees planted and wells dug for the benefit of domestic animals and human beings.

The final statement about planting trees and digging wells along roads may well refer to his activities within his own territory. Nevertheless, it is instructive that Ashoka thought that providing medical assistance was part of his *dharma* mission to foreign countries, as it was for domestic policy. Ashoka's *dharma*, thus, had a social and activist dimension. A point that we should keep in mind as we move to considering Manu is Ashoka's conviction that *dharma* is a moral force that stands above all kings and territories. It is a moral force to which all kings and all peoples must submit. And it is in this submission, in conforming to the demands of *dharma*, that Ashoka envisages domestic prosperity and, internationally, the elimination of wars and conflicts and the establishment of peace and tranquility. These points are elaborated by Rajeev Bhargava in chapter 4.

Kautilya. Kautilya, writing three centuries after Ashoka, provides a different voice with respect to domestic affairs and interstate relations. His work called *Arthaśāstra* (*KAS*) is a scientific treatise on political science encompassing both domestic and foreign affairs, and thus quite different from Ashoka's personal letters.

Except for the periods when the Maurya, the Gupta, and perhaps a few other regional empires ruled, the usual ancient Indian kingdom covered a relatively small territory. The result was that small states were butting against each other; they were thus forced to deal with each other either as enemies or as allies. Ancient Indian trade also was transregional and crossed state boundaries, forcing different kingdoms to establish relations with each other and to maintain trade routes. It was this political and economic reality that underlies the theories and policies enunciated by Kautilya in the second half of the *Arthaśāstra* devoted to foreign policy. It also underlies the theory of *maṇḍala* or circle of kingdoms espoused by Kautilya. His policies were developed within the scenario of numerous small states having to deal with and to outwit each other through military and diplomatic strategies. Foreign policy, therefore, occupies a central position in Kautilya's work.

Kautilya's attitude to foreign policy is based on the definition of the king as *vijigīṣu*, "one who desires to conquer." This adjectival term is derived from the desiderative form of the compound verb *vi-* √*ji*, (to conquer), from which are also derived common Sanskrit words such as *vijaya* (conquest). This is the pivotal concept in Kautilya's ideology of kingship as it relates to foreign affairs. In fact, this epithet is never used in the first half of his treatise, which deals with internal administration, bureaucratic structures, and law. Clearly the term in inapplicable when a king is dealing with his own territory and subjects. In all, this epithet occurs thirty-one times in the second half of the treatise. According to Kautilya, in his relations with other states and kings, the king he is addressing assumes the role of a "would-be-conqueror." It has been suggested in recent scholarship on the *Arthaśāstra* that *vijigīṣu* is "a potential conqueror state" (Shahi 2014: 71). This is incorrect and runs the risk I have already mentioned of introducing the notion of a modern state into the Kautilyan discourse. The term *vijigīṣu* always refers to an individual human being, in this case the king, rather than to an impersonal entity such as a state. This ultimate goal of conquest, which any individual *vijigīṣu* may have to postpone indefinitely or until the right circumstances prevail, dictates all the king's activities with respect to foreign affairs.

Kautilya thinks that the desire to acquire what one does not possess is an essential element of the very ideal of governance, which he calls *daṇḍanīti*. At the very beginning of his treatise, in dealing with economics, he notes the importance of economic activities: "By means of that, he brings under his power his own circle (*maṇḍala*) and his enemy's circle using the treasury and the army. . . . Government (*daṇḍanīti*) seeks to acquire what has not been acquired, to safeguard what has been acquired, to augment what has been safeguarded, and to bestow what has been augmented on worthy recipients" (*KAS* 1.4.3).[2] This was turned into a proverbial saying by Manu (7.99) and repeated frequently by later authors. Early in the section on foreign affairs, Kautilya offers a definition of *vijigīṣu*: "The seeker after conquest (*vijigīṣu*) is a king who is endowed with the exemplary qualities both of the self [enumerated at 6.1.6] and of material constituents [enumerated in 6.2.28], and who is the abode of good policy" (*KAS* 6.2.13).[3]

The whole point of being a king was to expand his territory by conquest or through diplomatic strategies. But, of course, all the neighboring kings were operating under the same assumption. Correct strategy and good foreign policy separated the successful conqueror from the failures. Good policy required good counsel or *mantra*. Although counsel was important for all state affairs, it was of paramount importance when dealing with foreign powers. The group of counselors (*mantrin*) headed by the chaplain did double duty in advising the king on both domestic matters and foreign affairs. There was, however, a bureaucracy that specialized in dealing with other states. With reference to diplomacy, the most significant official was the envoy (*dūta*).[4] Kautilya speaks of three levels of envoys (*KAS* 1.16.2–4). The highest, the plenipotentiary, has the broadest authority to negotiate with foreign governments, and he is expected to possess all the qualities of a minister. The mid-level envoys are given circumscribed and specific missions, while the low-level envoys merely conveyed royal edicts and messages.

Internal security was another important consideration, because kings were constantly attempting to undermine and to destabilize neighboring states by infiltrating secret agents, assassins, and spies. Given normal trade relations and the mobility of wandering ascetics and similar itinerants, this was a difficult task. Border guards headed by the frontier commander (*antapāla*), often residing in a fort and assisted by friendly forest tribes (*aṭavī*), were responsible for border security to prevent infiltration of enemy operatives. On the other hand, Kautilya recommends a robust secret service with a wide variety of covert operations directed both internally and against neighboring states.

Finally, there was the military organization headed by the chief of armed forces (*senāpati*). Books 9 and 10 deal extensively with the various kinds of military forces and their deployment. In general, an army was supposed to have four kinds of regiments: infantry, cavalry, chariot corps, and elephant corps. The kinds of troops one would deploy in an actual military conflict would, of course, depend on the terrain where the fighting was to take place and the kinds of troops deployed by the enemy.

Obviously, it was too expensive to maintain a large standing army. Therefore, Kautilya recommends a small army consisting mostly of hereditary soldiers called *maula*, belonging to the heartland of the kingdom. These are the best and the most loyal of troops. Other troops could be mobilized when a war was imminent. Kautilya at one place points to four kinds of troops besides the hereditary (7.8.27). The first consists of hired troops or mercenaries (*bhṛta*). Then there are corporate troops (*śreṇi*), who were probably men belonging to martial castes or guilds. They would offer their services to the highest bidder. The third comprised troops provided by an ally, and the last comprised those provided by a tribal chief (*āṭavika*). To this we should add troops provided by an enemy with whom the king may be temporarily allied, probably when he is attacking a common enemy.

In crafting his foreign policy Kautilya presents a theory of the foreign powers with which his ideal-typical king would have to contend. True to his desire to present abstract rather than historical realities, he enunciates the theory of *maṇḍala*, the circle of kingdoms. A king is surrounded in a circle by other states, and because they have common boundaries with him they are his natural enemies. Around these enemy kingdoms is a second circle of kingdoms. Given that they abut the territories of enemy kings of the first circle, they become his natural allies: my enemy's enemy is my friend. Those forming the third outer circle, by the same logic, are the enemies of his allies, and thus his own enemies—and so on. That this theoretical construct is artificial is obvious, but it also highlights the truism that you are most in conflict with your immediate neighbors. The only two kings Kautilya considers outside the *maṇḍala* theory of ally and enemy are the *madhyama,* who is an intermediate king located between two enemies, and the *udāsīna,* a powerful king who remains, or can afford to remain, neutral.

There is also a nonmonarchical type of state called *saṅgha* recognized by Kautilya. The term refers to confederacies where power is shared by leaders of clans. These confederacies, often erroneously termed republics (Jayaswal 1924), appear to have been common in the second half of the first millennium BCE. They are referred to in the Buddhist literature, and they probably gave their name to the Buddhist monastic order, the *saṅgha.* Kautilya is aware of both the strengths and the weaknesses of confederacies. I will discuss below his strategies with regard to these polities.

Although military might is important, Kautilya recognizes that it is a double-edged sword: one can lose a war just as easily—one might say, more easily—as one can win. War is inherently unpredictable. It is also expensive. So Kautilya recommends a variety of other strategies that are several steps removed from actual warfare and that can further the king's goals more effectively and less expensively.

One set of strategies called *upāya* (2.10.47) has four elements: conciliation (*sāma*), gifts (*dāna*), dissension (*bheda*), and military force (*daṇḍa*). The second set of strategies containing six elements is called simply *ṣāḍguṇya* (sixfold strategy; 7.1.1–19): peace pact (*saṃdhi*), initiating hostilities (*vigraha*), remaining stationary (*āsana*), marching into battle (*yāna*), seeking refuge (*saṃśraya*), and double stratagem (*dvaidhībhāva*). The four *upāyas* are discussed throughout the text, including the first half (Books 1–5), whereas the *ṣāḍguṇya* is confined mostly to Books 6 and 7. It appears that the former was a more general and widespread, and perhaps older, formulation of major foreign policy strategies, whereas the latter is a more sophisticated and nuanced strategy developed by the author of the sources

Kautilya used in crafting the second half of his treatise. Further, the *upāyas* appear to be concerned with policies both toward other kings and toward internal centers of power, whereas the *ṣāḍguṇya* is focused on strategies that a king himself would use vis-à-vis his external opponents. Although both lists contain the option of resorting to military force, the other components of these strategies are directed at achieving the desired objectives without war.

The central strategy that runs through all of Kautilya's foreign policy is captured in the word *atisaṃdhāna* and its nominal (*atisaṃdhi*) and verbal (*atisaṃdhatte, atisaṃdhīyate*) equivalents. There is an obvious connection between this term and *saṃdhi* as a peace pact or alliance. The origin of the term is probably to be located in precisely such a peace pact, which is used not to ensure peace but to outmaneuver and outwit the opponent—the prefix *ati* indicates the transgressive nature of this strategy. It uses the peace pact cunningly and skillfully—we could even say, deceptively, trickily, guilefully—to outsmart, outmaneuver, and finally overpower the king with whom he has concluded the pact. I have thus translated this term as "outwitting" (Olivelle 2011). At every step, Kautilya wants his king to pay attention to the larger picture and to use the tools at hand—whether it is negotiating a peace pact or initiating a state of hostilities, or even going on a military expedition with allied troops—in order to outwit and ultimately defeat the opponent. Much of Book 7 is given to the ways in which the strategy of outwitting an opponent can be used in diverse situations. This proverb highlights the centrality of good policy in foreign affairs:

> An arrow unleashed by an archer may kill a single man or not kill anyone; but a strategy unleashed by a wise man kills even those still in the womb.[5] (*KAŚ* 10.6.51)

Let us, however, take a step back, and look at Kautilya's views on alliances, which he calls *saṃdhi*.[6] This, as we have seen, is the first member of the sixfold strategy (*ṣāḍguṇya*), and it stands always in relation and contrast to the second member, hostilities (*vigraha*). The thesis I want to propose is that, contrary to how they have generally been depicted, *vigraha* and its verbal equivalents do not mean war, attack, fighting, or combat, and that *saṃdhi*, as also its verbal equivalents, does not mean peace or even a peace accord, at least in the modern sense of this expression. The terms used for warfare in the *Arthaśāstra* are the verb √*yudh* and the noun *yuddha*, as well as other terms such as *abhi-* √*han* and *abhi-* √*yuj*. Thus, for example, we have expressions such as: *aśvayuddha* ("cavalry charge": *KAŚ* 10.5.53), *hastiyuddha* ("attack with elephants": *KAŚ* 10.5.54), and the like, but never an *aśvavigraha*. The actual march into battle is always called *yāna*, along with its verbal equivalents. The suspicion that *vigraha* does not refer to actual warfare is further confirmed by several significant usages of this term, especially in its verbal forms.[7]

Let us now turn to the companion term *saṃdhi*, which does not imply a state of peace between two kingdoms or even a formal peace treaty, but a temporary and focused contract between two parties aimed at accomplishing a specific goal, such as attacking a common enemy. While that contract or pact lasts, naturally, the two sides will be in alliance rather than at war with each other. We see that it also entails a strategy to overcome and outwit another king rather than the initiation of a time of peace or the conclusion of a peace accord. The *Arthaśāstra* (7.1.6) defines *saṃdhi* as *paṇabandha*, that is, a negotiated agreement. That *saṃdhi* is a tactic is made clear at *KAŚ* 7.4.17–18:

> If he were to foresee that the result can be secured alone and within a brief period of time, then he should initiate hostilities (*vigṛhya*) with the rear enemy and his backer and march into battle (*yāyāt*). Under circumstances opposite of the preceding, he should enter into a peace pact (*saṃdhi*) and then march into battle.[8]

In a footnote to this passage, Kangle (1972: 333) comments in surprise: "This is downright duplicity, making peace and then attacking the enemy when he is least expecting such an attack." But that is the whole point! One should not be surprised; *saṃdhi* is as much a strategy seeking tactical advantage over other kings as *vigraha*. That it is so is explicitly stated in a long passage stating the conditions under which a king should resort to *saṃdhi* (*KAŚ* 7.1.32).

The clearest statement linking *atisaṃdhāna* with *saṃdhi* is in *KAŚ* 7.6. Here the opening sentence states:

> The seeker after conquests [that is, the *vijigīṣu*] should outwit (*atisaṃdadhyāt*) the second constituent of the circle [i.e., the *amitra* or enemy] in the following manner.[9]

It is interesting that in these passages the *saṃdhi* is done with the *amitra*, one's natural enemy, rather than with an ally. So if we translate *saṃdhi* as alliance, as is often done, we should be careful to distinguish such an alliance from the *mitra*, the natural ally of a king within the ideology of the *maṇḍala* (circle of kingdoms).

So, far from being a peace treaty, *saṃdhi* is a strategic move on the part of a king, either because he is in a difficult position and wants to buy time or because he thinks that such a pact could ensure victory either over the king with whom he is entering into the pact, or over another king whom he wants to attack with the support of his new ally, or, ideally, over both. Another point to remember is that an alliance formed through a *saṃdhi* is temporary and has nothing to do with the ally/enemy (*mitra*, *amitra*) configuration coming from the theory of the *maṇḍala*, the circle of kingdoms. These allies and enemies result from the very nature of territorial contiguity. As we have seen, one can indeed form a *saṃdhi* with one's natural enemy. On this point, *saṃdhi* is very similar to another form of compact or contract, namely *sambhūya*, the coming together of individuals, especially businessmen, to join forces and to combine resources in order to accomplish a particular common task (*KAŚ* 7.4.19–22).

Thus, we need to see these two terms, *saṃdhi* and *vigraha*, not as simple statements of facts—the states of war or peace—between kingdoms or states, but as deliberate political and military strategies employed by kings against each other. The one who is able to execute them better will outsmart the opponent. Within the Kautilyan political ideology, there really is no place for peace as a value and goal to be sought after; at best, peace is an interlude when no open hostilities are taking place. A state of stability where established states with boundaries respected by other states exist in mutual respect and cooperation—*à la* Ashoka—is something that Kautilya would have seen as an anomaly, as something antithetical to the very idea of kingship. The centrality of the concept of *atisaṃdhāna* in Kautilya's political strategy cannot be overstated, and it is a feature of his foreign policy that has often been ignored by scholars.

Before leaving Kautilya, let me briefly explore a kind of polity different from monarchy, namely the *saṅgha* or confederacy that I have already referred to. Kautilya devotes Book 11 of his work entirely to the topic of confederacies. He considered them the most stable and strongest form of government, and if a king could have a confederacy as an ally, it would be better than any gain he can expect to get: "Gaining a confederacy is the best among gains, whether it is army or ally, for confederacies, because they are closely knit, are impervious to enemy assaults" (*KAŚ* 11.1.1–2).[10] He refers by name to eleven confederacies: Kāmbojas, Surāṣṭras, Kṣatriyas, Śreṇis, Licchivikas, Vṛjikas, Mallakas, Madrakas, Kukuras, Kurus, and Pañcālas (*KAŚ* 11.1.4–5). Kautilya recognizes that open assault is not very effective against a confederacy, because they are united in their fight against an external enemy. Sowing dissension (*bheda*), the third of the four *upāyas*, is the principal means of overpowering a confederacy. Kautilya goes into great detail about how this might be accomplished. I will cite just a couple of examples. The first involves rivalry among chiefs of confederacies:

> In the case of all of these, secret agents operating nearby should find out the grounds for mutual abuse, hatred, enmity, and quarrels among members of confederacies, and sow dissension in anyone whose confidence they have gradually won, saying: "That person defames you." When ill will has thus been built up among adherents of both sides, secret agents posing as teachers should provoke quarrels among their young boys with respect to their knowledge, skill, gambling, and sports.[11] (*KAŚ* 11.1.6–8)

Here, Kautilya demonstrates a fine grasp of psychology in getting the adults involved in the quarrels of their children. The common method of sowing dissension involves, naturally, sex.

> An agent working undercover as an astrologer should describe to one man a girl who has been chosen by another: "That man's daughter is bound to become the wife of a king and the mother of a king. Get her by giving all you have got or by using force." If he fails to get her, he should stir up the opponent's side. If he gets her, a quarrel is assured.
>
> Or else, a female mendicant should tell a chief who loves his wife: "That chief, arrogant due to his youth, sent me to your wife. Because I fear him, I have come

carrying this letter and ornaments. Your wife is innocent. You should deal with him secretly."[12] (*KAŚ* 11.1.49–52)

Let me note, parenthetically, that a sentiment very close to that of Kautilya is expressed by the Buddha when King Ajātasattu sends his minister, Vassakāra, to the Buddha before he begins a military attack on the confederacy of the Vajjis, saying:

> I will root out these Vaggians, mighty and powerful though they be, I will destroy these Vaggians, I will bring these Vaggians to utter ruin! And bear carefully in mind whatever the Blessed One may predict, and repeat it to me. For the Buddhas speak nothing untrue!

Buddha replies to Vassakāra in a roundabout way, showing where he thought the strength of a confederacy lies:

> So long as the Vaggians hold these full and frequent public assemblies; so long may they be expected not to decline, but to prosper . . . So long as the Vaggians meet together in concord, and rise in concord, and carry out their undertakings in concord—so long as they enact nothing not already established, abrogate nothing that has been already enacted, and act in accordance with the ancient institutions of the Vaggians as established in former days . . . so long may the Vaggians be expected not to decline, but to prosper. *Mahāparinibbāna Sutta* (trans. T. W. Rhys Davids)

It is this unity that Kautilya is attempting to break by sowing dissensions within a confederacy through deviant strategies for which he is well known.

When everything fails, however, a king must resort to military force to attain his objective, namely, the conquest of adjoining lands. Books 9, 10, and 13 of the *Arthaśāstra* are devoted to war: mobilization, military preparation, march, and capturing the fort. I will leave out the intricate details of the march, the various military formations, the foraging raids to obtain food for the soldiers, the ambushes, and other military tactics. The ideal-typical battle is waged in an open field with the two armies arrayed facing each other, although battles in less ideal terrain, such as forests, marshes, and water, are also discussed. Besides open and formal warfare, there are various kinds of special operations aimed at weakening the enemy, including surprise night attacks, burning the crops, and poisoning water supplies. When everything is said and done, the enemy can always escape into his fortress and barricade himself there. The whole of Book 13 is thus devoted to how one can capture a fort, first by trickery—inciting the people within the fort to sedition, drawing the enemy out of the fort by various tricks, destroying its food and water supply, and the like—then by laying siege, and finally taking it by storm.

The discussion of foreign policy and war, as also the entire treatise, culminates with instructions regarding the conduct of the victor and how a newly conquered territory should be pacified and its people induced to shift their loyalty to the new ruler (*KAŚ* 13.5). The incorporation of conquered territories into one's own kingdom always posed challenges and dangers. Kautilya does not envisage a centrally controlled large empire. He instructs the victor to act magnanimously with the leaders and the people of the conquered land and "arrange for the veneration of all gods and hermitages" (*KAŚ* 13.5.11). He should not act as a foreign conqueror but as a local ruler: "Therefore, he should adopt the habits, dress, language, and conduct similar to theirs, and demonstrate his devotion to them during festivals in honor of the gods of the region, festivities, and recreational activities" (*KAŚ* 13.5.7–8).

Manu. Manu, writing a century or so after Kautilya, represents a very different intellectual and expert tradition from that of the *Arthaśāstra*. He was writing in a time and after a long period when Brahmanism faced strong challenges from a variety of sources, both religious—such as the Buddhist—and from foreign invasions setting up polities within India—such the Shakas and the Kushanas. Manu was within the mainstream of Brahmanism and was very much part of what Bronkorst (2016) has called the "reinvention of a tradition," in this case, of Brahmanism. A central element of this reinvention was making the Brahmin not simply the apex of a new pyramidal sociology—the system of social class or caste (*varṇa*)—but also the indispensable person for every king and ruler.

Manu's seventh chapter is devoted to the king, and, as has been repeatedly pointed out (McClish 2014; Olivelle 2004), he borrows much of his material on political science from Kautilya. I want here simply to focus on one aspect of Manu's discussion, namely the thesis that law—moral, civil, and criminal—defined as *dharma* is universal and not constrained by territory. In other words, law as *dharma* is supra-state and not dependent on legislatures or rulers. The view that moral law in some sense transcends the political structures of a state, or even general historical vicissitudes, is found in many cultures and religions—including, as we saw, in Ashoka—whether morality is viewed as based on some kind of natural law, divine revelation, or the will of god. But, what is significant for IR Theory, is that for Manu even law in the strict sense—that is, civil and criminal law—is also viewed as transcending any particular state or political structure, at least within the cultural geography of India. Kings don't make laws but only enforce them.

This view is not unique to Manu; it is articulated in other Brahmanical texts as well. But I have chosen Manu both because he more than any other author personifies the Brahmanical social and legal philosophy centered on the concept of *dharma*, and because his work has had a disproportionate impact on the development of Indian ethics, political science, and sociology.

In an early Vedic text, *dharma* is presented as a transcendent source of royal power connected with the cosmic king Varuṇa: "Varuṇa himself, the lord of *dharma*, makes him [the king] the lord of *dharma*. This, clearly, is supremacy, that he is the lord of *dharma*."[13] This statement, significantly, occurs in the ritual consecration of a king (*rājasūya*). Varuṇa is well known as the divine enforcer of moral law and order, called *ṛta* in the *Rig Veda* and, when that term became obsolete, *dharma*. The central duty of the king as the "lord of *dharma*," then, is to make sure that he himself and all his subjects follow *dharma*. Thus *dharma*, one text tells us, is "the power superior to the ruling power" or *kṣatra; dharma* stands above the king as the power that confers on him the power to rule:

It created *dharma*, a form superior to and surpassing itself. And *dharma* is here the ruling power (*kṣatra*) of the ruling power. Hence there is nothing higher than *dharma*. Therefore, a weaker man makes demands of a stronger man by appealing to *dharma* just as one does by appealing to a king. Now, *dharma* is nothing but the truth. Therefore, when a man speaks the truth, people say that he speaks *dharma;* and when a man speaks *dharma*, people say that he speaks the truth. They are really the same thing.[14] (*Bṛhadāraṇyaka Upaniṣad* 1.4.14)

Here we have a conception of *dharma* that is universal, that stands above temporary rules and rulers, and that permits weak individuals to make demands of those who are strong—quite the opposite of what happens with the "law of the fish," *matsyanyāya*, where, in the absence of an authority to impose *dharma*, the bigger fish eat the smaller ones. *Dharma* is truth, and this transcendent nature of *dharma* is noted in another verse of the *Bṛhadāraṇyaka Upaniṣad* (1.5.23):

From which the sun rises,
And into which it sets;
The gods make it *dharma*.
It's the same today and tomorrow.

yataś codeti sūryaḥ astaṃ yatra ca gacchati |
taṃ devāś cakrire dharmaṃ sa evādya sa u śva ||

The term and concept of *dharma*, however, were appropriated by different religious traditions, especially the Buddhist. During the last centuries before the common era, *dharma* was a site of contention. What is *dharma*? And how do we come to know it?—these were central issues in the epistemology of *dharma*. Within the Brahmanical tradition, the ultimate source of *dharma* came to be located in the Veda, which was thought to be eternal, self-existent, and without a human or divine author. Manu (2.6) spells out the sources of *dharma*, both ultimate and proximate:

The root of dharma is the entire Veda, as also the recollection and conduct of those who know it; likewise the practice of good people, and satisfaction of oneself.

vedo 'khilo dharmamūlaṃ smṛtiśīle ca tadvidām |
ācāraś caiva sādhūnām ātmanas tuṣṭir eva ca ||

There is no talk here of king, legislature, or state: *dharma* stands above all the contingent social and political formations. Manu also speaks of punishment called *daṇḍa* as a central aspect of *dharma*. The king wields *daṇḍa* against those who transgress *dharma*. The king's duty is not to create but to enforce *dharma*.

So, in Manu, as also in Ashoka, we have a concept of social order that is governed by a law that transcends any given political formation. This concept of *dharma* also governs what is lawful and permissible in the conduct of war, and in Ashoka even interstate relations.

Yet, Manu also allows for localized *dharma*: the *dharma* of a region, a village, or even a family. So we have a universal *dharma*, often articulated in legal treatises, and local *dharma* contained in the customs of the people. The only requirement is that the local *dharma* cannot contravene the *dharma* articulated in the authoritative legal texts.

CONCLUSIONS

The central conclusion from my brief foray into three major writers on ancient Indian political philosophy is that it is rich and diverse, and any attempt to distill it to one thing that we may prefer will both distort that complex reality and impoverish the rich Indian tradition. This was the main conclusion of my comments on methodology at the beginning of this paper.

Kautilya presents a unique view within Indian intellectual history, a view shared more broadly by the tradition of political science (*Arthaśāstra* or *daṇḍanīti*). His is the only extant scientific treatise from that tradition. His views on external relations are based on power politics that take as their central principle the enhancement of a king's power, wealth, and territory. It is a strong articulation of *realpolitik*, and it probably comes closest to the historical reality of ancient Indian kings vying for power and control against each other.

Ashoka is unique both in India and possibly in the world, because he is the only real king who has left us written documents of his own views and aspirations, his moral and political philosophy, in a deeply personal way.[15] Much of his political philosophy of coexistence and nonviolence based on *dharma*, nevertheless, soon disappeared from Indian political history, although it remained a cornerstone of Indian moral philosophy.

Manu and the mainstream of Brahmanical political thought were probably the ones that had the most influence on later political philosophy. I also think that Manu's views of law, both moral and civil, probably provide the best source for talking about a new IR Theory, although I am not competent to take that idea any further, let alone construct such a theory. But I think that, if IR Theory attempts to construct an international order based on laws that transcend any particular polity, then Manu's conception of *dharma* to which all Indian kings subscribed may offer some precedents. Manu, of course, envisaged only the cultural landscape of India, and his concept of *dharma* as transcending individual polities was easily accepted within that context. The task of a modern IR Theory would be to broaden that landscape to include a world constructed out of nation-sates.

I think such supra-state laws may have ecological dimensions as well. Manu, at least in the case of individuals, proposes punishments for what we would call ecological crimes. So, for example, Manu (11.143–145) talks about penances that people who cut down trees should observe:

> For cutting down fruit trees a person should recite softly one hundred ṛc verses; so also for cutting down shrubs, vines, creepers, or flowering plants. . . . For needlessly tearing out cultivated plants or ones that grow spontaneously in the forest, he should follow a cow for one day, subsisting on milk.

Similar penances are given for people who harm animals, even very small ones that lack bones (Manu 11.132–142).

Let me conclude with the caveat that I started out with: the states that we are dealing with in ancient India do not parallel the ones in contemporary times. The only ones that come close to such a parallel are the Greek kingdoms of west Asia mentioned by Ashoka. When attempting to construct theories for modern political realities, we must always guard against anachronism and the attempt to read ancient texts through modern lenses rather than taking them on their own terms. That is the respect we owe to these great thinkers of the past, the least we can do to their memory.

NOTES

1. Candragupta gained power in the aftermath of Alexander the Great's incursion into northwest India and his subsequent exit.

2. *tayā svapakṣaṃ parapakṣaṃ ca vaśīkaroti kośadaṇḍābhyām* | . . . *daṇḍanītiḥ alabdhalābhārthā labdhaparirakṣaṇī rakṣitavivardhanī vṛddhasya tīrthe pratipādanī ca* || The Sanskrit term *labdha* and its cognates refer to any acquisition, but in the case of the king they refer in particular to the acquisition of territory by conquest . This is clear in Ashoka's RE 13, where he refers to the Kaliṅga territory as acquired by conquest: *laddhesu kaliṃgesu* (Sk. *labdhesu kaliṅgeṣu*).

3. *rājā ātmadravyaprakṛtisaṃpanno nayasyādhiṣṭhānaṃ vijigīṣuḥ* ||

4. The *dūta* as envoy is mentioned also by Ashoka in RE 13.

5. *ekaṃ hanyān na vā hanyād iṣuḥ kṣipto dhanuṣmatā* | *prājñena tu matiḥ kṣiptā hanyād garbhagatān api* ||

6. We should also note that *saṃdhi* (normally spelled Sandhi) is a central concept in Sanskrit grammar. It refers to the way the last sound or letter in a word changes or is changed by sounds that immediately follow or precede it. So it refers to the euphonic combination of sounds, and in the political realm the political alliance of adjacent polities.

7. For further details and for a detailed analysis of *saṃdhi* and *vigraha*, see Olivelle 2011.

8. *yadā vā paśyet "na śakyam ekena yātum avaśyaṃ ca yātavyam" iti tadā samahīnajyāyobhih sāmavāyikaiḥ saṃbhūya yāyād, ekatra nirdiṣṭenāṃśena, anekatrānirdiṣṭenāṃśena* ||

9. *vijigīṣur dvitīyāṃ prakṛtim evam atisaṃdadhyāt* || KAŚ 7.6.1.

10. *saṅghalābho daṇḍamitralābhānām uttamaḥ* | *saṅghā hi saṃhatatvād adhṛṣyāḥ pareṣām* ||

11. *sarveṣām āsannāḥ sattriṇaḥ saṅghānāṃ parasparanyaṅgadveṣavairakalahasthānāny upalabhya kramābhinītaṃ bhedam upacārayeyuḥ "asau tvā vijalpati" iti* | *evam ubhayatobaddharoṣāṇāṃ vidyāśilpadyūtavaiharikeṣv ācāryavyañjanā bālakalahān utpādayeyuḥ* ||

12. *kārtāntikavyañjano vā kanyām anyena vṛtām anyasya prarūpayet "amuṣya kanyā rājapatnī rājaprasavinī ca bhaviṣyati, sarvasvena prasahya vaināṃ labhasva" iti | alabhyamānāyāṃ parapakṣam uddharṣayet | labdhāyāṃ siddhaḥ kalahaḥ | bhikṣukī vā priyabhāryaṃ mukhyaṃ brūyāt "asau te mukhyo yauvanotsikto bhāryāyāṃ māṃ prāhiṇot, tasyāhaṃ bhayāl lekhyam ābharaṇam gṛhītvāgatāsmi, nirdoṣā te bhāryā, gūḍham asmin pratikartavyam, aham api tāvat pratipatsyāmi" iti ||*

13. *varuṇa eva dharmapatir dharmasya patiṃ karoti paramatā vai sā yo dharmasya patir asad* (*Śatapatha Brāhmaṇa* 5.3.3.9).

14. *taccheyo rūpam atyasṛjata dharmam | tad etat kṣatrasya kṣatraṃ yad dharmaḥ | tasmād dharmāt paraṃ nāsti | atho abalīyān balīyāṃsam āśaṃsate dharmeṇa | yathā rajñaivam | yo vai sa dharmaḥ satyaṃ vai tat | tasmāt satyaṃ vadantam āhur dharmaṃ vadatīti | dharmaṃ vā vadantaṃ satyaṃ vadatīti | etad dhy evaitad ubhayaṃ bhavati ||*

15. Richard Salomon (2012) observes that Ashokan inscriptions "are highly untypical": "In terms of format, contents, and tone, there is practically nothing in the later inscriptional corpus of the Indian world that even resembles Ashoka's inscriptions." He comments on how unique Ashoka is even in world history: "It can hardly be denied that Ashoka stands as a unique figure in Indian, and indeed in world history. And if so, why shouldn't his inscriptions be unique?"

REFERENCES

Bellah, Robert. 1970. "Civil Religion in America." In *Beyond Belief: Essays on Religion in a Post-Traditional World*, 168–89. New York: Harper and Row.

Bloch, Jules. 1950. *Les inscriptions d'Asoka*. Paris: Société d'Édition «Les Belles Lettres».

Bronkhorst, Johannes. 2016. *How the Brahmins Won: From Alexander to the Guptas*. Leiden: Brill.

Jayaswal, K. P. 1924. *Hindu Polity*. 2 vols. Calcutta: Butterworth.

Kangle, R. P. 1969. *The Kauṭilīya Arthaśāstra*. Part I: A Critical Edition and Glossary, 2nd ed. (1st ed. 1960). Bombay: University of Bombay.

Kangle, R. P. 1972. *The Kauṭilīya Arthaśāstra*. Part II: An English Translation with Critical and Explanatory Notes. Bombay: University of Bombay.

McClish, Mark. 2014. "The Dependence of *Mānava Dharmaśāstra* Adhyāya 7 on the *Kauṭilīya Arthaśāstra*." *Journal of the American Oriental Society* 134: 241–62.

Olivelle, Patrick. 2000. *Dharmasūtras: The Law Codes of Āpastamba, Gautama, Baudhāyana, and Vasiṣṭha*. Delhi: Motilal Banarsidass.

Olivelle, Patrick. 2004. "Manu and the *Arthaśāstra*: A Study in Śāstric Intertextuality." *Journal of Indian Philosophy* 32: 281–91.

Olivelle, Patrick. 2005. *Manu's Code of Law: A Critical Edition and Translation of the* Mānava-Dharmaśāstra. New York: Oxford University Press.

Olivelle, Patrick. 2011. "War and Peace: Semantics of saṃdhi and vigraha in the Arthaśāstra." In *Pūrvāparaprajñābhinandanam: Indological and Other Essays in Honour of Klaus Karttunen*, edited by Bertil Tikkanen and Albion M. Butters, 131–39. Studia Orientalia 110. Helsinki: Societas Orientalis Fennica.

Olivelle, Patrick, ed. 2009. *Ashoka: In History and Historical Memory*. Delhi: Motilal Banarsidass.

Olivelle, Patrick. 2013. *King, Governance, and Law in Ancient India: Kautilya's* Arthaśāstra. New York: Oxford University Press.

Olivelle, Patrick, Himanshu P. Ray, and Janice Leoshko, eds. 2012. *Reimagining Ashoka: Memory and History*. Delhi: Oxford University Press.

Salomon, Richard. 2012. "Ashoka and the 'Epigraphic Habit' in India." In Olivelle, *Ashoka* 2009, 45–51.

Shahi, Deepshikha. 2014. "*Arthashastra* beyond Realpolitik: The 'Eclectic' Face of Kautilya." *Economic & Political Weekly* 49, no. 41: 68–74.

Thapar, Romila. 1997. *Ashoka and the Decline of the Mauryas*, 2nd ed. New Delhi: Oxford University Press.

Some Methodological Reflections

In Defense of Philosophy of Culture and Thick Generalizations

Roger T. Ames

In a single generation we have experienced nothing less than a seismic sea change in the economic and political order of the world. In the wake of this grand transformation, the Berggruen Institute in sponsoring the multiyear workshops on "Chinese and Indian Worldviews on Global Order" is prescient in anticipating the influence that the cultures of both East Asia and South Asia will have on the reshaping of a newly emergent geopolitical configuration. A point to be made at the outset: When we bring cultural "China" and "India" into conversation to inventory and assay the cultural resources available to us for a new geopolitical order, we must be wary of any uncritical assumption that we are referencing two nation-states in the ordinary sense of this term. The scale of these two "continents" (rather than "countries") is such that, when considered together, they not only constitute half of the world's population, but perhaps more importantly, they are heirs to and perpetuate antique cultural resources that take us back to human history's earliest memories. A second point: I am truly honored that, in the pairing up of sinologists with indologists, I have had this opportunity to work with and learn from Patrick Olivelle, one of the international academy's most distinguished scholars of Sanskrit literature.

Patrick and I have been tasked by the workshop organizers to think through some of the methodological issues in making cultural comparisons. In our exchange, I have had the benefit of receiving Patrick's essay as I prepared my own, and thus the opportunity to engage each of Patrick's important themes explicitly: the dangers of essentializing, making room for many voices, the problems of translation and definition, the importance of interpretive context, and the gleaning of resources from the past in our search for a new geopolitical order. As will be clear from what follows, Patrick and I are sometimes inclined to say things differently, and while some might want to make much of these differences, I think we are much closer than we are apart in the concerns we are expressing, and in the recommendations we chose to make. At the end of the day, both of us are cultural pluralists who over our lifetimes have been committed to promoting a better appreciation of, and respect for, the world's many diverse cultures.

Patrick is properly concerned about the issue of gross generalizations that would essentialize world cultures, and might have good reasons to associate my name with this *déformation professionnelle*. Indeed, on the sinological side, some contemporary scholars go so far as to believe that in discussing Chinese history and culture, we would do well to abjure generalizations altogether. And two of them, Paul Goldin and Michael Puett, have indicted me and my collaborators, happily in the company of some of the most distinguished sinologists of the past century, as offering what Goldin calls "an updated Orientalism." For Puett, Marcel Granet, Fritz Mote, Joseph Needham, Angus Graham, K. C. Chang, and Hall and Ames are all described as "cultural essentialists" in offering our best attempts to provide an interpretive context for understanding the evolution of Chinese culture. Goldin charges us along with these other scholars with presenting "China as a reified foil to a reified West, an antipodal domain exemplifying antithetic mores and modes of thought."[1] As his alternative to our "Orientalism," Goldin would argue that "if there is one valid generalization about China, it is that China defies generalization. Chinese civilization is simply too huge, too diverse, and too old for neat maxims."[2] And Puett, explicitly rejecting our self-conscious interpretive strategies, argues that "we should instead work towards a more nuanced approach in which we make no *a priori* assumptions regarding single statements made in single texts and the significance of any individual claims."[3]

I think that Goldin and Puett, while both presumably aspiring to some ostensive interpretive objectivity, are advocating for nothing short of a naïve realism that fails to acknowledge the inevitable and profound subjective coloration of all interpretative experience. We might appeal to Hilary Putnam to make this point. Putnam not only rejects "view-from-nowhere" objectivism, but further insists that the subjective dimension of experience is always integral to what the world really is. He would argue that

> elements of what we call "language" or "mind" *penetrate so deeply into what we call "reality" that the very project of representing ourselves as being "mapper's" of something "language-independent" is fatally compromised from the start.* Like Relativism, but in a different way, Realism is an impossible attempt to view the world from Nowhere.[4]

Putnam will not admit of any understanding of the real world that cleaves it off from its human participation and that does not accept our experience of it as integral to what the world *really* is:

> The heart of pragmatism, it seems to me—of James' and Dewey's pragmatism if not of Peirce's—was the supremacy of the agent point of view. If we find that we must

take a certain point of view, use a certain 'conceptual system,' when engaged in a practical activity, in the widest sense of practical activity, then we must not simultaneously advance the claim that it is not really 'the way things are in themselves.'[5]

In our earlier forays into translating the Chinese canons—a translation of both texts and culture—I and my collaborators, rather than advancing spurious claims to an erstwhile objectivity, have produced what we have called self-consciously interpretive translations. In describing our translations as "self-consciously interpretive," however, we are not allowing in any way that we are recklessly speculative or given to license in our renderings. Nor we are willing to accept the reproach that we are any less "literal" and thus more "creative" than other translators. On the contrary, we would insist first that any pretense to a literal translation is not only naïve, but is itself an "objectivist" prejudice of the first order. Just as each generation selects and carries over earlier thinkers to reshape them in their own image, each generation reconfigures the classical canons of world philosophy to its own needs. We too are inescapably people of a time and place.

At the most general level, I would suggest that modern English as the target language for translating the Chinese canons carries with it such an overlay of cultural assumptions that, in the absence of "self-consciousness," the philosophical import of the text can be seriously compromised. To conventionally translate the classical term *tian* 天 as a capital "H" "Heaven," for example, is to insinuate Abrahamic theological assumptions into what is a fundamentally an a-theistic cosmology. As the distinguished French sinologist Marcel Granet observes rather starkly, "Chinese wisdom has no need of the idea of God."[6] Again, a failure of naïve translators to be self-conscious and to take fair account of their own Gadamerian "prejudices" with the excuse that they are relying on an existing "objective" dictionary, is to fail to acknowledge that in the case of China at least, this lexical resource, given its missionary origins, is itself so heavily colored with cultural biases that Chinese philosophy is for the most part taught in religion or Asian Studies departments in our universities, and shelved in the religion section of our libraries. To fail to be self-conscious as translators is to betray our readers not once, but twice.[7] That is, not only do we fail to provide the "objective" reading of the text we have promised, but we also neglect to warn our unsuspecting readers of the cultural assumptions we willy-nilly insinuate into our translations.

This self-consciousness, then, is not to disrespect the integrity of the Chinese philosophical narrative, but to endorse one of the fundamental hermeneutical premises of this commentarial tradition captured in a cosmological postulate of the first among the Chinese classics, the *Yijing* 易經 or the *Book of Changes*, with its notion of "continuity in change" (*biantong* 變通):

According to the *Changes*, with everything running its full course, there is flux (*bian*), and where there is such flux, there is continuity (*tong*). And where there is such continuity, it is enduring.[8]

Risking here a thick generalization that emerges from a contrast between early Greek substance ontology and this Confucian process cosmology, this postulate might be used as an example that is revealing of a fundamental and resilient "continuity" integral to their different cultural identities. I would suggest that these early Confucian hermeneutically inclined philosophers were less disposed to ask *what* makes something real or *why* things exist, and more interested in *how* the complex relationships that obtain among the changing phenomena of their surroundings could be negotiated for optimum productivity and value. Rather than any predetermined necessity in teleologically derived assumptions about origins, or causal speculations about some grand design that are associated with ontological thinking, it is the pursuit of superlative quality in an achieved personal, social, and ultimately cosmic harmony (*he* 和), and the creative possibilities of enculturating the human experience (*wenhua* 文化), that served as a fundamental guiding value for these seminal Confucian thinkers.

What this postulate means when applied to the philosophical canons is that textual meaning at the intersection of change and persistence is irrepressibly emergent, and that, like it or not, we translators of the culture, far from being passive or secondary or epiphenomenal in our interpretive work, are integral to the growth of the tradition. The hundreds of translations of the *Daodejing* that have transformed it into world literature, for example, not only have extended its reach and influence but have dramatically appreciated the meaning and relevance that can be drawn from its pages.

As a self-confessed philosopher of culture, I am required to do my best to excavate, identify, and articulate generalizations that distinguish different cultural narratives. My premise is that only in being cognizant of these uncommon cultural assumptions will we, in some degree at least, be able to respect their most fundamental differences and to locate the philosophical discussion within their alternative worldviews. Just as in the watershed of the Western cultural narrative with the ontology made explicit by Plato and Aristotle, in the formative period of Confucian philosophy certain enduring commitments were reinforced by Confucius, Mencius, and Xunzi that are more persistent than others, and allow us to make useful generalizations about its evolution. In fact, one of the premises that allows for such generalizations is the importance of reading and understanding the earliest conditions available to us as the history of an organic process unfolds. Nathan Sivin observes that "man's prodigious creativity seems to be based on the permutations and recastings of a rather small stock of ideas," where the fundamental distinction between a Greek substance ontology and a classical Chinese process cosmology must number among this stock.[9]

We might take two historical examples of distinguished philosophers of culture—one from Europe and one from China—who were themselves willing to risk thick generalizations. In the Preface to his *Novissima Sinica* (News from China) written over the period of 1697–99, an astute and penetrating Gottfried

Wilhelm Leibniz offers a synoptic comparison between the contributions made by European and Chinese culture. In theoretical disciplines such as mathematics, logic, metaphysics, and in particular, theology, Leibniz argues, there is a clear European superiority. Indeed, for Leibniz, we Europeans "excel by far in the understanding of concepts which are abstracted by the mind from the material." We own the theoretical sciences and surpass the Chinese in those rational tools of the intellect that lead us to demonstrable truth, while the Chinese struggle with a kind of empirical geometry owned by most artisans.

On Leibniz's reading, by contrast with this European gift for theoretical and spiritual abstraction, the Chinese excel in the pursuit of civil philosophy where Chinese "civilization" in this important respect has set a standard far superior to that found in Europe. In Leibniz's own words:

> But who would have believed that there is on earth a people who, though we are in our view so very advanced in every branch of behavior, still surpass us in comprehending the precepts of civil life? Yet now we find this to be so among the Chinese, as we learn to know them better. And so if we are their equals in the industrial arts, and ahead of them in contemplative sciences, certainly they surpass us (though it is almost shameful to confess this) in practical philosophy, that is, in the precepts of ethics and politics adapted to the present life and use of mortals.

Considering the dearth of information on China available to Leibniz in his own time, this philosopher, resisting his own formalist and universalist philosophical proclivities that should have inclined him steeply in the opposite direction, was indeed a surprisingly keen and honest observer of cultural continuities and differences. He continues:

> Indeed, it is difficult to describe how beautifully all the laws of the Chinese, in contrast to those of other peoples, are directed to the achievement of public tranquility and the establishment of social order, so that men shall be disrupted in their relations as little as possible. . . . Certainly the Chinese above all others have attained a higher standard. In a vast multitude of men they have virtually accomplished more than the founders of religious orders among us have achieved within their own narrow ranks.[10]

Leibniz, in thus advancing his own generalizations about European and Chinese cultures, saw a clear contrast between the value invested in those abstract, theoretical disciplines in the European academy that are in search of axiomatic-deductive demonstration, and the more aesthetic and pragmatic applications of the Chinese tradition, a distinction that broadly distinguishes a European confidence in the dividends of the rational sciences from those alternative rewards that can be derived from virtuosity in the art of living. In fact, it was more than a fundamental sympathy and respect for Chinese culture that led Leibniz in the long-simmering Rites Controversy that came to a boil in Rome towards the end of his own life to defend Matteo Ricci's advocacy of an accommodationist Christianity. Leibniz's commitment to accommodationism was based upon his conviction that the precepts of any universal civil philosophy that would seek to construct a framework for optimizing the social, political, and indeed religious life of human beings in community would do well to take into account the substantial accomplishments of Chinese culture in this same effort.

As a second example of a distinguished philosopher of culture, Qian Mu 錢穆, in attempting to provide a corrective to the key Confucian philosophical terms that have been compromised by a Christian "conversion," is adamant that this vocabulary expressing the unique and complex Confucianism vision of a moral life simply has no counterpart in other languages.[11] Qian Mu's point in making this claim is not to argue for cultural purism and incommensurability; on the contrary, he would allow that with sufficient exposition made through thick generalizations (the ambitious objective of philosophers of culture), the Confucian world can be "appreciated" in important degree by those from without. Qian Mu's claim is in service to the uniqueness and the value of a tradition that has defined its terms of art through the lived experience of its people over millennia, and anticipates the real difficulty we must face in attempting to capture its complex and organically related vocabulary in other languages without substantial qualification and explanation.

In accordance with Qian Mu's project, I want to contest the resistance among some contemporary scholars to accept the kind of thick cultural generalizations being made by both Leibniz and Qian Mu that I believe are necessary if we are to respect the rich differences that obtain among traditions and if we are to avoid as best we can an impoverishing cultural reductionism. I would argue that the canopy of an always emerging cultural vocabulary is itself rooted in and grows out of a deep and relatively stable soil of unannounced assumptions sedimented over succeeding generations into the language, the customs, and the life forms of a living tradition. And further, I would argue that to fail to acknowledge the fundamental character of cultural difference as an erstwhile safeguard against the sins of either "essentialism" or "relativism" is not itself innocent. Indeed, ironically, this antagonism to cultural generalizations leads to the uncritical essentializing of one's own contingent cultural assumptions and to the insinuating of them into one's interpretation of the ways of thinking and living of other traditions.

I think that in my advocacy of "self-conscious generalizations" in translation, and in my appeal to the postulate of "continuities in change" from the *Book of Changes*, I am rehearsing what Patrick Olivelle has insisted upon when, in his own efforts at cultural translation, he rejects cultural essentializing while at the same time affirming the need to register and respect cultural continuities. In Patrick's own words:

> For sure, there are continuities and commonalities in both traditions, given that the cultural and religious ideas and institutions influenced thinkers of every age. But continuities do not constitute an essence. It is best for us to leave Aristotle behind

and follow the Buddha, who insisted on the absence of any substance, any soul, behind the composite entities we encounter, including ourselves. A culture, the Buddha would have said, is like a river; there is an illusion of substance but the water is never the same.[12]

Indeed, one might argue that the bugbear of "essentializing" that quite properly worries Patrick is itself, like any such corollary of "universalism," largely a culturally specific deformation. Indeed, I am anxious to defend a rather thick generalization that Patrick himself makes when he observes that "this assumption, I think, is a remnant of our Aristotelian heritage."[13] Such essentialism broadly conceived must be closely associated with Aristotle's substance ontology, and has been rejected broadly as a shared target in the post-Darwinian internal critique of the Western philosophical narrative beginning in the late nineteenth century with Nietzsche's "God is dead." After all, we can only "essentialize" if we are predisposed to believe there are such things as "essences," a way of thinking about things that did not recommend itself to the formative, analogizing philosophers of classical China. Essentialism itself arises from familiar classical Greek assumptions about ontology as "the science of being *per se*"—the self-sufficiency of being—and from the application of strict identity as the principle of individuation. It is this notion of "essences" that grounds Platonic idealism as well as Aristotle's doctrine of species (*eidos*) as immutable natural kinds. It is also the assumption of strict identity that grounds Aristotelian logic with its exclusionary "A or not-A" principle of noncontradiction.

In advancing the agenda of philosophy of culture, without going to the self-defeating extreme of essentializing, there are still important cultural continuities that must be registered. A point that was drilled into me by my teachers when my hair was still blonde was that different cultures think differently, and that we elide important distinctions among them at our peril. My teacher Angus Graham, for example, ascribes unique and evolving categories and conceptual structures to different cultural traditions, and in so doing, is challenging the Saussurian structuralist distinction between *langue* (universal and systematic linguistic structures and rules governing all languages) and *parole* (diverse and open-ended speech acts in any of our natural languages).[14] Like many (but not all) of us, Graham is persuaded that different populations within their always changing cultural milieus appeal to different concepts and ways of thinking and living. For Graham, getting at such conceptual differences is not an easy task:

> That people of another culture are somehow thinking in other categories is a familiar idea, almost a commonplace, but one very difficult to pin down as a topic for fruitful discussion.[15]

In trying to overcome this difficulty of stipulating conceptual differences, we might recall Nietzsche's appeal to a "common philosophy of grammar" as having anticipated Graham in this respect. Nietzsche asserts that a particular worldview has over time been sedimented into each member of the family of Indo-European languages to both shape and constrain the semiotic structures of these disparate yet in some ways continuous cultures. As a consequence of this shared history, our culturally specific Indo-European languages in their various modes of expression encourage certain philosophical possibilities while discouraging others:

> The strange family resemblance of all Indian, Greek, and German philosophizing is explained easily enough. Where there is an affinity of languages, it cannot fail, owing to the common philosophy of grammar—I mean owing to the unconscious domination and guidance by similar grammatical functions—that everything is prepared at the outset for a similar development and sequence of philosophical systems; just as the way seems barred against certain other possibilities of world-interpretation.[16]

Graham, like Nietzsche before him, looks to what languages reveal grammatically and by extension, conceptually, to get at the slippery issue of other cultures "thinking in other categories." Graham has consistently warned us that serious equivocations emerge when we elide the distinction between classical Greek ontological commitments and those assumptions grounding a classical Chinese processive, procreative cosmology. Ontology privileges "being *per se*" and a substance language with its "essence" and "attribute" dualism—that is, substances as property-bearers and properties that are borne, respectively. Process cosmology, on the other hand, gives privilege to "becoming" and to the vital, interdependent, correlative categories needed to "speak" process and its eventful content. Graham is quite explicit about the nature of these philosophical differences and their linguistic entailments:

> In the Chinese cosmos all things are interdependent, without transcendent principles by which to explain them or a transcendent origin from which they derive. . . . A novelty in this position which greatly impresses me is that it exposes a preconception of Western interpreters that such concepts as *Tian* "Heaven" and *Dao* "Way" must have the transcendence of our own ultimate principles; it is hard for us to grasp that even the Way is interdependent with man.[17]

Thus, my defense against the familiar charge made by some that philosophy of culture "essentializes" the Other, is first to acknowledge that cultural narratives are contingent. We are referencing holistic, protean, and always reflexively inflected historical *narratives* of populations—not reified *other minds*. Recently, and specifically in reference to the classical Chinese language, Graham concludes that in reporting on the eventful flow of *qi* cosmology, "the sentence structure of Classical Chinese places us in a world of process about which we ask . . . 'Whence?' and also, since it is moving, 'At what time?'"[18] I have followed him in consistently advocating a holistic, narrative understanding of Chinese culture as being more revealing of underlying cultural assumptions than any detemporalizing and essentializing analytical approach.

Further, the entertainment of other cultural narratives is always a reflexive exercise. If we acknowledge that the experiencing of other cultures is inevitably a matter of mutually shaping stories, then in failing to articulate apposite generalizations, we are at real risk of imposing on them cultural importances not their own. After all, without struggling with imagination to identify, refine, and ultimately defend such distinguishing characterizations, the default position is an uncritical cultural assimilation. Such cultural reductionism follows from the seemingly respectful and inclusive assertion that we are all the same, a claim that, far from being innocent, is in fact insisting that "they" are the same as "us." And in the cautionary language of Richard Rorty, such forced redescription is not only condescending but, indeed, is cruel and humiliating.

The distinguished scholar of comparative literature Zhang Longxi, for example, in his commitment to pursuing intercultural understanding, is quite critical of those of us (singling out Jacques Gernet as one primary example) who would describe the tension between Christianity and Chinese as not only one "of different intellectual traditions" but also "of different mental categories and modes of thought."[19] Zhang becomes impatient when "the cultural difference between the Chinese and the Western is formulated as fundamentally distinct ways of thinking and speaking, as the ability, or lack of it, to express abstract ideas." Zhang does not recognize that in thus giving abstract and theoretical ideas pride of place as the marker of the highest theoretical and spiritual ascent, he is advocating for decidedly Western philosophical assumptions that are not only absent in the classical Chinese tradition, but in fact are under assault within Western philosophy's own ongoing, internal critique.

My teachers thought that those who would claim that other peoples and cultures are too complex to make the necessary generalizations, or by default, that they are somehow "equal" in their ability to think, while probably intended to be inclusive and respectful, is anything but innocuous. Why would we assume that to allow that other traditions have culturally specific modalities of thinking is to claim such traditions do not know how to think, unless we ourselves believe that in fact there is only one way of thinking, and that this way of thinking—that is, *our* way of thinking—is the only way? The uncritical assumption that other cultures must think the same way as we do is for me the very definition of essentialism and ethnocentrism. I would argue that it is precisely the hard work needed to excavate, to recognize, and to appreciate the degree of difference obtaining among cultures in their modes of living and thinking that properly motivates cultural translation in the first place, and that ultimately rewards the effort. Surely arguing that there are culturally contingent modalities of thinking can itself be pluralistic rather than relativistic, and can be accommodating rather than condescending. At the very least, if comparative studies is to provide us with the mutual enrichment it promises, we must strive with imagination to take other cultures on their own terms and appreciate fully the differences that obtain among them.

This same point can be made another way. I would argue that the only thing more dangerous than striving to make responsible cultural generalizations is failing to make them. Generalizations do not have to preclude appreciating the richness and complexity of always evolving cultural traditions; in fact, it is generalizations that locate and inform specific cultural details and provide otherwise sketchy historical developments with the thickness of their content. There is no alternative in doing philosophy of culture, and in making the needed cultural comparisons, to an open, hermeneutical approach that is ready to modify always provisional generalizations with the new information that additional detail yields as it is interpreted within the grid of generalizations.

Edward Said, in his influential book *Orientalism* that was published in 1978, on behalf of the idea that "many voices should be heard," made the claim that largely for political reasons, "Oriental Studies" in the Western academy has constructed a distorted description of Islamic cultures in service to its own self-image and understanding. In the decades since the cautions of Said regarding the projection of "orientalist" prejudices in the study and teaching of other cultures, the tendency in academic circles has been to steer clear of what has come to be understood as "essentialist" constructions of culture. This cautionary corrective has resulted in valuable efforts to peel back layers of exotic and universalizing veneer that previous generations of scholarship had effectively laid over cultural realities, and to bring to light the often complex and convoluted striations of living and always changing cultures. In rejecting cultural essentializing, a genuine endeavor has been made in the scholarship to try with imagination to take other cultures on their own terms. However, this important attempt to rethink and to get past the naïve constructions of cultural others now runs the risk of obscuring the crucial and still vital role played by assaying differences in their ways of thinking and living, and of failing to acknowledge persistent cultural ideals in engendering and sustaining cultural change.

The story is complex. As a consequence of the challenge of new directions in historiographical thinking, the assumption that cultural families develop their distinctive patterns of values, norms, and practices in relative isolation from one another has become markedly less trenchant over the past several decades. Both historians and philosophers have come to recognize significant distortions that attend any unreflective tendencies to compartmentalize the ancient and premodern worlds according to currently prevailing spatial and conceptual divisions and their underlying (often highly political) rationales. In particular, critical assessment is now well underway regarding the degree to which persistent prejudices about metageography—especially the "myth of continents"—have shaped and continue to shape representations of history and cultural origins.[20] The classic assertion of "independently originating" European and Asian cultures on either side of the Ural mountains, for example, is being abandoned in favor of highlighting "Eurasian" characteristics in the complex cultural genealogies of both

"West" and "East." Indeed, since cultures arise interculturally, or better yet, *intra-culturally*, in wide-ranging, intimate commerce with one another over time, it would seem that no culture *can* be fully understood in isolation from others. There is a borderless ecology of cultures that has only an inside without an outside.

Again, we need to think genealogically as well as morphologically. That is, the development and growth of cultures does not take place only by way of historical interactions among them, resulting either in accommodations of differences as conditions for mutual contribution, or in competition for acknowledged superiority. Cultures change not only in adaptive response to others and to political, economic, or environmental exigencies, but are also animated by an internal impulse as an expression of their own particular aspirations. Quite often, this change involves and requires envisioning ways of life distinctively other than those that are near and familiar, revealing with greater or lesser clarity what present cultural realities are not, and do not promise. Cultural change *does* occur in response to differing circumstantial realities, but it also takes place as a function of pursuing new or not-yet-actualized ideals. Said differently, ideals as "ends-in-view"—what Charles Taylor calls "hypergoods"—are also realities that live in history, and that at least in degree, have the force of directing the patterns of change.[21]

This recognition of the indigenous impulse has as its own corollary the insight that the histories through which cultures narrate their own origins and development are not primarily aimed at accurately depicting a closed past, but rather at disclosing arcs of change projected into open and yet more or less distinctly anticipated futures. The cliché that history is written by the winners is perhaps better couched in terms of history being written to affirm that what has occurred *amounts to* a victory. Cultural change is inseparable from the process, at some level, of both valorizing and actualizing new (or at least alternative) interpretations of the changes that have occurred.

Thus, in seeking a new geopolitical order by trying to glean valuable resources from our several past cultural narratives, we must be self-conscious of the fact that our redescriptions of these cultures, *including our own*, while certainly being informed by their past, are also being reformulated to serve our own contemporary needs and interests. Patrick quite rightly gives us the example of how the notion of nation "state," that in our time has become the lowest common denominator in thinking about international relations (IR), is only of recent origin and has little relevance for the cultures of either ancient India or China. He asks, in formulating an alternative to our contemporary notions of IR, whether the Indian and Chinese traditions offer an alternative to what is a conflicted and fragmenting Westphalian model of independent, sovereign states. One example provided in Patrick's own answer is to select what he recommends as the most influential model of IR in Indian history, the *dharma* of Manu as it is consonant with the Brahmanical *Vedas*.

Let me try to summarize what Patrick says about this Manu tradition in his own words as preliminary to offering at least my own interpretation of an alternative but equally robust classical Confucian notion of IR captured in the expression *tianxia* 天下, or "All-under-the-heavens." First, Patrick draws from the *dharma* of Manu "the thesis that law—moral, civil, and criminal—defined as *dharma* is universal and not constrained by territory or government," an idea captured in the insistence that "kings don't make laws; they only enforce them." Further, what makes Manu particularly relevant to our search for new resources for a changing global world order is that "this concept of *dharma* also governs what is lawful and permissible in the conduct of war, and in Ashoka even interstate relations."

To this universal and capacious reach of *dharma*, Patrick offers a further, seemingly inclusive refinement:

> Manu allows for localized *dharma:* the *dharma* of a region, a village, or even a family. So we have a universal *dharma*, often articulated in legal treatises, and local *dharma* contained in the customs of the people, called *ācāra*. The only requirement is that the local *dharma* cannot contravene the universal *dharma* articulated in the authoritative legal texts.

There is a Confucian alternative to this "one-behind-the-many," universal and self-sufficient conception of Manu's *dharma* that might have some immediate relevance to the precipitous change in the geopolitical order of the world we have witnessed over the last decade with the rise of China. At the end of 2013, China introduced what it calls the "One Belt, One Road Initiative" (*yidaiyiluchangyi* 一带一路倡議) (usually referred to in English-language reports as BRI). From the Chinese perspective, this bold BRI initiative is touted as nothing less than an evolving program of collaboration between China and its extended neighbors that will transform the existing world order from top to bottom and in all of its parts. Rhetorically there are two espoused values that ground this vision of BRI, "equity" (*gongying* 共贏) and "diversity" interpreted through the language of a "shared future for the human community" (*renleimingyun gongtongti* 人類命運共同體). Rhetorically at least, China has on offer here an inclusive "win-win" vision of what we might call a doctrine of "*intra*-national relations" in the sense that it advocates for an ecological model of IR within which "transformation" (*hua* 化) means that just as the one changes the many, so the many change the one. And the BRI claim is that the roots of this new Chinese IR initiative are grounded in traditional Chinese thinking—cosmological and political—reaching back as early as the *Book of Changes*.

One important distinction Confucian philosophy might bring to BRI and its corollary IR theory is the difference between "*inter*-national relations" and "*intra*-national relations." We use the prefix "*inter*-" to suggest a joint, external, and open relationship that conjoins two or more separate and in some sense comparable entities. By way of contrast, "*intra*-" meaning—"on the inside," "within"—references internal and constitutive relations contained within a given entity itself. "*Intra*-" has immediate organic, ecological implications—an inside without an outside. It references a radical contextuality—the inseparability of the one and the many (*yiduobufen* 一多不分)—where the global order is the always provisional and emergent totality of all orders without any single privileged and dominant order among them. What recommends the neologism "*intra*-national" over "international" is that, rather than referencing the external relations that obtain between or among separately individuated and sovereign polities, the assumption behind *intra*-national is that we are describing a matrix of internal relations—a "field of polities" or a "political ecology"—where each "polity" owns its unique aspectual perspective on the unsummed totality, and where together in their constitutive relations with each other, these polities comprise our shared, interdependent, interpenetrating, and irreducibly social and political identities.

Intra-national gives us a focus-field understanding of our relationality, where each polity is holographic as a specific construal of all relations within the unbounded ecology of intra-national relations. In contrast to a world of "things" that follows from Aristotle's substance ontology and the doctrine of external relations that define them, this Confucian ecological cosmology is a world of interpenetrating "events" defined in terms of organic, internal, and constitutive relations. This model resonates immediately with Patrick's appeal to a nonessentialist description of cultures wherein all identities are interdependent, interpenetrating, and mutually entailing, ideas immediately associated with the Buddha's doctrines of "no-self" (*anattā*) and "co-dependent arising" (*pratītya-samutpāda*).

One corollary of this Confucian process cosmology is that in the absence of a nature-nurture dualism, human culture is not only perceived as being integral to nature, but in the Confucian canons, erstwhile distinctively human values such as "sincerity" (*cheng* 誠) and "family reverence" (*xiao* 孝) are themselves elevated to cosmic status.[22] As Patrick would suggest with the Manu conception of a universal *dharma*, the coincidence of the human and natural norms means that the *yiduobufen* global order has immediate environmental and ecological implications as well. Again, applying this insight to IR, we have to allow that there is no one true world order, but only the many, equally revealing perspectives on a planetary order that, in their totality, come to constitute its always emergent, continuous and yet multivalent order.

While the uncritical Western assumption that China's ambitious strategy for effecting an alternative world order must necessarily be a contemporary iteration of the West's own imperialistic history, this notion of *tianxia* so conceived through a traditional Confucian process cosmology provides an alternative explanation. *Tianxia* provides an ecological model of IR that begins from an acknowledgment of interdependence in all political and economic activity, and that advocates for hybridity rather than assimilation. As with the *yiduobufen* syncretism, in the absence of one universal *dharma* order to which all particular *dharma* orders must conform, there is only a continuity and interdependence among a manifold of geopolitical orders, each of which is construed from one particular polity or another.

China, in its unwavering commitment to proceed with this geopolitical strategy for an unprecedented scale of world economic development, if viewed sympathetically in terms of its understanding of its own history and identity, might be seen as parlaying *tianxia* into a new world politics. BRI has a political, an economic, and a cultural dimension. Such an idealized cultural reading of *tianxia*, laid out clearly by the Chinese academy as the interpretive context for BRI, might have the positive benefit, both domestically and internationally, of setting in a concrete way the appropriate aspirational targets for this initiative for the economic and political forces, and of providing a basis for evaluating their successes and failures. If BRI is to be successful, it needs to take into account China's earlier attempts at collaboration over the past few decades, such as its very mixed African adventure. A standard can be established for assaying and defending the successes of BRI, and at the same time, for recognizing and thus acting to minimize its failures. BRI to be successful must certainly have an economic and a political component. But absent the cultural assumptions that must guide these forces, a failed BRI would become an Asian imperialism that simply replaces one race with another. Intellectual China must get past its reticence of being "tutor to the emperor" (*dishi* 帝師), and step up to fulfill its responsibility to bring real clarity to these assumptions. Indeed, the notion of *tianxia* as a way of articulating and promoting the values of a cultural and spiritual China drawn from its own canonical texts must be used to exhort the economic and the political Chinas to live up to their own rhetoric, and to thus lead the way into a more equitable world order.

Patrick Olivelle and I think somewhat differently about cultural translation and have set our own priorities in how we should proceed. But in service to a healthy pluralism, these differences can certainly be read as cautionary and in many cases compensatory for one another. His essay has certainly inspired me to continue to reflect carefully on my own assumptions, and to try to make them more explicit.[23] If we can rise above any exclusivity in our critical dialectic, we might well have to concede that there is something to recommend each of our positions, and that we would certainly have less if we had only one of them.

NOTES

1. Paul R. Goldin, "The Myth That China Has No Creation Myth," *Monumenta Serica* 56 (2008): 3.

2. Ibid., 21.

3. Michael Puett, *To Become a God: Cosmology, Sacrifice, and Self-Divinization in Early China* (Cambridge, MA: Harvard University Asia Center, 2003), 24–25.

4. Hilary Putnam, *Realism with a Human Face* (Cambridge MA: Harvard University Press, 1990), 28. Emphasis in original.

5. Hilary Putnam, *The Many Faces of Realism* (La Salle, IL: Open Court, 1987), 83.

6. Marcel Granet, *La pensée chinoise* (Paris: Editions Albin Michel, 1934), 478.

7. Hans-Georg Gadamer uses "prejudices" not in the sense that prejudice is blind, but on the contrary, in the sense that our prejudgments can facilitate rather than obstruct our understanding. That is, our assumptions can positively condition our experience. But we must always entertain these

assumptions critically, being aware that the hermeneutical circle in which understanding is always situated requires that we must continually strive to be conscious of what we bring to our experience and must pursue increasingly adequate prejudgments that can inform our experience in better and more productive ways.

8. *Book of Changes* B2: 《易》，窮則變，變則通，通則久。

9. Nathan Sivin, foreword to Manfred Porkert, *The Theoretical Foundations of Chinese Medicine* (Cambridge, MA: MIT Press, 1974), xi.

10. Gottfried Wilhelm Leibniz, *Writings on China*, trans. Daniel J. Cook and Henry Rosemont Jr. (Chicago: Open Court, 1994), 46–47.

11. Jerry Dennerline, *Qian Mu and the World of Seven Mansions* (New Haven, CT: Yale University Press, 1988), 9.

12. See Patrick Olivelle's chapter in this same volume, p. 40.

13. Ibid.

14. Saussure uses the analogy of a chess game, where *langue* are the fixed rules that govern the game while *parole* are the actual, varied moves made by different people that come to constitute any particular game.

15. A.C. Graham, *Studies in Chinese Philosophy and Philosophical Literature* (Albany: State University of New York Press, 1990), 360.

16. Friedrich Nietzsche, *Beyond Good and Evil*, trans. W. Kaufmann (New York: Vintage, 1966), 20.

17. A.C. Graham, "Replies," in *Chinese Texts and Philosophical Contexts: Essays Dedicated to Angus C. Graham*, ed. Henry Rosemont Jr. (La Salle, IL: Open Court, 1991), 287.

18. Graham, *Studies in Chinese Philosophy*, 360–411.

19. See Zhang's "Translating Cultures: China and the West," in *Chinese Thought in a Global Context: A Dialogue between Chinese and Western Philosophical Approaches*, ed. Karl-Heinz Pohl (Leiden: Brill, 1999), 44. His reference is to Jacques Gernet, *China and the Christian Impact: A Conflict of Cultures*, trans. J. Lloyd (Cambridge: Cambridge University Press, 1985), 8.

20. See Martin W. Lewis and Kären Wigen, *The Myth of Continents: A Critique of Metageography* (Berkeley: University of California Press, 1997).

21. "Hypergoods" is a useful neologism introduced by Charles Taylor in his *Sources of the Self: The Making of the Modern Identity* (Cambridge, MA: Harvard University Press, 1989), 62–63: "Most of us not only live with many goods but find that we have to rank them, and in some cases, this ranking makes one of them of supreme importance relative to the others. . . . Let me call higher-order goods of this kind 'hypergoods,' i.e. goods which not only are incomparably more important than others but provide the standpoint from which these must be weighed, judged, decided about."

22. See elevation to cosmic status of the human values of "resolution" (*cheng* 誠) and "family reverence" (*xiao* 孝) in Roger T. Ames and David L. Hall, *Focusing the Familiar: A Translation and Philosophical Interpretation of the* Zhongyong (Honolulu: University of Hawai'i Press, 2001); and Henry Rosemont Jr. and Roger T. Ames, *The Chinese Classic of Family Reverence: A Philosophical Translation of the* Xiaojing 孝經 (Honolulu: University of Hawai'i Press, 2009).

23. Inspired by this exchange with Patrick Olivelle, I have recently written a more comprehensive essay defending philosophy of culture against the "essentialism" charge: "Unloading the Essentialism Charge: Reflections on Methodology in Doing Philosophy of Culture," in *Comparative Philosophy and Method: Contemporary Practices and Future Possibilities*, ed. Steven Burik, Robert Smid, and Ralph Weber (London: Bloomsbury Academic Press, 2022).

Political Leadership

How Do Xunzi and Kautilya Ponder Interstate Politics?

Yan Xuetong

Xunzi/Xun Kuang (313–238 BCE), a Chinese philosopher, and Kautilya/Chanakya (between first century BCE and first century CE), an Indian philosopher, lived in an era of frequent interstate warfare. It is always helpful to explore the ideas of ancient thinkers of different civilizations and draw useful insights on understanding contemporary international politics. Indian scholars view both Sun Tzu and Kautilya as strategists and have done many comparative studies about their thoughts on strategies.[1] Although Han Feizi and Kautilya are often categorized as Machiavellian thinkers, the former's work does not touch extensively on interstate relations. However, Xunzi and Kautilya both have plenty to say about interstate politics. Thus, this article explores and compares their thoughts on the aspect of interstate politics, based on two corpora, *Xunzi* and the *Arthaśāstra*. Since Xunzi and Kautilya were not aware of each other's work, their shared thoughts reflect a cross-cultural understanding of interstate politics, and their differences of views may result from, but are not limited to, different personal experiences and interstate systems.

METHODOLOGY OF STUDYING INTERSTATE POLITICS

Although both books are about political governance, *Xunzi* focuses on political ideas while the *Arthaśāstra* addresses mainly governmental strategies. The former is more concerned with basic concepts of political studies, the latter primarily with policy making. The methodology used in *Xunzi* is historical induction, while that used in the *Arthaśāstra* is logical deduction. The methodological differences between the books may be due to the personal experiences and cultural differences of the authors or editors. Despite these differences, both *Xunzi* and the *Arthaśāstra* adopt an individual level of analysis, treating political leadership as the independent variable and ministers as the intermediate variable.

Historical Induction vs. Logical Deduction

As mentioned above, *Xunzi* and the *Arthaśāstra* make arguments using historical inductive and logical deductive methods, respectively. Xunzi illustrates his arguments by bringing forward a viewpoint before or after presenting historical cases. For instance, when he argues that morality enables a king to conquer the world quickly, he says, "They uniformly applied moral principles throughout the land, and in a single day it was plainly evident. Such were Tang and Wu."[2] Differing from Xunzi's inductive methodology, Kautilya applies a deductive method. Every book of the *Arthaśāstra* illustrates arguments with detailed literal explanations but rarely with historical cases. For instance, when he discusses strategies for dealing with allies, Kautilya comments on more than forty scenarios but provides neither successful nor failed historical examples.[3]

Xunzi's methodology makes his arguments empirically convincing, and Kautilya's makes his arguments rigorously logical. Unfortunately, Xunzi's arguments cannot be applied to every case because he does not set up rigorous conditions for them. The defect in Kautilya's methodology is that many of his arguments cannot be proven by empirical experiences. Inductive methodology makes Xunzi's thought concrete and deductive methodology makes Kautilya's abstract.

Xunzi's thoughts blend the ideas of Confucianism and Legalism but not religious thinking.[4] Since both Confucianism and Legalism are secular political thoughts rather than religious ideologies, he attributes different political phenomena to rulers' or ministers' mentality and capability rather than a nonhuman power. His writings are loaded with historical records of human activities but say nothing about the power of a god. Differing from Xunzi, Kautilya is a religious believer and his analysis treats human capability and supernatural power as equally important factors in the fate of a state: "[Acts] of human agency are good policy and bad policy; of divine agency, good fortune and misfortune. For it is acts of human and divine agency that make the world go. . . . That [human acts] can be thought about; the divine is incalculable."[5] The abstract style of the *Arthaśāstra* might have been influenced by the religious practice of Kautilya or this book's unknown editors. It is full of conversations between Kautilya and other people, all of which are presented in the name of Kautilya or the third person.

Individual Analysis: Treating Kings as the Independent Variable

For modern IR theoretical studies, the level of analysis comprises system, state, and individual.[6] Xunzi's and Kautilya's analyses can be interpreted at the individual level, for they treat rulers as the fundamental independent variable. They define the nature of states as an instrument used by rulers. Xunzi says:

> The state is the most powerful instrument for benefit in the world. The ruler of men is the most influential position of authority for benefit in the world. If a ruler

employs the Way to maintain these two—the state and his position—then there will be the greatest peace and security, the greater honor and prosperity, and the wellspring for accumulating what is beautiful and fine. If a ruler does not employ the Way to maintain them, then there will be the greatest danger and peril and the greatest humiliation and adversity. It would be better not to have these two than to have them.[7]

Kautilya also views rulers, namely kings, as the most important factor for the survival of a state. "The king, the minister, the country, the fortified city, the treasury, the army and the ally are the constituent elements (of the state),"[8] Kautilya says. "The king and (his) rule, this is the sum-total of the constituents."[9] Treating kings as the most important element of a state, every book of the *Arthaśāstra* engages with the theme of what policy a king should adopt for the survival and improvement of his state.

Although they hold the same view about the role of kings and the nature of states, Xunzi differs from Kautilya in his understanding of the components of states. Xunzi views people and land as two independent components, but Kautilya views people and land as one. In Kautilya's writings, the term "country" refers to the land with people ruled by a king outside his fort: "For there is no country without people and no kingdom without a country."[10] Nevertheless, he regards people as just one of many components of a country:

> Possessed of strong positions in the center and at the frontiers, capable of sustaining itself and others in times of distress, easy to protect, providing neighboring princes, devoid of mud, stones, salty ground, uneven land, with agriculture land, mines, material forests and elephant forests, beneficial to cattle, beneficial to men, with protected pastures, rich in animals not depending on rain for water, provided with water-routes, with valuable, manifold and plenty of commodities, capable of bearing fines, and taxes, with farmers devoted to work, with a wise master, inhabited mostly by the lower *varnas*, with men loyal and honest—these are the excellences of a country.[11]

Xunzi and Kautilya hold different views about the relations between land and people, possibly because the Chinese feudal system makes every individual's identity tied to the state where he/she is born; for instance, Xunzi is still identified as a native of the State of Zhao. In ancient China, people with different state identities often lived on the land of a same state; Xunzi regards land and people as separate elements of a state. In ancient India, there were groups of wandering people without state identity. For instance, Buddha and his followers were stateless and landless people. This situation may have caused Kautilya to make no distinction between people and land and to consider the combination of people and land as country.

Triadic Categorization

Niraj Kumar noticed that both Kautilya and Xunzi prefer triadic categorization when they analyze political subjects: "We find various triads all through [the *Arthaśāstra*]. The war itself is to be launched in three ways: open war (*praka-shayuddha*), secret war (*kutayuddha*) and silent war (*gudayuddha*). There are three kinds of neighbours—hostile (*aribhavi*), friendly (*mitrahavi*) and vassal (*bhrib-havi*). The aggressor is one of three kinds—righteous (*dharmik*), greedy (*lobhi*) and tyrannical (*atyachari*)—and appear[s] to be resonating [with] Xunzi's thought during the same period."[12] It is true that there are also many triads in *Xunzi*, such as the three desires of rulers— desire for security (*an*), desire for glory (*rong*), and desire for establishing his fame and meritorious accomplishments (*gongming*)— and the three types of leadership—humane authority (*wang*), hegemony (*ba*), and tyrant (*qiang*).[13]

Kumar suggests that the geopolitical shape of India had an impact on Kautilya's triadic framework of thinking: "Since India has a perfect triangular peninsula, this landscape had profound influence over Indian thought-structure. Indian mind is encapsulated in triadic thinking that possibly stems from the geophilosophical domain."[14] Regardless of whether Kumar's argument is popular among Indian scholars, the geographical analysis of Kautilya's concept does not sound convincing. However, it is quite certain that Chinese scholars have never thought Xunzi's triadic thinking to have been influenced by the geographic shape of ancient China. The geographic shape of ancient China changed frequently both before and after Xunzi.

Viewing Ministers as the Intermediate Variable

Both Xunzi's and Kautilya's individual analyses are not limited to the rulers. They treat ministers as the intermediate variable in their arguments, with ministers fulfilling the roles of policy consultation and implementation. Xunzi says:

> Those who are to maintain the state certainly cannot be so alone. Since this is the case, the strength, defensive security, and glory of country lie in the selection of its prime minister. Where a ruler is himself able and his prime minister is able, he will become a True King. Where the ruler is personally incapable, but knows it, becomes apprehensive, and seeks those who are able, then he will become powerful. When the ruler is personally incapable, but neither realizes it, nor becomes apprehensive, nor seeks those who are able, but merely makes use of those who fawn over him and flatter him, those who form his entourage of assistants, or those who are related to him, then he will be endangered and encroached upon, and, in the extreme case, annihilated.[15]

Xunzi illustrates his arguments with historical cases, such as the following:

> Thus, the relation between King Cheng and the Duke of Zhou was that he heeded the duke's advice on everything that transpired, for he realized what was valuable. The relations of Duke Huan to Guan Zhong were that in the business of state he used Guan for everything that developed, for he knew what was beneficial. The kingdom of Wu had Wu Zixu but was incapable of using him, so ultimately the country was destroyed, for it turned against the Way and lost this worthy man. Thus, those who honored sages became king; those who valued the worthy became

lords-protector; those who respected the worthy survived; and those who scorned them were destroyed.[16]

Kautilya also suggests that the correct principle for appointing ministers should be based on capability rather than personal relations to the king: "For from the capacity for doing work is the ability of a person judged. And in accordance with their ability, by (suitably) distributing rank among ministers and assigning place, time and work (to them), he should appoint all these as ministers, not, however, as councilors."[17] He provides details about the appointments of ministers, councilors, and chaplains; the administration of secret tests to determine the integrity of ministers; the appointments of persons to the secret service; and so on. But he does not provide any imperial references to support his views.[18]

Kautilya does not view the capability of ministers as equally important to that of the capability of rulers, whereas Xunzi does. For instance, Xunzi believes that capable ministers can make a state strong even when the ruler is incapable: "Where the ruler is personally incapable, but knows it, becomes apprehensive, and seeks those who are able, then he will become powerful."[19] Kautilya suggests that the capability of ministers is secondary to the capabilities of the ruler because the ruler can replace impotent ministers at any time: "It is the king alone who appoints the group of servants like the councilor, the chaplain and others, directs the activity of departmental heads, takes counter-measures, secures their advancement. If the ministers are suffering from calamities, he appoints others who are not in calamities. . . . For the king is in the place of their head."[20]

VIEWS ABOUT THE NATURE
OF THE INTERSTATE SYSTEM

Xunzi and Kautilya have different concepts about interstate systems, mainly because the ancient Chinese and Indian interstate systems were not the same. Xunzi lived in the Warring States period, which was experiencing the power decentralization of the unipolar Zhou Dynasty, but the norms of that interstate system were still hierarchical. Kautilya lived in a nonhierarchical and competitive interstate system, although his normative aim was that the king he was advising and who was bent on conquest (*vijigīṣu*) could eventually emerge victorious and even become a universal emperor (*cakravartin*) within the Indian subcontinent. Their distinct conceptualizations of the interstate system can be observed in their views about the nature of interstate systems and understandings of peace and war.

Anarchy or Hierarchy

In ancient China and India, people had no knowledge of modern geography; thus, neither Xunzi nor Kautilya knew that the earth is spherical, believing it to be a flat square. Xunzi describes the earth with the concept of "the Four Seas"[21] and Kautilya with the concept of "the four ends of the earth."[22] Therefore, they imagine the geographic shape of an interstate system as a flat square.

Based on the belief that human beings do not like to be controlled, both Xunzi and Kautilya view the nature of the interstate system as anarchic. For instance, Xunzi says: "It is of the inborn nature of human beings that it is impossible for them not to form societies. If they form a society in which there are no class divisions, strife will develop. If there is strife, then there will be social disorder; if there is social disorder, there will be hardship for all. Hence, a situation in which there are no class divisions is the greatest affliction mankind can have."[23] Kautilya also views the world as an anarchic system, with all states playing the same roles. He describes the interstate system as a chessboard, with states as the chess pieces:

> There are the constituents (of the circle of kings). Or the conqueror, the ally and the ally's ally are the three constituents of the (circle of kings). They, each individually united with its five constituent elements, the minister, the country, the fort, the treasury and the army, constitute the eighteen-fold circle. By that is explained a separate circle (for each of) the enemy, the middle and the neutral kings. Thus there is a collection of four circles. There are twelve constituents who are kings, sixty material constituents, a total of seventy-two in all.[24] (See figure 3.1.)

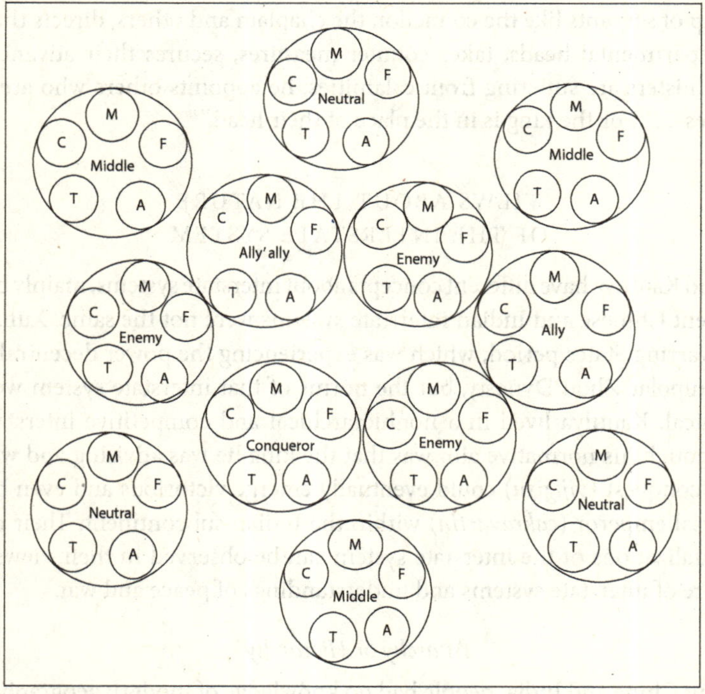

FIGURE 3.1. Kautilya's concept of the ancient Indian interstate system. Acronyms: Minister (M), Country (C), Fort (F), Treasury (T), Army (A).

Differing from Kautilya, who never discusses the possibility of a hierarchic interstate system, Xunzi believes the interstate system can be either anarchic or hierarchic, depending on whether there is a class arrangement of states. He suggests that a hierarchic interstate system can be established by a strong interstate leading power via regulating a social estate of states: "A situation in which there are class divisions is the most basic benefit under Heaven. And it is the lord of men who is the indispensable element wherewith to 'arrange the scale' of the classes of men."[25] He also notes, "The Ancient Kings abhorred such disorder. Thus, they instituted regulations, ritual practices, and moral principles in order to create proper social and class divisions. They ordered that there be sufficient gradations of wealth and eminence of station to bring everyone under supervision. This is the fundamental principle by which to nurture the empire."[26]

Xunzi's concept of a hierarchic interstate system is based on the Five Ordinances System said to be established in the Xia Dynasty and improved in the West Zhou Dynasty.[27] He says:

> Accordingly, all states of Xia Chinese have identical obligations for service to the king and have identical standards of conduct. The countries of the Man, Yi, Rong, and Di barbarians perform the same obligatory services to the king, but the regulations governing them are not the same. Those who are enforced within [the royal domain] do royal service. Those who are enforced without [the royal domain] do feudal service. Those who are in the feudal marches zone do guest service. The Man and Yi nations do service according to treaty obligations. The Rong and Di do irregular service. Those who do royal service provide offerings for the sacrifices of thanks; those who do feudal service provide offerings for the cult sacrifices; those who do guest service provide for the drinking ceremonies; those who do service according to treaty present tribute offerings; and those who do irregular service come to pay their respects at the succession of the new king. Each day, offerings of thanks are made; each season, there is the drinking ceremony; each year, tribute is offered; {and once a generation there is the succession of the new kin}. This is just what is meant by they observed the qualities inherent in the land forms and regulated with ordinances the vessels and implements; they judged the various distances and so differentiated grades of tributes and offerings—for such is the perfection of true kingship.[28]

Figure 3.2 shows the diagram of the Five Ordinances System.

Divergent Views on Interstate Relations

According to Xunzi, a state's foreign relations are crucial to its security, and the formation of foreign relations mainly depends on a state's policies toward others:

> A humane man would keep in good order the obligations between small and large countries, between the strong and weak, and would sedulously maintain them. The

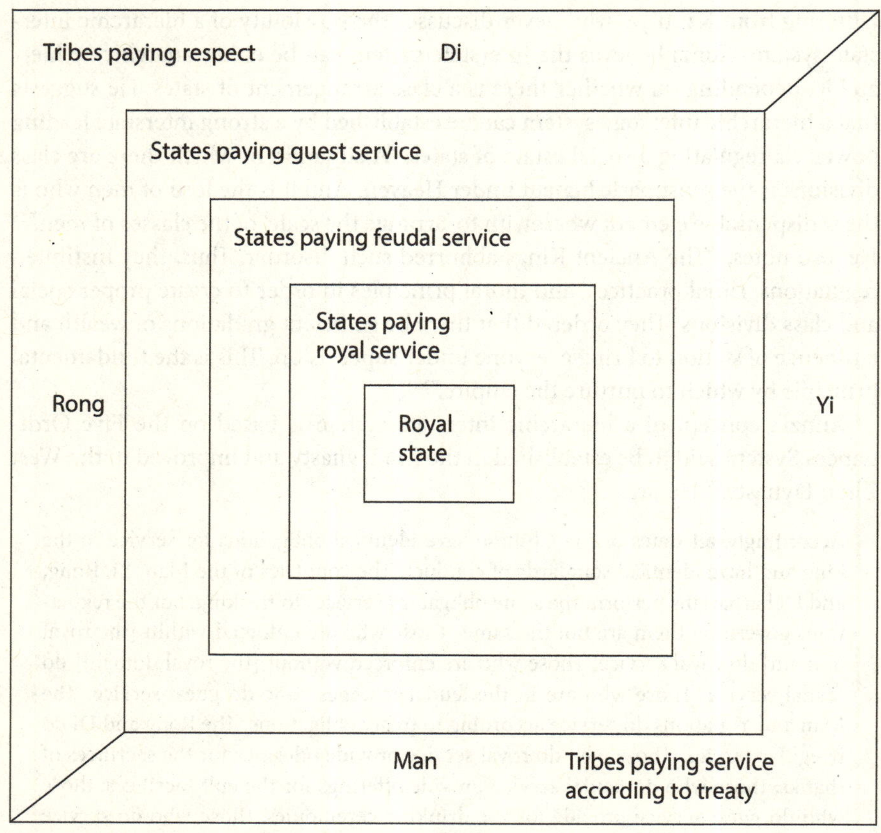

FIGURE 3.2. Xunzi's concept of the ancient Chinese interstate system.

important point of ritual would be observed with the extreme of good form. The *gui* jade baton and the *bi* jade insignia would be very sumptuous. The presents and contributions would be very munificent. The means he uses to persuade others must be those of a gentleman who is elegantly correct in form and of discriminating intelligence. Should others have designs against him, who among them could become angry with him? This being so, those who act out of anger will not commit aggression against him. If for the sake of a reputation, or for the sake of profit, or because of anger, others do not commit aggression against him, then his country will be as secure as a boulder and as long-lived as the Winnowing Basket and Wings constellations.[29]

Kautilya also regards foreign relations as an important factor in a state's security. He identifies friends and enemies in terms of geopolitics, blood lineage, and interests:

One with the immediately proximate territory is the natural enemy; one of equal birth is the enemy by birth; one opposed or in opposition is the enemy made (for the time being). One with territory separated by one other is the natural ally; one related through the mother or father is the ally by birth; one who has sought shelter for wealth or life is the ally made (for the time being).[30]

Kautilya regards ally as an element of state, but Xunzi does not. The divergent views of ally might be a result of their respective experience in the ancient Indian and Chinese interstate system. The ancient Indian interstate system was normally multipolar and rarely unipolar. The configuration consisted of two components: the power structure and strategic relations between major powers. In a multipolar configuration, the balance of power among major states is critical to the survival of a state and the stability of that interstate system. Based on his observation of the characteristics of a multipolar system, Kautilya theoretically types states according to relations between kings, such as conqueror, ally, ally's ally, enemy, middle states, and neutral states.[31] Since ally is so important to the fate of a king, it is very reasonable for Kautilya to view ally as a component of state.

Unlike the ancient Indian interstate system, the ancient Chinese interstate system irregularly shifted among unipolar, bipolar, and multipolar configurations. In general, unipolar configuration rests on an asymmetric power structure between a solo superpower and other major powers. Their strategic relations are less important in shaping a unipolar configuration than in a bipolar or multipolar configuration. A unipolar configuration lays the foundation for a hierarchic interstate system, in which the survival of states greatly relies on the protection from the solo superpower. The royal state serves as the interstate leadership who arranges the class of states. Based on his observation of the ancient Chinese hierarchic interstate system, Xunzi categorizes interstate actors into three groups, including six classes according to their relations with the royal state, namely the kingdom of the son of heaven. They are the royal state, states of three classes, and tribes of two classes.[32]

Although Kautilya views the interstate system as an anarchic system, he also realizes the unequal relationship between the strong and the weak. He suggests making allies according to relative material strength between states rather than the principle of equality: "He should seek shelter with one whose strength is superior to the strength of the neighboring (enemy). . . . Or if situated between two stronger kings, he should seek shelter with one capable of protecting him or with one whose intervening weak neighbor he may be, or with both."[33] Kautilya's idea of seeking shelter with both friendly and threatening states at the same time may appear, to foreign eyes, as an Indian diplomatic tradition similar to the principle of nonalignment during the Cold War.

Different from Kautilya's way of studying the types of states according to relations or material strength only, Xunzi stresses the political nature of states. Xunzi views the political nature of a state as a more important criterion than material strength and foreign relations for its identity. According to the foreign policies adopted by each country, Xunzi divides leading powers into three types: "*wang*" (the true king or the humane authority), "*ba*" (the lord-protector/hegemony), and "*qiang*" (the powerful/tyranny).[34] He says, "The True King tries to win men; the lord-protector to acquire allies; the powerful to capture land."[35] In his view, the state with a moral leadership will be supported by talented people of other states, including its enemies; the state with strategic credibility will be supported by its allies only; and the state with material strength only will get no support from others, although it is able to conquer others by military force.

Views about Peace and War

Xunzi views peace as an opposite state of security to war. The word "*heping*" (peace) was coined in modern Chinese and its corresponding ancient Chinese character is *an* (peace, order, and stability) or *zhi* (order by governance). Studying the peace between states in a hierarchic interstate system, Xunzi views peace as a result of good interstate governance by the leading state rather than an approach adopted by the leading power to achieve security. For instance, Xunzi says, "Order is born of the gentleman; chaos is produced by the small man."[36] Although Xunzi treats war as both a state of security and a strategy for security, he does not study peace from an instrumental perspective.

Differing from Xunzi's view of peace, Kautilya believes that both peace and war have dual characteristics; namely, they are both states of and strategies for security. Viewing peace as a state of security, Kautilya says, "Peace is that which brings about security of enjoyment of the fruits of works."[37] Regarding peace as a strategy for security, he says that "entering into a treaty is peace."[38] When addressing the six major measures of foreign policy, he parallels peace and war: "Peace, war, staying quiet, marching, seeking shelter and dual policy constitute the six measures."[39] It is reasonable for Kautilya to examine both peace and war in an anarchic interstate system from an instrumental perspective. His instrumental perception of peace leads him to believe that peace is a less expensive strategy than war to achieve the same profit: "If there is equal advancement in peace and war, he [king] should resort to peace. For in war there are losses, expenses, marches away from home and hindrance."[40] He rigorously calculates the costs and benefits of peace and war in an instrumental way: "For, when the gain is equal there should be peace, when unequal war is considered (desirable) for equal, weaker and stronger kings. Thus have peace and war been described."[41]

As for war, Xunzi regards it as both a state of and a strategy for security, but he worries about the negative political results of military victory:

When others defend the ramparts of their cities and send out knights to do battle with me and I overcome them through superior power, then the number of casualties among their population is necessarily very great. Where casualties have been extreme, the population is bound to hate me with vehemence. If the population detests me, then each day their desire to fight against me will grow. Where others defend the ramparts of their cities and sends out knights to do battle with me and I overcome them through superior power, then the number of casualties among my own people is certain to be very great. If the number of casualties among my own people has been great, they are certain to have a fierce dislike for me. If my own people hate me, then each day they will have less desire to fight for me; so as others grow more willing to fight, my own people will grow less willing to defend me. In this way, the cause of my former strength is reversed and produces weakness. Lands may be acquired, but their inhabitants will flee. As involvements become more numerous, accomplishments decrease. Although there is more to defend, the wherewithal to defend it diminishes. In this way the basis of my former greatness is reversed and is taken piece by piece from me.[42]

It would be wrong to suppose that Xunzi is a pacifist. In fact, he does not oppose the idea of achieving political goals through war, nor does he oppose the annexation of other states. In his view, different types of annexation bring different political results. Annexation based on moral principles will make a state a humane interstate authority, while immoral military attacks will undermine a state's interstate status: "One who uses moral power to annex people will become a True King; one who employs raw power to annex them will become weak; and one who employs wealth to annex them will become poor. In this regard, antiquity and today are one and the same."[43]

Differing from Xunzi's emphasis on the moral legitimacy of war, Kautilya focuses on the military capability of winning a war: "When in decline as compared to the enemy, he should make peace. When prospering, he should make war."[44] Kautilya also adds: "The conqueror should employ the six measures of policy with due regard to this power. He should make peace with the equal and the stronger; he should make war with the weaker. For going to war with the stronger, he engages as it were in a fight on foot with an elephant. And (at war) with the equal, he brings about loss on both sides, like an unbaked jar struck by an unbaked jar. (At war) with the weaker, he attains absolute success, like a stone with an earthen vessel."[45] Kautilya touches on the legitimacy of war on some occasions, but his emphasis on the military capability of war leaves readers with a much deeper impression than his concern for legitimacy. This could be the reason for many comparative studies about his strategic thoughts in the *Arthaśāstra* and Sun Tzu's in *Art of War*.

ANALYSIS OF THE POWER OF A STATE

Both Xunzi and Kautilya study the power of a state from the aspects of material and nonmaterial strength, but they have different views about the components of both kinds of strength. They hold similar views about the importance of political leadership to a state's comprehensive strength. Both of them believe that the morality of leadership is crucial to a state's interstate status, but Xunzi values strategic credibility to a state's security more than Kautilya does. Xunzi views strategic credibility as the basic element of interstate leadership morality. The cost of obtaining strategic credibility is lower than that of practicing other higher moral norms. For example, it is easier for a leading power to keep its promises effectively than to aid other states generously. Other states will view a leading power as an immoral leader when it has no strategic credibility.

Components of a State's Power

Both Xunzi and Kautilya regard power as strength, but Xunzi categorizes power into two types—material strength and nonmaterial strength—while Kautilya divides power into three types—counsel, might, and energy. Kautilya says, "Power is (possession of) strength. . . . Power is threefold: the power of knowledge is the power of counsel, the power of the treasury and army is the power of might, the power valour is the power of energy."[46] Regarding material strength, Kautilya views geographical conditions of land as elements of material strength: "endowed with agricultural land, mines, material forests and elephant forests, beneficial to cattle, beneficial to men, with protected pastures, rich in animals, not depending on rain for water, provided with water-routes and land-routes, with valuable, manifold and plenty of commodities . . . these are the excellences of a country."[47]

Xunzi also discusses the military, the economy, and land, but he stresses the use of material resources: "One who knows the way of true strength does not rely on military strength. Rather, he considers how to use the king's mandate as the means to collect together his physical power and consolidate his inner power. . . . The way of the Lord-protector is quite different. He opens up wilderness lands to cultivation, fills the granaries and storehouses, and provides useful implements."[48] However, their different views on material strength are less important and evident when compared to their differing views on nonmaterial strength.

Xunzi treats political leadership as the only nonmaterial strength, while Kautilya views knowledge and valor as two types of nonmaterial strength. Xunzi believes that every individual is born with the same nature; thus, he does not think that anyone is born with leadership capability: "Now, since human nature is evil, it must await the instruction of a teacher and the model before it can be put alright, and it must obtain ritual principles and a sense of moral right before it can become orderly. Nowadays, since men lack both teacher and model, they are prejudiced, wicked, and not upright. Since they lack ritual principles and precepts of moral duty, they are perverse, rebellious, and disorderly."[49] In contrast to Xunzi, Kautilya assumes that every individual is born differently in nature; thus, he makes the distinction between valor, an inborn strength, and knowledge, an acquired strength. He asserts that "the excellences of the king are: Born in a high family, endowed with good fortune, intelligence and spirit, given to seeing elder, pious, truthful in speech, not breaking his promise, grateful, liberal, of great energy, not dilatory, with weak neighboring princes, resolute, not having a mean council (of ministers), desirous of training—these are the qualities of one easily approachable."[50]

Political Leadership as the Basis of Comprehensive Power

Both Xunzi and Kautilya view political leadership as the foundation of a state's comprehensive strength. They believe that all of the other components of a state's strength, including the economy, the military, and natural resources, will be improved when its political leadership is strong; otherwise, no matter how immense a state is, it will lose strength when political leadership is weak. Xunzi argues that strong leadership will make a weak state rise and weak leadership will make a strong state decline:

> Hence, one who cultivates ritual principles becomes a king; one who effectively exercises government become strong; one who wins over the people will be secure; and one who merely collects tax levies will perish. Accordingly, the True King enriches the people; the lord-protector enriches his scholar-knights; a state that can barely manage to survive enriches its grand officers; and a state that is doomed enriches only the ruler's coffers and fills up his storehouses.[51]

Similarly, Kautilya emphasizes that the personal qualities of the leader are fundamental to the successful functioning of the other elements of a state, of which he suggests there are seven. That is, these seven elements cannot properly function, or can even be undermined, when the personal qualities of a king are poor.

> A king endowed with personal qualities endows with excellences the constituent elements not so endowed. One not endowed with personal qualities destroys the constituent elements that are prosperous and devoted (to him). Then that (king) not endowed with personal qualities, with defective constituent elements, is either killed by the subjects or subjugated by the enemies, even if he be ruler up to the four ends of the earth. But one possessed of personal qualities, though ruling over a small territory, being united with the excellences of the constituent elements, (and) conversant with (the science of) politics, does conquer the entire earth, never loses.[52]

Both Xunzi and Kautilya argue that morals and ethics of political leadership have direct impacts on a state's military strength. Xunzi stresses that military power is reliable when a state's leadership is viewed as ethical by the ruled, otherwise it could lead to the destruction of its military might: "If the ruler does not exalt ritual principles, then the army will be weak. If he does not love his people, then the army will be weak. If when he prohibits or approves something he is untrustworthy, then the army will be weak. If his commendations and rewards do not penetrate down to the lower ranks, then the army will be weak. If the generals and marshals are incapable, then the army will be weak."[53] It is obvious that Xunzi attributes the appointment of incapable officers to the poor morality of a state's leadership.

Kautilya also thinks that a ruler's morality has decisive impacts on the state's military strength. He views military capability as a combination of soldiers and military equipment. Among the two components, he suggests that the loyalty of soldiers, cultivated by the morality of their ruler, should be more important than military equipment. A ruler cannot rely on his state's military capability when his soldiers' loyalty is broken by his immoral behavior: "(When the choice is) between a strong king unjustly behaved and a weak king justly behaved, he should march against the strong king unjustly. The subjects do not help the strong unjust king when he is attacked, they drive him out or resort to his enemy. But the subjects support in every way the weak but just king when he is attacked or follow him if he has to flee."[54]

Moral Principles and a State's Interstate Status

Xunzi stresses that moral principles adopted by a king will make his state the leading power of the world:

> The Way of a True King is not like this. His humanity is the loftiest in the world, his justice the most admirable, and his majesty the most marvelous. His humanity being the loftiest is the cause of none in the world being estranged from him. His justice being the most admirable is the cause of none failing to esteem him. His majesty being the most marvelous is the cause of no one in the world presuming to oppose him. His majesty permitting no opposition coupled with a way that wins the allegiance of others is the cause of his triumphing without having to wage war, of his gaining his objectives without resort to force, and of the world submitting to him without his armies exerting themselves.[55]

Kautilya also regards the morality of a ruler as the key to a state's status. He lists four qualities of a king, including being easily approachable, intellect, energy, and personal excellence.[56] Each of the four qualities includes many aspects. The quality of being easily approachable includes "truthful in speech, not breaking his promise, grateful, [and] liberal."[57] He views immoralities as putting a country in danger of being destroyed by other countries: "Not royal descent, greedy, with a mean council (of ministers), with disaffected subjects, unjust in behavior, not applying himself (to duties), vicious, devoid of energy, trusting in fate, doing whatever pleases him, without shelter, without a following, impotent, ever doing harm (to others)—these are excellences in any enemy. For an enemy of this type becomes easy to exterminate."[58]

Xunzi regards strategic credibility as the basis for a state to win support from other states. Since every state may have enemies, it must seek the support of other states in order to survive or to rule. Xunzi knows that it is difficult for most kings to have a high level of morality, so he suggests they at least maintain strategic credibility . He believes that strategic credibility is the basis of winning support from others.

> Although the moral force of their inner power had not yet reached perfection and although moral principles had not yet been fully attained, yet, in a general way, they

displayed rational principles for ordering the world. Their punishments and rewards, their prohibitions and assents, were believed by the world. Their ministers and subjects fully and clearly knew that they were capable of exercising constraints over them. When the rules and edicts of government had been set forth, then although they might see opportunity for profit or danger of loss, they would not deceive their people. When agreements had already been settled, then although they might see the opportunity for profit or danger of loss, they would not deceive their allies. Since they behaved in this fashion, their army was strong, their cities well defended, and hostile countries stood in awe of them. Then the unity of their own countries was a brilliantly evident beacon, and their allies had faith in them.[59]

Xunzi argues, relying on historical cases, that morality can help a weak state to become strong:

> Although from despised and backward countries, their majestic authority shook the whole world. Such were the five Lords-Protector . . . Thus, that Duke Huan of Qi, Duke Wen of Jin, King Zhuang of Chu, King Helu of Wu, and King Goujian of Yue, all of whom were of despised and backward countries, held majestic sway over the world and [that] their might held peril for all the Central States was due to no other cause than that they were in the main trustworthy. This is what is called "established trust and becoming a lord-protector."[60]

Kautilya also perceives strategic reputation as an important element in shaping foreign relations. He believes that strategic reputation is politically more important in ancient times than in his time because kings of his time were no longer as true to their word as were their ancestors.

> Peace, treaty, hostage, there are one and the same thing. The creation of confidence among kings is (the purpose of) peace treaty or hostage. . . . Plighting one's troth or taking an oath is a pact stable in the next world as well as here, a surety or a hostage is of use only in this world, depending on strength. "We have made a pact," thus kings of old, faithful to their word, made pacts by plighting their troth. In case of (fear of) its transgression, they touched fire, water, a furrow in the field, a clod of earth from the rampart, a gem, seeds, a fragrant substance, a liquid, gold or money, affirming with an oath, "May these kill or abandon him who would break the oath."[61]

Kautilya certainly considers allies' loyalty as an important criterion for judging the quality of an ally: "Allied from the days of the father and the grandfather, constant under control, not having a separate interest, great, able to mobilized quickly—these are the excellences of an ally."[62]

Nevertheless, his thinking about strategic credibility seems a one-way concept, different from Xunzi's. He suggests a king cautiously consider how loyal his allies are to him, but none of his comments on alliance suggests that a king be loyal to his allies. Whereas Xunzi stresses that "when agreements had already been settled, then although they might see the opportunity for profit or danger of loss, they would not deceive their allies."[63]

CONCLUSION

The shared thoughts of Xunzi and Kautilya on important concepts and issues of interstate relations as reflected in this article can help us to enrich existing IR theories. Ancient Chinese and Indian thinkers have paid attention to the paradigm of many theoretical concepts such as leadership determinism and leadership morality. These ideas have laid a good basis upon which Chinese and Indian scholars can construct a new IR theory. In regard to establish non-Western IR theories, Amitav Acharya suggests that "these theories need to incorporate and adapt to the realities of the non-Western world. ... It is not enough to 'test' existing theories in non-Western contexts and revise them if there is a mismatch. We also need to go beyond the existing theories. Global IR calls for developing whole new theories and perspectives from other societies on their own terms."[64] I would like to propose that Chinese and Indian scholars develop universal IR theories covering both Western and non-Western historical realities. That means our thinking should travel beyond China and India and produce a general framework for both analyzing and forecasting international changes on major issues. For the sake of developing universal IR theories, Chinese and Indian scholars should refrain from the nationalist impulse to establish a Chinese or Indian school of IR theories.

Xunzi's and Kautilya's thoughts on interstate politics both reflect leadership determinism. While the paradigm of their thinking is very traditional, it is more efficient than economic determinism and political system determinism in explaining changes in economic growth of China and India. These two countries are distinctive in their political systems, but historical comparison shows that they have experienced quick as well as slow economic growth under the reigns of different national leadership since their independence. Horizontal comparison shows that their economies have grown at a similar speed in recent years, but faster than those countries that shared the same political system, such as Cuba and the UK respectively. Their bilateral relations experienced both amicable and antagonist periods in the last seven decades. Both friendly and hostile relations were shaped by the policies adopted by the leadership of the two nations. These facts imply that their future bilateral relations will continue to be shaped by their decision makers despite differences in their political systems or economic productivity.

Both Xunzi and Kautilya regard morality as an important component of leadership qualities. For quite a long time, people around the world have believed that democratic institutions determine American global leadership. During Donald Trump's presidency, which began in 2017, American leadership in global governance deteriorated dramatically while American democratic institutions have remained, for the most part, unchanged. Faced with the global pandemic that began in December 2019, Trump's administration failed to lead the world to contain the epidemic's expansion. People may have different judgments as to the morality of Trump's leadership, but most people, including many Americans, have a similar view of his leadership's strategic credibility. Nowadays, people are worried about regressive changes in the world order, mainly because they have little hope of expecting a moral international leadership by any great power in the near future.

Xunzi's thought has had a strong influence on some Chinese IR scholars' theories, such as with regard to moral realism,[65] but it does not have a clear impact on contemporary Chinese foreign policy. Unlike Confucius and Mencius, Xunzi's arguments have never been quoted in any contemporary Chinese official documents or speeches. However, Kautilya's thought leaves tangible marks on both Indian scholars and decision makers. Kautilya's impact on modern Indian strategic thinking is generally recognized, although there are debates about the depth of his impact among scholars.[66] Nehru often referenced the *Arthaśāstra* in his speeches and writings, even commending the book to his daughter Indira in his *Selected Works of Jawaharlal Nehru*.[67] In regard to Kautilya's thoughts on interstate relations, L. N. Rangarajan states: "Kautilya gives us a detailed theoretical analysis of all possible political situations with recommendations on ways of meeting them."[68] I interpret his remark to suggest that the *Arthaśāstra* provides rich resources for scholars who seek to develop new IR theories.

NOTES

1. Akshay Joshi, "Strategic Wisdom from the Orient: Evaluating the Contemporary Relevance of Kautilya's Arthashastra and Sun Tzu's Art of War," *Strategic Analysis* 43, no. 1 (January–February 2019): 54–74; K. N. Ramachandran, "Sun Zi and Kautilya: Towards a Comparative Analysis," *Strategic Analysis* 38, no. 3 (May–June 2014): 390–408; Anusmita Dutta and Manish S. Dabhade, "Diplomatic Theory of Kautilya and Sun Tzu: Assessing Interpretations," *International Studies* 51, nos. 1–4 (2014): 162–79; Giri Deshingkar, "Strategic Thinking of Kautilya and Sun Zi," *China Report* 32, no. 1 (1996): 1–13.

2. John Knoblock, trans., "Book 11, Of Kings and Lords-Protector," *Xunzi I* (Changsha: Human People's Publishing House, 1999), 319.

3. R. P. Kangle, "Book 7, The Six Measure of Foreign Policy," *The Kautilya Arthaśāstra Part II* (Delhi: Motilal Banarsidass, 2014), 339–53.

4. Xu Jin, "The Two Poles of Confucianism: A Comparison of the Inter-state Political Philosophies of Mencius and Xunzi," in *Ancient Chinese Thought, Modern Chinese Power*, ed. Yan Xuetong (Princeton, NJ: Princeton University Press, 2011), 161.

5. Kangle, "Book 6, The Circle of Kings as the Basis," *The Kautilya Arthaśāstra Part II*, 317 (6.2.6–7, 12).

6. James E. Dougherty and Robert L. Pfaltzgraff, Jr., *Contending Theories of International Relations: A Comprehensive Survey*, 5th ed. (New York: Addison Wesley Longman, 2001), 28–29.

7. Knoblock, "Book 11, Of Kings and Lords-Protector," *Xunzi I*, 315.

8. Kangle, "Book 6, The Circle of Kings as the Basis," *The Kautilya Arthaśāstra Part II*, 314 (6.1.1).

9. Kangle, "Book 8, Concerning the Topic of Calamities," *The Kautilya Arthaśāstra Part II*, 390 (8.2.1).

10. Kangle, "Book 13, Means of Taking a Fort," *The Kautilya Arthaśāstra Part II*, 486 (13.4.5).

11. Kangle, "Book 6, The Circle of Kings as the Basis," *The Kautilya Arthaśāstra Part II*, 315 (6.1.8).

12. Niraj Kumar, "Building Grand Strategy with Indian Characteristics for Rebounding India," *Journal of Indian Research* 2, no. 1 (January–March 2014): 12.

13. Knoblock, "Book 9, On the Regulations of a King," *Xunzi I*, 217, 221.

14. Kumar, "Building Grand Strategy," 12.

15. Knoblock, "Book 11, Of Kings and Lords-Protector," *Xunzi I*, 329.

16. Knoblock, "Book 24, On the Gentleman," *Xunzi II*, 783.

17. Kangle, "Book 1, The Topic Training," *The Kautilya Arthaśāstra Part II*, 16 (1.8.27–29).

18. Ibid., 17–27 (1.9–12).

19. Knoblock, "Book 11, Of Kings and Lords-Protector," *Xunzi I*, 329.

20. Kangle, "Book 8, Concerning the Topic of Calamities," *The Kautilya Arthaśāstra Part II*, 386 (8.1.13–14, 18).

21. Knoblock, "Book 15, Debate on the Principles of Warfare," *Xunzi I*, 457.

22. Kangle, "Book 6, The Circle of Kings as the Basis," *The Kautilya Arthaśāstra Part II*, 317 (6.2.3).

23. Knoblock, "Book 10, On Enriching the State," *Xunzi I*, 273.

24. Kangle, "Book 6, The Circle of Kings as the Basis," *The Kautilya Arthaśāstra Part II*, 319 (6.2.23–28).

25. Knoblock, "Book 10, On Enriching the State," *Xunzi I*, 273.

26. Knoblock, "Book 9, On the Regulation of a King," *Xunzi I*, 215.

27. The royal kingship city is located at the center of the system. The *dian* ordinance, which occupied the 500 *li* surrounding the kingship city, was for planting various grains and acted as the king's food supplier. The next surrounding 500 *li* was the *hou* ordinance, which mainly provided the king with labor and territorial protection. The next surrounding 2,500 *li* was the *bin* ordinance, which comprised the vassal states of China. This area was subdivided into five 500-*li qi*, in this order—*hou qi, dian qi, nan qi, ai qi, and wei qi*—that were mostly responsible for cultural education and military support. The next areas contained the *yao* ordinance and the *huang* ordinance, each 1,000 *li*, but their distance from the center is uncertain. The *yao* ordinance was further divided into the *man* and *yi* ordinances, each 500 *li*, of similar political order but reduced taxation. The *huang* ordinance was further divided into the *zhen* ordinance and *fan* ordinance, each also covering 500 *li*, which had simple political systems and norms, and where population mobility was high.

28. Knoblock, "Book 18, Rectifying Theses," *Xunzi II*, 571, 573.

29. Knoblock, "Book 10, On Enriching the State," *Xunzi I*, 309.

30. Kangle, "Book 6, The Circle of Kings as the Basis," *The Kautilya Arthaśāstra Part II*, 318 (6.2.19–20).

31. Ibid., 319 (6.2.23–28).

32. Knoblock, "Book 18, Rectifying Theses," *Xunzi II*, 571, 573.

33. Kangle, "Book 7, The Six Measures of Foreign Policy," *The Kautilya Arthaśāstra Part II*, 325 (7.2.6, 13).

34. It should be noted that in Xunzi's works, *ba* is similar to the linguistically neutral "hegemony," which has no negative meaning such as aggression toward or bullying of weak states.

35. Knoblock, "Book 9, On the Regulations of a King," *Xunzi I*, 221.

36. Ibid., 215.

37. Kangle, "Book 6, The Circle of Kings as the Basis," *The Kautilya Arthaśāstra Part II*, 317 (6.2.3).

38. Kangle, "Book 7, The Six Measures of Foreign Policy," *The Kautilya Arthaśāstra Part II*, 321 (7.1.6).

39. Ibid., 321 (7.1.2).

40. Ibid., 325 (7.2.1).

41. Ibid., 348 (7.8.34).

42. Knoblock, "Book 9, On the Regulations of a King," *Xunzi I*, 221, 223.

43. Knoblock, "Book 15, Debate on the Principles of Warfare," *Xunzi I*, 497.

44. Kangle, "Book 7, The Six Measures of Foreign Policy," *The Kautilya Arthaśāstra Part II*, 321 (7.1.13–14).

45. Ibid., 327 (7.3.1–5).

46. Kangle, "Book 6, The Circle of Kings as the Basis," *The Kautilya Arthaśāstra Part II*, 319 (6.2.31, 33).

47. Ibid., 319 (6.1.8).

48. Knoblock, "Book 9, On the Regulations of a King," *Xunzi I*, 223, 225.

49. Knoblock, "Book 23, Man's Nature Is Evil," *Xunzi II*, 743.

50. Kangle, "Book 6, The Circle of Kings as the Basis," *The Kautilya Arthaśāstra Part II*, 314 (6.1.2–3).

51. Knoblock, "Book 9, On the Regulation of a King," *Xunzi I*, 219.

52. Kangle, "Book 6, The Circle of Kings as the Basis," *The Kautilya Arthaśāstra Part II*, 317 (6.1.16–18).

53. Knoblock, "Book 10, On Enriching the State," *Xunzi I*, 134–35.

54. Kangle, "Book 7, The Six Measures of Foreign Policy," *The Kautilya Arthaśāstra Part II*, 335 (7.5.16–18).

55. Knoblock, "Book 9, On the Regulation of a King," *Xunzi II*, 227.

56. Kangle, "Book 6, The Circle of Kings as the Basis," *The Kautilya Arthaśāstra Part II*, 314–15 (6.1.3–6).

57. Ibid., 314 (6.1.3).

58. Ibid., 316 (6.1.13–14).

59. Knoblock, "Book 11, Of Kings and Lords-Protector," *Xunzi I*, 319, 321.

60. Ibid., 321.

61. Kangle, "Book 7, The Six Measures of Foreign Policy," *The Kautilya Arthaśāstra Part II*, 375 (7.17.1–7).

62. Kangle, "Book 6, The Circle of Kings as the Basis," *The Kautilya Arthaśāstra Part II*, 316 (6.1.12).

63. Knoblock, "Book 11, Of Kings and Lords-Protector," *Xunzi I*, 321.

64. Amitav Acharya, "From Heaven to Earth: 'Cultural Idealism' and 'Moral Realism' as Chinese Contributions to Global International Relations," *Chinese Journal of International Politics* 12, no. 4 (2019): 491.

65. Yan Xuetong, *Leadership and the Rise of Great Powers* (Princeton, NJ: Princeton University Press, 2019), 259.

66. Aparna Pande, *From Chanakya to Modi: Evolution of India's Foreign Policy* (New York: HarperCollins India, 2017), 24–25.

67. Jawaharlal Nehru, *Selected Works of Jawaharlal Nehru* (Delhi: Orient Longman, 1972), 462.

68. L. N. Rangarajan, *Kautilya: The Arthashastra* (Hayana: Penguin Books, 1987), 506.

4

Ashoka's Dhamma as a Project of Expansive Moral Hegemony

Rajeev Bhargava

INTRODUCTION

Ancient, pre-modern, pre-democracy rulers and their states can be classified into three kinds. First, those rulers who conquer territories and rule people by brute force and elaborate surveillance. They enslave people, treat them as subhuman, subject them to arbitrary power, and tyrannize them. Second, those rulers who seize power in the territory that they inhabit or conquer other territories, but then form alliances with subsidiary rulers, neutralize opposition, and impose or compel others to accept their worldview. This is rule by domination. In such states, the elementary needs of people may be met but their conception of the good life is utterly disregarded. Political domination is accompanied by cultural domination. Third, and finally, there exists the ruler who rules neither by brute force nor by domination. Instead, he provides political, cultural, and intellectual leadership. He wishes to arrive at a political ethic that accommodates the worldview of his subjects; that is, he seeks to find a common ground, allowing multiple conceptions of the good life to exist and then to integrate these conceptions into his political ethic. In short, he encourages discussion among different groups within his territory, and once a common political ethic is identified, he becomes its guardian. He leads by example, doing everything in his power to provide ethical education to his subjects.

Although formulated in an entirely different era and context, the modern Italian philosopher Antonio Gramsci coined the term "expansive hegemony," which can be used to describe such rule. When a ruler is morally hegemonic in this sense, he manages to arrive at a new ethic that coalesces the multiple ethical perspectives of all the groups in his society. Expansive hegemony is entirely consistent with pluralism. This new ethic provides a social cement to his rule within the territory

96

and could be equally valuable to rulers and subjects beyond the boundaries of its originator. Therefore, this ethic may take root not only within the territorial boundary of the hegemon's rule but also spread beyond it. This diffusion does not happen automatically, but is undertaken by suitably trained moral educators. This establishes the basis of a new kind of imperial order where brute force and domination is replaced by the intellectual and moral leadership of the hegemon. Word is spread not just by the traveling trained officials of the state but by the ruler himself, who leads by example.

Asoka, who ruled in the third century BCE in India, is probably the first leader in the world of this third kind. Knowledge about him comes from his inscriptions or edicts that lie scattered in more than thirty places throughout India, Nepal, Bangladesh, Pakistan, and Afghanistan.[1] Most of them are written in Brahmi script from which all Indian scripts and many of those used in Southeast Asia later developed. The language of the edicts in the eastern part of the subcontinent is Prakrit, associated with the people of Magadh; in the edicts of western India it is closer to Sanskrit in the Kharoshthi script, with one extract of Edict 13 in Greek and one bilingual edict in Kandahar, Afghanistan, written in Greek and Aramaic. Asoka's edicts, the earliest decipherable corpus of written documents from India, have survived throughout the centuries because they are written on rocks, cave walls, and stone pillars. These edicts appear to be in Asoka's own words rather than in the more formal language in which royal edicts or proclamations in the ancient world were usually written.

Excessive self-praise was common in oral cultures, especially among rulers. Modesty was not a political virtue. Thus, many of his inscriptions describe his achievements. He claims to have ushered in a new era, to have broken away from the past, a feature that already distinguishes him from other empire-builders of his time. However, other significant features need highlighting. His self-praise is almost always tempered by self-criticism. Talk of his achievement is disrupted by intense self-reflection about the difficulties faced by a leader who wishes to be ethical. Rock Edict 5 states: "It is easy to commit sins, or do wrong, and far more difficult to do something good or morally right. Nor is it easy to follow the example of a righteous person." Pillar Edict 3, for example, reflects on human nature: "We all notice only the good deeds we have done but not always our wicked deeds." To confront oneself, to ask if one has been cruel, harsh, unjustly angry, or proud, is hard; Asoka speaks of how he had been close to failure and expresses regret for the harm he might have caused to humans and animals. He reflects also on human frailty and vulnerability, and more generally on the human predicament. Some of these inscriptions are less like the edicts of a ruler and more like a personal diary, often confessional, that he nonetheless shares with the public, a sort of published personal notebook in stone or iron.

Second, it was a normal royal custom, particularly in his times, to affix a long chain of self-glorifying honorific titles before one's own name. For example, the

Achaemenidian inscriptions of Darius begin thus: "I, Darius, the Great King, king of kings, king of countries, king on this earth, son of Hystaspes, the Achaemenid" (the Elamite text of the inscription DPf).[2] Contrast this with Asoka, who humbly eschews such titles and wishes to be known simply as "devanam priya" (the beloved of the gods or other rulers). Third, the moral worldview propagated by him does not ask others to abandon their own idea of the good life but seems to say to them, "Keep yours, but also embrace my own."

This essay explores the Asokan politico-moral ethic, called Dhamma, and the role of moral and intellectual leadership in it both within the king's own territory and beyond it. It shows that one of the central aspirations of Asoka's Dhamma is a form of universalism, to shape the global order by sending emissaries all over the world. At appropriate junctures, it shows similarities of Asoka's views to Xunzi's as enunciated and compared by Yan Xuetong in this volume with Kautilya's political vision. Kautilya provides somewhat of a contrast to Xunzi, whereas Asoka and Xunzi share many similarities. A comparison between Xunzi and Asoka is equally interesting, perhaps even more appropriate.

ASOKA'S DHAMMA AS CIVIC RELIGION

At the core of Asoka's edicts lies his conception of Dhamma, a set of precepts about how to lead a good individual and collective life. Dhamma is generally understood in India's scholarly tradition to mean "law." But in a recent essay, Patrick Olivelle has proposed that Dhamma be reconceived as civic religion, a term revived by Robert Bellah, after Rousseau first coined it in his classic work, *The Social Contract*.[3]

Dhamma as Personal Morality (Interpersonal Morality)

For Olivelle, Dhamma has far more to do with the cultivation of personal and religious virtues, with spiritual growth, and with the development of character than with obedience to civil and criminal law. He cites Rock Edicts 2 and 3, which explicitly speak of Dhamma: "Obedience to mother and father. Giving to friends and acquaintances and relatives, to brahmanas and sramanas. Showing kindness and abstaining from killing living beings." Asoka extols "spending little and storing little" and "speaking the truth." Both Rock Edicts 9 and 11 and Pillar Edict 7 add that "proper regard to slaves and servants" is morally important.[4]

In Pillar Edict 2, Asoka explicates further: "It is having few faults and doing many good deeds (*Kalyana*), compassion (*Daya*), charity (*Dana*), truthfulness and purity (*Sochaye*)." Later two other virtues are added: *Samyama* (self-control) and *Bhavashuddhi* (purity of mind). Olivelle rightly points out that Asoka's Dhamma does not discriminate between individuals and groups. Dhamma is applicable to all, regardless of social station, economic status, gender, or ethnicity. Its aspiration, like Buddha's, is universal.[5]

But I wish to push Olivelle further. I do this by making explicit two distinctions implicit in his remarks on Asoka: first, between the personal and the social, and second, between morality and law. Olivelle is right that Asoka's Dhamma is not obedience to law, civil or criminal. Force and coercion are not part of the moral and political lexicon of the epigraphs.[6] Asoka relies on persuasion (*Nijjhati*) rather than legislation, but it does not follow that Dhamma is thereby equated with personal or individualistic morality. Individual morality is not the only alternative to law. As important for Asoka is collective or intergroup morality—what we owe each other as members of religio-philosophical groups. Dhamma is then more than interpersonal morality— what we owe each other as individuals and to members of one's own family, those who are extensions of one's self.

Interpasandic (Intergroup) Morality

Among historians, a consensus exists today that Asoka lived at a time when urbanization was well under way. New towns had arisen, and with them a new, separate class of traders and merchants. In large tracts of land, different categories of people—Brahmins, Kshatriyas, merchants, and ordinary people—freely lived or were compelled to live together, and to interact. This was also a period of the emergence of larger state formations. One new function of state officials was to address the possibly troublesome interaction among these groups and individuals. These state officials possibly lived among and jostled with these groups. Since, as one of the epigraphs tells us, members of each of these socioeconomic groups attached themselves to different *pasandas*, these *pasandas* too interacted with one another. As they regularly met face to face, the quality of their interaction would surely have depended on the moral and ethical character of their respective *pasandas*, and the different content of their worldviews. Profound disagreement and conflict were likely if these differences were major.

What was the nature of these differences? First, those who agreed on the ethical centrality of ritual sacrifice began to differ on its form—some accepted that it involved several Brahmins, was large, complicated, and expensive, while others thought this baroque quality obscured its real meaning, which lay in simplicity and economy. A second difference also emerged within practitioners of ritual sacrifice. Some claimed that the main purpose of ritual sacrifice was to propitiate the gods, to persuade benevolent gods to work in favor of the *yajamana* and prevent malevolent gods from obstructing *yajamanas* from receiving the desired goods. Others thought that the gods, even if they existed, were irrelevant to this entire process. The correct, meticulous, flawless performance of the ritual by the Brahmins was sufficient to beget all the desired goods. Third, there was a straightforward disagreement between those who affirmed the centrality of ritual sacrifice and those who denied it or who claimed that the act of sacrifice was meaningless unless related to knowledge, unavailable to or hidden from the empirical self, what later came to be viewed as the identity of the Brahman and the Atman (the

Upanishadic Thinkers). Fourth, among those who denied its significance were those who disregarded Karma (Ajivikas) and those who believed that any alternative ethics must make it its pivot (Jainas, Buddhists). Fifth, among those who gave Karma a central place in their ethics, there were the radical ascetics who evaluated all Karma negatively and believed that cessation of all Karma—physical and mental motionlessness—was the only way to individual salvation (Nirgranthas or Jainas) and there were those who argued that Karma could be both positively and negatively evaluated and that salvation depends not just on self-focused action but even more on other-related actions of kindness and compassion (Buddhists). Finally, in the broadest possible terms, a straightforward conflict existed between ritual specialists (Brahmins) and all those who rejected the ethical significance of ritual sacrifice (*Shramanas*, i.e., the Jains, Buddhists, Ajivikas, and some ascetic Brahmins).[7]

What, despite profound differences in worldviews, could be the basis of such coexistence? For a start, the possibility of coexistence depended on toleration, the capacity to put up with the practices of others, despite deep moral disagreement. Better still, it needed mutual adjustment and accommodation: to the extent possible, Vedic, Brahmanical ethics needed to be moralized; the shramanic worldview, the worldview of Buddhists, Nirgranthis, and Ajivikas, needed to accept some value in rituals and rites. This could hardly have been easy, given the Shramanic contempt for rituals and the Brahmanic distaste for anti-ritualistic, transcendental morality. The edicts encourage partial reconciliation. Rock Edict 9 notes that rituals and ceremonies play an important role in the daily lives of people. They are also significant on the occasions of births, the marriages of sons and daughters, journey, sickness, and death.[8]

Several edicts mention, however, the limited value of rituals and ceremonies.[9] Rock Edict 9 says, "It is right that ceremonies are performed but this kind bears little fruit and is of 'doubtful value.'"[10] The only ceremonies worth performing are Dhamma-related, i.e., those good deeds that concern others: ceremonies of Dhamma, the Dhamma-*mangalas* that celebrate the proper treatment of slaves and employees, restraint of violence toward living creatures, reverence toward teachers, and liberality toward Brahman and Sramana ascetics.[11] Yet rituals do not address one of the most burning moral issues of the times: interpasandic disagreement and conflict. Hence, Edict 12 says, "The beloved of the Gods does not wish to overvalue gifts and sacrifice. More important than these is the reverence one's faith commands or the number of its followers or its core ethical values. Even more important than these ethical values are the essentials of all faiths and *pasandas*. It is these essentials that constitute the common ground of these seemingly conflicting conceptions."[12]

What then are these essentials? Interpreters here give differing answers: Dhamma is sometimes seen as virtue, religious truth, or simply piety. But the most convincing answer, consistent with what is mentioned above, is that Dhamma is akin to a social ethic.[13] If so, it is fair to say that for Asoka, rites and rituals have no meaning unless embedded within an ethical perspective, and the ethical import of these gifts is overshadowed or overridden by their lack of moral significance. This is why only those rituals may be performed that are not injurious to anyone (humans as well as nonhumans). No animal may be killed in order to be sacrificed. Nor should there be any *samaja* (assembly) for such a purpose, implying that other kinds of assemblies, especially the Sangha, are permissible.[14]

What then is the social content of Dhamma? The fundamental principle of Dhamma is *vacaguti*, variously interpreted as restraint on speech or control of the tongue. Why is such importance attributed to *Vaca*? We do not have much evidence of the verbal battles and hate speech of that period, but the edicts imply that verbal wars in that period were intense and brutal. They simply had to be reined in. And what kind of speech had to be curbed? Edict 12 says that speech without reason that disparages other *pasandas* must be restrained. Speech critical of others may be freely enunciated only if one has good reasons to do so.[15] However, even when one has good reasons to be critical, one may do so only on appropriate occasions; and even when the occasion is appropriate, one must never be immoderate. Critique should never belittle or humiliate others. Thus, there is a multilayered, ever-deepening restraint on one's verbal speech against others. Let us call it "other-related self-restraint." However, the edicts do not stop at this. They go on to say that one must not extol one's own *pasanda* without good reason. Undue praise of one's own *pasanda* is as morally objectionable as unmerited criticism of the faith of others. Moreover, the edicts add that even when there is good reason to praise one's own *pasanda*, it too should be done only on appropriate occasions, and even on those occasions, never immoderately. Undue or excessive self-glorification is also a way to make others feel small. For Asoka, blaming other *pasandas* out of devotion to one's own *pasanda*, as well as unreflective, uncritical, effulgent self-praise, can only damage one's *pasanda*. By offending and thereby estranging others, it undermines one's capacity for mutual interaction and possible influence. Thus, there must equally be multi-textured, ever-deepening restraint with respect to oneself. Let this be "self-related self-restraint."

Elsewhere, in Edict 7, Asoka emphasizes the need not only for self-restraint, *samyama*, but also *bhavashuddhi*, again a self-oriented act. But in my view, *bhavashuddhi*, purity of mind, here includes cleansing one's self of ill will toward others. Self-restraint and self-purification are not just matters of etiquette or prudence. They have an other-related, moral significance.

For Asoka, hate speech and self-glorification produces discord and dogma. He wishes instead to advance mutual understanding and mutual appreciation, for which it is better to have *samovaya*, concourse, an assembly of *pasandas* where they can hear each other out and communicate with one another. This may or may not result in agreement and consensus, but it certainly makes them *bahushruta*, i.e., one who listens to all, the perfect listener, or one who hears or has heard the many, and thereby becomes open-minded. In this way they can tease out the impurities and imperfections from their own collective ethical self-understanding. This is the only path to *atma pasanda vaddhi*, growth in the ethical self-understanding of one's own *pasanda*, and to *par pasanda vaddhi*, growth in the ethical self-understanding of others. It also brings growth of the essentials of all (*saravadhi*). The edicts here imply that the ethical self-understanding of *pasandas* is not static but constantly evolving, and such growth is crucially dependent on mutual communication and dialogue with one another. Blaming others without good reason or doing so immoderately disrupts this process and, apart from damaging Dhamma, diminishes mutual growth of individual *pasandas*. In another passage, Asoka says that those seeking improvement in their own ethical views should not only communicate with others with different ethical perspectives in order to learn from them but even follow their precepts, "obey" them. Thinking as if you were in someone else's shoes may not on occasion be sufficient; you have to act with their shoes on. This practical ethical engagement brings an experiential dimension that could be ethically transformative.

Vacaguti and *samovaya* are social virtues irreducible to personal or individual virtues because they involve a set of dispositions and comportment not only regarding one's own self—the particular beliefs and practices that are dear to me—but also regarding other selves. Like civility, openness, and tolerance, they too are associated with individuals, but even more, they are relational. They are an attribute of whole societies. We may legitimately speak of a civil (with *samyama* and *vacaguti*) society, an open society, a tolerant society, and a harmonious rather than an acrimonious society. Asoka himself conveys strongly that he has in mind "harmony" as an attribute of social life.[16] The social dimension of Dhamma requires that each group act in a manner that generates harmony in society.

This point needs to be made more centrally than Olivelle does. Doing so lends greater weight to his argument that Asokan Dhamma be seen as civic religion, for a key feature of civic religion is that it is neither opposed to any particular religio-philosophical perspective nor associated exclusively with it. The need to have a space for it arises precisely under conditions of diversity, as Olivelle recognizes. In a multi-religious, multi-philosophical society, civic religion draws attention to core values around which citizens can unite, rise above, or discover commonality beneath radical diversity and conflict. *Samyama* and *vacaguti* are crying out to be included in a list of virtues and values around which everyone, disagreeing on much else, can agree. For Bellah, civic religion is the moral glue, a common reference point that gives people a sense of unity amidst radical differences. It exists only where multiple religions and philosophies cohabit. Furthermore, in Bellah's use of the term, in the American context, this individual and social morality is called a religion because it includes rituals and a variety of other spiritual elements, not the least of which is the symbolic role played by "God," an empty sign which means so little that it can be filled in as each person wishes. In Asokan edicts this role is performed by Dhamma; as long as they agree on the broad idea, each religio-philosophical group can read into it whatever else they wish.

DHAMMA AS POLITICAL ETHIC
(RULER-RULED MORALITY)

Equally important, there exists a crucial political component of Dhamma that outlines how political power is to be used for ethical purposes, what ethical relation there must be between the ruler and the ruled, and what is expected of royal officials. It is also about what the ruler owes to people who are not directly his subjects—in short, concerning interstate relationships, or what ethical principles shape the global order. True, these are not present explicitly in the list of virtues or norms associated with Dhamma, but, I would argue, nor is Dhamma conceivable without them. Indeed, I would argue that unlike other conceptions of Dharma or Dhamma extant in Indian society, Asoka offers us a uniquely political conception. In the remaining part of this essay, I elaborate this point, which is somewhat less emphasized by scholars on Asoka. This strong political dimension should also have been underlined by Olivelle. Adding it to the idea of civic religion does not contradict Olivelle's claim; rather, it strengthens it. For civic religion, as I have already mentioned, is also a political idea. It refers not only to widely held social principles but also to political principles. In the American context it refers primarily to values of democracy and citizenship equality. These two values define the relationship between the ruler and the ruled. American civic religion is not possible in the absence of democracy or if citizenship is reduced to subjecthood. These values, and others such as justice, tolerance, and freedom, must be pursued by the president and the citizens alike. No one is above them. The president also becomes the point of reference, acting as a moral exemplar, sometimes as a pastor, sometimes as a priest, and sometimes as a prophet. Obviously, Asoka is no democrat, but it does not follow that the idea of civic religion is not deployable within the framework of kingship.

Three points must be kept in mind before I elaborate the political dimension of Dhamma. First, Buddha's teachings opened up the possibility of the radical sociopolitical restructuring of the world and the self by politico-moral action from above. Buddha's ethic included the pivotal importance of moral action. Once one stands outside the whole cosmos and is able to see its limitations, and once the transcendental point from which one examines the cosmos is viewed as emanating a moral vision, it becomes possible to imagine a profound restructuring of society and polity in accordance with that vision. Once again, D. D. Kosambi imaginatively engages this point when he says that more than a personal conversion of the emperor, there appears to have taken place in Asokan times a deeper conversion of the whole previous state apparatus. The king not only preaches a new morality but is able to launch radically new political and administrative measures that include public morality as an essential ingredient, and provide a framework within which radically differing ethics can coexist and nourish one another.[17] Indeed, Asoka never tires of saying that he is breaking away from the past, that he is inaugurating a new order, something unlike any of his predecessors. His is a radically new vision of kingship.[18]

Second, also emerging at this time in India is the idea of the *Cakravartin*, the wheel turner. The wheel that these great rulers turn is the wheel of Dhamma. Whereas the Buddha turned the wheel of the Dhamma in the religious sphere, the Cakravartin turns it in the political sphere. The Cakravartin represents the Buddhist political ideal of the just ruler, who brings peace and prosperity to his subjects.[19] The normative king, it seems, is intrinsic to the social and moral order of the world.[20]

Third, with the birth of the idea of a moral ruler or the "normative king," Asoka's Dhamma is seen in a new light.[21] Before Asoka, right and wrong actions were possibly determined by the king himself. The law must not have been applied in a consistent or legitimate manner but in a highly personal and arbitrary one. Thus, rajas are often depicted as rewarding or punishing according to how their personal interests were served.[22] By fashioning the idea of Dhamma, Asoka attempts to tame the institution of kingship itself and to contain the absolute exercise of power by the king. Indeed, the reconceptualization of Dhamma may also be viewed as an attempt to transform power into authority by infusing it with certain norms. It is also, as far as possible, to place strategic considerations secondary to the moral vision of Dhamma.[23] Dhamma was an immutable moral principle that was above even the Cakravartin. The Cakravartin conquers other kingdoms not by physical force but by moral appeal.[24] Wherever he travels he is welcomed and people voluntarily "submit" to his rule out of respect for his adherence to the principles of Dhamma.

It is obvious that Asokan Dhamma presupposes neither democracy nor citizenship. But does this make the idea any less political, or the term "civic religion" entirely inapplicable to the Asokan period? Like civic religion, Dhamma also presupposes a certain politico-moral relationship between the ruler and the ruled. Dhamma specifies what the king and his officials owe to the subjects and what subjects owe to the king and all his men. What subjects owe to the king and his officials is obedience to his commands. They must follow Dhamma. Yet, Pillar Edict 7 makes it clear that this compliance must arise from *Nijjhati* (persuasion), not *Niyama* (law). Everyone must follow Dhamma out of an inner disposition to comply with one's conscience, as it were. This is precisely where the roots of his notion of hegemony lie. Indeed, Asoka follows Dhamma as conscientiously as his subjects. Quite like a good democratic leader, Asoka is a moral exemplar to his people, acting sometimes as teacher, sometimes as healer, and always as father.

This does not exhaust the political dimension of Dhamma, however. For it must also include what the king owes his subjects. The politico-moral order stands above the king, at least partially. Just as the head of the family is as much part of the family as his wife and children are, the king is part of the political order as much as his subjects are. And just as all members of the family owe something, though not the same, to each other, the king owes something to his subjects, though it is qualitatively different from what the subjects owe him. Pillar Edict 6 clarifies what this is: *Sarvajana*, or *sarvaloka hita* (welfare of all living beings in this world and hereafter) or *Sukha* (happiness) in this world and *swarga* (heaven) in the other. Asoka declares that even those condemned to death must have the possibility of attaining *swarga*. Furthermore, another quality or virtue is expected of the king and all his officials: *viyohala* or *vyavahar samata* (procedural impartiality in the judicial domain) and *danda samata* (impartiality in the domain of retributive punishment).

Like Xunzi, Asoka insists that the ruler's role in day-to-day ruling is central.[25] Rock Edict 6 indicates that the primary duty of the ruler is to rule for his subjects. Once again, he is keen to establish a break from the administrative system of the past. Official matters in the past were not dispatched quickly and reports were neither composed nor received by the king at all times. Political administration was inefficient, everything was done leisurely, and the king did not devote enough time to this task. The king was not involved in day-to-day administration, for there was no real interest in ensuring the welfare of the subjects. But now, in his time, by his conduct, things are transformed because anybody could approach him at any time, is allowed to interrupt him while he is dining, in his own apartment or in the apartments of his women, in his carriage or in the cattle shed. Information is being fed to him all the time; reports are given about what is happening in the country, on the basis of which he can act and transact public business. When he gives a verbal instruction to his officers, concerning, say, a donation or a proclamation, and if there is any ambiguity, difference of opinion, or dispute over what it means, and if as a result there is any deliberation or discussion over it among the officers, then it is reported to Asoka immediately. He adds, "But simply hard work and efficiency in doing things, in dispatching business is not enough; you have to get results." The main result he hoped for was the happiness and welfare of his subjects in this world and in heaven. The other crucial quality is the attitude and motive by which the ruler acts. Any good deed of significance or consequence that he has performed and for which he is known has been done solely to discharge his debt to all beings.

The Role of Officials

Asoka believes that no king can rule on his own but needs a team of committed officials.[26] Rock Edict 5 tells us that state officials are crucial for Dhamma. These officials must work for all sections, among the servants and the nobles, among the poor and the aged, among the wealthy householders, and in women's residences.[27] They must work with all classes of people and all pasandas. They must even be committed to promoting the welfare of prisoners, and those who have children, are sick, or are aged must not be kept overly long in prison. They must ensure not only that Dhamma is practiced by everybody, but everywhere, regardless of age, gender, wealth, social status. There is no aspect of Dhamma that they can ignore. They must scrutinize every little detail.

The king must appoint different categories of officers to perform different functions. These officers, who increase the glory of Dhamma throughout the world, act on behalf not only of him but his queens, his sons, and other princes.[28] Yet the king must play a direct, active role in ensuring that officials follow Dhamma. In the First Separate Edict, he gives instructions directed at officers and city magistrates: "If I (morally) approve of something, I desire it. And anything I desire I seek to achieve by taking appropriate action." It follows that only a ruler who himself follows Dhamma has the ability to appoint the best person suited for this job.[29] In this respect too, Asoka's views are similar to Xunzi's.

Asoka tells his officers that "they can influence the many thousands of living beings under their charge, only if they gain their affection." But personal affection does not come in the way of performing dhammic functions. Impersonality is not a condition of impartiality. These officials are expected to be impartial, to conduct judicial proceedings, to reward and punish impartially (*viyohala samata* and *danda samata*). Besides, only if the ruler leaves the offer of rewards and punishments to the discretion of the officials will they exhibit responsibility, and confidently and fearlessly discharge their duties.

In sum, that everyone must follow Dhamma does not entail a spurious universalism in which each person is required, at all times, in all contexts, and regardless of their role, to follow the same moral precepts. That is an absurd demand. Undoubtedly, some moral precepts are to be followed by everyone, but there are parts of Dhamma meant for one section in relation to the other section. What one section does, the other doesn't have to do. For example, the precepts for the educator or the instructor cannot be the same for the instructed or the educated. But the point is that these precepts are relevant for everybody and must be known to everybody.

The Turning Point: Rock Edict 13

Buddha's teachings certainly played a role in Asoka's vision. But the turning point in his life came in the eighth year of his rule, after the war waged on Kalinga.[30] The scale of wanton destruction at Kalinga left Asoka distraught and changed his perspective on war. The edicts mention the displacement and deportation of 150,000 people, and the death of at least 100,000. They speak of "many more who perished unknown." The slaughter, death, and deportation has "caused immense grief to the beloved of the gods and weighs heavily on his mind." The war, he discovered, had tragic consequences not only for those who directly suffered violence, but practically every resident of Kalinga, for even those who were fortunate to have escaped its direct impact suffered from the misfortunes of their friends, acquaintances, colleagues, and relatives. No one then is unaffected by the horrors of war, and everyone participates in suffering. The survivors of war are the ones who are left to grieve. Thapar rightly notes that "the regret and remorse at the suffering in Kalinga is not the regret of a man moved by a passing emotion, but the meaningful contrition of a man who was consciously aware of the sorrow he had caused."[31]

The realization that those who suffered were followers of Dhamma made things worse. For ordinary people living in his territory, those who were not themselves warriors, but brahmanas, sramanas, followers of other pasandas, and householders, all follow Dhamma when they obey their mothers and fathers and their teachers and behave well and devotedly toward their friends, acquaintances, colleagues, relatives, slaves, and servants. The thought of what happened to such dhammic people during the Kalinga war weighed heavily on Asoka's mind and, at the time of inscribing the thirteenth edict, he writes, "If even a thousandth of that were to occur now, he would be filled with horror." It has been said that it was easy for Asoka to renounce war after he had already established a large empire. But imperial ambitions have no limit, and at whatever stage this was done, it must be seen as a significant self-limitation. Indeed, Asoka not only began to discourage war but publicly denounced the very idea of glorifying continuous conquest.

In other words, Asoka made a valiant attempt to move away from the warrior ethic, i.e., the ethics of physical courage and manly prowess, particularly on the battlefield. He firmly refused to play war games, dismissing the idea that fame and glory are goods in themselves. The only kind of fame and glory he desired is one that is achieved by obeying and following the Dhamma. Alternatively, he can be seen to be changing the very idea of what counts as glory; Dhammic glory is achieved by getting rid of all evil tendencies that give us no merit. Indeed, there is glory and dignity in siding with victims of plunder and conquest, with the poor and the downtrodden rather than with the heroic chieftains. It also lies in elevating the sustaining goods of ordinary life (life-goods) well above power, conquest, and glory. To secure life-goods for his subjects is central to the king's Dhamma.

Life-Goods for Ordinary People

The ruler's commitment to provide material welfare to his subjects in Asokan inscriptions is echoed elsewhere in Buddhist texts. "After the *cakkavatti* had brought the entire universe under his umbrella, he must proceed to ensure that his people live in comparative comfort, in a world where destitution has been wiped out."[32] Asoka takes it upon himself to care for the sick and the aged, to plant mango groves, dig wells, build rest houses along main routes, to grow banyan trees on the road in order to provide shade to both humans and animals.[33] Thus, he provides two kinds of medical services, one for humans and the other for animals. Medicinal herbs for humans and for animals are planted in places where they did not grow earlier.[34] The care of animals is very interesting here because with respect to basic material needs—water, food, shelter, medical treatment—the distinction between humans and animals is irrelevant. He commits himself not just to human universalism but to a universalism across species.

It is the moral duty of the king to provide material welfare. The king owes this to the people and the people know that the king has these obligations to them. He neither excludes life-goods from morality nor reduces Dhamma to the acquisition of this-worldly goods. So, he takes a middle path between hedonism and asceticism. The attainment of life-goods is a very important benefit and everybody should enjoy them. Not that this was entirely absent from the plans of earlier rulers. "But I have done these things in order that my people might conform to Dhamma," Asoka says.[35] I suppose it means that all these acts are part of a larger moral vision which he explicitly formulated. It is part of Asoka's Dhamma, his moral vision that people live and travel in comfort, be happy, and enjoy material benefits. War, conquest, and the pursuit of glory upset both the physical security of humans and their valid pursuit of life-goods. They violate Dhamma. Therefore, they must be avoided.

The masculine Kshatriya culture is also relentlessly un-self-critical and unforgiving. For Asoka, however, the ruler is required to develop two further virtues. First, the ability to self-correct. Since a leader learns from his followers and his mistakes, he must be ready to own up to them. This is already demonstrated in Edict 13. But this self-reflective, self-critical tone is present in other inscriptions too. For instance, in Edict 14 he says, "In some places there are inaccuracies, some passages have been omitted or the engraver has made some errors and in acknowledging them, he is acknowledging inadequacies in his edicts." Second, as far as possible, one who does wrong should be forgiven. One must reconcile with adversaries. He says this in the context of forest dwellers. He says that "he wants to reconcile with the forest dwellers, he doesn't want to have any kind of hostility with them but he also warns them that while he feels remorseful and is prepared to atone, he still has power and can use it against them."[36] The tribes must repent for the wrongs they have done and follow Dhamma or else he warns them they might not be spared. Asoka here admits that there are limits to political toleration and forgiveness.

Thus, by formulating Dhamma and elaborating how it is to be realized, Asoka attempts to reshape the entire Brahmana-Kshatriya culture. What Buddha appears to have done to the brahmanas and their ideology, Asoka appears to be doing to the Kshatriyas and their ideology. The introduction of the idea of civility too must be understood in this context. Asoka wants a change not only in the warrior ethic but what might be called the word-warrior ethic, in the reckless display of manliness in verbal fighting, in hostility conveyed through words, in attempts at braggadocio and using language to humiliate others. He strongly advises against *himsa* (violence) through *vaca* (speech). It seems he is not just against killing but against any assault on human dignity.

From now on he considered only one victory to be important: the victory of Dhamma, a moral conquest, a transformation from a warrior ethic of conquest to a political ethic of moral hegemony. In the past, there were war drums and a spectacle of arms and weaponry. Now he wishes a moral spectacle, wishing through these festivities to stoke the moral imagination of the people. Likewise, in the past, people conquered territories and built kingdoms in order to enhance their own pleasure. They worked for their own good, for their own benefit, but Asoka says that he has changed all that. He thinks that all his descendants should also be like him and receive all the pleasure and delight from following Dhamma rather than vanquishing other people's territories, which only brings suffering to everyone and torture to all moral beings. The purpose of kingship, of state-building, Asoka claims, is not to benefit the king himself but to benefit everybody, to bring happiness to everybody, illuminated by Dhamma.[37] This brings personal gain for the king. He earns spiritual revenue (merit).[38]

Further evidence of the disavowal of the warrior ethic comes from his views on hunting. In Rock Edict 8, he speaks once again of a break with the past when it was mandatory for kings to go on pleasure tours that consisted of hunting and other amusements.[39] The king, he says, goes on tours but these are dhammic tours. During these journeys he meets *brahmanas* and *sramanas* and bestows gifts on them. But it is important that everybody understands and follows Dhamma, so he gives instructions in Dhamma to others; if there are any questions on Dhamma then these questions are answered by him. These moral assemblies, discussions, deliberations, conversations, dialogues, and question-and-answer sessions on ethics, on what is good and bad, how to do the right thing, give him great pleasure. The pleasure derived from the ethically significant is qualitatively different from the pleasures of self-seeking. In short, Asoka wishes to have moral education as an important component of his politics. He wishes to embody this morality in his person, to educate others by his own example. When he leads by example, he gives *cakhudane* (spiritual insight)[40] with which to lead the good life.

The idea that political morality can be taught by instruction and example is what really distinguishes him from all his predecessors. Some kings in the past had probably glimpsed the idea of Dhamma, he says.[41] They may even have genuinely searched for ways by which to foster Dhamma, to make it a part of everyday life and popular consciousness. But they didn't succeed in getting people to respond. For Asoka, education ensures the development of an interest and relationship with Dhamma. Inculcation, teaching, and instruction help people to devote themselves to Dhamma. There is an element of formality here. Practical initiation seems to Asoka to be insufficient. Custom alone will not help. A whole discourse on Dhamma is required, which in turn needs specialists, a new class of intellectuals employed and trained by the ruler's administration. These intellectuals are responsible for teaching Dhamma, to make its content explicit, to explain it in moral assemblies. Besides, it is not enough to know Dhamma. One has to be moved by *kamataya* (the love) of it, and have the energy to realize it.[42] This intense love generates conviction and commitment. Dhamma requires that it be taught by educators who love and are committed to it and can communicate both to all subjects. Inculcating this enduring commitment is as important as careful examination, obedience, and a fear of committing wrong or sin.[43]

It is important for Asoka that Dhamma grows. Growth can be of two kinds, however. First, deepening of its meaning, as when its content is enriched in mutual encounters between different *pasandas*; but growth also refers to its spread among the people. Dhamma needs moral and intellectual refinement but also a vertical spread. Asoka seems to have a universal aspiration for Dhamma. He wishes that its moral appeal not be restricted only to elites but to move among ordinary folks. It must become part of common sense, popular imagination, and the entire social imaginary. Dhamma is a social project, a kind of mission to transform popular consciousness. This means that moral educators and intellectuals must take Dhamma everywhere within the kingdom to help raise popular ethical awareness. Engraving and inscribing Dhamma is one way to realize this mission, but the message also needs to travel to other countries, to distant places. Asoka believed that Dhamma was continuously growing in his own time by virtue of his own love of morality, instructions, and education and by the effort of all the officers—the moral educators and frontier officials.

It is this idea that rulers must be committed to impart Dhamma, through pedagogical techniques such as public meetings, discussion, and question-and-answer sessions, that pushes me to deploy a concept developed two millennia later by the Italian philosopher Antonio Gramsci: expansive hegemony.[44] Hegemonic rule is different from other, more common forms of rule.[45] One form, rule by violent conquest and brute force, is discussed in Kautilya's *Arthashastra*, which, although not a text about imperial rule, encourages rulers to be desirous of conquests (*vijigisu*), to have as their ultimate goal conquest in all four directions.[46] A second form, rulers who seize power by violent conquest of an alien territory and then rule by compelling the conquered to assimilate to their own worldview, is rule by domination. All kinds of methods are deployed to identify how these other countries are ideologically opposed to them and then to neutralize this opposition. This too is discussed extensively in the *Arthashastra*. As Olivelle puts it, "A king's success hinged to a great extent on his ability to 'outwit' his foreign rivals. The Arthaśāstra has a technical term for this, *atisaṃdhā-*. The 'outwitting' or 'overreaching' of rivals was the goal of all deliberations on foreign policy. Whether through diplomacy, intimidation, supplication, or open hostility, a king always sought some kind of advantage against ally and enemy alike."[47] In this form of rule, different strategies are used to cause other populations to acquiesce to the conqueror, even if it means that their cultural identity is subsumed in the cultural identity of the conqueror. Although, here, a king's rule depends on ideas, not on brute force alone; the ruling ideas must be the conqueror's own.

Finally, there exists a third form of rule that is without brute force or cultural domination. Here, the ruler provides ethical education to his subjects and takes active measures to arrive at a consensus. This is rule by hegemony. This is done by leaving untouched a country and its people's conception of the good, its substantive ethic and individuality; however, by emphasizing some elements already present in the country and its people's views and building upon them, by finding a common ground from within, the basic objectives of rulers are no longer in conflict; and indeed, at some level there is a unity or active consensus on values. This is strikingly similar to some points made by Xunzi. "His majesty being the most marvelous is the cause of no one in the world presuming to oppose him, his majesty permitting no opposition coupled with a way that wins the allegiance of others is the cause of his triumphing without having to wage war, of his gaining his objectives without resort to force, and of the world submitting to him without his armies exerting themselves."[48]

When a ruler is morally hegemonic in this sense, he manages to arrive at a new ethic that coalesces the multiple ethical perspectives of all the groups in his society. Expansive hegemony is entirely consistent with maintaining diversity and an endorsement of pluralism. This new ethic provides a social cement to rule within, as well as beyond, the boundary of his own territory. Therefore, this ethic spreads beyond the territorial boundary of the hegemon's rule, establishing the basis of a new kind of imperial order where brute force and domination is replaced by the intellectual and moral leadership of the hegemon, which shows the way, inspiring and improving upon the status quo. In this way the ruler of one country is able to provide intellectual leadership and moral direction to others so that those who are led feel their own lives enriched. This is achieved pedagogically, by moral education.

Asoka claims that his efforts at education in and about Dhamma and all other practices and ceremonies that surround these pedagogic efforts bear fruit. The hard work by him and his officials achieve at least two things. One, certain moral virtues such as mercy, truthfulness, purity, gentleness, charity, and liberality grows, as do the quality of social relations, both interpersonal and interpasandic. There is greater obedience to mother and father and to teachers. There is deference to people who are aged. There is greater regard for *brahmanas* and *sramanas*, for the wretched and the poor, the slaves and servants. This regard increases as never before, perhaps as in no other century. Besides, this is not just something that happens in his own time; he is convinced that it will continue in the future. This certainty results from his belief that his good work will be carried forward by his sons, grandsons, and great-grandsons. All of them have committed themselves to the practice and instruction of Dhamma.

If the hegemon is interested in gaining the affection and consent not only of his own people but also people of other countries, he must relinquish an instrumental attitude toward them. He must also be moved by a commitment to their "identity" and welfare. The idea is to provide transformational leadership in which leaders and "followers" have a reciprocal relationship that raises everyone to higher levels of motivation and morality, alongside or perhaps beyond life-goods. Although Asoka does not explicitly mention this, he seems to abandon the view presupposed by the old warrior ethic that interstate relations are anarchic, a view held possibly by Xunzi and quite certainly by Kautilya[49] for whom the origin or basis of kingship is not to be found in transcendent moral principles or social contract but solely in the staff (*danda*) or coercive political power.[50] Unlike Asoka, who is guided primarily by Dhamma, Kautilya's principal motivation is *artha* or worldly success. The importance of every moral principle, if recognized, is secondary. Patrick Olivelle sums up his political ideology succinctly:

> Ultimately, Kauṭilya's focus on *daṇḍa* does not reduce the king to a naked tyrant. Kauṭilya does not jettison tradition, whether it concerns royal or religious practice. It is simply that he measures all things in the end according to how well they support the material power of the king. Ordinarily, the king is quite happy to conform to the traditions of kingship and Brāhmaṇism. At heart, however, Kauṭilya's true faith lies in power, and he does not hesitate to subvert these traditions if it will further the king's interests. It is perhaps best not to interpret this as cynicism, but to take Kauṭilya at his word: the fruitfulness of all human activities—many of which are quite worthwhile—relies ultimately on effective governance.[50]

CONCLUSION

It could be said, with due caution, that Asoka tried to establish a paternalistic perfectionist state. What makes it perfectionist is its embrace of an objective theory of the good life (or of human well-being) and the belief that it is the business of the state to (sometimes) promote it. This point needs emphasizing: Dhamma is not what Asoka wills it to be or merely desires. In this sense, it is not subjective. Rather, Asoka is as bound to and by it as are his subjects and follows whatever action Dhamma implores him to do. Though objective, this good is not to be equated with any particular thick, substantive conception of the good of a specific pasanda, however. Instead, the good it promotes is common to all pasandas, and thin. To follow Dhamma is to avoid vices such as cruelty, envy, arrogance, fierceness, and wrath and to cultivate virtues such as compassion, truthfulness, purity of mind, and self-restraint. None of these dictate any particular thick idea of the good life. Asoka's Dhamma takes a stand against the violent, warrior ethic and promotes any ethic that abjures a violent culture of glory and vainglory. What makes it paternalistic is that the ruler views himself as the father, his subjects as his own children, and puts his entire apparatus of rule toward the realization of what is objectively considered to be good for them.[51] He sees it as his personal and direct responsibility to do so. If and when the subjects go against Dhamma, it becomes his duty to intervene in their lives, not coercively but largely through education and persuasion.

To break away from this warrior ethic, Asoka underscores the moral significance of nonviolence and noninjury to others. He strongly discourages ill-treatment of the aged, servants, and even slaves. Asoka had seen this warrior ethic creep into intellectual life. While elites viewed themselves as rival warriors, at the more popular level, people acted as word-warriors, living in a culture of verbal abuse and mutual humiliation. Through hate speech people did violence to each other, saying the wrong things on the wrong occasions. Asoka addresses this problem of verbal violence, particularly among pasandas, and through a variety of self-restraints, seeks a change in this culture by bringing in the idea of general moral concern and dignity.

In short, Asoka wants to launch a new, sustainable moral order. He tries to offer a new paradigm for kingship, specifying how power is to be ethically wielded. He tries to specify what it is to be a proper king, and to be an exemplar of good rule.

This ethical perspective, more relevantly for this volume, is meant potentially for the entire world, to guide interstate relations. He wants a new global order led by Dhamma and its main propagator, whoever that happens to be. As he says, "The Beloved of the Gods considers the victory by Dhamma to be of foremost significance." In Rock Edict 13, he claims:

> In this moral endeavor, he has gained victory on all frontiers to a distance of six hundred yojanas [about 1,500 miles], where reigns the Greek king named Antiochus, and beyond the realm of that Antiochus in the lands of the four kings named Ptolemy, Antigonus, Magas, and Alexander, and in the south over the Colas and Pandyas as far as Sri Lanka. Likewise here in the imperial territories among the Greeks and the Kambojas, Nabhakas and Nabhapanktis, Bhojas and Pitmikas, Andhras and Parindas, everywhere the people follow the Beloved of the Gods' instructions in Dhamma. Even where the envoys of the Beloved of the Gods have not gone, people hear of his conduct according to Dhamma, his precepts and his instruction in Dhamma, and they follow Dhamma and will continue to follow it.[52]

This insight—that we could find an alternative to the violent chaotic world order in a moral vision that is common to all countries and can bind them together into a harmonious world order—is what makes Asoka a fascinating figure even in our own times. In *Glimpses of World History*, Jawaharlal Nehru, India's first prime minister, writes:

> Men of religion have seldom, very seldom, been as tolerant as Asoka. In order to convert people to their own faith they have seldom scrupled to use force and terrorism and fraud. The whole of history is full of religious persecution and religious wars, and in the name of religion and of Gods perhaps more blood has been shed than in any other name. it is good therefore to remember how a great son of India, intensely religious, and the head of a powerful empire, behaved in order to convert people to his ways of thought. It is strange that any one should be so foolish as to think that religion and faith can be thrust down a person's throat at the point of the sword or a bayonet.[53]

In the mythology of India's secular nationalism, Asoka is the tolerant and wise king par excellence, one who rules by moral persuasion rather than by force or domination. He acknowledges substantive religio-philosophical differences, but proposes that through self-restraint and mutual discursive encounters, each society can live with these differences, learn from and enrich each other. By working out an ideological vision that incorporates and accommodates substantive differences within each society and between societies, Asoka develops a model of intellectual leadership and moral hegemony that has relevance for the entire world.

The world today, reeling in the aftermath of the disguised imperialisms of two major ideological blocs, and threatened with new forms of colonization and imperial conquests, would do well to heed these wise voices from China and India. It would be a happier place and morally more worthy if countries abandoned the path of physical conquest and domination and pursued the course of multiple, even if contesting, moral hegemonies.

NOTES

1. I do not wish to read ancient texts as a mirror in which I see my own socially embedded self. On the contrary, I wish to acknowledge their radical otherness, their remoteness from us. I begin with the presumption that they would appear to us strange and puzzling. I hope to be surprised by their resemblance to us. In short, I wish to first discover what these ideas meant in their own time and place before raising the question of their relevance to us. I hope these texts would challenge some of our deeply cherished assumptions, both those taken for granted in contemporary India and presupposed by mainstream Western epistemic frameworks. Nietzsche is my guide here, as is Bernard Williams, who quotes him in *Shame and Necessity*: "I cannot understand what would be the meaning of classical philology in our own age if it is not to be untimely, that is to act against the age and by doing so to have an effect on the age and let us hope to the benefit of a future age." To give ideas of the ancient text the power to change our own thoughts, it is crucial that we be familiar with the social history of these ideas, to know the sociology of that period.

2. Pierre Briant, *From Cyrus to Alexander: A History of the Persian Empire*, trans. Peter T. Daniels (Winona Lake, IN: Eisenbrauns, 2002), 168.

3. Patrick Olivelle, "Asokan Inscriptions as Text and Ideology," in *Reimagining Asoka: Memory and History*, ed. Patrick Olivelle et al., 170–83 (Oxford: Oxford University Press, 2013).

4. Asoka speaks also of taking care of the aged and the sick, but among the group that might be called incapacitated, he does not mention "the physically challenged." Xunzi, possibly, enjoins the king to include them in his social welfare policies. This is suggested in passing by Henry Rosemont Jr. in "State and Society in the Xunzi: A Philosophical Commentary," in *Virtue, Nature and Human Agency in the Xunzi*, ed. T. C. Kline III and Philip J. Ivanhoe (Cambridge, MA: Hackett, 2000), 8.

5. Olivelle, "Asokan Inscriptions as Text and Ideology," 172.

6. The similarities with Confucius are striking for he too argued against relying exclusively or strongly on law to effect social harmony or ethical development. See Joel Kupperman, "Tradition and Community: Formation of the Self," in *Confucian Ethics*, ed. Kwong-Lui Shun and David B. Wong (Cambridge: Cambridge University Press, 2004).

7. For a fuller account of these differences, see my "Beyond Toleration: Civility and Principled Co-existence in Asokan Edicts," in *The Boundaries of Toleration*, ed. Alfred Stepan and Charles Taylor (New York: Columbia University Press, 2014). There is little supra-mundane about their ambition. This is underlined by the fact that life in heaven was a further continuation of a pleasant life on earth. In the Rig Veda, man is born and dies only once. There is no rebirth. Indeed, *amratva* (immortality) in some passages of the Rig Veda appears to be nothing but the continuation of a long life on earth.

8. Major Rock Edict 9.

9. In this respect, there appears to be some difference between him and Xunzi. See Yan Xuetong, chapter 3, this volume, pp. 12–13.

10. See Rock Edict 9, in N. A. Nikam and Richard McKeon, *The Edicts of Asoka* (Chicago: University of Chicago Press, 1962), 44.

11. Rock Edict 9, ibid., 44.

12. See Heinrich Zimmer, *Philosophies of India*, ed. Joseph Campbell (Delhi: Motilal Banarsidas, 2000 [1951]), 469–70: "Asoka, rather than trying to uphold one view or the other—and thereby identifying himself with one school or the other—sought to emphasise what he held to be the 'essence' common to all sects and schools. Doing otherwise would have been to encourage a more vociferous conflict of ideas and practices among these sects and schools, thereby compromising the concord and cohesion he was trying to build up within his kingdom."

13. The term is used by Romila Thapar in "Is Secularism Alien to Indian Civilization?" in *The Future of Secularism*, ed. T. N. Srinivasan, 83–108 (Delhi: Oxford University Press, 2007).

14. Rock Edict 12, in Nikam and McKeon, *The Edicts of Asoka*.

15. "There should not be condemnation of others without any grounds. Such slighting (*lahuka*, from *laghu*) should be for specified grounds only." See Radhakumud Mookerji, *Asoka* (London: McMillan, 1928), 159.

16. Both K. R. Norman and Patrick Olivelle have used the term harmony for Asoka's normative ideal for society.

17. Finally, the rules governing ordinary people and the ruler himself stemmed from the same moral source. This was quite unlike the statecraft recommended by Chanakya, where an entirely amoral ruler committing all kinds of crimes against subjects and neighbors reigned over a morally regulated population.

18. See, for instance, Rock Edicts 4, 6, 8.

19. See Damien Keown and Charles S. Prebish, eds., *Encyclopedia of Buddhism* (New York: Routledge, 2010), 274.

20. Ibid., 167.

21. This normative king—one who rules by a moral vision—is, as Xunzi puts it, a true king. The similarities between the two are striking. See Yan Xuetong, chapter 3, this volume, p. 10. On Xunzi's occasional references to the "sage-king," see Siufu Tang, *Self-Realization through Confucian Learning: A Contemporary Reconstruction of Xunzi's Ethics* (New York: SUNY Press, 2016).

22. *Samyutta Nikaya*, III, 301–3.

23. Here there may be a marginal difference in the views of Xunzi and Asoka. See Yan Xuetong, chapter 3, this volume, p. 11.

24. The reference to conquerors by physical force is to those who perform the Brahmanical *asvamedha* rite. In contrast to the *asvemedhi*, rival kings welcome and submit to the Cakravartin and ask him to teach them (*anusasa maharajati*). See Keown and Prebish, *Encyclopedia of Buddhism*, 273.

25. See Yan Xuetong, chapter 3, this volume.

26. The Delhi-Topra 7th Pillar Edict, as described in Jules Bloch, "Les inscriptions d'Asoka," in *Collection Émile Senart* (Paris: Société d'édition, 1950), 134: "The rajukas are appointed for hundreds of thousands of people who are supposed to instruct the people to follow the dhamma."

27. Ibid.

28. In these passages Asoka seems to imply that only people with certain virtues and education can be appointed as state officials. This seems to be similar to Xunzi's views, expressed by Yan Xuetong in chapter 3 of this volume and endorsed by Henry Rosemont Jr., that moral qualities and character are an important part of the criteria for the selection of officials. Xunzi further appears to suggest that "although a man be the descendant of a king, duke, prefect or officer, if he does not observe the rules of proper conduct and justice, he must be relegated to the common ranks; likewise, even when he is the descendant of a commoner, if he has acquired learning, developed a good character, and is able

to observe the rules of proper conduct and justice, then he should be elevated to be minister, prime minister, officer or prefect." Quoted in Rosemont Jr., "State and Society in the Xunzi," 7.

29 The Delhi-Topra Fourth Pillar Edict, in Bloch, "Les inscriptions d'Asoka," 124–25.

30. Asoka's views on the adverse impact of war seem similar to Xunzi but with a crucial difference. Xunzi appears to think of the political consequences of war that will eventually threaten the king's rule. Asoka is concerned more about the social and moral consequences of war. See Yan Xuetong, chapter 3, this volume, p. 10.

31. Romila Thapar, *Asoka and the Decline of Mauryas* (Delhi: Oxford University Press, 1961), 36.

32. "The ideal king Maha Sudassana, for instance, establishes a perpetual grant (*evarupangdan-angpatthapeyyang*) to provide food for the hungry, drink for the thirsty, gold for the poor, money for those in want, as well as wives for those who required them. Digha Nikaya, 2:137; Dialogues of the Buddha, 2:211. This dhammikodhammaraja "patronizes samanas and brahmanas who are worthy, providing them with all the things necessary to pursue their goals." Digha Nikaya, 2:141; Dialogues of the Buddha, 2:217."

33. Pillar Edict 7. Rock Edict 2

34. Rock Edict 2.

35. Pillar Edict 7.

36. Rock Edict 13.

37. Pillar Edict 7.

38. The contrast with the tradition of thinking articulated later by Kautilya could not have been sharper. For Kautilya, the king's rule is explained in the last instance by the ambitions of the king and animated by the king's unique capacity to coerce and compel others.

39. Rock Edict 8.

40. The Delhi-Topra Second Pillar Edict, 120–21.

41. The Delhi-Topra Seventh Pillar Edict, 134.

42. The Delhi-Topra First Pillar Edict, 119–20.

43. The Delhi-Topra Third Pillar Edict, 121–22. The sins mentioned here include fierceness, cruelty, anger, pride, and envy. Sinful actions are motivated by these negative passions.

44. For a discussion of the idea of expansive hegemony, see Chantal Mouffe, "Hegemony and Ideology in Gramsci," in *Gramsci and Marxist Theory*, ed. C. Mouffe, 168–203 (London: Routledge, 1979).

45. Yan Xuetong shows that Xunzi too divides leading powers into three types: *wang* (the true king or the humane authority), *ba* (the lord-protector/hegemony), and *qiang* (the powerful/tyranny).

46. He says, "The True King tries to win men; the lord-protector to acquire allies; the powerful to capture land." This threefold classification is similar to mine, except that I use the term hegemony in a different Gramscian sense.

47. Mark McClish and Patrick Olivelle, "Introduction to *The Arthaśāstra*," in *Arthaśāstra: Selections from the Classic Indian Work on Statecraft, ed.* Mark McClish and Patrick Olivelle (Cambridge, MA: Hackett, 2012), lxxi..

48. Quoted in Yan Xuetong, chapter 3, this volume, p. 15, from Knoblock, "Book 9, On the Regulation of a King," *Xun Zi II*, 227. At least in this passage, it seems that Xunzi wishes the ruler to rule without using force but by winning their allegiance. Yet it is unclear whether this allegiance is to be gained by propaganda or consent through proper education. It seems certain, however, that for Xunzi, moral qualities were essential for effective political leadership.

49. Yan Xuetong, chapter 3, this volume, p. 9.

50. McClish and Olivelle, "Introduction to *The Arthaśāstra*."

51. He presents himself as a father figure and says that "just as I would desire welfare and happiness in this world and the next for my children, just so, I desire the same for all men."

52. Rock Edict 13, trans. Romila Thapar, in Thapar, *Asoka and the Decline of the Mauryas*, 256.

53. J. L. Nehru, *Glimpses of World History* (Oxford: Oxford University Press, 1989), 62–63.

THEME III

Amoral Realism

A Comparative Study on the International Political Thoughts of Han Feizi and Kautilya (Chanakya)

Xu Jin

INTRODUCTION

China and India are the two ancient civilizations in the East, with long histories and splendid cultures. However, in recent times Western civilization has been dominant internationally, resulting in Eurocentrism. Eastern civilizations are being marginalized and excluded. The dominant theories of international relations—realism, liberalism, constructivism—are all based on the philosophy and history of the West. Today, however, Eastern states continue to rise, China in particular. It has become increasingly important to pay attention to and investigate the international political thoughts from the East.

In recent years, Chinese scholars have been drawing ideational resources from their own country's ancient political thought, with an aim to construct a theory of international relations from China's experience, and with some success.[1] Among the "Hundred Schools of the Sages" in China pre-Qin periods, the Legalist school has a leading figure named Han Feizi. Political realism is deeply rooted in his thoughts. His belief in the supreme role of power in diplomacy is still valuable for reference.

The ancient Indian political thoughts of Chanakya resurfaced at the beginning of the twentieth century, but then faded into the background. Recent years have witnessed a rediscovery of ideological value from the *Arthashastra*, and scholars have initiated in-depth studies on Chanakya. Both Han Feizi and Chanakya are considered political realists. Similarities and differences coexist in their international political thoughts.

While seemingly following different paths—China insisting on the path of peaceful rise and India seeking great power status—there have been occasional frictions between China and India over territorial disputes. The history, current status, and future development of Sino-Indian relations have also been the subject of ongoing research in the International Relations community. One approach to gaining a deeper understanding of Sino-Indian relations is to conduct a comparative study of the traditional ideologies and cultures of the two countries. China's Han Feizi and India's Chanakya are undoubtedly representatives of realism in ancient international political thought. The study of the two ideologies is conducive to promoting academic and cultural exchanges between China and India.

Hence, this paper attempts to compare the international political thoughts of China's Han Feizi and India's Chanakya. Their similarities and differences are explored, with an aim to consider the implications of such comparative research results on modern international relations.

1. LITERATURE REVIEW

Most of the current academic research on Han Feizi's thoughts focuses on the rule of law, management, and human nature. There are only a few studies on Han Feizi's international political or diplomatic thoughts: Cai Xinde, "A Study on Han Feizi's Diplomatic Thoughts"; Sun Xuefeng and Yang Zixiao, "Han Feizi's Thoughts on International Politics"; Ye Zicheng and Pang Xun, "The Schools of Chinese Diplomatic Thoughts during the Spring and Autumn and Warring States Periods and their Comparison with the West"; *Ye Zicheng, Chinese Diplomatic Thoughts during the Spring and Autumn and Warring States Periods* (the book includes a chapter titled "Han Feizi's Power—Interests Matter the Most"). The prevailing view of these research results is that Han Feizi focuses on the realist world. He believes that human nature is seeking interests, as is the state. He emphasizes that the state can increase its capability through the rule of law, and that it should be tactful in its diplomacy.

There are more studies on Chanakya's *Arthashastra* outside China than in China. Among the latter are Wang Yan, "An Interpretation of the International Political Thoughts in the *Arthashastra*" and "The *Arthashastra* and the Roots of India's International Strategies"; Zhang Jincui, "The *Arthashastra* and the Classical Roots of Indian Foreign Strategies"; Jin Jie, "The Thoughts and Strategies in the *Arthashastra*"; and Liao Xuesheng, "What a Country the *Arthashastra* Describes." Most of these studies are based on the text of the *Arthashastra*. They provide interpretations of the international political and diplomatic thoughts in the *Arthashastra*, and analyze Indian foreign policies from their interpretations. Chanakya also highlights the realist world. He considers national interests as the core interests, and believes that states can do whatever it takes to pursue their interests. His diplomatic thoughts include the circle of nations doctrine and the principle of sixfold diplomacy.

In comparative studies, there are scholarly articles comparing Chanakya with Machiavelli, such as Jin Haipeng's "A Comparative Study on the Political Thoughts of Chanakya and Machiavelli." There are also scholarly studies comparing Han Feizi with Machiavelli. But rarely are there studies comparing Han Feizi and Chanakya, and thus a study comparing Han Feizi's international political thought with Chanakya's presents a fresh perspective.

2. COMPARISON OF THE INTERNATIONAL POLITICAL THOUGHTS OF HAN FEIZI AND CHANAKYA

The international political thoughts of Han Feizi and Chanakya are scattered, respectively, in the *Complete Works of Han Feizi* and the *Arthashastra*. This essay initiates a comparative analysis of their international political thoughts in terms of background, political purpose, philosophical foundations, moral ideas, views of state relations, foreign policy, and war perspectives and strategies.

2.1 Background

The ideas of thinkers can be analyzed logically and with historical insights only by seeking to understand the thinkers' backgrounds, which is the soil out of which their ideas grow. This approach requires a clear understanding of the sociopolitical realities of their times.

Both Han Feizi and Chanakya were living in periods of great historic transition from slavery to feudal monarchy. At that time, numerous wars broke out. A state's primary goal was to ensure its survival, and afterwards to compete for hegemony. In order to promote unity, a state needed to centralize power and enhance monarchical rule. Han Feizi says, "A wise ruler will make the people under the rule his eyes and ears,"[2] and by doing so will be able to gather information. Han Feizi highlighted the power of a ruler to rule and to make decisions. He was living in the Spring and Autumn and Warring States periods, and Chanakya was living in the Buddha's period in ancient India. Similar zeitgeists prompted both Han Feizi and Chanakya to construct their own systems of thought based on the political realities of the time. It was the brutal competition and the era of war that made them both focus on realistic material interests and national strength.

Han Feizi, as mentioned above, was living in the Spring and Autumn and Warring States periods, from 280 BC to 233 BC. At that time, vassals contended for supremacy; wars of annexation broke out frequently; and states sought to change their laws to become stronger. It was a time of competition for power. In the *Complete Works of Han Feizi*, it says, "In the ancient times states competed in morality; in the middle times states competed in wisdom and strategy; and nowadays states compete in strength."[3] This means that, in ancient times, to win or lose, people competed by morality; in the middle times, people competed by strategic wisdom; and in today's society, people compete by power. "A fundamental goal of states in that time is survival. After state survival is guaranteed, it is possible for a state to be the hegemon."[4] The base goal for a state is survival, and the highest goal for a state is hegemony. The slave-owning aristocrats from that society began to lose power, and the new landowning class became increasingly active.

Chanakya was living in ancient India in the fourth century BC, a century before Han Feizi. The goals of ancient India were warding off invasion by Alexander from Macedonia, the unification of India, and the establishment of a new dynasty. The ancient Indian society had a strict hierarchical caste system and a strong religious atmosphere. To some degree, the ancient India in which Chanakya lived was experiencing a much more difficult era than ancient China at that time. Therefore, the strength of a state appeared vital. The differences in their backgrounds due to the times they lived in contributed to the differences in their thinking.

2.2 Political Purpose

The political thinking of Han Feizi and Chanakya is closely related to reality. They did not write and theorize for the purposes of a book—they intended to help their own states and rulers to achieve certain political ends.

Against the common backdrop of frequent wars and competition for power, Chanakya and Han Feizi shared a common political purpose. Namely, they both wanted to ensure that national interests were protected and the state was empowered. For one thing, they aimed to ensure the survival of the state; for another, they wanted the state to prosper in order to be the hegemon. Han Feizi was a native of Han at that time. The country was in political turmoil domestically and foreign enemies surrounded the country. He wrote several times to the king of Han, asking him to adopt his political policies. Most scholars speculate that the *Arthashastra* was Chanakya's and others' synthesis and reflection of the empire's experience in waging foreign wars after it was unified. They also summarized the strategies for imperial governance.[5]

Han Feizi and Chanakya had different political purposes because of the different times that they were living. Han Feizi's political ideas were to rule by law, reform the country, win the war of annexation, and become a hegemon. The social life to which Han Feizi aspired was not the unworldly paradise depicted by Laozi and Taoism. The political reality of the time did not allow the fulfillment of this dream. The stabilization and unification of society could only be achieved by war.

Chanakya's political aim was to assist Chandragupta Maurya in fighting against Alexander's invasion and overthrowing the Nanda empire. Thus, a new dynasty could be established, which would become the empire of mainland India and conquer additional territories. In the *Arthashastra* he mentioned repeatedly the conquest of the "earth" or the conquest of the "quadrilateral earth." The earth appears to refer to the Indian subcontinent, south of the Himalayas.[6] Chanakya was equally concerned with the well-being of the people. He thought that security and abundance of material wealth were the foundations for a powerful state.

2.3 Philosophical Foundations

Complete philosophical foundations underpin all sets of political thoughts. Ideas grow from their philosophical foundations. Han Feizi and Chanakya's thinking was no exception. Consistent threads run through their thoughts. And those threads are the key to grasping their ideas comprehensively.

Both Han Feizi and Chanakya are characterized by political realism. Seeking power and profit are at the core of their thoughts. This is a conclusion deduced on the basis of humanistic theory. Both take a pessimistic view of human nature as evil, selfish, unreliable, and untrustworthy. Han Feizi described the relationship between parents and children: "Parents congratulate each other if a son is born. If it is a girl, they will murder her." "Both parents and children are calculative in their relationship."[7] "Husband and wife are not connected by blood. If they love each other, they stay close. Otherwise, they leave each other."[8] "The relationship between the monarch and the vassals is a direct exchange of interests. Their relationship is not father-and-son bloodline but trading relations. Vassals do their best to work for the monarch; and the monarch rewards them with big titles and handsome money." All the people in the court hope the monarch dies in order to gain more interests.[9] "The consorts, ladies, and princes form their interest group behind the emperor's back. They hope he dies early. Otherwise, they grab little power." They do not necessarily hate the emperor. Yet the death of the emperor is beneficial to their interests. Everyone from all walks of life think about their own interests.

> Doctors suck the blood of the patients from their wounds. The poisoned blood is in their mouth. They do it not out of familial love, but for their own interests. A carmaker wishes everyone to be rich so he can sell his car. A craftsman makes enough coffins and he will wish other people to die young. Their motivations are not caused by the carmaker's kind heart and craftsman's cold blood but interests. If people are not rich, cars will not sell well. If people do not die, coffins will not sell well either. The intention is not to hate others, but the benefit lies in the death of others.

In short, Han Feizi believes that when it comes to one's own safety and interests, the first reaction of the human subconscious is to pursue one's own interests and avoid harm, to do what is beneficial for oneself and find solutions to save oneself. This is just human nature.[10]

Chanakya sees man as unreliable and untrustworthy, "a mixture of cowardice, folly, and villainy. Their nature makes them a victim of deceitful predators and tyrants."[11] However, the two also admitted the good part of humanity. Han Feizi recognized Confucius's benevolence, and Chanakya appreciated the altruism of human beings.

The philosophical underpinnings of the two ideas are also quite different. Han Feizi mainly started his logical argument from a theory about human nature, believing that humans tended to seek profit. "What people mostly want is the satisfaction in daily life. They are quite materialistic. They want to avoid danger and escape poverty."[12] Therefore, the state represented by the monarch is also profit-seeking. Hence, the state should seek to build up its capability to protect the national interest. What is the national interest that the monarch protects? "It is hegemony. The biggest interest that a monarch can pursue is to compete for hegemony and become a hegemon."[13]

Chanakya's thought, on the other hand, is more complex. His thinking combines religious and nonreligious components. Chanakya used number theory, yoga, and breathing as philosophical foundations. He combined religious philosophy with *realpolitik*. Chanakya created his own set of moral ethics, inspired by religious and nonreligious philosophies. Among them, Samkhya and Yoga were religious philosophies and Lokayata was not. Chanakya instructed rulers to follow these ethical principles in order to rule righteously (or rule by the law of Buddhism). Thus, the law of Buddhism (moral ethics) in his thinking is more about "justice" than religion. Chanakya did not attempt to separate Buddhism (moral ethics) from his political thoughts and decisions. He paid more attention to the strengths of *artha* (material well-being) than *dharma* (moral ethics).[14]

2.4 Moral Ideas

Another reason why both Han Feizi and Chanakya are considered political realists lies in their similar attitude toward morality. Morgenthau, the renowned classical realist, argued in one of the six principles of political realism that morality should not be above the national interests. Rulers must make decisions for the national interests by rational prudence. This coincides with the views of Han Feizi and Chanakya, both of whom defined morals in light of political reality. They did not blindly promote or abide by morality. At the right time, it was considered acceptable to defraud the enemy, use violence, secretly punish, and so on. Han Feizi attached more importance to the public interest, that is, the national interest. He believed that "the interests of the public" were more important than "the private interests." A wise monarch must make a distinction between public and private interests:

> The principle of being a wise ruler is that one must understand the difference between the public and private interests. He should uphold the rule of law and avoid personal favors. When this wise sovereign rules, his bureaucrats leave personal interests aside and protect public interests. When a crooked sovereign rules, his bureaucrats harm the public interests to protect their own interests.[15]

The moral views of Han Feizi and Chanakya are also different. Han Feizi had his greatest attachment to strength and held contempt for the role of morality. He believed that morality was not useful for politics and profit was the most important. He was ruthless and did not care about the weaknesses and needs of other countries. Han Feizi's moral-free stance was based on his observation of a chaotic historical and realistic world. His conclusion from such observation was that politics should be independent from morality. He thought politics and morality were totally different things. In the game of competition between states, states win or die and there is no middle ground for morality. States have to use all means available to ensure their survival and strength. Han Feizi affirmed that ethical, aesthetic, and philosophical values issued from the moral concept of benevolence and righteousness, but he denied their political value. He supported a unified theory of law and virtue, but considered law above virtue and that virtue should supplement law. Han Feizi emphasized the importance of justice for the ruler and bureaucrats to rule the country:

> Bureaucrats are clean, honest and impartial; they maintain justice. They protect public interest. Bureaucrats are corrupted and indulgent of his own desires; they secure interests for himself and his family. They protect their private interests. When a wise sovereign rules, bureaucrats leave personal interests aside and protect public interests. When a crooked sovereign rules, bureaucrats harm the public interests and protect personal interests.[16]

Han Feizi also opposed the hypocrisy of benevolence that had no political utility. "One should not be praised for preaching benevolence and righteousness. Otherwise it would be detrimental to social utility; and academicians should not be appointed in governmental positions. Otherwise, it will undermine the rule of law."[17] "Therefore, a wise monarch should do what is practical and beneficial, and ignore what has no practical significance. He does not need to preach about benevolence and morality and buy into what the so-called scholars say."[18] Han Feizi also defined what benevolence and righteousness was in his mind:

> A true benevolent and righteous person worries about the chaotic situation in the world and suffering of the country. He is not concerned about his own low position and humiliation. Yi Yin thought ancient China was in chaos. He tried to be the cook of the then emperor Cheng Tang and get close to him. Thus, he would have the chance to be his advisor. Bai Lixi thought the Qin dynasty was in chaos. He tried to be a captive soldier under the Duke Mu of Qin and get close to him. Thus, he would have the chance to be his advisor. They both worried about the chaotic situation of the world and suffering of the country. At the same time, they were not concerned their own sufferings and humiliation. What they did was true benevolence and righteousness.[19]

Han Feizi believed that the key to ruling the country was to treat the people in a benevolent manner. "Being a benevolent ruler, is the key to face and tend the people."[20]

In Chanakya's opinion, force was not the first option for solving problems. Extremely immoral measures could be taken after other measures such as negotiation, mediation, economic inducement, etc., had all failed. He was concerned about the relative capability of other countries. He was concerned about not only the pursuit of material enjoyment and worldly happiness but also the spiritual fulfilment and ultimate meaning of human life. The two pursuits were not in conflict. In chapter 6 of this volume, Deepshikha Shahi mentions that the comprehensive philosophical basis of Chanakya's *Arthashastra* goes beyond the boundaries of realpolitik (or political realism).[21] Chanakya's morality should not be understood as politics in opposition to ethics, which is a kind of Western dichotomous thinking. Rather, Chanakya's *Arthashastra* should be placed somewhere between realpolitik and moral politics.[22] He was employing immoral political means to achieve a moral goal—the welfare of the people. At the same time, Chanakya laid down a number of moral conduct codes for monarchs and advocated a wise and moral ruler for the country. In his opinion, it is most important for a monarch to learn self-control, which includes being free from lust, anger, greed, conceit, arrogance, and recklessness. He also asks the ruler to abide by other principles: "Keeping away from others' wives, not coveting other people's property, no killing, no daydreaming, be consistent, no lying, no extravagance, not contacting with harmful people, not indulging in harmful activities."[23]

2.5 Views of State Relations

In terms of interstate relations, both Han Feizi and Chanakya believed that such relations were competitive and involved game-playing. The international environment is described thusly: the strong do what they can and the weak suffer what they must. A state has to build up its own capability and be attentive to other states' purpose and action. However, the two differ in the details. Han Feizi thought the competition between states was fierce. It was a zero-sum game: you win or you die; there is no middle ground. Therefore, he did not hold high expectations for interstate relations. He did not believe that alliances between states were reliable. At critical moments, big states often refuse to assist small states due to their own interests. A state's priority is increasing its own capability. As long as it is powerful, it does not need to be concerned about other states.

The international environment, according to Chanakya, was following the "law of the fish." It is a world where the big fish eat the small fish. So that the king should be the conqueror of the world in order to ensure the state's survival. Only empires of great size and power, with no domestic instability, can contain the big fish and foreign invaders. He highlighted the importance of geopolitics. He forwarded the idea of "Mandala"—state circle theory to describe state relations. It refers to a series of circles where states are located. The closest neighbor to the state is the enemy; another state on the circle closest to the enemy is a friend, and vice versa. Chanakya found enemies and friends by geography. He was not hostile to other states blindly. His foreign policies were formulated according to realistic interstate relations.

2.6 Foreign Policy

In the opinions of both Han Feizi and Chanakya, the primary goals of foreign policy were to increase state capability, realize national interests, and conquer other countries. Both believed that the monarch should be the key figure in making foreign policy decisions. Both stressed the importance of conspiracies, strategies, and tactics. They advocated for the necessary deception of the enemy and appropriate war as one approach.

Variation exists in their foreign policy ideas, however. The core of Han Feizi's foreign policy thought is to rule by law in order to build a strong nation. He believed that ruling by law was fundamental to increasing the state's capability. The monarch should use rewards and punishment to govern the state. Ruling by law could increase the state's economic and military capability. "States would not be forever rich or strong, nor would they forever be poor and weak. Those who enforced the law are decisive and the nation would be rich and strong; those who enforced the law are irresolute and the nation would be poor and weak."[24] "A state that was strict with the rule of law would be strong, and a state that lacked the rule of law would be weak."[25] How strict the law was implemented directly determined the rise and fall of nations: "If a state is strict with its rule of law, it should be peaceful and powerful. If a state implements unjust law, it should be in chaos and poverty."[26] At the same time, Han Feizi believed that a state could solve its all international political problems by increasing its strength. Hence it did not have to be concerned about the strength of other states. "The mentality of interdependence will lead to blaming and complaining; however, the mentality of self-reliance will lead to success in a course."[27] Therefore, it is most important for a country to rely on its own strength and achieve independence. It should not want to depend on another state. "To be invaded or not, it all depends on oneself. It is not a question for others. Self-reliance leads to no invasion. Why bother with others' strength or weakness? The only mistake is that a state does not seek to help itself but instead hopes for the goodness of its enemies. A state like that is lucky not to be invaded."[28] Thus, Han Feizi highlighted the importance of state self-reliance, not the function of diplomacy. In addition, Han Feizi did not trust state alliances. He considered them to be unreliable and even dangerous.

> Bailing out small states is not necessarily beneficial. Instead, a state has to mobilize its army and make an enemy of big powers. Small states may still disappear after assisting them. Miscalculations can occur when attacking big powers. Once a state fails in its military adventure, the small state will be controlled by big powers. Sending an army then will be a military defeat. Retreating will lead to the fall of cities. One has not yet received the benefits from making alliances to save the small states but already saw the annexation of its homeland and defeat of its army.[29]

Chanakya valued the role of diplomacy and proposed a sixfold foreign policy. First, peaceful coexistence: it was possible for states to enter into agreements and make commitments; second, war: states could invade others; third, neutrality: states could be indifferent and take no action; fourth, offense: states could attack others; fifth, alliance: states could seek assistance; sixth, double-edged policy: states could be friendly with one side yet at war with another. These six types of foreign policies could be used individually or in combination. Compared to Han Feizi, Chanakya's thoughts about diplomacy were more prudent and flexible. His thought was systematic and responsive to the changing circumstances. It encouraged states to actively handle relations with other states. Alliance is valued in his thought. If one's own state is at a disadvantage, it should seek help from others. In addition, it could advocate for peaceful coexistence.

2.7 War Perspectives and Strategies

Both Han Fiezi and Chanakya placed great importance on force in their perspectives about war. They valued the meaning of war. They advocated the use of war at the right time. Both invented highly developed war strategies. As Han Fiezi says, "War effects the survival of states."[30] He adds that big powers are no exception to this rule:

> If you win the war, you will secure your country and throne. And your army will be strong and your reputation will be established. And even if the same thing happens later, you won't be able to find bigger benefits more than this victory. Winning the war is for the long-term interests. If the war is not won, your country will be in jeopardy, the army will be weakened, the monarch will be killed and his name will be dust and ashes. You cannot even escape from immediate disaster if you lose. You will not be able to gain any long-term interest at all.[31]

In terms of war strategy, however, the two are different. According to Han Feizi, war could test whether a state had increased its capability. Only a success in war could guarantee the survival of states. In order to win a war, decision makers had to be cautious in making war decisions. Before making a decision about war, they must examine the situation carefully. They should not fight an unprepared war. To be more specific, first they should figure out the comprehensive power of the states. Second, they should determine the perfect timing to initiate a war. Third, they should fight to the degree that is justified. Also, both rewards and punishments should be clearly established. Han Feizi believed that humans tended to seek profits. He proposed to manage the army with clear rewards and punishments in accordance with human nature. "Governance for the world has to be based on human circumstances. Humans have the tendency to judge things good or bad. Hence rewards and punishment can be placed and prohibitions can be made. Finally, the rules to govern can be complete."[32] First, severe penalties should be imposed. Second, soldiers should be attended to. Lastly, one should be attentive to the strategy of war. When attacking the enemies, he should choose the weaker one first, then the stronger one. At times, he should deceive the enemy if necessary. He should use these tactics to take down the enemy.

According to Chanakya, decisions about war should be made based on the situation and interests. When peace and war have the same function, peace should be the choice. Neutrality should be maintained when it is believed that the enemy cannot harm you and at the same time you are not strong enough to destroy the enemy. The side with the better advantage should initiate the war if war is coming. If a state has the necessary means to attack, it should go on the offensive. A state could purposefully build peace with another state in order to wage war against the third.

3. IMPLICATIONS FOR THE CURRENT WORLD

From the comparison of Han Feizi and Chanakya, we can see that there are profound and rich international political thoughts embedded in the Eastern cultural traditions. Academic multiculturalism can be built by digging into and revitalizing Eastern ideas. Hence Eurocentrism can be avoided.

The ideas of Han Feizi and Chanakya still shed light on the reality of international relations today. We are more than two thousand years beyond the time of Han Feizi and Chanakya. The current international society is much different from their war-ridden societies with brutal state competition. Yet the security dilemma of the great powers, and zero-sum games, still exist and some of the less developed regions are still in turmoil. National interest is fundamental and paramount. It must be the starting point for all foreign policy. This is the commonsense reality for every state. The question becomes, How is morality now viewed? In the modern globalized world, human civilization is already highly developed. Is it still necessary to defend national interests through unethical means? The game of interests still remains the reality in international society. This game is played based on a state's capabilities and there is still incessant militarized conflict. Nevertheless, international norms and institutions keep developing. International cooperation based on economic interests and the benefits for solving global issues is also proceeding in an orderly manner. Where is the balance between realpolitik and moral politics? Which one carries the heavier weight? Are the realization of national interests and the pursuit for human peace and justice doomed by conflict? Undoubtedly, the way that we understand politics, ethics, and decision making has to be firmly grounded in the background and in reality. It should not deal in fantasy. For one thing, we need to think about political issues realistically, as Han Feizi did; for another, we need to be concerned about the well-being of the people, as Chanakya was.

CONCLUSION

China and India, as two ancient civilizations, have accumulated rich histories and outstanding cultures. Han Feizi and Chanakya are two great political thinkers.

A comparative study of their international political thought reveals many similarities and differences.

Both Han Feizi and Chanakya are recognized as political realists. They placed great importance on realistic political interests and on the survival and strength of the state. Both believed that immoral means could be appropriately employed to achieve the national interests.

Both lived in a time of ceaseless wars and fierce competition. But each faced a different task: Han Feizi aimed to promote unification, whereas Chanakya purported to defend against foreign enemies and establish a new dynasty. Han Feizi deduced that states sought profits due to human nature's tendency to seek profits. He drew a clear line between politics and ethics and searched for the independence of politics from ethics. Chanakya synthesized and constructed his own philosophy, absorbing resources from religious and nonreligious ideas. He advocated for using immoral political means to achieve moral goals: accumulating wealth, protecting the people, and ensuring their well-being.

Both Han Feizi and Chanakya clearly found that the law of the jungle existed in state competition. Hence, they stressed the need to increase their own state's capability to ensure survival. But Han Feizi was extremely distrustful of interstate relations and opposed alliances, while Chanakya developed the Mandala theory of the state circles: distinguishing friends and enemies according the location on the circles. Han Feizi focused on domestic construction for the rule of law to increase state power. He dismissed diplomacy. Chanakya proposed the principle of sixfold diplomacy and applied it in a comprehensive and flexible manner. Both Han Feizi and Chanakya valued the role of war and also proposed different war strategies.

The international political thoughts of Han Feizi and Chanakya have similarities and relate to each other because of the similarities of their times and backgrounds. And their thinking was based on reality. Yet they are different because they were influenced by different cultures and social environments.

NOTES

1. Yan Xuetong, *Leadership and The Rise of Great Powers* (Princeton, NJ: Princeton University Press, 2019); Yan Xuetong, *Ancient Chinese Thought, Modern Chinese Power* (Princeton ,NJ: Princeton University Press, 2011).

2. Han Feizi: Jian jie shi chen.

3. Han Feizi: wu du.

4. Han Feizi: Yu lao.

5. Wang Yan, "Zheng shi lun guo ji zheng zhi si xiang jie du" [An interpretation of the international political thoughts in *the Arthashastra*], (Graduate thesis, Party School of the Central Committee of CPC, July 2017).

6. Ibid.

7. Han Feizi: liu fan.

8. Han Feizi: bei nei.

9. Ibid.

10. Sun Xuefeng and Yang Zixiao, "Han Feizi de guo jia jian zheng zhi si xiang" [Han Feizi's thoughts on international politics], *Quarterly Journal of International Politics* 2 (2015): 85–101.

11. Jin Haipeng, "Kao di li ye he ma ji ya wei li de zheng zhi si xiang bi jiao" [A comparative study on the political thoughts of Chanakya and Machiavelli], *Theory Research* 32 (2014): 33–34.

12. Han Feizi: wu du.

13. Han Feizi: Liu Fan.

14. The author thanks Prof. Deepshikha Shahi.

15. Han Feizi: Shi Xie.

16. Han Feizi: Shi Xie.

17. Han Feizi: Wu du (Five Vermin).

18. Han Feizi: Xian Xue.

19. Han Feizi: Nan Yi.

20. Han Feizi ji jie xu (A review on Han Feizi).

21. Deepshikha Shahi, chapter 6, this volume.

22. Ibid.

23. Haipeng, "Kao di li ye he ma ji ya wei li de zheng zhi si xiang bi jiao," 33–34.

24. Han Feizi: you du.

25. Han Feizi: shi xie.

26. Han Feizi: wai xu shuo.

27. Ibid.

28. Han Feizi: nan san.

29. Han Feizi: wu du.

30. Han Feizi: chu jian qin.

31. Han Feizi: nan yi.

32. Han Feizi: ba jing.

REFERENCES

1. Gao Huaping and Wang Qizhou, trans. and ed. Zhang. 2015. *Han Feizi*. Beijing: Zhonghua Book Company.

2. Zeng Xiangyu and Wei Chuxiong. 2019. *Zheng shi lun guo ji zheng zhi si xiang yan jiu* [A study on the international political thought of the *Arthashastra*]. Beijing: Current Affair Press.

3. Guan Lixin. 2012. "Han Feizi si xiang yan jiu" [A study on Han Feizi]. PhD Dissertation, Heilongjiang University.

4. Sun Xuefeng and Yang Zixiao. 2008. "Han Feizi de guo jia jian zheng zhi si xiang" [Han Feizi's thoughts on international politics]. *Quarterly Journal of International Politics* 2: 81–97.

5. Cai Xinde. 2006. "Han Feizi wai jiao si xiang yan jiu" [A study on Han Feizi's diplomatic thoughts]. Graduate Thesis, Jilin University, April.

6. Yang Zhicai. 2008. "Fei dao de de dao de: Ping Han Feizi de zheng zhi dao de guan" [The morals behind the immorality: A review of Han Feizi's political moral views]. *Jiaozuo Normal College Review* 24(3): 42–45.

7. Wang Yan. 2017. "Zheng shi lun guo ji zheng zhi si xiang jie du" [An interpretation of the international political thoughts in the *Arthashastra*]. Graduate Thesis, Party School of the Central Committee of CPC, July.

8. Zhang Jincui. 2013. "Zheng shi lun yu yin du wai jiao zhan lue de gu dian gen yuan" [The *Arthashastra* and the classical roots of India's foreign strategies]. *Foreign Affairs Review* 2: 123–34.

9. Jin Jie. 1986. "Zheng shi lun si xiang yu ce lue" [The thoughts and strategies in the *Arthashastra*]. *South Asian Studies* 4: 3–14.

10. Wang Yan. 2016. "Cong zheng shi lun kan yin du guo ji zhan lue si xiang gen yuan" [The *Arthashastra* and the roots of India's international strategies]. *Shanxi Youth* 3: 24–29.

11. Liao Xuesheng. 1993. "Zheng shi lun miao su de jiu jin shi zen yang de guo jia" [What country does the *Arthashastra* describe?]. *Historiography Quarterly* 4: 161.

12. Jin Haipeng. 2014. "Kao di li ye he ma ji ya wei li de zheng zhi si xiang bi jiao" [A comparative study on the political thoughts of Chanakya and Machiavelli]. *Theory Research* 32: 33–34.

13. Ye Zicheng and Pang Xun. 2011, "Zhong guo chun qiu zhan guo shi qi de wai jiao si xian liu pai ji qi yu xi fang de bi jiao" [The schools of Chinese diplomatic thought during the Spring and Autumn and Warring States Periods and the comparison with the West]. *Journal of World Economics and Politics* 12: 24–29.

14. Ye Zicheng. 2003. *Chun Qiu Zhan Guo Shi Qi De Zhong Guo Wai Jiao Si Xiang* [Chinese diplomatic thought during the Spring and Autumn and Warring States Periods]. Hongkong: Hongkong Social Sciences Press.

The Spectre of "Amoral Realism" in International Relations

A Classical Indian Overview

Deepshikha Shahi

As per the conventional wisdom on international relations (IR), it is presumed that the pursuit of Political Realism or realpolitik calls for a rational political action which is "amoral"—either "immoral" (opposed to moralpolitik) or "neither immoral nor moral" (apathetic to moralpolitik). Also, it is held that all Asian philosophical traditions are amoral as they project a form of awareness that is inconsistent with any notions of morality or moralpolitik. However, this chapter shows how the classical Indian text of Kautilya's *Arthaśāstra* uses an amoral framework—supported by the eclectic philosophical substructures of *Sāṃkhya*, *Yoga*, and *Lokāyata* (literally meaning "numbers," "aggregate," and "worldly ones" respectively)—to not only temper apparently immoral methods, but also attain concrete moral goals in IR. In this sense, Kautilya's *Arthaśāstra* deviates from both Eurocentric and Chinese Political Realism. The chapter illustrates how Kautilya's Amoral Realism can be resourcefully mobilized to bridge the gulf between realpolitik and moralpolitik in contemporary global politics.

THE AMORAL ROOTS OF POLITICAL REALISM IN EUROCENTRIC IR

The idea of amoralism in Eurocentric IR oscillates between "immoralism" and "moral relativism." A few scholars assert that Amoral Realism involves "rational strategic actions" (Loriaux 1992) that have "no room for moral considerations" (Frankel 2013) and, thus, they are "not subject to calculations of morality" (Antunes and Camisão 2018); the cynical view of Amoral Realism "rationalizes immoral conducts with high-minded talk about state interests and international realities" (Brilmayer 1999). Other scholars argue that "amorality is not immorality"

(Hom 2018), and Amoral Realism is "neither driven by morality nor especially immoral" (Kissane 2013); it is, rather, an evolving theory that relates to specific circumstances, and its relevance is judged in terms of its ability to make prudent political decisions (Morgenthau 1962). Even if Realism is pushed as an amoral approach, it does not translate into an immoral foreign policy (Conces 2009). And despite the claim that the human mind is amoral, as it does not have innate conceptions of (im)moral and is prone to certain instincts that are necessary for survival (Al-Rodhan 2015), Realists use their own moral convictions. As Realists use their own moral convictions to suggest how states can best survive, their theories retain an "amoral character" by remaining silent on whether the survival of a particular state/government is morally desirable (Walt 2010).

In Eurocentric IR, Amoral Realism creates an uncomfortable, if not unfeasible, relation between realpolitik and moralpolitik: moralpolitik prefers to look for "abstract/ideal notions of morality," whereas realpolitik sees more merit in "rational/ prudent approach to reality" which can protect the "self" (own state) against the potential/actual use of violence by "other/s" (other states). This concept of realpolitik has developed within the boundaries of Classical Realism (Morgenthau) and Neorealism (Waltz) among others.[1] Unlike Waltz, who excludes the subjective questions of morality to work as a pure "scientist," Morgenthau shows greater moral sensitivity in confessing a dynamic link between two concepts of power: "empirical" (power as domination/*pouvoir*) and "normative" (power as human capabilities/*puissance*) (Rösch 2015). For Morgenthau, the normative power is an "end" that reestablishes a value-system that has the potential to confine empirical power (Frei 2001). But until and unless that value-system is reestablished, Morgenthau seems skeptical about the use of normative power (as a "means," not as an "end") along with empirical power, thereby verifying those studies that problematize Morgenthau as a champion of realpolitik, yet label him as an "uneasy Realist" (Scheuerman 2009).

Classical Realism and Neorealism—as major variants of Amoral Realism in Eurocentric IR—sanction a dualistic reality characterized by the struggle-of-power between "self" and "other/s." To causally arrive at the centrality of this struggle-for-power, Morgenthau's Classical Realism arouses the assumed aggression in "human nature" (*animus dominandi*), and Waltz's Neorealism awakens the supposed "anarchy" in world's political structure (*absence of a world government*). Against the competitive pretext set by this struggle-for-power (which turns into a perennial security-dilemma for "self"), the probability of self-help arises only if the "self" goes for maximization-of-power and adjusts itself with ever-shifting balance-of-power among "other/s." Morgenthau (1986) observes this maximization-of-power as "superiority (not equality) of power" vis-à-vis "other/s," and defensive realists like Waltz (1979) warn that this maximization-of-power vis-à-vis "other/s" must not be limitless because the state that acquires too much of a share in zero-sum power[2] is likely to be damaged by antagonistic coalition among "other/s."

Furthermore, offensive Realists suggest that it makes a good strategic sense for each state to possess as much zero-sum power as possible and, if the situation is right, to pursue hegemony over "other/s" (Mearsheimer 2001).

Despite an emphasis upon human lust for power, Morgenthau does not intend to repress morality in political life. He opines that the universal moral principles cannot be applied to the acts of the states in their abstract formulation; they must be filtered through concrete circumstances; the states must imagine the political consequences of a seemingly moral action (Eisikovits 2016). For Morgenthau, the sphere of IR is "autonomous"; the states in this autonomous sphere cannot subordinate their acts to the abstract universal ideals manageable in individual/ domestic sphere (Karpowicz and Julian 2018); the abstract universal ideals do not supply the "political restraints" that bring successful consequences in IR (Williams 2005). Conversely, Waltz laments that the pinning of political evil on human nature occurs in the nonscientific thinking of Augustine, Spinoza, Niebuhr, and Morgenthau (Voina-Motoc 1999). Waltz adopts a "scientific" outlook in treating the anarchical structural conditions as a stimulus behind the functional similarity of the states: all states follow the moral principle of survival. But this moral principle of survival makes sense only in anarchical structural conditions ridden with violence: even for Waltz, the abstract universal ideals beyond relations of violence become untenable/undesirable (Lundborg 2018).

Analogous to the apprehensions of R. Aron (1966) and E. H. Carr (2001),[3] Morgenthau's Classical Realism and Waltz's Neorealism undercut the abstract universal ideals as a feasible option in IR. Hence, moral reflections in Classical Realism and Neorealism get compressed into a single core principle—the principle of realpolitik whereby rational/prudent exercise of power protects the "self" against the potential/actual use of violence by "other/s," thereby enabling the "self" to secure survival and, in some cases, hegemony. Classical Realism and Neorealism marginalize the abstract/ideal exercise of power that can attain extra–Political Realist goals: the extra–Political Realist goals (as in moralpolitik) that surpass the concerns of survival/hegemony for "self," and attempt to secure all that brings benefit to both "self" and "other/s." From a comparative perspective, Kautilya's Arthaśāstra digresses from Eurocentric Political Realism in two respects: (i) it does not anticipate "rational/prudent" and "abstract/ideal" as mutually opposed; and (ii) it is not restricted to realpolitik, but consistently embraces moralpolitik.

KAUTILYA'S *ARTHAŚĀSTRA*: A CLASSICAL INDIAN ACCOUNT OF AMORAL REALISM

It is alleged that all Asian philosophies are amoral as they imbibe a logic which is incompatible with morality (Zelinski 2003). Arguably, the amoralism of Daoism (which finds extension in Han Fei's Legalism) prompts Chinese IR, and the amoralism of Kautilya stimulates Indian IR. So, they say, Kautilya's amoralism not only depicts reality "as it is," not "as it ought to be" (Boesche 2003), but also presents a "statement of the immoral practices of kings/ministers" (Sarkar 1985). M. Winternitz (1923) laments that one should look in vain for anything that could be called "law" in *Arthaśāstra* as Kautilya is ready to not only make treaties but also break them in appropriate conditions, thereby showing no preference for peace. But J. Jolly (1913) contends that Kautilya's *Arthaśāstra* is a branch of "Dharmaśāstra"—a text that contains a few rules that fall within the domain of "law proper" (Kangle 1997). At one point, one wonders as to what was the (im)moral impulse behind the law proper in Kautilya's *Arthaśāstra*. Tracing the controversy around Kautilya's (im)morality, U. Thakkar (1999: 2) narrates:

> This controversy arises because of the fact that two distinct lines of thought are evident in Kautilya . . . namely the theological . . . and the political . . . if Kautilya upholds the high authority of the Brāhmanical [theological] canon, he allows himself to make religion the instrument of statecraft, or in other words, to sacrifice Theology at the altar of Politics.

But does Kautilya really sacrifice theology at the altar of politics? R. Shamasastry (1915: 8–9) translates an intuitive extract from this treatise:

> [i] *Anvikshaki* ["philosophy of science"] [ii] the triple *Védas* ["religious scriptures"], [iii] *Várta* ["economics"], and [iv] *Danda-niti* ["political science"] are the four sciences . . . it is from these sciences that all that concerns righteousness and wealth is learnt . . . *Anvikshaki* comprises *Samkhya, Yoga,* and *Lokayata* . . . Light to all kinds of knowledge, easy means to accomplish all kinds of acts . . . is the science of *anvikshaki.*

The science of Kautilya's *Arthaśāstra* emanates from the (ir)religious philosophical substructures of *Sāṃkhya, Yoga,* and *Lokāyata,* which, in turn, convey a meticulous approach to the dilemmas of morality in life. So, what are the central propositions of *Sāṃkhya, Yoga,* and *Lokāyata?* How do these propositions surpass Eurocentric Political Realism, thereby emitting extra–Political Realist elements? And how do these extra–Political Realist elements blend realpolitik and moralpolitik? The classical Indian philosophies are divided into two clusters: "orthodox" (that approve the infallibility of God/*Védas*); and "unorthodox" (that disapprove the infallibility of God/*Védas*). *Sāṃkhya* and *Yoga* subscribe to orthodox cluster,[4] but *Lokāyata* belongs to unorthodox cluster. Kautilya's *Arthaśāstra* plans an eclectic mix of both the clusters, thereby combining *Sāṃkhya, Yoga* and *Lokāyata* as its integrated philosophical base. P. Olivelle (1998: 21) comments:

> *Sāṃkhya* posits a primal matter, called *prakrti* . . . This primal matter, originally unmanifest, contains three qualities: goodness, energy, and darkness. The visible and manifest universe has proceeded from the original primal matter; the three qualities are distributed in different proportions within the various constituents of the universe.

Sāṃkhya confirms a "dualistic reality" wherein the primordial equilibrium of *prakṛti* (matter) gets disturbed when it is modified by *puruṣa* (spirit)—an incident that marks the beginning of the evolution of the world! R. W. Perrett (2007: 150–51) elaborates:

> First, the pure contentless consciousness of the *puruṣa* becomes focused on the *prakṛti* and out of the delimitation evolves intelligence . . . then evolves the ego consciousness which leads to the misidentification of the true self with the ego. From [it], evolves the mind; [then] the five sensory organs and the five motor organs; then the five subtle elements (sound, touch, form, taste and smell) and the five gross elements (ether, air, fire, water and earth) . . . *Yoga* broadly accepts this *Sāṃkhya* ontology. [Remembering this evolutionary process], the *Sāṃkhya-Yoga*[5] ethics . . . mentions five . . . moral precepts or "restraints": non-injury, truthfulness, non-stealing, chastity, and greedlessness.

These "restraints" coupled with some "observances" (e.g., contentment, self-study etc.) facilitate the knowledge of manifest world. The knowledge of manifest world is acquired through the methods of "perception," "inference," and "valid testimony" (Radhakrishnan and Moore 1967). *Lokāyata*, unlike *Sāṃkhya-Yoga*, sponsors "perception" as the sole means to know "this-world." D. P. Niles (2017: 178) observes:

> *Lokāyata* teaching is that all aspects of matter, including humanity, are particular combinations of the four basic elements, earth, water, fire and air . . . Matter can think . . . consciousness arises from matter . . . the soul is nothing but the conscious body. Enjoyment is the only end of human life. Death alone is liberation. At death all matter reverts to its constitutive elements.

In Indian history, *Lokāyata* progressed as a dissent against the "elite" enthusiasts of those texts that contained *Sāṃkhya-Yoga*: the elite enthusiasts formed the dominant social group called brahmin, whereas *Lokāyata* grew as a creed of the "mass." This elite-mass conflict fuels the conjecture that *Lokāyata* is irreconcilable to *Sāṃkhya-Yoga*. But a closer scrutiny unfurls some overlaps: *Lokāyata* discards unmanifest primordial nature/*prakṛti*, but it supports the study of manifest world as experienced by the bodily-self/*puruṣa*. For the study of manifest world, *Lokāyata* uses a few methods of *Sāṃkhya-Yoga*: it rejects inference and valid testimony, but accepts perception as a mode of inquiry; it rejects ether, but accepts air, fire, water, and earth as parts of holistic reality. The hedonistic ethics of *Lokāyata* abandons the rituals meant to protect future life, and elevates the joy of bodily-self (Sharma 2000), but it does not do so at the expense of the soul-oriented-self; it, rather, defends the "identity of body and soul" (Joshi 1987)—*Lokāyata* allows sexual rituals, but it does not cancel out the spiritual values of noninjury, truthfulness, nonstealing, and greedlessness when it comes to protect the interests of bodily-self.

The joint propositions of *Sāṃkhya-Yoga* and *Lokāyata*, which underpin Kautilya's *Arthaśāstra*, are as follows: the device to navigate and cope up with the reality of this-world is "perception"; the bodily-self (as it uses perception to navigate and cope up with the reality of this-world) wishes to defend the "identity of body and soul": that is, the interests of the body (material enjoyment/*artha* and physical pleasure/*kāma*) and the interests of the soul (righteousness/*dharma* and self-liberation/*moksha*) are not mutually exclusive. Moreover, the identity of body and soul can be defended by implementing some moral principles: noninjury, truthfulness, nonstealing, and greedlessness. Assigning the ideal rule of a "saintly-king" who is ought to act in accordance with these moral principles, Kautilya commands:

> [A saintly-king] . . . shall keep away from hurting the women and property of others [follow noninjury and nonstealing]; avoid . . . falsehood [follow truthfulness]; Not violating righteousness [*dharma*] and economy [*artha*], he shall enjoy his desires [*kāma*]. He may enjoy in an equal degree the three pursuits of life, charity, wealth, and desire, which are inter-dependent upon each other. Any one of these three, when enjoyed to an excess, hurts not only the other two, but also itself [i.e. follow greedlessness]. (Shamasastry 1915: 17)

In spite of the vision of dualistic reality (akin to Eurocentric Political Realism),[6] the Realism of *Sāṃkhya-Yoga* and *Lokāyata* makes the rational/prudent quest for material enjoyment/*artha* and physical pleasure/*kāma* dependent upon the abstract/ideal apparatus of righteousness/*dharma*, i.e., morality-ethics (Gray 2014). R. W. Perrett (1998: 52) illustrates:

> One view . . . holds *dharma* ["righteousness"] to be an instrumental value . . . which leads inevitably to the good of prosperity conceived in both this-worldly [rational/prudent] and other-worldly [abstract/ideal] terms . . . [*dharma*'s] superiority over *artha* and *kāma* is its unfailing reliability in affecting this good.[7]

Accordingly, Kautilya's *Arthaśāstra* monitors both rational/prudent and abstract/ideal concerns while exercising power for achieving extra–Political Realist goals: these extra–Political Realist goals exceed realpolitik as they outdo the need to secure survival/hegemony, and pave the way for occasional pursuance of moralpolitik. An instance of occasional pursuance of moralpolitik is found when Kautilya asks the conqueror state to boost not only its own power, but also the enemy's power. Kautilya directs:

> Power is of three kinds . . . Intellectual strength provides the power of good counsel; a prosperous treasury and a strong army provide physical power, and valour is the basis for morale and energetic action. The success resulting from each one is, correspondingly, intellectual, physical and psychological . . . the conqueror shall . . . add to his own power . . . [But] he may in situations wish power . . . even to his enemy. If a powerful enemy is likely to antagonize his subjects by harming them . . . it will be easy to overpower him. (Rangarajan 1992: 525–26)

Kautilya asks the conqueror state to boost its power by crushing an unjust enemy state. But he also asks the conqueror state to win the subjects of that unjust enemy state: the conqueror state must not terrorize those subjects for self-glory and do what was beneficial to them, thereby behaving as if the conqueror state belonged to them (Chande 1998)—an instance that suspends self-other distinction! These acts are guided by Political Realist goals of "protection/survival" (*yogakshema*), and extra–Political Realist goals of "benefit for all" (*lokasamgraha*) (Jai 1999). These extra–Political Realist goals cross those barriers of realpolitik that prefer rational/prudent quest for survival/hegemony: the will to promote the abstract universal ideals of "benefit for all," that aim to discover the world's potential for virtue and to derive happiness therefrom for "self" and "other/s" (Iyer 2000), positions Kautilya's *Arthaśāstra* between realpolitik and moralpolitik. It is pertinent to see how Kautilya's *Arthaśāstra*—as an Asian model of Amoral Realism that tempers immoral methods to attain moral goals—differs from Chinese Political Realism, especially, Han Fei's Legalism.

KAUTILYA VERSUS HAN FEI

What are the traits of Kautilya's Amoral Realism that set it apart from other Asian models, such as the Amoral Realism behind Han Fei's Legalism? Like Kautilya's *Arthaśāstra*, Han Fei's text, *Han Feizi*, is a classical work of "eclecticism" (Ivanhoe 2011). As a precursor to Han syncretism (Goldin 2013), *Han Feizi* borrows insights from many sources, such as Daoism, Confucianism, and Legalism (or Realism). A. Waley (1939: 202–3) informs:

> With Daoism, Realism has a very close connection. Both doctrines reject "the way of the Former Kings", upon which the whole curriculum of the Confucians was based . . . even the mystical doctrine of *wu-wei*, the Non-activity of the ruler by which everything is activated, finds a non-mystical counterpart in Realism. When every requirement of the ruler has been embodied in law and the penalities for disobedience have been made so heavy that no one dares to incur them, the Realist ruler can . . . enjoy himself; "everything" (just as in Daoism) "will happen of its own accord."

"Just as in the [D]aoist and Confucian interpretations of *wu wei*, in the Han Fei[zi's Legalism], there is an attempt to correlate the operation of the cosmos and the proper functioning of the political state. Characteristics attributed to the [cosmic D]ao are projected onto the ideal ruler . . . *wu wei* [i.e., nonactivity] and the related techniques of rulership [a]re intended to prevent any insight into the ruler's personality which might interfere with the operation of the governmental machinary" (Ames 1983: 51–53). By mixing *wu-wei* with Legalist polity, Han Fei resembles Kautilya's all-encompassing methodological skills that simultaneously deals with the metaphysical, epistemological, practical, ethical, and aesthetic aspects of reality. But Han Fei differs from Kautilya with regard to the appraisal of the "ruler's action": while Kautliya sees the ruler's action as a form of power, Han Fei gives ample weightage to the ruler's nonactivity. Quoting *Han Feizi*, R. N. Bellah (2011: 457–58) writes:

> Do not let your power be seen, be blank and actionless. Government reaches to the four quarters, but its source is the centre. The sage[-king] holds to the source, and the four quarters come to serve him . . . Do not be the first to move . . . If you show delight, your troubles will multiply; if you show hatred, resentment will be born. Therefore discard both delight and hatred, and with an empty mind, become the abode of the Way.[8]

Even *Sāṃkhya-Yoga* agrees that the primordial eqilibrium of nature/*prakriti* (comparable to "the Way") gets disturbed in the evolutionary process activated by the human spirit/*purusa*. But the propositions of *Sāṃkhya-Yoga-Lokayata* in Kautilya's *Arthaśāstra* never endorse nonactivity: rather, they envision the ruler's moral-energetic action as a source of "psychological power." Kautilya states:

> Of a king, the religious vow is his readiness to action [here, readiness to action testifies to the ruler's morality/energy, whereas inaction indicates the ruler's immorality/lethargy; in times of crises, the ruler's action, not inaction, boosts the psychological power of the state, including the subjects]. The king who [acts] in accordance with sacred law, evidence, history, and edicts of kings . . . will be able to conquer the whole world bounded by the four quarters. (Shamasastry 1915: 52, 215)

Contrary to Han Fei's "sage-king," who is asked to sit at the center of the governmental structure and judge the efficiency of his ministers, but refrain from any active personal intervention in the administrative affairs, Kautilya's saintly-king, as he occupies the center of the states-system, is asked to use his personal qualities to enrich the other elements of his state, especially when they are less than perfect: these elements include ministers, population, fort, treasury, army, and ally. Kautilya states: "whatever character the king has, the other elements also come to have the same" (Sihag 2004: 146). Dissimilar to the king's "impersonal" conduct styled after *wu-wei* by Han Fei (Winston 2005), Kautilya counts on the king's "personal" qualities. But this does not mean that Kautilya ignores the importance of detachment. As Han Fei praises the king's detachment from delight/hatred, Kautilya lauds the king's "active engagement with" yet "conscious detachment from" the immediate moments of success and failure in politics (Ganeri 2003). The detachment of Kautilya's saintly-king aims to achieve "protection/survival" and "benefit for all," whereas the detachment of Han Fei's sage-king intends to preserve "order."

Though Han Fei's Legalist "order" is measured as the single necessary condition for a decent life (Flanagan and Hu 2011), it runs the risk of manufacturing an "entrapped sovereign" whose "God-like omnipotence" is submerged by the system he ostensibly runs (Pines 2018). This system, sooner or later, transforms into a de facto "bureaucratic Legalism" (Schneider 2018), wherein it is the ministers who do the real ruling (Graham 1989), the ministers whom Han Fei himself identifies as the king's "most dangerous foes" (Graziani 2015). In theory, the sage-king aspires to materialize a "social engineering" (Pines 2016) by using his impersonal power/*shu* to change laws/rules/techniques/*shi* in accordance with the change in circumstances. In practice, this social engineering is expected to satiate the egocentric human nature whose morality is distorted in times of economic deprivations. Nonetheless, this social engineering rests upon an "award and punishment mechanism" (*hsing-ming*) whereby the sage-king not only tallies "names" (or offical-positions) with "performances" (or work-proposals) for separating solid talent from idle chatter (Witzel 2012), but also confers harsh punishment upon an ever-increasing population for the purpose of aligning individual interest with public interest (*fa*) (Craig 1998). B. Watson (1964: 98–99) quotes a passage from *Han Feizi*:

> Though his penalities may be severe, this is not because he is cruel, he simply follows the custom appropriate to the time. Circumstances change according to the age, and ways of dealing with them changes with the circumstances.

Bellah (2011: 458) continues: "In ancient times, people were few and resources plentiful; today people are many and resources few. What required little government then requires harsh punishment today." Slowly, Han Fei's "bureaucratic Legalism" turns into "authoritarian Daoism" (Hansen 2000) wherein one is rewarded and punished in accordance with the "positive laws": even a moral deed is severely punished if it violates the positive laws (Chen 2016). Although this authoritarian Daoism says nothing against Daoism *per se*, it maintains a distance from Daoist spiritual-abstract forms (Moody 2008). At last, what links Daoism and Legalism is an opposition to moralism; "the danger is that together they reject morality" (Bellah 2011: 458). Han Fei rebuffs Daoist spiritual-abstract forms of benevolence, righteousness, love and kindness as useless political virtues (Vogelsang 2016), thereby allowing immorality to preserve "order." Even Kautilya, who is motivated by the goals of "protection/survival" and "benefit for all," is not averse to the temporary use of immoral means (e.g., assasination, etc.), but he firmly upholds the spiritual-abstract forms of morality when he addresses the king:

> In the happiness of his subjects lies his happiness; in their welfare his welfare; whatever pleases himself he shall not consider as good, but whatever pleases his subjects he shall consider as good . . . satisfactory discharge of [his] duties is his performance of sacrifice (Shamasatry 1915: 52).

It is appealing to inquire if these premodern ideas of Kautilya could be put into practice in today's (post)modern global politics.

PREMODERN KAUTILYA AND POST(MODERN) GLOBAL POLITICS

Today's global politics neither justifies a separation of "moral-domestic-order" from "amoral-international-anarchy" (Ashley 1987), nor awaits an import of moral-ethical-principles from "outside" (the sphere of international) to "inside" (the sphere of domestic) (Walker 1993). Rather, the present international community, which gives a crucial role to morality in the determination of global order (Kapstein and Rosenthal 2009), grapples with the crisis of "plurality of values" (Amstutz 2018)—any single moral-value subsists with plural moral-values represented at diverse local-global levels (Nancy 2000). Amid the anxiety that this "chaotic condition of moral conceptions and beliefs" (Dewey 1923) might be a harbinger of "messy morality" (Coady 2008), there is little disagreement about the need for a "moral theory of international law" (Buchanan 2003) which could collaborate scholars and practitioners at all levels of governance (Garofalo 2008), thereby connecting "public opinion" and "foreign policy" via moral sentiments (Kertzer et al. 2014). As this moral theory of international law follows the "golden rule of humanity," it demands a fresh global politics centered upon not only rights, but also duties (Kung, 1998), and one of the duties is the avoidance of "double standards": that is, "one [set of moral-values] for other people, and a different and more permissive one for oneself" (Harries 2005). Here, the idea is to condemn the use of violence for 'securing one group of citizens by placing others in danger" (Burke 2004) and prioritize the ethics of care for "self" and "other/s" in a globalized world with greater international interdependence (Held 2011).

So, how can Kautilya's *Arthaśāstra* encourage the moral agenda of contemporary global politics? Nowadays, global politics sees the inside-outside-demarcation (or fixed borders of Westphalian states-system) as a moral hurdle (Ling 2017). Kautilya's *Arthaśāstra* seems promising as it does not instill a demarcation between domestic politics (inside) and international politics (outside) (Acharya and Buzan 2009). As this demarcation cultivates a self-other dualism that hampers the ethics of international responsibility, the absence of this demarcation in Kautilya's *Arthaśāstra* permits many alternative forms of self-other relationship to grow, e.g., the self-other relationship wherein the subjects of own state stay connected to the subjects of other states for many reasons (e.g., for expressing discontent with certain policies), thereby mirroring the transnational realities of current global politics: recent studies show how anti-government protests worldwide have brought together dissatisfied individuals/groups that were assumed unlikely to unite for a common cause due to ideological differences (Axford, Gulmez, and Gulmez 2018); and how popular dissatisfaction with governance frameworks is resulting in new transnational sites of authority built around new coalitions of actors/interests (Breslin and Nesadurai 2018). Because the subjects of different states stay connected, the just exercise of power becomes a fundamental international responsibility. Quoting *Arthaśāstra*, R. P. Kangle (1997: 120) writes:

> An unjust or improper use of . . . power by the ruler might lead to serious consequences, the most serious being a revolt of the subjects against the ruler . . . large number of acts on the part of the ruler . . . are likely to make the subjects disaffected with his rule . . . if the subjects become disaffected [at the domestic level], they may join hands with the ruler's enemies [at the international level] . . . [This] threat . . . is

expected to serve as a check on the wanton use of coercive power by the ruler. This shows at the same time how the ruler's authority is, in the last analysis, dependent on the contentment of the subjects.

Since the subjects' contentment, as a vital aspect of public opinion, decides the ruler's authority, Kautilya announces that the ruler's authority is harmed if s/he does not pay what ought to be paid, or if s/he does exact what ought not to be taken (Shamasastry 1915: 386–87): these acts damage the economic prospects of the subjects of own state and/or other state/s. Kautilya further suggests that a conqueror state is prudent if it is just toward the subjects because the subjects, when impoverished, become greedy; when greedy, they become disaffected; when disaffected, they either go over to the enemy state or themselves kill the unjust ruler (Kangle 1997: 120). Therefore, the conqueror state should not allow these causes of decline, greed, and disaffection among the subjects to arise, or, if arisen, should instantaneously counteract them (Deb 1938). Also, Kautilya cautions that the ruler's authority is harmed if s/he attacks a state that has a virtuous ruler (who takes good care of the subjects) or a prevalence of loyal subjects (who put up a resilient fight for their ruler) (Olivelle 2013: 275). Even when the ruler attacks an unjust state where a morally diseased king is likely to bring harm to his subjects, the ruler's authority is enforced if s/he saves the "value-systems" of the subjects of that unjust state. Kautilya preaches:

> Having acquired a new territory (after defeating a morally-diseased enemy), he should cover the enemy's vices with his own virtues, and the enemy's virtues by doubling his own virtues ... he should follow the friends and leaders of the people ... he should adopt the same mode of life, the same dress, language, and customs as those of the people. He should follow the people in their faith with which they celebrate their national, religious and congregational festivals. (Shamasastry 1915: 581–82)

The urge to keep the plurality of values shows the known connection between "public opinion" and "foreign policy" in Kautilya's *Arthaśāstra*. Because of this connection, Kautilya allows a minimal use of organized violence in foreign policy (that could badly affect the public opinion): to begin with, Kautilya prioritizes the "skills for intrigue" (understood as ingenious application of the "science of polity") for achieving intended goals, not enthusiasm or physical power that often lead to organized violence, such as war. But in case the war becomes a necessity, then Kautliya advises the conqueror state to declare war against an unjust state with disaffected subjects who would not put up a resilient fight for their ruler, thereby minimizing the scale of violence in war. Kautilya broadly classifies three types of war: "open war" fought with preset place-time and stipulated rules; "concealed war" fought with an element of surprise; and "silent war" similar to modern guerrilla war. The moral legitimacy of war is contingent on the state's relative power: the states with evenly matched militaries should use open war, and the states that are weaker than their opponents, or that are not sure about their relative power, should use concealed/silent war. Kautilya can be seen as a forerunner of "just war traditions" (Morkevičius 2018) because he engages with the ideas of *jus ad bellum* (conditions that justify participation in war), *jus in bello* (rules about how war should be fought once it has started), and *jus post bellum* (instructions on how war should be ended).

Besides, Kautilya denounces the use of organized violence to torture those who, after being defeated in war, have reached a psychological terrain whereby they are ready to lay down their lives. Kautilya cautions: "the vehemence of someone who reenters a battle without regard for his life becomes irrepressible," thus, it is not only morally sound, but also rationally proper to not "harass a man who has been crushed" (Olivelle 2013: 380). One can draw parallels between the irrationality inherent in the torture of crushed individuals in Kautilya's *Arthaśāstra* and the ongoing research on moral psychology and torture in existing IR (Wisnewski 2010). Far from torture, Kautilya exhibits an empathy toward "rights" (Chandrasekaran 2006): e.g., he attaches a huge importance to the compassionate treatment of invaded rulers/ministers. Kautilya also puts an accent on duties/responsibilities. J. Chemburkar (1999: 65) explains:

> [Kautilya] classifies duties as *viśesa dharma* and *sāmānya dharma* . . . *sāmānya dharma* includes duties . . . which are common to all irrespective of any distinction such as class, caste, creed, sex, time-space [e.g., the spiritual-value of "forgiveness" is *sāmānya dharma* (Shamasastry 1915: 11)]. [But] there are certain duties which are . . . determined by the role one is playing . . . [these peculiar duties are called *viśesa dharma* which] differ from individual to individual . . . *viśesa dharma* is determined by an individual's relation with other fellow beings . . . e.g. the king is bound by *rajadharma* [i.e., the king's peculiar duty to obtain material prosperity for the subjects (Kangle 1997: 131)] as he is . . . related to the whole social fabric in a specific way.

As the ruler is related to the whole social fabric in a specific way, s/he shoulders the duty to derive material well-being. But when the ruler acts to derive material well-being, these acts should not become a hurdle in the path of spiritual well-being: here, the duty toward utilitarian material well-being is to be reconciled with an obligation toward altruistic spiritual well-being. R. P. Kangle (1997: 2) clarifies:

> With *artha* understood, by implication, in the sense of the earth where men live and seek their material well-being, it ceases to be a goal pursued by individuals and appears as the means of ensuring the well-being of men in general. And since state activity alone can make such general well-being possible, the protection of earth [becomes] an essential part of state activity. [*Arthaśāstra*] is thus defined as the . . . [knowledge] which shows how this activity of the . . . protection of the earth should be carried out.

R. Eckersley (2004) echoes a Kautilyan sentiment when she goes against the grain of much current IR thinking to argue that the state is still the preeminent institution for tackling environmental issues on earth. Kautilya focuses upon moralpolitik (i.e., abstract universal ideals of protecting the earth, minimizing the organized violence, nurturing the plural values, defending the subjects' contentment, and practicing the value of forgiveness) as a necessary condition for realpolitik (i.e., rational/prudent struggle for maximization-of-power). As Kautilya focuses upon moralpolitik as a necessary condition for realpolitik, he dilutes some of the basic dichotomies that haunt the conventional study of global politics (Abbott, 2004)—namely, "self vs. other/s," "material vs. ideational," "spiritual vs. sensual," and so on. Indeed, it is this theoretical-practical temper of Kautilya—which amorally mediates between the spiritual and sensual aspects of life (Shahi 2018)—that stands to upgrade the customary ways of handling the persisting challenges of global politics, such as climate change, pandemic, economic crisis, humanitarian intervention, and war on terror.

CONCLUDING REMARKS

"Realism between realpolitik and moralpolitik" is the hallmark of Kautilya's Amoral Realism. Against the Eurocentric idea of a zero-sum world (wherein rational/prudent, not abstract/ideal, hunt for power by "self" can deplete the power of "other/s"), Kautilya's Amoral Realism complements the image of a zero-sum-world with a "variable-sum world": Kautilya agrees that different states must seek to augment their power (in order to retain growth, or to make progress from decline to stability, and then, from stability to growth); but when different states seek to augment their power, they must know that they do not always share a competitive relationship with each other; at different points in time in dealing with different states, the growth in power of own state ("self") requires not only depletion in power of "other/s" (zero-sum view), but also coordinated growth in power of "other/s" (variable-sum view). To attain this coordinated growth in power of "self" and "other/s," Kautilya's Amoral Realism, unlike Han Fei's Amoral Realism, prescribes a proactive (not nonactive) upkeep of the abstract-spiritual bureaucratic-legal forms. As Kautilya's Amoral Realism tracks coordinated growth in power of "self" and "other/s," it unleashs a robust vision of global politics that strives to reconcile the seemingly disjointed spheres of "the domestic" and "the international."

GLOSSARY

artha: material well-being; **kāma:** physical pleasure; **dharma:** righteousness; **yogakshema:** protection/survival; **lokasamgraha:** benefit for all

NOTES

1. Neoclassical Realism (Fareed Zakaria) emerged as the "logical extension" of Neorealism. But some IR scholars claim that Neoclassical Realism undermines the core of Neorealism (Legro and Moravcsik 1999).

2. The notion of zero-sum power holds that the gain of power by "self" leads to an equivalent loss of power by "other/s." By contrast, the variable-sum view on power—which is infrequently described in Kautilya's *Arthaśāstra*—assumes that it is possible to have mutual gains of power not offset by equivalent losses somewhere else (positive-sum), and mutual losses of power not offset by equivalent gains somewhere else (negative-sum).

3. R. Aron (1966) admits the "morality of struggle" and "morality of law," but recommends what he calls the "morality of prudence," thereby conveying that the morality in IR is equivocal. Likewise, E. H. Carr (2001) considers the coexistence of "utopia" and "reality" as two irreconcilable forces in IR.

4. Since *Sāmkhya* does not consider God as the creator of the world (Larson 1969), it is seen as an "atheistic" (not religious) philosophy. Nevertheless, a few scholars suggest that *Sāmkhya* is not an atheistic philosophy as it does not falsify the existence of God, but only denies the role of God as the sole creator of the world (Bronkhorst 1983). *Yoga* considers the belief in God as the "first teacher" (Dickstein 2015).

5. As *Sāmkhya* (Sāmkhyakārikā, 350–450 CE) lends support to *Yoga* (Yogasūtra, 200–300 CE) (Perrett 1998), *Sāmkhya* and *Yoga* are often jointly referred to as "*Sāmkhya-Yoga*."

6. The dualistic reality of *Sāmkhya-Yoga* assumes the separate existence of *prakrti*/matter and *purusa*/spirit. *Lokāyata* proposes a more nuanced picture of this dualistic reality when it argues that "spiritual-consciousness" originates from "material-body" (Bhattacharya 2011). Though *Lokāyata* ranks the material-body over and above the spiritual-consciousness, it does not refute the separate ontological existence of these two kinds of reality.

7. Is Kautilya equally motivated by *dharma, artha*, and *kāma*? N. P. Sil (1985: 125–26) writes: "One major problem in determining the extent of Kautilya's moral susceptibility is that he is seldom consistent in his contentions . . . He might occasionally appear . . . amoral, though, on closer scrutiny, his fundamental moralism becomes obvious. For instance, he observes that . . . material well-being[/*artha*] alone is supreme, for, spiritual good[/*dharma*] and sensual pleasures[/*kāma*] depend on material well-being . . . Yet, on another occasion, Kautilya comments that a king must preserve his body, not wealth; for, what regret can there be for wealth that is impermanent?" S. Gray (2014: 640) asserts: "Kautilya . . . does not argue for *artha*'s superiority but rather for its harmonious integration with the other goals of human life . . . *dharma* [righteousness], *kāma* (desire, including the sphere of physical, sensual delights), and *moksha* (liberation from the cycle of birth and death) all depend upon *artha* [material well-being] to flourish in a codependent fashion . . . Kautilya's claim concerns material dependence, not qualitative superiority." Even for K. J. Shah (1982), Kautilya does not negate, at least in theory, that *artha* has to be pursued in accordance with *dharma*.

8. "Dao" (or "The Way") denotes an absolute entity which is the source of the universe. However, cosmic Dao is not a transcendent source beyond the physical world; rather, it is something which is "always present" / "always emerging": as such, it is creative but is not a supreme creator God. Since it continually creates multiple things in manifest world, it gives birth to "complementary polarities" (*yin/yang*). Human beings—whose sociocultural presence is marked by artifice and restraints—can only strive to attune themselves to the mysterious fluctuations of cosmic Dao. It is said that the cosmic Dao is no special lover of humanity. For a study on how the Dao of inner saint and outer king are linked, see Shan (2012).

REFERENCES

Abbott, A. (2004). *Methods of Discovery: Heuristics for the Social Sciences*. New York: W. W. Norton.

Acharya, A., and Buzan, B., eds. (2009). *Non-Western International Relations Theory: Perspectives on and beyond Asia*. London: Routledge.

Al-Rodhan, (2015). "The 'Emotional' Amoral Egoism of States." http://www.themontreal review.com/2009/the-emotional-amoral-egoism-of-states.php

Ames, R. T. (1983). *The Art of Rulership: A Study in Ancient Chinese Political Thought*. Honolulu: University of Hawai'i Press.

Amstutz, M. R. (2018). *International Ethics: Concepts, Theories, and Cases in Global Politics*. London: Rowman and Littlefield.

Antunes, S. and Camisão, I. (2018). "Introducing Realism in International Relations Theory." https://www.e-ir.info/2018/02/27/introducing-realism-in-international-relations-theory/

Aron, R. (1966). *Peace and War: A Theory of International Relations*, trans. R. Howard and A. B. Fox. New York: Doubleday.

Ashley, R. (1987). "The Geopolitics of Geopolitical Space: Toward a Critical Social Theory of International Politics." *Alternatives* 12(4): 403–34.

Axford, B., Gulmez, D. B., and Gulmez, S. B. (2018). *Rethinking Ideology in the Age of Global Discontent: Bridging Divides*. London: Routledge.

Bellah, Robert N. (2011). *Religion in Human Evolution*. London: Harvard University Press.

Bhattacharya, R. (2011). *Studies on the Carvaka/Lokayata*. London: Anthem Press.

Boesche, R. (2003). *The First Great Political Realist: Kautilya and His Arthashastra*. Lanham, MD: Lexington Books.

Breslin, S., and Nesadurai, H. E. S. (2018). "Who Governs and How? Non-State Actors and Transnational Governance in Southeast Asia." *Journal of Contemporary Asia* 48(2): 187–203.

Brilmayer, L. (1999). "Realism Revisited: The Moral Priority of Means and Ends in Anarchy." *Nomos* 41: 192–215.

Bronkhorst, J. (1983). "God in Sāṃkhya." *Wiener Zeitschrift für die Kunde Sü-dasiens* 27(6): 149–64.

Buchanan, A. (2003). *Justice, Legitimacy, and Self-Determination: Moral Foundations for International Law*. Oxford: Oxford University Press.

Burke, A. (2004). "Just War or Ethical Peace? Moral Discourses of Strategic Violence after 9/11." *International Affairs* 80(2): 329–53.

Carr, E. H. (2001). *The Twenty Years' Crisis: An Introduction to the Study of International Relations*. New York: Palgrave.

Chande, M. B. (1998). *Kautilyan Arthasastra*. New Delhi: Atlantic.

Chandrasekaran, P. (2006). "Kautilya: Politics, Ethics and Statecraft." https://mpra.ub.uni-muenchen.de/9962/

Chemburkar, J. (1999). "Kautilya's Arthaśāstra and the Early Dharmasūtras: Some Observations on Rājadharmas." In *Perceptions on Kauṭilīya Arthaśāstra: In Commemoration of Prof. R.P. Kangle's Birth Centenary*, edited by K. P. Jog. Mumbai: Popular Prakashan.

Chen, X. (2016). "Positive Law and Natural Law: Han Feizi, Hobbes, and Habermas." *Journal of East West Thought* 1(6): 11–32.

Coady, C. A. J. (2008). *Messy Morality: The Challenge of Politics*. Oxford: Oxford University Press.

Conces, R. (2009). "Rethinking Realism (or Whatever) and the War on Terrorism in a Place Like the Balkans." *Theoria: A Journal of Social and Political Theory* 56(120): 81–124.

Craig, E. (1998). *Routledge Encyclopedia of Philosophy: Genealogy to Iqbal*. London: Routledge.

Deb, H. K. (1938). "The Kautilya Arthasastra on Forms of Government." *Indian Historical Quarterly* 14: 366–79.

Dewey, J. (1923). "Ethics and International Relations." https://www.foreignaffairs.com/articles/1923-03-15/ethics-and-international-relations

Dickstein, J. (2015). "Īśvara as He Is: Devotional Theism in the Pātañjala Yogaśāstra." MA thesis, University of Colorado. https://scholar.colorado.edu/cgi/viewcontent.cgi?article = 1037&context = rlst_gradetds

Eckersley, R. (2004). *The Green State: Rethinking Democracy and Sovereignty*. London: MIT Press.

Eisikovits, N. (2016). *A Theory of Truces*. New York: Palgrave Macmillan.

Flanagan, O., and Hu, J. (2011). "Han Fei Zi's Philosophical Psychology: Human Nature, Scarcity, and the Neo-Darwinian Consensus." *Journal of Chinese Philosophy* 38(2): 293–316.

Frankel, B., ed. (2013). *Realism: Restatements and Renewal*. London: Routledge.

Frei, C. (2001). *Frustration and Fulfillment: Hans J. Morgenthau—An Intellectual Biography*. Baton Rouge: Louisiana State University Press.

Ganeri, J. (2003). *Philosophy in Classical India: An Introduction and Analysis*. London: Routledge.

Garofalo, C. (2008). "Ethical Challenges in Global Governance." *Viešoji Politika IR Administravimas* 23: 16–22.

Goldin, P. (2013). *Dao Companion to the Philosophy of Han Fei*. London: Springer.

Graham, A. C. (1989). *Disputers of the Tao: Philosophical Argument in Ancient China*. La Salle, IL: Open Court.

Gray, S. (2014). "Reexamining Kautilya and Machiavelli: Flexibility and the Problem of Legitimacy in Brahmanical and Secular Realism." *Political Theory* 42(6): 635–57.

Graziani, R. (2015). "Monarch and Minister: Reflections on an Impossible Partnership in the Building of Absolute Monarchy in the Han Feizi." In *Ideology of Power and Power of Ideology in Early China*, edited by Y. Pines, P. R. Goldin, and M. Kern. Leiden: Brill.

Hansen, C. (2000). *A Daoist Theory of Chinese Thought: A Philosophical Interpretation*. Oxford: Oxford University Press.

Harries, O. (2005). "Morality and Foreign Policy." *Policy* 21(1): 24–29.

Held, V. (2011). "Morality, Care, and International Law." *Ethics & Global Politics* 4(3): 173–94.

Hom, A. R. (2018). "Truth and Power, Uncertainty and Catastrophe." In *Routledge Handbook of Ethics and International Relations*, edited by Brent J. Steele and Eric A. Heinze. London: Routledge.

Ivanhoe, P. J. (2011). "Hanfeizi and Moral Self-Cultivation." *Journal of Chinese Philosophy* 38(1): 31–45.

Iyer, S. (2000). "Religion and Economics of Fertility in South India." PhD thesis, University of Cambridge. https://doi.org/10.17863/CAM.16513

Jai, H. (1999). "Lokasamgraha in Kautilya." In *Perceptions on Kauṭilīya Arthaśāstra: In Commemoration of Prof. R.P. Kangle's Birth Centenary*, edited by K. P. Jog. Mumbai: Popular Prakashan.

Jolly, J. (1913). "Arthashastra und Dharmashastra." *Zeitschrift der Deutschen Morgenländischen Gesellschaft* 67: 49–69.

Joshi, R. V. (1987). "Lokāyata in Ancient India and China." *Annals of the Bhandarkar Oriental Research Institute* 68(1/4): 393–405.

Kangle, R. P. (1997). *The Kauṭilīya Arthaśāstra: A Study (Vol. 3)*. Delhi: Motilal Banarsidass.

Kapstein, E. B., and Rosenthal, H. (2009). *Ethics and International Relations.* Farnham: Ashgate.

Karpowicz, K., and Julian, W. (2018). "Political Realism in International Relations." https://plato.stanford.edu/entries/realism-intl-relations/

Kertzer, J. D., et al. (2014). "Moral Support: How Moral Values Shape Foreign Policy Attitudes." *Journal of Politics* 76(3): 825–40.

Kissane, D. (2013). "From Moral to Amoral." https://www.e-ir.info/2013/05/15/from-moral-to-amoral/

Kung, H. (1998). *A Global Ethic for Global Politics and Economics.* Oxford: Oxford University Press.

Larson, G. J. (1969). *Sāṃkhya: An Interpretation of Its History and Meaning.* Delhi: Motilal Banarsidass.

Legro, J. W., and Moravcsik, A. (1999). "Is Anybody Still a Realist?" *International Security* 24(2): 5–55.

Ling, L. H. M. (2017, November 22). "The Very Fact That You're Thinking Differently, Is Already an Action." Press Releases. Centre for Global Cooperation Research, University of Duisburg-Essen.

Loriaux, M. (1992). "Saint Augustine and the Realists: Skepticism, Psychology, and Moral Action in International Relations Thought." *International Studies Quarterly* 36(4): 401–20.

Lundborg, T. (2018). "The Ethics of Neorealism: Waltz and the Time of International Life." *European Journal of International Relations* 25(1): 229–49.

Mearsheimer, J. J. (2001). *The Tragedy of Great Power Politics.* New York: W. W. Norton.

Moody, P. R. (2008). "Rational Choice Analysis in Classical Chinese Political Thought: The 'Han Feizi.'" *Polity* 40(1): 95–119.

Morgenthau, H. J. (1962). *The Decline of Democratic Politics: Politics in the Twentieth Century,* Vol. 1. Chicago: University of Chicago Press.

Morgenthau, H. J. (1986). *Politics among Nations: The Struggle for Power and Peace* (6th ed., revised by K. W. Thompson). New York: A. A. Knopf (originally published in 1948).

Morkevičius, V. (2018). *Realist Ethics: Just War Traditions as Power Politics.* Cambridge: Cambridge University Press.

Nancy, J.-L. (2000). *Being Singular Plural.* Stanford, CA: Stanford University Press.

Niles, D. P. (2017). *Is God Christian? Christian Identity in Public Theology—An Asian Contribution.* Minneapolis: Fortress Press.

Olivelle, P. (1998). *The Early Upanisads: Annotated Text and Translation.* New York: Oxford University Press.

Olivelle, P. (2013). *King, Governance, and Law in Ancient India: Kautilya's Arthasastra.* New York: Oxford University Press.

Perrett, R. W. (1998). *Hindu Ethics: A Philosophical Study.* Honolulu: University of Hawai'i Press.

Perrett, R. W. (2007). "Sāmkhya-Yoga Ethics." In *Indian Ethics: Classical Traditions and Contemporary Challenges (Vol. 1),* edited by P. Bilimoria, J. Prabhu, and R. M. Sharma. Hampshire: Ashgate.

Pines, Y. (2016). 2016. "Social Engineering in Early China: The Ideology of the Shangjunshu (Book of Lord Shang) Revisited." *Oriens Extremus* 55: 1–37.

Pines, Y. (2018). "Legalism in Chinese Philosophy." https://plato.stanford.edu/cgi-bin/ency clopedia/archinfo.cgi?entry = chinese-legalism

Radhakrishnan, S., and Moore, C. A. (1967). *A Sourcebook in Indian Philosophy*. Princeton, NJ: Princeton University Press.

Rangarajan, L. N. (1992). *The Arthashastra*. New Delhi: Penguin Books.

Rösch, F. (2015). *Power, Knowledge, and Dissent in Morgenthau's Worldview*. New York: Palgrave Macmillan.

Sarkar, B. K. (1985). *The Positive Background of Hindu Sociology: Introduction to Hindu Positivism*. New Delhi: Motilal Banarsidass.

Scheuerman, W. E. (2009). *Hans Morgenthau: Realism and Beyond*. Cambridge: Polity Press.

Schneider, H. (2018). *An Introduction to Hanfei's Political Philosophy: The Way of the Ruler*. Newcastle: Cambridge Scholars.

Shah, K. J. (1982). "Of Artha and the Arthaśāstra." In *Way of Life: King, Householder, Renouncer: Essays in Honour of Louis Dumont*, edited by T. N. Madan. Delhi: Motilal Banarsidass.

Shahi, D. (2018). *Kautilya and Non-Western IR Theory*. Cham, Switz.: Palgrave Macmillan.

Shamasastry, R. (1915). *Kautilya's Arthashastra*. Bangalore: Government Press.

Shan, C. (2012). *Major Aspects of Chinese Religion and Philosophy: Dao of Inner Saint and Outer King*. Beijing: Springer.

Sharma, C. (2000). *A Critical Survey of Indian Philosophy*. Delhi: Motilal Banarsidass.

Sihag, B. S. (2004). "Kautilya on the Scope and Methodology of Accounting, Organizational Design and the Role of Ethics in Ancient India." *Accounting Historians Journal* 31(2): 125–48.

Sil, N. P. (1985). "Political Morality vs. Political Necessity: Kautilya and Machiavelli Revisited." *Journal of Asian History* 19(2): 101–42.

Thakkar, U. (1999). "Morality in Kautilya's Theory of Diplomacy." In *Perceptions on Kauṭilīya Arthaśāstra: In Commemoration of Prof. R.P. Kangle's Birth Centenary*, edited by K. P. Jog. Mumbai: Popular Prakashan.

Voina-Motoc, I. (1999). *Moral-Rule and Rule of Law in International Politics: Common Sense, Political Realism, Skepticism*. http://www.iwm.at/wp-content/uploads/jc-08–021.pdf

Vogelsang, K. (2016). "Getting the Terms Right: Political Realism, Politics, and the State in Ancient China." *Oriens Extremus: Journal of Language, Art and Culture of the Far East* 55: 39–71.

Waley, A. (1939). *Three Ways of Thought in Ancient China*. London: Allen and Unwin.

Walker, R. B. J. (1993). *Inside/Outside: International Relations as Political Theory*. Cambridge: Cambridge University Press.

Walt, S. M. (2010). *Realism and Security*. International Studies Association and Oxford University Press. https://doi.org/10.1093/acrefore/9780190846626.013.286

Waltz, K. (1979). *Theory of International Politics*. Boston: McGraw-Hill.

Watson, B. (1964). *Han Fei Tzu: Basic Writings*. New York: Columbia University Press.

Williams, M. (2005). *The Realist Tradition and the Limits of International Relations*. Cambridge: Cambridge University Press.

Winston, K. (2005). "The Internal Morality of Chinese Legalism." *Singapore Journal of Legal Studies*, 313–47.

Winternitz, M. (1923). "Kautilya and the Art of Politics in Ancient India." *Vishva Bharati Quarterly* 1(3): 265.

Wisnewski, J. J. (2010). *Understanding Torture*. Edinburgh: Edinburgh University Press.

Witzel, M. (2012). "The Leadership Philosophy of Han Fei." *Asia Pacific Business Review*, 18(4): 489–503.

Zelinski, D. (2003). Dōgen's Ceaseless Practice. In *Action Dharma: New Studies in Engaged Buddhism*, edited by Christopher S. Queen, Charles S. Prebish, and Damien Keown. London: Routledge.

Empire

The Particularity of Ancient China as an Empire

Zhou Fangyin

Empire is a Western discourse, but it is also used to analyze ancient China. However, ancient China is different from the empires of the Western world as they are commonly understood, and has its particularity. This is reflected not only in the internal organizational framework of ancient China but also in its relations with the outside world.

ANCIENT CHINA AS AN EMPIRE?

After the second half of the seventeenth century, in descriptions of China by Western scholars, it has gradually become a common phenomenon for them to call China an "empire." On the other hand, it was not until the late Qing Dynasty that the Chinese began to use the word "empire," and later on, the term "empire" was used by Chinese to address the Manchu Dynasty itself, resulting in the designator "Qing Empire."[1] On this basis, the use of "empire" has been accepted by more and more Chinese, resulting in the emergence of references to the Qin Empire, the Han Empire, the Tang Empire, and so on. There is a famous TV series called *The Great Qin Empire*, with a first season and three sequel seasons, totaling 126 episodes by 2019.

On the whole, empire is a rather vague concept that originated in the West. To a large extent, it is based on the practice of the Roman Empire. Although ancient China was a very powerful country in the Eastern world for a long period, the concept of empire was not very appropriate for analyzing the dynasties of ancient China. It is easy to mislead outsiders who do not have a comprehensive understanding of the history of ancient China. In the analysis of ancient Chinese history, it is not that the concept of "empire" cannot be used, but that great care should be taken, especially to distinguish the situation in ancient China, to avoid unnecessary misunderstandings.

When some people use the term "Chinese empire," they may simply use the term "empire" to refer to a huge and powerful country; that is, to some extent equating an empire with a great power or a regional hegemony. But empires are conceptually different from great powers and regional hegemonies. A great power mainly refers to the state of strength of a country. A country does not automatically become an empire just because its strength grows so that it surpasses other countries around it.

Doyle defines empire as "relationships of political control imposed by some political societies over the effective sovereignty of other political societies."[2] Of course, empires do not just mean high-handed political control over other political societies; they often can be grounded in legitimacy.[3] There are two basic important elements comprising the concept of empire. One element is the absorption of and rule over different nationalities and different political entities. This is true of the Roman Empire and the Mongolian Yuan Empire, among others. During the transition of the Ming and Qing dynasties, Westerners began to use empire to describe Manchu, an important factor being that the Qing Dynasty was established on the basis of Manchu rule over a large number of Han people.[4] A second basic element is the hierarchical relationship between the center and the periphery, where the center is not the geographical center but the political center. Empires involve the control of dominant political entities (often the center state) over other political entities (colonies, autonomous or semi-autonomous regions, other countries, etc.) and the formation of a hierarchical order between the two sides. The empire can interfere with the political entities under its rule in military, economic, foreign relations, and other aspects, and such interference is often accepted by the latter.

The establishment and maintenance of hierarchical order is an important part of imperial governance. Now, people gradually realize that hierarchy is a quite common phenomenon in international relations,[5] which has led some scholars today to believe that the United States is also an empire.[6] There is no doubt that ancient China established and maintained a hierarchical order in East Asia, and itself was also a very complex political entity. When people use the concept of empire in a broad sense, it is more or less acceptable to call ancient China an empire. But there is no doubt that China has some distinctive features.

THE CONCEPT OF GREAT UNIFICATION HAS LED TO THE FORMATION OF A POLICY ORIENTATION IN CHINA THAT EMPHASIZES THE INTERIOR OVER THE EXTERIOR

A rather unique aspect of the Chinese Empire, compared to many other empires in world history, is its continuity over the course of its long history. From the unification of China by the Qin Dynasty in 221 BC and the establishment of the Qin Empire until the late Qing Dynasty, the Chinese Empire has undergone several processes of disintegration and reconstruction. On a territory roughly comparable in size to Europe, China has not experienced an irreversible breakup and has always been able to reunify after a period of division. In this process, the concept of great unification played an important role.

In Chinese history, there has been a rich practice of realizing the great unification, which began in the Qin and Han periods, but the ideology of the great unification predates the political practice of the Qin and Han dynasties. The thinkers of the pre-Qin period used spatial concepts such as *Wufu* (five dresses) and *Sifang* (four directions) in an attempt to construct an ideal model of an inclusive, hierarchical, unified state.[7]

At the ideological level, the most important feature of the "Great Unification" is the "veneration of unification" and the pursuit of the political unification of the country and the stability of the political order. Since the Qin and Han dynasties, the completion of the task of unification has been an important quest of every ruler of a dynasty that considers itself orthodox in China, and it is also his responsibility to do so. Even during the period of great division between the Three Kingdoms and the North and South Dynasties, the separate regimes did not give up their quest for national unity. It can be said that the pursuit of great unification became an important "logic of appropriateness" for the rulers of the ancient Chinese dynasty,[8] which also constituted a basis for their legitimacy in maintaining domestic rule. "Great unification" is a political ideology that has had an important influence on political practice, but it has also influenced many aspects of political governance and political culture in ancient China.

Ancient China was a vast country with a diverse range of people living within its territorial boundaries and with a diverse culture. Such cultural differences often result in centrifugal forces within the state, a challenge that needs to be overcome in order to sustain a grand unified state. After gaining power, all the Chinese dynasties transcended cultural differences to a certain extent in order to achieve a greater level of homogeneous cultural identity, to consolidate the political identity of the people within their territory toward the state, and to maintain the stability of the dynasty. From this, we can see the "order complex" that has existed in traditional Chinese culture since the reign of the first emperor of the Qin Dynasty.[9]

The recurring practice of the great unification reinforced the idea of "Great Unification" in ancient Chinese society, making it a universal collective social consciousness, and even the Chinese minority regimes, once they were deeply influenced by Confucianism, and formed the Chinese identity, also developed a strong consciousness to maintain the unified regime. Since ancient China developed the strong ability of imperial governance based on the county system during the Qin and Han dynasties, it led to a number of great unification regimes in Chinese history to achieve national strength, social stability, economic prosperity, and popular tranquility. In other words, the well-being of the people is often associated with a stable unified regime and is rarely achieved through a separatist regime. In this way, the Chinese people's pursuit of great unification becomes a strong social consciousness. This was further reinforced by the promotion of the concept by the central government in Chinese history.

Wang Gengwu, a famous scholar, emphasized the uniqueness of the central empire of China, arguing that it was characterized by "historical unity," which is not applicable in other countries. Although China has been divided, the driving force behind all regimes has been to reunite the empire.[10]

For ancient China, the concept of great unification did not mean that a unified China would be bigger and better, and it did not translate into a highly expansionary foreign policy. What it actually pursued was the unification of the core area of Chinese civilization. In this light it is interesting that the Northern Song rulers, although they were aware of some relatively weak regimes in the southwest of the country that offered them room for expansion, did not show any obvious interest in absorbing them, but never forgot the Yanyun Sixteen Prefecture (*Yanyun shiliu zhou*) under the rule of Liao Dynasty and tried to reclaim the region through force, economic redemption, and so on. Because the Yanyun Sixteen Prefecture had both important national defense significance and very important cultural significance for the Central Plains dynasty, it was traditionally a very important part of the Central Plains region.

The existence of the great unification consciousness, to some extent, shaped the "logic of appropriateness" of the rulers of the Chinese Empire, which led them to be quite obsessed with the unification of the country. As a result, in ancient China, there was a situation in which emphasis was placed much more on the interior than the exterior.[11] It was considered more important to achieve the "cultivation of morality and peace" and maintain harmony, stability, and prosperity in the central part of the country than to annex foreign territory. As long as the Central Plains, as the main body of the empire, was stable, the fluctuation of borders did not hinder the integrity of the concept of "Tianxia" (All-Under-Heaven). In contrast, active border expansion was often not a matter of any urgency.[12]

Such a concept has also influenced the basic features of the Chinese-dominated international order in East Asia in what is known as the tribute system. On the whole, the tribute system is a kind of regional order arrangement with a low degree of compulsion, which is manifested in that, on the one hand, the degree of coercion within the scope of this order arrangement is very low, and there is not much substantive content.[13] On the other hand, China does not forcefully promote this order arrangement to the outside world. The extending logic of this order has two main aspects. The first is that "if remoter people are not submissive, all the influences of civil culture and virtue are to be cultivated to attract them to be so";[14] that is, to bring other countries into the order arrangement by increasing China's own attractiveness rather than by coercion. The second is based on the idea that "the king does not rule the barbarians, those who come do not reject, those who go do not pursue."[15] The international order established in East Asia under the leadership of China is also an order with a relatively low level of institutionalization. In the tribute order, there are not many specific mechanisms and arrangements in the political, economic, security, and other aspects, apart from very detailed rules on rituals and ceremonies. This is a very loose regional order in general.

THE RELATIONSHIP BETWEEN ANCIENT CHINA AND ITS NEIGHBORS

Ancient China did establish a hierarchical order in East Asia, which was called the tribute system by some scholars.[16] But this hierarchical order is different from many of the hierarchical orders that people see elsewhere. David Kang claims that East Asian international relations emphasized formal hierarchy among nations while allowing considerable informal equality, which contrasts with the Western tradition of international relations, which has consisted of formal equality between nation-states, but with substantial informal hierarchy.[17]

The hierarchical order in East Asia is more obvious in nominal inequality, but the exchange of material interests is more equal, and even there is often a clear preference for the interests of neighboring countries, that is, the so-called "giving more and getting less (*Houwang bolai*)." In particular, China usually does not exercise effective administrative control over its neighboring countries, does not collect taxes, does not control their armed forces, and has limited impact on their foreign relations. As a result, there was a phenomenon that Korea and Ryukyu paid tribute to both China and Japan. China's moderate foreign policy has been accompanied by a relatively low frequency of wars in the history of this region.

1. China is a strong force but is cautious in its use of force abroad

The ancient East Asian international system was a typical unipolar system in which China had a significant power advantage over its neighbors over the long term. In such a system, such opportunities were often present if ancient China attempted to expand into the periphery. But ancient China, without facing strong external constraints, was generally quite cautious in its use of external force.[18] For realists, this is to some extent a self-contradictory phenomenon. Because it is costly to maintain a large army, it seems wasteful not to use it for external conquest and colonization.

In its long historical process, ancient China did not show a strong tendency to colonize other places, and such an opportunity, at least in the process of Zheng He leading his huge fleet to sail the world, presented itself to China many times. If China had shown a colonial tendency in ancient times and exercised effective control over countries other than China, it would be more in line with the normal understanding of empire. This situation cannot be said to be completely absent in Chinese history—for example, the Mongolian Yuan Empire—but it is generally an exception rather than a norm.

Even when it was quite powerful, ancient China showed moderation or reluctance to focus on the operation of overseas territories. Its foreign relations have long been managed by the etiquette department. Relations between foreign countries and China are mainly reflected in regular tributes rather than in the search for treaties in favor of China's interests, or in efforts to strengthen control over the outside world.

Historically, the regional order in East Asia under the leadership of China is an order arrangement with great freedom and flexibility for neighboring countries. It is not a regional order arrangement that forcibly brings these countries together on the basis of China's power primacy. The interests, considerations, and behavioral logic behind this arrangement were clearly stated by Ban Gu:

> We should keep them outside not inside, to alienate them so as not to be close with them; we cannot administrate over the barbarians, and the edicts, decrees and our calendar cannot be applied to the barbarians; if the barbarian invades, we shall defend ourselves and punish them; if they leave away, we shall be prepared and defensive. If the barbarians desire to pay tribute to China and follow the customary rituals, their tribute shall be received properly, and we shall give unto them in return. We shall appease and bind them for the long time, and never lose our propriety. This is the customary way that has prevailed since ancient times, and the accepted way of handling the barbarian peoples.[19]

Zhu Yuanzhang, the founding emperor of the Ming Dynasty, expounded his basic idea of dealing with foreign relations in his *ancestral discipline* (*Zuxun lu*), to which he attached great importance and asked future emperors to follow strictly:

> All overseas countries, such as Annan, Zhancheng, Koryo, Siam, Ryukyu, the West, Dongyang and small southern countries, are confined to mountains and seas and are located in a remote place; the land is not enough to supply, and the people are not easy to govern. If they do not speculate to disturb our border, then they will be ominous. It will also be ominous for us if they do not cause trouble to China, and we easily send troops to crusade. I am afraid that future generations will rely on the prosperity and strength of China, be greedy for a moment's military merit, sent troops for no reason, and injure people's lives, we must bear in mind not to do that. But the northern barbarian tribes approach the northwest of China, which has always been a frontier problem in China. We must train our troops and be prepared for them.[20]

Zhu Yuanzhang, who participated in many wars as the founding emperor of the Ming Dynasty, was generally a realist rather than a pacifist. The basic idea of his foreign policy for the Ming Dynasty was to adopt a policy of military vigilance against the northwest Mongolian forces, which posed a great threat to China's security. However, for countries that did not threaten China's national security, he stressed the adoption of a pacifist policy and the inadmissibility of "easily sending troops to attack," let alone "sending troops to attack for no reason but to gain war credits."

Ban Gu's logic and Emperor Zhu Yuanzhang's admonition do not represent the whole of ancient China's foreign policy. Since the foreign policy of a great power must adapt to the international environment it faces, it requires inherent complexity, and can't be completely pacifist. However, the ideas and propositions put forward by them did exert great influence on ancient China, and similar policy thinking was rare, or at least not dominant, in the foreign policy of other major empires in the western world.

Although ancient China had obvious advantages in East Asia over a long period, it did not exist as an expansionary country for most of that time. China's territorial boundaries were far from being limited by external restrictions on its ability to expand abroad. In this respect, China's self-restraint (which, of course, has its rational basis) has played a significant role. Similar to Zhu Yuanzhang, many emperors in ancient China were alert to the drawbacks of the expansionist behavior of an empire. In this respect, Zhu Di, the Yongle emperor of the Ming Dynasty, was a rare exception.

Corresponding to ancient China's restraint in the use of force abroad is the perception of the low-level threat from neighboring countries, which is particularly reflected in the building up of military power in neighboring countries. Even with a powerful empire as a neighbor, the Joseon Dynasty during the Ming Dynasty maintained a military force that was only sufficient to maintain domestic security. According to Parker's statistics, the Joseon Dynasty maintained a force of only 10,000 combat-capable soldiers, the minimum required for internal security and policing.[21] Such a military commitment undoubtedly reflected the sense of security that the Joseon Dynasty had when it was a neighbor of Ming Dynasty China.

Although China has been generally moderate in its external relations (relative to its strength and the limited external constraints it faced), strength is undoubtedly an important and indispensable material basis that enables China to play a leading role in East Asia and to better realize its political intention.

2. The boundaries of China's great unification dynasty were largely defined by culture rather than by the capacity of its armed forces

For most of its history since the Qin and Han dynasties, China was more of a cultural empire than an empire based on military conquest. The relatively short-lived Mongolian Yuan Empire (which ruled the Central Plains for 98 years) may have been a notable exception in this regard. The Mongolian Yuan Empire also underwent a gradual process of Sinicization, and its external expansion declined rapidly as it established a stable regime in the Central Plains.

The Ming Dynasty was a powerful dynasty in ancient China, with a very strong army during the reign of Taiju Zhu Yuanzhang (1368–1398), the founder of the Ming Dynasty. Zhu Di, emperor Yongle of the Ming Dynasty (reigned from 1402 to 1424), made five northern expeditions to Mongolian Yuan. Zhu Di also built up a navy that was the most powerful in the world at the time, led by Zheng He.

But such a powerful dynasty, with no rival in its vicinity, was far less in size than the Han and Tang dynasties in past history. Nor did the Ming Dynasty make an aggressive effort to regain such a vast territory. An important reason is that the Ming Dynasty considered its territory to be sufficient to support its need for legitimacy as a grand unified regime. The founding emperor of the Ming Dynasty also deliberately cautioned his descendants not to use his country's power advantage easily for foreign military purposes. This, to some extent, reflects the identity of the ancient Chinese Empire as a cultural empire rather than an empire of force, although military power is essential to the maintenance of any huge empire.

Another typical example is the Northern Song Dynasty. The Northern Song Dynasty fought several wars with Liao in its early years and maintained peace with Liao for a hundred years after the Chanyuan Treaty (*Chanyuan zhi meng*). In the unified dynasties of China, the military strength of the Northern Song Dynasty was relatively weak in general, and it faced great military pressure from the Liao Dynasty to the north. But the centennial peace of Northern Song and Liao actually greatly relieved the pressure faced by the Northern Song.

The Northern Song had relatively good opportunities for expansion in the southwest at the beginning of the founding and for quite some time thereafter. In 960 AD, Zhao Kuangyin founded the Song Dynasty and then launched a unification war, and in 965, the Northern Song Dynasty sent its general, Wang Quanbin, to attack Later Shu state and unified Sichuan.[22] This also brought the Northern Song to the border with the Dali State in the southwest. As to how to deal with the relationship between the Northern Song and Dali, Wang Quanbin, the Northern Song general, hoped to take advantage of the victory to attack it. Zhao Kuangyin, the Northern Song Emperor, decided to adopt a policy of peaceful coexistence with the Dali regime in Yunnan in view of the military mutiny caused by the military difficulties in the border areas at the end of the Tang Dynasty,[23] and he used a jade axe (a paperweight) to draw a line along the area west of the Dadu River on the map, saying, "Beyond this line, it's not mine."[24] From this, the boundaries of the southwestern border of the Northern Song Dynasty were established. This decision of the Northern Song Dynasty was undoubtedly made out of political rationality, but strategic prudence and self-restraint were fully demonstrated in such rationality.

Song Gaozong (reigned 1127–1162) once commented on Zhao Kuangyin's policy:

> The barbarians are wild and cunning, this is their nature from ancient times. Because of being harassed by the southwest forces, the Tang Dynasty entered Sichuan several times to fight back. After Zhao Kuangyin, the founding emperor of Song Dynasty, sent troops to settle down, Song and Dali state took the Dadu River as the boundary. Since then, Dali state did not dare to harass the border areas. However, defensive officers and soldiers on the border need to have appropriate personnel.[25]

From here we can see that from the founding emperor of the Northern Song Dynasty and the emperors of the Song Dynasty adopted the policy of peaceful coexistence, especially not taking the initiative to attack neighboring countries in the southwest direction, which reflected a consistent strategic restraint. The Northern Song Dynasty did not hold a positive attitude toward establishing a closer hierarchical order with Dali state even in a peaceful way. From 965 AD to 1115 AD, the Northern Song Dynasty rejected Dali state's request for canonization as many as eleven times.[26] It was not until 1115 AD that the Song Dynasty finally agreed to the request of the State of Dali and formally established vassal relations. Even so, the relationship between the two sides remained very loose.

Judging from the long process of Chinese history, China has adopted a series of practices such as a policy of loose reins; the chieftain system; replacing local chiefdoms by the central government branches in some border areas; and setting up corresponding officials and institutions, which gradually formed a strong sense of belonging in these areas, and established effective governance of some border areas in the late dynasty of China.

It is worth noting that the practices of ancient Chinese dynasties differed significantly from the colonialism of Western countries. China's effective governance of frontier areas has evolved over a period of nearly a thousand years or more. Such a long period of time in itself shows that it was not a policy rationally designed by a particular government, and it shows that ancient China did not give high priority to external expansion and land annexation. China was not in a hurry to integrate the frontier regions with insufficient cultural centripetal force into its territory, but rather took a highly cautious and even somewhat rejectionist approach to the integration.

Another aspect of this is reflected in the fact that the Great Unification dynasties of ancient China (with the possible exception of the Mongolian Yuan) were often unwilling to bear the costs of ruling heterogeneous regions and cultures. In this regard, even the Manchu, which had a strong force, had been very cautious about using troops in the southeast.

3. Ancient China did not develop the idea of external colonization, nor did it act systematically

Whiles Western scholars tend to describe ancient China as an empire, it is easy to find the reverse—that ancient China has long had a significant power advantage in East Asia, and even in the broader geography, but has basically shown no tendency to colonize abroad. Otherwise, one would see an important colonial power in the east of the world. For the Ming Dynasty, which occupies an important position in Chinese history, it had a quite obvious military advantage over the surrounding countries most of the time. Such a dynasty, which lasted 276 years, did not carry out colonial acts in Asia.

One notable figure among the Ming emperors was Zhu Di or Emperor Yongle, known as the "Emperor on Horseback," who has also been cited by some scholars as an example of how ancient China was in fact a realist state.[27] However, Zhu Di was an obvious anomaly rather than a convention among the emperors of ancient China. In addition to several northern expeditions to Mongolian Yuan, Zhu Di also waged a war against Annan (part of today's Vietnam). Scholars engaged in international relations theory tend to subconsciously view this as a typical act of realism. However, there are quite a few inexplicable aspects of realism in Emperor Yongle's military operations toward Annan. The use of military force against Annan was the first large-scale military operation of Emperor Yongle's reign. It seems somewhat difficult to understand Emperor Yongle's large-scale military action against Annan without taking into account factors such as the ritual order, cultural perceptions, and so on, but mainly the realist concerns about the power distribution and sources of threat. The military advantage of the Ming Dynasty over Annan was unquestionable, but neither the previous Ming emperors nor the subsequent Ming emperors had shown any enthusiasm for using military force toward Annan, which was still true in the Qing Dynasty.

An important reason for Emperor Yongle to send his troops to attack Annan is that the state minister, Li, had arrogated power in Annan and abolished King Chen and installed his son as King of Annan. In the first year of Yongle, Annan sent a tribute envoy to the Ming Dynasty claiming that there was no one in the clan of the former king of Annan, and the current king of Annan was the grandson of the former king. Emperor Yongle suspected that there was deceit, and sent officers to investigate, but did not find out the truth, so under such circumstances, he crowned Hu Han Cang as King of Annan. But in the second year of Yongle, Chen Tianping, the younger brother of the former king of Annan, Chen Rifu, came to the capital of China and pleaded with Emperor Yongle to send troops to punish Li. In the fourth year of Yongle, Annan lured and killed Chen Tianping in the name of welcoming him back as king. This made Emperor Yongle so angry that he decided to use his army against Annan. This fact shows that Emperor Yongle had a strong motivation to maintain the stability of the tributary order through his military operation against Annan, and this military operation would not have taken place without the abolition of Annan's legitimate king. Moreover, if the Ming government was motivated by realism, then the Ming could have continued to fight south toward Champa Kingdom because Yongle's military operations had been very successful and Annan had quickly calmed down, but the Ming Dynasty did not do so.[28]

In addition, as early as the sixteenth and seventeenth centuries, a large number of Chinese from Fujian, Guangdong, Zhejiang, and other southeast coastal provinces went to Southeast Asia to do business and live there. By 1586, the Chinese population in Manila, Philippines, had reached 10,000. Despite repeated massacres by the Spaniards, the number of Chinese in the area continued to increase, and by 1750, the Chinese population had risen to 40,000.[29] During the Ming and Qing dynasties, a large number of Chinese went to Southeast Asia and gained influence there, but their behavior had little to do with the central government of the Ming and Qing dynasties. This would have been an ideal resource to exploit if ancient China had the colonial consciousness of modern Western countries.

In fact, for most of ancient China's history, China did not understand what colonization was, and it was not until after the Opium War, when China was reduced to a semi-colony, that some Chinese gradually gained a basic understanding of colonial policy. The earliest work by Chinese scholars on the phenomenon of colonization is *The Colonial Policy* (*Zhimin Zengce*, 1905) by Zhou Zhongzeng. The book begins by pointing out that colonial policy is the latest thinking in the West.[30] And at this point, 400 years after Columbus discovered the new continent, colonial policy was far from being the latest wave of thought in the West.

Knowledge of the colonial practices of Western countries led some Chinese intellectuals at the end of the Qing Dynasty and for some time afterwards to hope that China would also become a colonial power, such as can be found in a high school history textbook in the 1930s which argued that the failure of the previous dynasty to run the Nanyang Islands as a colony had been a great mistake. "In the past, we thought that we should not care about things in the distance, so that although there was such a good foundation, the state did not make efforts to help people to move forward; this is really a big mistake."[31] This aspiration of the intellectuals was somewhat anachronistic at the time, but their views reflected in another way the fact that China had not carried out effective colonial action in the past, despite its great power advantage and many opportunities.

CONCLUSION

Several dynasties in ancient China were considered by some scholars as "empires" because of their huge land area, great strength, internal ethnic diversity, and other factors. The historical Chinese Empire, however, was far different from empire in the Western sense. We should avoid using the concept of empire in the Western world to simply correspond to the dynasties of ancient China. A considerable number of Chinese do not see ancient China as an empire, but more as a great power in East Asia. While the fact that China once dominated the East Asian region as a great power for a long time may be analyzed as a model of empire, this model cannot simply be compared to the West.

Historically, China has long held primacy in East Asia, but it has not constructed a strict regional order in which it is the center and has a strong binding force on other countries in the system. China has generally shown restraint in its foreign policy, pursuing only limited foreign policy objectives in the region and, on that basis, has developed a mutually acceptable and stable relationship with neighboring countries in the course of interaction, which has given rise to the particularities of the historical East Asian order.

Ancient China was not an empire in the sense of maximizing power or maximizing security. An important feature of the Chinese Empire has been that when the security pressure of the international system was at a relatively low level, its special political culture, especially Confucianism, had a significant influence on its foreign policy: (1) compared with external expansion, the maintenance of the stability of internal order was obviously given higher priority; (2) foreign affairs were often in a secondary position in ancient China's unified dynasty, and in many cases they were not highly valued; (3) in terms of foreign policy, ancient China tended to be less proactive and more often responded to the problems and challenges posed by its neighbors, without adequate institutional design and arrangements, and without establishing treaty-based obligation relations with its neighbors; (4) although ancient China had a power advantage in East Asia or even across a larger region for a long time, it did not pursue a colonial policy in the periphery; and (5) while ancient China had had ample time to construct an institutionalized regional order in its favor, what does exist in the region is a rather loose order in which China has only very limited influence over other countries, an influence far less than would be expected of an empire in the Western sense.

From the perspective of comparing China and India, if we treat both ancient China and ancient India as empires, they not only have some similarities but also great differences. Their commonality is demonstrated by the fact that both China and India have a long history, occupy large geographical areas, have internal ethnic diversity, and have very complex cultural compositions. Moreover, there has been a clear opposition to war in the dominant culture of both, which contrasts sharply with the prevalence of force in some Western empires.[32] In addition, neither ancient China nor ancient India carried out a systematic colonization of foreign countries and neither showed a strong expansionary nature. On the whole, they all have the characteristics of cultural empires.

There are also some important differences between ancient China and ancient India, one important difference being that the recurring great unification dynasties were an important feature of ancient China, and although it went through some periods of division, ancient China was always able to achieve reunification under new dynasties. After the first great unification of Qin, there were several famous great unification regimes, such as Han, Tang, Yuan, Ming and Qing, among which, except for the Mongolian Yuan, all lasted more than 200 years. Ancient India, on the other hand, was divided for a much longer period of time, and did not exhibit the obvious historical cycle of "division—unification—division—unification" as China did. Such a state of unity and division also influenced the political culture of both sides—in ancient China, the idea of "great unification" had an important influence on dynastic politics, while in ancient India, similar ideas with important influence were not formed, and thus cannot play an important role in the political aggregation of ideas. In addition, China has played a greater role in shaping the regional order, not only establishing a tribute order in East Asia but also forming a Confucian cultural circle around China that has profoundly influenced regional order and behavior pattern in East Asia by providing institutional templates and exerting cultural appeal. In contrast, ancient India seems to have had much less influence on the regional order.

NOTES

1. Mark C. Elliott, "When We Talk about the 'Empire', What Do We Talk About: Discourse, Method and the Archaeology of an Idea (Dang women tan diguo shi, women tan xie shenme—huayu, fangfa yu gainian kaogu)," *Exploration and Free Views (Tansuo yu zhengmin)*, no. 6 (2018): 49–57.

2. Michael Doyle, *Empires* (Ithaca, NY: Cornell University Press, 1983), 19.

3. Barry Buzan and Richard Little, *International Systems in World History: Remaking the Study of International Relations* (Oxford: Oxford University Press, 2000), 176.

4. Mark C. Elliott, "Was Traditional China a Empire? (Chuantong zhongguo shi yige diguo ma?)," *Reader's Magazine (Dushu)*, no. 1 (2014): 29–40.

5. John M. Hobson and J. C. Sharman, "The Enduring Place of Hierarchy in World Politics: Tracing the Social Logic of Hierarchy and Political Change," *European Journal of International Relations* 11, no. 1 (2005): 63–98; David A. Lake, *Hierarchy in International Relations* (Ithaca, NY: Cornell University Press, 2009); T. V. Paul, Deborah Welch Larson, and William C. Wohlforth, eds., *Status in World Politics* (New York: Cambridge University Press, 2012); David C. Kang, "Hierarchy and Legitimacy in International Systems: The Tribute System in Early Modern East Asia," *Security Studies* 19 (2010): 591–622; Brantly Womack, "Asymmetry and China's Tributary System," *Chinese Journal of International Politics* 5, no. 1 (2012): 37–54; Sun Xuefeng, Liu Ruonan, and Ouyang Xiaomeng, "The Trend of American Unipolar System from the Perspective of Hierarchy (Dengji shijiao xia de meiguo danji tixi zouxiang)," *Foreign Affairs Review (Waijiao Pinglun)*, no. 2 (2015): 80–103.

6. Niall Ferguson, "America as Empire, Now and in the Future," *The National Interest*, July 23, 2008, https://nationalinterest.org/article/america-as-empire-now-and-in-the-future-2390; John J. Mearsheimer, "Imperial by Design," *The National Interest*, December 16, 2010, https://nationalinterest.org/article/imperial-by-design-4576; Christopher Layne and Bradley A. Thayer, *American Empire: A Debate* (New York: Taylor & Francis Group, 2007).

7. Bu Xianqun, "An Analysis of the Concept of Great Unification and National Governance in Chinese History (Tan woguo lishi shang de dayitong sixiang yu guojia zhili)," *Journal of Chinese Historical Studies (Zhongguo shi yanjiu)*, no. 2 (2018): 14–20.

8. As to "logic of appropriateness," see J. G. March and J. P. Olsen, "The New Institutionalism: Organizational Factors in Political Life," *American Political Science Review* 78, no. 3 (1984): 738–49; J. G. March and J. P. Olsen, "Institutional Perspective on Political Institutions," *Governance* 9, no. 3 (1996): 247–64.

9. Zhang Desheng, *Confucian Ethics and Social Order (Rujia lunli yu shehhui zhixu)* (Shanghai: Shanghai People's Publishing House, 2008), 110.

10. Wang Gungwu, *The Chinese Way: China's Position in International Relations* (Oslo: Scandinavian University Press, 1995), 52–53. Quoted from Zheng Yongnian, "Organizing China' s Inter-state Relations: From 'Tianxia' (All-Under-Heaven) to the International Order (Zhongguo guojia jian guanxi de goujian: cong 'tianxia' dao guoji zhixu)," *Journal of Asia-Pacific Studies (Dangdai Yatai)*, no. 5 (2009): 33–66.

11. Piao Zhijun, "On the Ideal and Practice of the concept of 'Zhongnei Qingwai' in the Northern Song Dynasty (Beisong shiqi 'zhong nei qing wai' guannian de lixiang yu xianshi lun)," *Studies on the History of Song Dynasty (Songshi yanjiu luncong)* (Beijing: Science Press, 2008), 22–41.

12. Sun Jianmin, *A Study of China's Border Governance Strategies through the Dynasties* (*Zhongguo lidai zhibian fanglue yanjiu*) (Beijing: Military Science Press, 2004), 85–86.

13. Davad Kang, "Getting Asia Wrong: The Need for New Analytical Frameworks," *International Security* 27, no. 4 (Spring 2003): 57–85; David Kang, *China Rising: Peace, Power, and Order in East Asia* (New York: Columbia University Press, 2007).

14. The Analects of Confucius, on politics.

15. As Su Shi said 900 years ago: "The barbarians cannot be ruled in the way of ruling China. If we seek its great governance, it will lead to great chaos. The former kings knew it, so their way of ruling them is not to rule them. To rule them in a way that does not rule is a profound way of ruling." See Su Shi, "The King Does Not Rule over the Barbarians (Wangzhe bu zhi yidi lun)," in Zhang Zhigang, Ma Defu, and Zhou Yukai, *The Complete Collection of Su Shi* (*Su Shi quanji jiao zhu*) (Shijiazhuang: Hebei People's Press, 2010), 84.

16. John K. Fairbank, ed., *The Chinese World Order: Traditional China's Foreign Relations* (Cambridge, MA: Harvard University Press, 1968).

17. David C. Kang, "Getting Asia Wrong: The Need for New Analytical Frameworks," *International Security* 27, no. 4 (2003): 57–85.

18. Meng Weizhan, "International Relations Theories and Applicability in the Study of Inter-state Relations of Ancient China (Guoji guanxi lilun zhi yu zhongguo gudai guojia jian guanxi yanjiu de shiyongxing wenti)," *Journal of Central South University* (*Zhongnan daxue xuebao / Social Science*) 18, no. 6 (2012): 22–31; Zhu Zhongbo and Zhou Yunheng, "China' s Strategic Culture of Peace: A Reassessment of Cultural Realism (Zhongguo zhanlue wenhua de hepingxing: wenhua xianshi zhuyi zaifansi)," *Journal of Contemporary Asia-Pacific Studies* (*Dangdai yatai*), no. 1 (2011): 36–51.

19. *Hanshu* (Chronicles of the Han Dynasty), Scroll 94, *Xiongnu zhuan*.

20. *Ancestral Discipline: Proverbs and Precepts* (*Zuxun lu: Jian jie*), in May of the sixth year of Hong Wu, quoted from Wan Ming, *A Draft of the History of Sino-Foreign Relations in the Ming Dynasty* (*Mingdai zhongwai guanxi shi lun gao*) (Beijing: China Social Sciences Press, 2011), 142.

21. Eugene Y. Park, "War and Peace in Premodern Korean: Institutional and Ideological Dimensions," in *The Military and Korean Society*, edited by Young-Key Kim-Renaud, R. Richard Grinker, and Kirk W. Larsen, Sigur Center Asia Papers (Washington, DC: George Washington University, 2006), 6.

22. "The History of Song, Ben Ji I (Song Shi, Ben Ji I)", and "The History of Song, Ben Ji II (Song Shi, Ben Ji II)."

23. At the end of the Tang Dynasty, Xuzhou troops were transferred to Guilin to defend the Nanzhao (Dali), which was scheduled for a three-year period, and was delayed for three years, triggering a mutiny. This mutiny was suppressed, but five years later, there was an uprising led by Huang Chao that eventually destroyed the Tang Dynasty. Thus, *The New Tang Book—The Southern Barbarians* (*Xin Tang Shu, Nanman zhuan*) commented: "The Tang was destroyed by Huang Chao, and the disaster was based on Guilin."

24. *Continuation of Zizhi Tongjian* (*Xu Zizhi Tongjian*), vol. 4, Song Ji IV. See also Taiwan Armed Forces University, *History of War in China* (*Zhongguo lidai zhanzheng shi*), vol. 11, Song, Liao, Jin, Xia (I) (Beijing: Citic Press, 2013), 139.

25. *Compile Manuscripts of Song Dynasty* (*Song huiyao jigao*), vol. 195, geographical area 21 (Beijing: Zhonghua Book Company, 1997), 7661.

26. Liu Yongsheng, "The Relationship between Two Song Dynasties and Dali Kingdom (Liangsong wangchao yu daliguo guanxi yanjiu)," *Journal of Social Science of Jiamusi University* (*Jiamusi daxue shehui kexue xuebao*) 24, no. 1 (2006): 80–82.

27. Yuan-kang Wang, *Harmony and War: Confucian Culture and Chinese Power Politics* (New York: Columbia University Press, 2011); Feng Zhang, *Chinese Hegemony: Grand Strategy and International Institutions in East Asian History* (Stanford, CA: Stanford University Press, 2015).

28. For the background of Emperor Yongle's military operation toward Annan, see Chao Zhongchen, *The Legend of Ming Chengzu* (*Ming Chengzu zuan*) (Beijing: People's Publishing House, 2008), 342–54.

29. Nicholas Tarling, ed., *The Cambridge History of Southeast Asia*, vol. 1, *From Early Times to c. 1800* (Cambridge: Cambridge University Press, 1993), 348–49.

30. Zhou Zhongzeng, *The Colonial Policy* (*Zhimin Zengce*) (Wuhan: Hubei Law and Politics Editorial Office, 1905), 1, quoted from Li Yongdong, "Colonized 'Empire' and the Colonial Will of Semi-Colony (Bei zhimin de 'diguo' yu ban zhimindi de zhimin yiyuan)," *Shandong Social Sciences* (*Shangdong shehui kexue*), no. 3 (2017): 17–23.

31. Lv Simian, "National History of Senior Middle School Textbooks (Gaoji zhongxue jiaokeshu: Benguo shi)," in Lv Simian, *Five Kinds of Primary and Middle School Textbooks by Lv Simian(I)* (*Lv zhu zhongxiaoxue jiaokeshu wu zhong*) (Shanghai Ancient Books Publishing House, 2011), 543, quoted in Li Yongdong, "Colonized 'Empire' and the Colonial Will of Semi-Colony."

32. About the features of the Indian Empire, see Upinder Singh, chapter 8, this volume.

Ideas of Empire in Ancient India in a Comparative Frame

Upinder Singh

This essay examines ideas of empire in ancient Indian thought, primarily during the period circa 600 BCE to 600 CE. This is done by analyzing the idea of the *cakravartin* (world victor) and the various other ways in which political paramountcy was understood and proclaimed in political ideology and practice. This allows a reflection on the military and moral aspects of rulership, the treatment of the violence involved in war, and the tension between imperium and renunciation. The various expressions of imperial ideals are discussed, including those in Jaina and Buddhist texts, the inscriptions of the Maurya emperor Aśoka, Hariṣeṇa's account of Samudragupta's conquests in the Allahabad pillar inscription, and Kālidāsa's description of the legendary king Raghu's triumphant "victory over the quarters." The last section of the paper compares ancient Indian and Chinese ideas of empire and rulership.

The emergence of the state in India dates to the Harappan civilization (ca. 2600–1900 BCE), but since the Harappan script has not yet been deciphered, details of political organization are not known. A framework of the dynastic history of north India emerges from the sixth/fifth century BCE, and this was swiftly followed by sophisticated intellectual inquiries into kingship and empire, especially concerning the issues of power and violence.[1]

Ancient Indian political discourse distinguished kings from emperors. The Sanskrit epics and Purāṇas distinguish the first righteous and consecrated king (Manu in one account and Pṛthu in another) from the first *cakravartin* (emperor), the legendary Bharata. In the *Mahābhārata* epic, the contest for power involves a terrible war among the Kauravas and Pāṇḍavas, who are descendants of Bharata. Jaina texts refer to Bharata as the first *cakravartin* of this era, but describe him as the son of the first Jaina *tīrthaṅkara* (saint) of the current era, Ṛṣabhanātha. When texts spoke of the emperor being victorious over the whole world, the geographical space that they had in mind was the Indian subcontinent, bounded by the

Himalaya mountains in the north and the oceans in the east and west; the northeastern and northwestern boundaries remained fuzzy.

The dichotomy between the civilized and barbarian formed an important backdrop to ideas of empire. The term Āryavarta (land of the *āryas*—the cultured, civilized people) was an expanding geocultural space, identified with sacrifice (*yajña*) and the Brahmanical social order of the four *varṇa*s (hereditary social classes). Āryavarta was often contrasted with the lands of the *mlecchas* (barbarians), an umbrella term for "Others" including foreigners and tribals.[2] Some barbarians are mentioned frequently by name. Thus, the *mlecchas* of the northwest include the Yavanas, Gāndhāras, Barbaras, Cīnas (we see an echo of the Qin here), Śakas, Tuṣāras, Kankas, Pahlavas, Madrakas, Ramaṭhas, and Kāmbojas.[3] The border between Āryavarta and *mleccha* country was a moving cultural and political one and there were *mlecchas* within Āryavarta as well. In the long run, *mleccha* groups were segregated as well as partially assimilated into the normative social order. For instance, while there are many pejorative references to the *yavanas* (the Greeks, also a generic term for "westerners"), they were eventually absorbed into the normative social order by being described as an example of the mixture of social classes (*varna-saṁkara*).

The Mauryas (ca. 324–187 BCE) are credited with creating the first virtually subcontinental empire in Indian history, although continuous or effective Maurya military and fiscal control over such a vast area is highly unlikely. But the *idea* of empire was much older. Early Vedic texts (composed during ca. 1500–1000 BCE) allude to extensive conquest and political paramountcy; the imperial idea is reflected in words such as *sāmrājya* (empire) and *samrāṭ* (emperor) and in elaborate Vedic sacrifices such as the *aśvamedha* (horse sacrifice) which celebrated imperial status.

Kings were distinguished from emperors. The five royal insignia are the white umbrella, fly-whisks, shoes, turban, and throne.[4] However, the symbol that emerged fairly early as a symbol of empire is the wheel (*cakra*). The *cakravartin* is an emperor, a great paramount king, universal victor, whose chariot wheels roll everywhere unimpeded, and who is victorious over the four quarters of the earth. The wheel is an important multivalent symbol with deep roots in the Indian cultural traditions. With a form that combines all-encompassing totality with motion, it is not an accident that it became a potent symbol which acquired a variety of important religious, moral, and political meanings.

The idea of the *cakravartin* is important in Brahmanical, Buddhist, and Jaina texts. In fact, it is Buddhism and Jainism—the religions of renunciation and non-violence—that engaged most intensely with the concept and made the *cakravartin* central to their discourse on ultimate power and ultimate values. Both traditions have the idea of the great man (*mahāpuruṣa* in Buddhism, *śalākāpuruṣa* in Jainism), who can be either a world victor (i.e., emperor) or world renouncer; both assert the superiority of the latter over the former. As we shall see, apart from the idea of the *cakravartin*, the idea of empire or paramountcy was also expressed in other ways as well.

THE CAKRAVARTIN IN JAINISM

The extant Jaina texts were compiled at a fairly late date and the *cakra* and *cakravartin* feature prominently in them. According to Śvetāmbara Jaina tradition,[5] the twenty-fourth Jaina *tīrthankara* Mahāvīra was initially conceived in the womb of a Brāhmaṇa woman named Devānandā. However, at the orders of the god Indra, the embryos in the wombs of Devānandā and the Kṣatriya (warrior class) queen Triśalā were exchanged, because great men, including *cakravartin*s and *arhat*s (those who had attained enlightenment), could not possibly be born in low, poor, or Brāhmaṇa families. In Jainism, the *arhat* is greater than the *cakravartin*.

The *cakravartin* is one of sixty-three *śalākāpuruṣa*s (excellent men).[6] Consistent with the emphasis in Jaina precepts and practice on extreme nonviolence, he is a great emperor who follows the wheel and brings the whole earth under his sway *without indulging in violence*. Several such emperors are described in the *Triṣaṣṭiśalākāpuruṣacaritra* and Jaina Purāṇas, which describe their victory over the four quarters in the manner of elaborate ceremonials. For instance, Bharata, the first *cakravartin* of this era, followed a wheel that appeared before him and proceeded to become victorious over the whole world. Before confronting each rival king, he performed a lay vow (the *pauṣadha-vrata*) in which he became a renunciant for a time and concentrated his mind on the guardian deity of the enemy kingdom. The enemies realized that it was futile to resist and submitted to him. No battle was fought, no blood spilt. But the greatness of Bharata is overshadowed by that of his younger brother Bāhubali, who realized the utter futility of political ambition and violence in the midst of a dramatic combat with his ambitious elder brother, and who gave up kingship to lead the life of a renunciant.

In the Jaina tradition, several great kings became *cakravartin*s and thereafter renounced kingship and attained perfection, some of them even becoming *tīrthankara*s.[7] The *cakravartin* Nami of Mithilā attained enlightenment while he was a ruler and renounced the world, leading to great consternation all around. The god Indra came before him and urged him to return to his palace, to be a true Kṣatriya warrior and king. But Nami resolutely refused. The sixteenth *tīrthankara* Śāntinātha too was once a *cakravartin*. Jaina texts connect the etymology of the name of the twenty-second *tīrthankara* Nemīnātha with the wheel (*nemi*, from the root *nam*, refers to the outer rim of a wheel). According to one account, the circumference of his body was like that of the *dharmacakra* (the wheel of *dharma*); according to another, before he was born, his mother saw a wheel made of black jewels.[8] Jaina texts refer to the fourteen jewels (*ratnas*) of the *cakravartin*. The fourteen jewels are the *cakra*, umbrella, sword, rod, cowrie, leather piece, gem, the nine treasures, general, steward, *purohita* (chaplain), carpenter, elephant, and horse.[9] A fifteenth jewel—the wife—was added to this list.

In Jaina sculpture, *tīrthaṅkaras* are often shown seated on a throne, flanked by symbols including fly-whisks and umbrellas, a blending of royal and religious imagery. The *dharmacakra* (wheel of *dharma*) can be seen on the base of Jina images from the first century CE onwards. From the fourth century, the wheel is flanked by a pair of bulls or deer. The *tīrthaṅkara* Śāntinātha is specifically associated with the wheel flanked by two antelopes.

THE CAKRAVARTIN IN THE BUDDHIST TRADITION

Although the *cakra* has a remote ancestry and an importance in the Jaina tradition, it is the Buddhist appropriation of the symbol to represent the world victor and world renouncer, and Aśoka's subsequent deployment of this symbol (discussed further on), that catapulted it to much greater prominence. The Buddhist tradition seems to have made the greatest investment in the idea of the *cakravartin*.

The *cakkavatti* (Pali of *cakravartin*) is central to Buddhist ideas of empire and true greatness. A great man can be recognized by thirty-two signs (*lakṣaṇa*s) on his body.[10] In early Buddhist texts, at any given time, there can be only one Buddha and one *cakkavatti* in the world, and both have their own wheel. The two wheels reflect an important division of labor and complement each other; they can also follow each other sequentially. In later hagiographies of Buddha Śākyamuni, his first sermon in the deer-park at Sarnath is known as the *dharmacakra-pravartana* ("the turning of the wheel of dharma") and the wheel figures prominently in sculptural depictions of this event.

In the Mahāparinibbāna Sutta (in the Dīgha Nikāya of the *Sutta Piṭaka*), as the Buddha lies on the threshold of death, his disciple Ānanda asks him repeatedly and anxiously about the funerary arrangements that should be made for him. The Buddha tells Ānanda that his post-cremation remains should be treated like those of a *cakkavatti*—they should be placed in a *stūpa* (funerary mound) built at the crossroads, and people who went there and made offerings of garlands, perfumes, or colored paste would be rewarded with enduring benefit and joy.[11] However, there was a significant difference between the funerary remains of great kings and enlightened beings: *stūpa*s, sometimes containing bodily relics of the Buddha or other famous monks, became places of cultic worship and pilgrimage. Relics came to be coveted, distributed, and redistributed across the Buddhist world and sometimes became objects of competition, contention, and conflict. Although there are frequent parallels between the *cakkavatti* and the Buddha in the Buddhist tradition, there is never any doubt about the Buddha's superiority. The *cakkavatti* implements the Buddha's *dhamma* (teaching) in his realm. *Dhamma* is the king of the *cakkavatti* king.

Early Buddhism associates the *cakkavatti* with the seven treasures (*ratanas*): the wheel, elephant, horse, jewel, woman, landed householder, and the counselor/adviser. The seven treasures of the *cakkavatti* are further correlated with the seven treasures of the *arhat*, which lead to enlightenment: mindfulness, discrimination of states, energy, rapture, tranquility, concentration, and equanimity.[12] While the emperor's power and authority are proclaimed through the seven treasures and ceremonial insignia, the enlightened one does not require any outer paraphernalia as advertisement.

In the Mahāsudassana Sutta and Cakkavatti Sīhanāda Sutta, the idea of the *cakkavatti* is combined with that of the *dhammiko dhammarāja*, the righteous king who follows the wheel and rules according to morality. In the Mahāsudassana Sutta, king Mahāsudassana sees a magnificent wheel treasure with a thousand spokes. As the wheel rolled in different directions, he followed it with his fourfold army. Wherever the wheel stopped, kings welcomed Mahāsudassana and invited him to rule over them. The king instructed his new subjects to refrain from taking life, taking what was not given, sexual misconduct, lying, consuming strong alcoholic drinks, and overeating. One by one, the other six treasures then appeared before Mahāsudassana. The king reached the heights of power but was eventually drawn towards a life of renunciation and compassion. The Cakkavatti Sīhanāda Sutta narrates what happens when a king does not follow the prescribed path and decides to think for himself.[13] King Dalhanemi had attained victory over the entire earth up to the oceans through *dhamma*, without the use of force; he possessed the seven treasures, foremost among which was the wheel. One day, he saw that the wheel treasure had slipped from its position. The king recognized this as a sign that he did not have much time to live, and handing the reins of power over to his son, he became a renouncer. Under his successors, whenever the wheel vanished, the ruler sought the advice of Dalhanemi; the latter told him to rule according to *dhamma* and the wheel treasure reappeared. However, the seventh ruler in line did not seek Dalhanemi's advice and ruled the people according to his own ideas. The results were disastrous—morality disappeared; there was evil and violence everywhere.[14] In both these accounts, the wheel appears before the king. It leads, he follows. It appears and disappears. It is beyond the king's control. The wheel is a premonition and portent. King and wheel are tied to teach other by an irresistible bond.

Unlike the early Buddhist texts which talk about a generic *cakkavatti/cakravartin*, later ones distinguish between different types of *cakravartins*. They describe the Maurya emperor Aśoka as a *cakravartin* who ruled over one of the four continents (*caturbhāga-cakravartin*) and one who wielded force (*bala-cakravartin*). In the Chinese translation of the *Aśokāvadāna*, he is called an iron-wheeled monarch who ruled over Jambudvīpa (an area that included the subcontinent). Vasubandhu's fourth/fifth century *Abhidharmakośa* correlates the material out of which the conqueror's wheel was made, the number of continents over which he ruled, and the method whereby he achieved his great victories.[15] The golden-wheeled *cakra-vartin* (*suvarṇa-cakravartin*) establishes his rule over four continents by simply going forth. The silver-wheeled one (*rūpya-cakravartin*) establishes his rule over three continents as a result of encounters with some petty kings. The copper-wheeled one (*tāmra-cakravartin*) establishes his rule over two continents after some resistance. The iron-wheeled one (*ayaś-cakravartin*) establishes his rule over one continent, namely Jambudvīpa, through the use of weapons, although no one is actually killed in the process. Other ideas about the *cakravartin* are found in the *Lotus Sutra*, which talks about a *caturdvīpaka-cakravartin* (a *cakravartin* who rules over the four continents), *bala-cakravartin*, and *maṇḍalin* (who rules over a small region).[16] The Buddhist tradition accepts that the king's force is compatible with *dharma*.

Although *cakravartin*s were incredibly powerful, they were not always wise or perfect. The Mandhātu Jataka highlights the dangers of the emperor's arrogance and lust for power.[17] Mandhātā was a great, powerful *cakravartin*. When he clenched his left fist and touched it with his right hand, seven kinds of jewels poured down. He ruled the earth for thousands of years but was dissatisfied. On hearing that heaven was a better place, he rolled the wheel of empire and traveled to the heaven of the four great kings, who invited him to rule over their domain. After a long time, Mandhātā was once again seized with dissatisfaction and longed to rule over a better place. On being told that the heaven of the thirty-three gods was more beautiful than this one, he rolled along the wheel of empire and headed toward it. The god Sakka (Indra) welcomed him and gave him half his kingdom. After millions of years of power-sharing, during which thirty-six Sakkas came and went, Mandhātā was again seized by a desire for greater power. He thought to himself that half of this heaven was not enough; he should kill Sakka and rule alone. These violent and greedy thoughts were his undoing. Mandhātā's power and life started ebbing, and because a human body cannot die in heaven, he fell earthward and landed in a park. There he breathed his last. The story of Mandhātā, the *cakra-vartin* with an insatiable lust for power, drives home the destructive potential of excessive ambition and arrogance.

The *cakra* and *cakravartin* were also represented visually. The wheel appears on third-century BCE Aśokan pillar capitals. In the post-Maurya period, it became a ubiquitous symbol of the Buddha's teaching at all Buddhist *stūpa*-monastery sites, where it occurs repeatedly and prominently in the sculptural program. At Nagarjunakonda (in Andhra Pradesh in South India), the wheel-based plan of some of the *stūpa*s (with varying number of spokes) reflects an interesting manifestation of the importance of the wheel in Buddhism.

The *cakkavatti* with his "treasures" is represented in relief sculptures at several early Buddhist sites such as Amaravati and Nagarjunakonda in South India. The scene often occurs in abridged form, showing some and not all seven "jewels." What is especially interesting is the fact that the *cakkavatti* is usually in a powerful stance, raising his fisted right hand, his left hand about to strike or having just struck that fist in order to release a shower of money and jewels. This reflects the ability of the great emperor to bestow enormous wealth on his subjects.

THE MAURYA EMPEROR AŚOKA

The military foundations of the Maurya empire were laid by Candragupta and his son and successor, Bindusāra, but the first two Maurya rulers have been eclipsed in fame by the third king, Aśoka (ca. 268–232 BCE). Aśoka boldly made *dhamma* (the Prakrit form of the Sanskrit *dharma*; meaning goodness, morality, or virtue) the cornerstone of his political agenda. He had his discourses on morality inscribed and reiterated on rocks and pillars in far-flung areas of the subcontinent, part of his massive propaganda project to make people good. Although Aśoka's *dhamma* was inspired by Buddhism, it carried his own individual stamp and the inscriptions (which frequently use the first person) clearly convey his ideas in his own words.

Aśoka is not described as a *cakravartin* in his inscriptions (he usually has the titles *devānaṁpiya*, "beloved of the gods," and *piyadasi*, "of gracious mein"), but he did not consider himself an ordinary king. As I have argued in my recent book, he had two ideas of empire—one political, the other moral, the latter encompassing the former.[18] His conception of his constituency extended to all living beings, including humans and animals. In making *dhamma* a central issue, Aśoka emphasized the moral foundations of royal authority and empire, connecting it with the good, merit, happiness, and heaven. He directly engaged with the problem of violence and conflict in the political and social spheres, emphasized nonviolence, and presented himself as not only a primary mediator but a prophet in the moral domain.

Aśoka's idea of empire explicitly condemned and rejected war. In major rock edict 13, war and military victory are described as undesirable and reprehensible. The message of this inscription is as follows: The king had fought a terrible war against the people of Kalinga (in eastern India), nine years after his consecration; this made him realize that war was deplorable because it caused incalculable, universal suffering. Action against rebellious forest people, however, was different from regular war and was justified. Aśoka replaced military victory with a new kind of victory called *dhamma-vijaya* ("victory through *dhamma*"), which consisted of propagating and inculcating virtue and goodness among people in his own political domain and those of neighboring kings. His welfare measures—such as the provision of medical treatment, the planting of herbs, trees, and roots for men and animals, and the digging of wells along roads—and his *dhamma*-propagation activities extended into the kingdoms of others. This clearly indicates that Aśoka thought his moral jurisdiction extended far beyond his political domain to the whole world.

Aśoka's imperial ideal was also expressed visually through the combination of epigraphic texts with carefully chosen sculptural motifs—the lion, elephant, bull, horse, lotus, and wheel. The most resplendent of his pillar capitals is the Sarnath capital, which was chosen as the symbol of the modern Indian republic. It consists of four lions sitting back to back on a circular abacus, which has an elephant, horse, humped bull, and lion carved in high relief. The abacus rests on an inverted lotus. The majestic, still repose of the four crowning lions contrasts with the animals moving clockwise on the abacus, separated from one another by wheels. The discovery of fragments of a wheel nearby suggests that the Sarnath lions may have once supported a wheel. The careful combination of sculptural motifs and written words created a unique expression of imperium.

THE IMPERIAL IDEAL IN OTHER SOURCES

The Sanskrit epics, the *Mahābhārata* and *Rāmāyaṇa*, too have the idea of a paramount king who combined extensive conquest with exceptional martial and moral qualities. Issues related to kingship and political paramountcy are central in the *Mahābhārata*. The text connects an old-world warrior ethic with new political concerns related to empire and governance and adds new religious elements to them. It combines a belief in the decrees of fate with an assertion of the importance of human effort. It combines the old Kṣatriya idea of the warrior who asks no questions and fights unto death, with a new age warrior who is assailed with questioning and doubt. While political paramountcy is an important concern in the *Mahābhārata*, the term *cakravartin* occurs only eleven times in the voluminous work.[19]

In the *Rāmāyaṇa* epic, great and powerful kings usually have the modest epithet *rājan*. Although Rāma is a great king and his rule is the ideal rule, he is not described as a *cakravartin*. This term occurs only once in the epic, where Rāma's father Daśaratha is described as having been born in a lineage of *cakravartins*.[20] But even though Rāma is not described as a *cakravartin*, it is clear that he is lord of the whole earth.

The earliest epigraphic reference to the *cakravartin* occurs in an inscription in the Hathigumpha cave on the Udayagiri cave in eastern India; it is that of king Khāravela, who ruled over Kaliṅga in Orissa in eastern India in the first century BCE. The inscription contains a reference to the king's expedition against Bharadhavasa (i.e., Bhāratavarṣa), which here refers to north India in general. An inscription in the nearby Manchapuri cave, recording a donation by the chief queen of Khāravela, seems to refer to Khāravela as the *cakavati* (that is, *cakravartin*) of Kaliṅga.[21] It can be noted that Khāravela was an ardent follower of Jainism, but his inscriptions boast about his various successful military campaigns.

The idea of empire is also found in Kauṭilya's *Arthaśāstra*, a sophisticated political treatise whose dates are debated (they range from the third century BCE to the second century CE). Kauṭilya's discussion of interstate relations is based on a context of multiple states, a "circle of kings" (*raja-maṇḍala*). Kauṭilya saw war as a natural part of political expansion, but advocated a careful cost-benefit analysis before initiating military confrontations. The word *cakravartin* occurs in only one place in the text, where the *cakravartī-kṣetra* ("field of the *cakravartin*") is described as the region between the Himalayas and the sea, one thousand *yojanas* across in extent.[22] But the idea of empire-building is present throughout the *Arthaśāstra*. It is reflected in the idea of the *vijigīṣu* (the king desirous of victory) aiming to become the hub of the "circle of kings" and the discussion of the strategies that he should adopt to attain his goals. The goal of political paramountcy is also implied in the idea that a king should aim at enjoying the earth without sharing it with any other ruler.[23]

The idea of the *cakravartin*, based on the chariot-wheel, suggests a land-based imperial ideal. A glance at ancient Indian political history indicates that wars were generally land-based affairs.[24] Given the enormously long subcontinental coastline, the essentially landlocked nature of the military aspirations of ancient Indian empires is noteworthy.

THE EMERGENCE OF A CLASSICAL INDIAN IDEA OF EMPIRE

While there were differences in perspectives across texts and traditions, in about the middle of the first millennium, we see the emergence of a "classical idea" of empire that held sway for many centuries and was expressed in inscriptions and texts. The concept of the *cakravartin* was not part of this. From the time of the imperial Guptas, that is, from the fourth century CE, three titles came to signify political paramountcy—*mahārājādhirāja* ("great king of kings"), *parama-bhaṭṭāraka* ("supreme lord"), and *parameśvara* ("supreme lord"). Political paramountcy and empire-building were also proclaimed through the performance of sacrifices such as the *aśvamedha* (horse sacrifice).

The idea of a hierarchy of kings with a paramount king at the apex, his many subordinate kings bowing their bejeweled heads before his feet, was described eloquently by poets. Poets vied with each other to describe the military invincibility and great fame of paramount kings in royal inscriptions. Imperial power was also expressed through analogy with the gods in inscriptions and art. Although kings were not deified, they were associated with the gods in order to exalt their status, often through double entendre, for instance in the Gupta-period relief sculpture of Varāha (the boar incarnation of the god Viṣṇu) in the Udayagiri cave in central India.

The most important way in which a ruler put forward his claim to political paramountcy was through a detailed listing of military victories in his *praśastis* (epigraphic panegyric). The Allahabad pillar inscription, a eulogy of the Gupta emperor Samudragupta (ca. 350–370) composed by a high-ranking official and military commander named Hariṣeṇa, is an important inscription in this respect. It describes the Gupta empire as the hub of a political network which had different kinds of political control over and relationships with other states—direct annexation, defeated rulers, feudatories, and those who acknowledged his suzerainty.[25] The military career of the emperor is presented in detail and presented as a *digvijaya* ("victory over the quarters"), but the violence of war is aestheticized through the use of poetic language. Further, the vigorous descriptions of the emperor's military accomplishments are regularly punctuated and tempered by references to his nonmartial qualities and achievements, including to his benevolence, learning, and musical accomplishments.

Another important work of the mid-first millennium is Kālidāsa's *Raghuvaṁśa* (fourth/fifth century CE), a highly influential work of political poetry which deals both with the ideals and realities of kingship and empire. The long poem contains a very specific and detailed mapping of the subcontinent as a politico-geographical space which is encompassed by king Raghu's conquest of the quarters (*digvijaya*). Kālidāsa's description of the *digvijaya* is a carefully constructed clockwise circumambulation of the subcontinent.[26] Raghu's victorious march spans the entire subcontinent extending from the Indus valley and Himālayas in the north to Assam in the east, ocean to ocean. The description is accompanied by references to the landscape, trees, flowers, and produce of the various regions. It is a masterful geopolitical mapping of the subcontinent, marked by great poetic beauty and elegance. By and large, Kālidāsa avoids graphic descriptions of the violence of war in favor of abstract aestheticized descriptions of adversaries who are overwhelmed and submit to Raghu; those who are uprooted; others who are uprooted and reinstated; and still others who offer presents, tribute, and obeisance.[27] War is idealized and aestheticized; its mundane objectives and its violence are almost completely erased. The idea of empire and sovereignty reflected in the *Raghuvaṁśa* does not involve annexation; it involves the decisive demonstration of military superiority by the great victor and the acceptance of this superiority by defeated kings.[28] The emperor is victorious over the "world" without conquering it.

Notwithstanding the importance of victories in battle, Kālidāsa makes it clear that great kings do not seek political paramountcy for the sake of land or riches but for the sake of fame. After his conquest of the quarters, Raghu performs a grand sacrifice in which he uses up all the wealth he had obtained in his wars—the sacrifice is called the *viśvajit* ("victory over the world"). He then hands over the reins of power to his son, and goes off to the forest, where he lives out the rest of his life performing yoga and meditation, realizing the ultimate reality before he dies. For Kālidāsa, the great king is a sage king (*rājarṣi*) possessed of discipline and self-control (*vinaya*); the greatest kings are renouncers.

While the idea of renunciation as part of the imperial ideal was not universally accepted, the idea that empire consisted of victory and not conquest, that it should involve reinstating defeated kings who acknowledged the emperor's paramountcy, became part of what can be described as the "classical Indian" notion of empire.

The idea of empire in ancient India essentially visualized a multistate system where one king succeeded in establishing his suzerainty over a series of others, without necessarily displacing them or annexing their territory. Further, this idea of empire coexisted with a recognition of tribal, regional, and subregional identities. In fact, regional geocultural terms (e.g., Tamilakam, Kaliṅga, Āndhra, Kosala, Mahākosala, etc.) are mentioned very often in ancient texts and inscriptions. It can be argued that notwithstanding the existence of the idea of a subcontinental empire, it was the aggrandizing regional kingdom that was the more frequent historical phenomenon and formed the more frequently invoked model of political success.

COMPARING IDEAS OF EMPIRE AND RULERSHIP IN ANCIENT INDIA AND ANCIENT CHINA

There is an interesting similarity between the imperial acts of the third-century BCE Maurya emperor Aśoka and the first Qin emperor: both toured the land and set up stone pillars proclaiming their achievements.[29] As in India, in ancient China too, political discourse was variegated and changed over time (in China, it included Confucian, Daoist, Legalist, and neo-Confucian thought).[30] In both India and China, the dominant political discourse was pro-monarchy. There was a conceptual dichotomy between the civilized and barbarian (*yi, man* in China); the onward march of empire was marked by conflict and a partial absorption of groups that were initially considered outsiders or barbarians. The idea of empire was important in both India and China. A difference is that in India, it is the ideology of kingship that is emphasized, while in China it is the ideology of empire. Many an ancient Indian text states that if there were no kings, chaos and violence would prevail. In China, it is the absence of the emperor that leads to chaos. The position of the paramount king in ancient India was exalted, but not as exalted as that of the emperor in China.

There are some similarities between the ideas of the ideal ruler, for instance, in their qualities of impartiality and self-control. The Indian idea of the sage-like king (*rājaṛṣi*) may perhaps be compared with that of the emperor as a superhuman sage (*sheng*). But the idea that the ideal ruler should be inactive (found in China) is absent in India, where the prowess, energy, and vigorous activity of the great king are emphasized. In India, kings and emperors were compared with the gods, but they were not considered sacred. The position of the emperor in China was qualitatively different.[31] In India, the idea of kingship and empire constantly intersected with the ideas of renunciation and nonviolence, and there was a continuing tension between engaging with the world and turning one's back on it.

The ideas of *Tianxia* (All-under-Heaven) and *Dayitong* ("great unification") are central to ancient Chinese political discourse, and these are only partially comparable with the idea of the *cakravartin's digvijaya*. What is emphasized in India is political paramountcy among a hierarchy of rulers rather than political unification. An ancient Indian emperor did not have to eliminate other kings; he had to get them to acknowledge his paramountcy. Further, the idea of empire coexisted with the idea of expansionist regional kingdoms. In China, a multistate order was not considered sustainable or legitimate; in India, it was the considered the norm. According to Yuri Pines, the ideology of *Dayitong* had great impact on political developments over two millennia, facilitated by the politically and culturally influential role of the literati (*shi*).[32]

In India, the dissemination of the ideas of the political theorists was more diffuse and indirect, and their impact on political culture more difficult to assess. Brāhmaṇas in royal courts, who crafted royal panegyrics and advised kings, obviously exerted influence and were responsible for the emergence of certain pan-Indian elements in royal ideology, but they lacked the kind of collective identity or defined roles of the Chinese literati. In ancient China, the literati and bureaucracy seem to have been both facilitators as well as checks to the power of the ruler. In India, there was no system of institutional checks and balances.

The people/subjects (*prajā*) are important in some of the ancient Indian theories of the origins of kingship and ensuring their well-being and prosperity is considered as part of the *dharma* (duty) of the king. Kauṭilya's enumeration of the elements of the state includes *janapada* (people and territory). His great achievement is to demonstrate through cold calculating logic that it is in the interest of the king to ensure the welfare and prosperity of the people. In Chinese political thought too, people figure as the foundations of the polity and there is a connection between political legitimacy and ensuring the well-being of the people.[33] However, the idea of *yung-chung* ("using the people") was understood in radically different ways. While the Legalists had the idea of the ruler using/manipulating the people to serve his own interests, the second-century BCE "Art of Rulership" chapter of the *Huai Nan Tzu*, which has a strong Daoist influence, considers the state harnessing the talent and abilities of the people as an end in itself. This is how the emperor could attain the state of *wu-wei*.[34]

The discourse of the ideal ruler could be used to exalt the ruler but also to highlight his inadequacies. In China, the idea of the True Monarch and the self-image of the literati as being above the ruler permitted a critique of bad rulers, and sometimes rather outspoken criticism.[35] Ancient Indian texts mention many kings who did not live up to the ideals of kingship and who met a bad end. In both cases, the aim was not to incite rebellion or regicide, but to warn rulers. This can be extended to comparing the attitude towards righteous rebellion. The *Arthaśāstra* has the idea of popular rebellion (*prakṛti-kopa*), the anger of the people. The *Mahābhārata* states that a cruel king who does not protect his people, who robs them in the name of levying taxes, should be killed by his subjects, as though he were a mad dog.[36] But while there were intra-elite contests for power, military coups, and rebellions by powerful landholders, there is no documented large-scale popular or peasant rebellion in ancient India. In contrast, Chinese history has a large number of small-scale and large-scale "popular rebellions" and civil wars, which sometimes resulted in dynastic change. The idea of righteous rebellion percolated down; it was cited by rebels; the role of the literati, who sometimes joined in and offered support to the rebels, was no doubt important in this.[37]

Violence of various kinds is woven into the political histories of India and China. The conflict between imperial ideology and nomadic traditions in China can only partially be compared with the conflict between the state and the forest tribes in ancient India.[38] This is because in China, on certain occasions, the nomads succeeded in taking over the empire, even if they were ultimately assimilated. In India, tribal chieftains often metamorphosed into kings, but never succeeded in overthrowing the great kingdoms or empires.

Another difference is the ceremonial, performative aspect of the conduct of interstate (including foreign) relations. In ancient India, a ruler's position of paramountcy was established through subordinate kings entering into matrimonial alliances, offering gifts and tribute, and acknowledging his overlordship in their official pronouncements. But the level, scale, and outreach of ceremonial and gift exchange of the Chinese tributary system was not present in India.

Indian political thought displays a constant engagement with the problem of distinguishing necessary coercive force from violence, and a constant awareness that the desirability of nonviolence was countered (if not cancelled) by the need for kings to use violence in order to rule. This was especially discussed in the context of the king's punishment and war. There is a similarity in Kauṭilya and Sunzi's recognition that war should be a last resort and that the costs of war must be carefully weighed against its likely outcome and benefit. There are some similarities in Indian and Chinese political and military traditions, for instance in the importance attached to chivalry and to military and matrimonial alliances. There is the idea of righteous warfare—war against those who had acted against the Way of Heaven in China; and against *dharma* in the Indian case. But there are also several striking differences—the written covenants, elaborate war rituals and ritual pronouncements, and regular hostage exchange that are part of Chinese warfare[39] are absent in ancient India.

One of the biggest contrasts is how war featured in political ideology. Bloody warfare was endemic in both ancient India and ancient China, but the treatment of war in political discourse was strikingly different. In China, there were different ways of thinking about war and peace, including that of the Mohists who advocated complete disarmament. As we have already seen, in mainstream political thought, the consensus was that it was only unification under a single ruler who united All-under-Heaven that could be the basis of enduring peace and order.

After the Qin unification, during the Han period, the Confucian literati down-played the importance of warfare and put forward the idea that it was virtue (*de*), and not military prowess, that had led to the Han success. The idea of the inauspicious (*xiong*) nature of warfare and it being seen as a way of exorcizing the impure or polluted emerged in Han times and lived on in later centuries. The purification of the ruler before issuing weapons to his troops was connected with the idea of the inauspicious nature of war.[40] For these reasons, war and military victories—although sought by all rulers—were not to be advertised or glorified.[41] Indian monarchs—except Aśoka—advertised and celebrated their martial victories, even though war was aestheticized and military accomplishments balanced with irenic virtues. In both ancient India and China, however, the attempt was the same—to erase the violence involved in ruling and in political expansion.

A comparison between the ideologies of empire in ancient India and China thus reveals some affinities, but many more differences, which may possibly have relevance for understanding how these countries see themselves as part of the contemporary world.

NOTES

1. I have discussed these in detail in my book, *Political Violence in Ancient India* (Cambridge MA: Harvard University Press, 2017). State formation in South India began a few centuries later.

2. Aloka Parasher, *Mlecchas in Early India: A Study in Attitudes towards Outsiders Up to AD 600* (New Delhi: MunshiramManoharlal, 1991). The term occurs in the *Śatapatha Brāhmaṇa*, but comes into frequent use only in post-Vedic texts.

3. Parasher, *Mlecchas in Early India*, 250.

4. Variations of the list sometimes include the sword.

5. The Jainas are divided into two sects—the Digambara ("sky-clad" tradition of naked ascetics) and Śvetāmbara ("white-clothed" ascetics); both have their respective monastic orders and lay following.

6. These comprise five types of men— 24 Jinas, 12 Cakravartins, 9 Baladevas, 9 Vāsudevas (also known as Ardha-cakravartins, "half-*cakravartins*"), and 9 Prativāsudevas.

7. These are listed in the *Uttarādhyāyana Sutra* and the Jaina Purāṇas.

8. Helen M. Johnson, trans., *Triṣaṣṭiśalākāpuruṣacaritra*, vol. 1, *Adīśvaracaritra* (Baroda: Oriental Institute, 1931), 261.

9. The nine treasures (*nidhi*) of the *cakravartin* are the following figures: Naisarga, Pāṇḍuka, Piṅgala, Sarvaratnaka, Mahāpadma, Kāla, Mahākāla, Māṇava, and Śaṅkhaka (Johnson, trans., *Triṣaṣṭiśalākāpuruṣacaritra*, vol. 1, 252).

10. The Lakkhana Sutta lists the thirty-two signs. They include long earlobes, long arms, a protuberance on top of the head, and webbed hands and feet. The idea of the physical markers of greatness is there in Jainism as well, in a more elaborately developed form. For instance, the thirty-four *atiśaya*s (eminences) of a *kevalin* (one who has attained knowledge but is not fully liberated from *karma*) include that his breath is as fragrant as the lotus; he is always accompanied by a pleasant breeze and good weather; his teaching is immediately comprehended by listeners in their language; and the following do not exist in his proximity—disease, enmity, seasonal calamities, epidemics, excessive rain, drought, famine, fear of rulers, and enemies.

11. E. M. Hare, trans., *The Book of the Gradual Sayings (AṅguttaraNikāya) or More-Numbered suttas*, vol. 3 (Oxford: Pali Text Society, [1934] 2001), 264.

12. Bhikkhu Bodhi, *The Connected Discourses of the Buddha: A Translation of the SaṁyuttaNikāya* (Boston: Wisdom, 2000), 1594–95.

13. Bodhi, *Connected Discourses of the Buddha*, 395–405.

14. In the future, *dhamma* would be restored under the future king Sankha, who would renounce the world under the tutelage of Metteyya Buddha.

15. John Strong, *The Legend of King Aśoka* (Princeton, NJ: Princeton University Press, 2016), 50–54.

16. The four continents are Uttarakuru in the north, Jambudvīpa in the south, Pūrvavideha in the east, and Apara Godāniya in the west.

17. E. B. Cowell, ed., *The Jātaka*, vol. 3, Jataka no. 258, pp. 216–18.

18. Upinder Singh, *Political Violence in Ancient India*, 267–72.

19. *Cakravartin* occurs in *Mahābhārata* 1.67.29; 1.69.47; 3.88.7; 3.107.1; 3.188.91; 5.114.4; 6.110.10; 12.27.10; 13.75.26; 13.151.42; 14.4.23. Paramountcy is more usually indicated by terms such as *samrājya* (empire) and *samrāṭ* (emperor).

20. *Ram.* 5.29.2. Apart from this, there is one reference each to other imperial epithets, *samrāṭ* and *sārvabhauma*; John L. Bockington, *Righteous Rāma: The Evolution of an Epic* (New Delhi: Oxford University Press, 1984), 125.

21. R. D. Banerji, "Inscriptions in the Udayagiri and Khandagiri Caves," *Epigraphia Indica* 13 (1915–1916): 158–60.

22. *Arthaśāstra* 9.1.18. A *yojana* is usually taken to be equivalent to nine miles. This would be a little over nine thousand, which is much more than the actual breadth of the subcontinent.

23. *Arthaśāstra* 1.5.17.

24. There is debate over whether or not the early kingdoms and empires of India had a navy. The *Arthaśāstra* does not mention a navy, but Megasthenes does. Perhaps the Greeks were projecting onto India something that they were very familiar with in their part of the world. Although we encounter allusions to navies and sea battles in a few inscriptions, most of them belong to the post–600 CE period. Hero stones in the Goa area on the western coast depict sea battles, and some of the Ajanta murals show fleets of ships, but the overall evidence of naval warfare is not very strong. The Gupta emperor Samudragupta claimed victory over the island of Siṁhala (Sri Lanka) "and all the other islands." Many centuries later, in the eleventh century, Rājendra Coḷa is said to have launched a naval attack on the kingdom of Śrīvijaya, a polity based on the island of Sumatra.

25. This includes Sri Lanka and "all the other islands," which, we are told, acknowledged Samudragupta's suzerainty.

26. The act of circumambulation is also a central religious act in Indian religions.

27. It has been suggested that Kālidāsa modeled his account of Raghu's *digvijaya* on Hariṣeṇa's description of Samudragupta's victories. There are some similarities, but also several differences.

28. See Singh, *Political Violence in Ancient India*, 353–57.

29. Yuri Pines, *The Everlasting Empire: The Political Culture of Ancient China and Its Imperial Legacy* (Princeton, NJ: Princeton University Press, 2012), 20–21.

30. "India" and "China" are being used as a shorthand for the sake of convenience, with an awareness that the idea of the nation-state with fixed territorial boundaries is a modern one and that these cannot be simplistically projected onto ancient times. Similarly, a comparison between "Indian" and "Chinese" thought should not amount to essentializing that thought or to ignore the elements of internal diversity and change.

31. Pines, *Everlasting Empire*, 45, 51.

32. Pines, *Everlasting Empire*, 41–42.

33. Pines, *Everlasting Empire*, 134.

34. Roger T. Ames, "'The Art of Rulership' Chapter of the Huai Nan Tzu: A Practicable Taosim," *Journal of Chinese Philosophy* 8 (1981): 225–44; Roger T. Ames, "Wu-wei in 'The Art of Rulership'

Chapter of Huai Nan Tzu: Its Sources and Philosophical Orientation," *Philosophy East and West* 31, no. 2 (April 1981): 183–213.

35. Pines, *Everlasting Empire*, 50, 83, 149.

36. *Mahabharata* 13.60.19–20.

37. Pines, *Everlasting Empire*, 139–40, 160.

38. On the complex relationship between the state and the forest in ancient India, see Singh, *Political Violence in Ancient India*, chap. 5.

39. Robin D. S. Yates, "Making War and Making Peace in Early China," in *War and Peace in the Ancient World*, ed. Kurt Rafflaub (Oxford: Blackwell, 2007), 34–52.

40. Yates, "Making War and Making Peace," 41.

41. Robin D. S. Yates, "Early China," in *War and Society in the Ancient and Medieval Worlds: Asia, the Mediterranean, Europe, and Mesoamerica*, ed. Kurt Rafflaub and Nathan Rosenstein (Center for Hellenic Studies Colloquia 3, Washington, DC: Center for Hellenic Studies; Cambridge, MA: Harvard University Press, 1999), 35–36.

Just War

9

The *Mahābhārata*, Mencius, and the Modern World

Reflections on Dharmayuddha *and* Ānṛśaṃsya

Kanad Sinha

1

Undeniably, we were on God's side in World War II and the Cold War.
But were we ourselves without sin in those just struggles?
—PAT BUCHANAN

I remember coming across the quoted statement of the conservative American politician Pat Buchanan while browsing through the attention-seeking quotes of several American politicians before the last presidential election in the United States. The statement is both intriguing and disturbing. On one hand, it shows how even an ardent conservative has self-doubt despite a self-righteous confidence of being on the right side of a war. However, it also shows how, even after having doubts about one's own methods and actions, one can claim to be on "God's side," with a confidence that the "other side" (here the fascists and the communists respectively) is necessarily the evil/demonic. Buchanan is no colossus in the political history of mankind, but the tendencies inherent in the statement contain implications much wider than Buchanan's political agenda. It leads us to some questions pondered over by thinkers of different civilizations over centuries, concerning the issue of "just war." Is war justified in any time? Is pacifism a sign of weakness or of moral superiority? Should one fight for a just cause or avoid war by all means? How does one decide if one is necessarily on the right side? Even if a side proves to be morally superior, are they necessarily perfect and right in all their steps? What if one resorts to unfair means to assure a fair end (the victory of the "right" side)?

189

In ancient India, the text that engaged most closely with all these questions is the *Mahābhārata*. The text revolves around a family feud that turns into a bloody catastrophic war, known as the Bhārata War / Kurukṣetra War, which is traditionally described as a *dharmayuddha* (just war / righteous war). The word *dharma-yuddha* can have several connotations. It may mean a war fought for the right cause (establishment of *dharma*), a war between good and evil (*dharma* and *adharma*), a war which itself is *dharma* (since *dharma* could be based on *varṇa* or caste in a caste-divided society, and warfare was a sacred duty of the militant *kṣatriya* caste), or a war fought following the right codes of warfare. The *Mahābhārata* deals with all these aspects of the question of *dharmayuddha*. However, the most basic of all these questions is if war can be the right thing to do in any situation. Can any war be *dharmayuddha?* This question is not only central to the *Mahābhārata* but utterly relevant to our contemporary world politics. In recent years, we have seen a peculiarly growing popularity of aggressive nationalist politics. Several popular leaders all over the world, from Donald Trump to Vladimir Putin, have considered a display of aggressive and militant masculinity a marker of a "strong state." The recent verbal showdowns between the American and North Korean premiers, the prevalent political sentiments regarding India-Pakistan relationship on both sides of the border, the seemingly endless Arab-Israel clashes and the recent Russian invasion of Ukraine—all show that even the end of the Cold War could not free the world from consistent doubts about war and peace: whether aggressive nationalism is to be celebrated or denounced, whether pacifism is desirable prudence or undesirable weakness, whether to settle for peace or intimidate by force an enemy whose standpoint seems unrighteous, and so on. To find an ancient Indian engagement with such questions, we shall start with the heated debates in the "Udyogaparvan," the fifth book of the *Mahābhārata,* where both the contending parties of the catastrophic Bhārata War start their war preparations.

The *Mahābhārata* tradition, in all probability, originated as an *itihāsa* (one of the historical traditions of early India, possibly with a bardic origin) of the Later Vedic Kuru kingdom which, according to Michael Witzel, was not just the earliest proto-state of the Indian subcontinent but possibly the location where the *varṇa*-based Vedic orthodoxy and orthopraxy were formulated.[1] Although the composition of the text has probably gone through multiple tellings and retellings before its final canonization and has usually been dated between 500 BCE and 500 CE, historians like Romila Thapar and R. S. Sharma—who have pointed out the difference between the narrative and didactic sections of the text—note that the older narrative sections represent the context of the period of the Later Vedas (ca. 1000–600 BCE).[2] Although I am inclined to support this view and place at least the core narrative of the *Mahābhārata* in its Later Vedic context, separating the layers of the *Mahābhārata* and ascertaining its nature as either a bardic historical tradition of Later Vedic times or a memory of the Later Vedic past or a revised mythological/didactic unified text are questions that have attracted intense debates beyond the scope of this paper. Leaving these debates aside, it can be said that the central narrative of the *Mahābhārata* revolves around a succession struggle in the most important polity of Later Vedic North India, the Kuru kingdom.

Simon Brodbeck and Brian Black rightly describe the main issue of the text as the conflict of primogenitive birthright and behavioral fitness.[3] Primogeniture appears to be a new idea in kingship, not yet completely established. The tribal notion of selecting the ablest as the chief was still present, by virtue of which the great king Bharata chose Bhūmanyu—son of Bharadvāja—as his successor, neglecting all of his own sons.[4] The system continued up to the period of Śaṃtanu, in whose favor his elder brother, Devāpi, abdicated the throne.[5] However, Śaṃtanu's passion for the fisherwoman Satyavatī brought a disjuncture. Śaṃtanu's son Devavrata (Bhīṣma), who was the fittest to succeed to the throne, made a vow to Satyavatī's father, assuring the unborn children of Satyavatī the throne.[6] Bhīṣma's famous vow unfolded into a crisis, as both the sons of Satyavatī died early.[7] In this situation, Satyavatī asked Vyāsa, her son born out of a premarital union, to beget children from the two widows of Vicitravīrya, Ambikā and Ambālikā. Born of this levirate, Dhṛtarāṣṭra—the eldest of the next-generation princes—failed to obtain the throne because of his blindness, and younger Pāṇḍu became the king. However, this choice of the fitter over the legitimacy of primogeniture created a frustration in Dhṛtarāṣṭra, which manifested itself in his son Duryodhana, who fought hard to establish his legitimate claim to the throne and remained a staunch advocate of the martial *varṇadharma* of the *kṣatriyas* throughout the text. Thus, there was a constant conflict between Duryodhana and the five surrogate sons of king Pāṇḍu (Yudhiṣṭhira, Bhīma, Arjuna, Nakula, and Sahadeva). The latter group, headed by the eldest Yudhiṣṭhira, known as the Pāṇḍavas, escaped the early attempts of Duryodhana to kill them off, and became powerful enough to force a partition of the kingdom, after Draupadī, the princess of the strong kingdom of Pāñcāla, became the common wife of the five brothers. The conflict reached its height when Yudhiṣṭhira not only lost all of his property in a dice game against Duryodhana and his party, but in desperation staked and lost Draupadī, who was molested in the open court. After this, war seemed the only option left, despite Yudhiṣṭhira's reluctance to fight. Yudhiṣṭhira, still unwilling to fight, followed the conditions of the dice game by accepting an exile of thirteen years for himself and his brothers. Twelve years of forest-dwelling followed by a year of masquerade was supposed to get them their share of the kingdom back. They spent the thirteenth year in the kingdom of Matsya, at the end of which a marriage between Abhimanyu, a son of Arjuna, and Uttarā, the daughter of Virāṭa (the king of Matsya), sealed a political alliance between the Pāṇḍavas and Matsya. The "Udyogaparvan" began in this situation when the marriage party also became the site of a political conference to decide what course the Pāṇḍavas were to take if Duryodhana refused to give them their kingdom back.

Right from this initial assembly, the "Udyogaparvan" presents several ethical dilemmas. After fulfilling their commitment about the exile, what should the Pāṇḍavas do? Did not they deserve their share of the kingdom back? What if Duryodhana refused to return it? One solution was war. But that would involve the killing of numerous people, including his own kinsmen. So which was better: war or peace? Peace and nonviolence were eternal virtues. It was a *kṣatriya*'s duty to fight for his property. Between one's caste duty and the eternal *dharma*, which was to be followed? Then there was another aspect to the problem. The conflict was not only about a share in the kingdom. Even if the Pāṇḍavas forgot their political interest, what about the humiliation of Draupadī? Should not it be avenged? But should a wrong necessarily be avenged by violence? Was a crime by the opponent enough justification for initiating a war that would endanger the existence of the entire clan? Draupadī's humiliation was wrong. But how right was a war that pitted a noble-hearted grandfather against his dear grandchildren, a famous teacher against his favorite student, and cousins against their equally capable cousins?

In this huge conundrum of ethical questions, everybody would provide an answer and add more questions. Yudhiṣṭhira and Duryodhana, Arjuna and Karṇa, Drupada and Dhṛtarāṣṭra, Kuntī and Gāndhārī—everyone would have a say in the matter. But the finality had to be provided by Vāsudeva Kṛṣṇa, a distant cousin of the Pāṇḍavas, who had practically become their friend, philosopher, and guide and had established himself as the most charismatic diplomat of the time.

In the very first meeting, Kṛṣṇa made his stand crystal clear:

This being the case, think of what will profit
The Dharma's[8] son and Duryodhana,
And profit the Kurus and Pāṇḍavas,
Consistent with Law, correct, earning fame.

King Dharma is not one to covet the realm
Of even the Gods, if it were under Unlaw,
He would strive for lordship even in some village
If it were consistent with Law and Profit.[9]

Therefore, we can see that Kṛṣṇa's primary ambition was a combination of Law (*dharma*) and Profit (*artha*), the first representing the eternal virtue while the second represented the practical and material interest. However, while deciding on this ground, Kṛṣṇa no longer intervened as an ally of the Pāṇḍavas, but reminded a totally pro-Pāṇḍava gathering of the need to think of a solution benefitting both parties. His sympathy for Yudhiṣṭhira was not for their friendship and alliance but because of the latter's dedication in performing the *dharma*. That *dharma*, according to Kṛṣṇa, focused on the defense of a right rather than personal gain. Therefore, even the rulership of heaven was not to be coveted unjustly, but the rightful lordship over even a village had to be carefully defended.

Thus, Kṛṣṇa indicated that Yudhiṣṭhira should defend his right to a share in the kingdom, but did not yet advocate war as the means. Rather, he emphasized the interest of both parties and wanted to know Duryodhana's stance before making any decision. Therefore, he suggested the sending of an ambassador for such purpose.[10]

Both parties, however, were sure that a war was imminent. Therefore, Kṛṣṇa had to logically resolve the doubts about war and peace in the Pāṇḍava camp to establish his viewpoint. The doubts were bound to be there, particularly with Yudhiṣṭhira's obsession in observing the *dharma*. Even the Kuru court knew it well, and tried to bank on it. Therefore, Dhṛtarāṣṭra's message in reply to the demand of a share of the kingdom for Yudhiṣṭhira, by Drupada's ambassador, turned out to be an ethical quiz. Saṃjaya, the envoy of Dhṛtarāṣṭra, presented war as an evil, a cause of total devastation, infernal and destructive. A victory in such a war would be equivalent to defeat, according to him.[11] The imminent war was shown as even more evil, since it involved the death of kinsmen.[12] Saṃjaya also suggested that begging would be better than reigning by undertaking such a war.[13]

The ploy did not work. Yudhiṣṭhira made it clear that he did not covet any wealth through *adharma*,[14] but referred the matter to Kṛṣṇa to decide what *dharma* was at that moment. Kṛṣṇa readily pointed out how empty the peace proposal was.[15] He noted that the Kurus were recommending the Pāṇḍavas to follow the path of peace without themselves undertaking any effort in the matter. In his long reply to Dhṛtarāṣṭra's message, we find the first clear exposition of Kṛṣṇa's teachings in the *Mahābhārata*. And there, Kṛṣṇa emphasized the concept that *dharma* lay in performing one's own duties properly and nothing else. That was how all divinities and natural forces also functioned, by performing their roles ceaselessly.[16] Then he extended this natural law of action to the society and envisioned a separate set of duties for the king:

> A king should protect all classes without
> Distractions and yoke them each to his task,
> Be not given to lusts and be fair to the subjects
> And not comply with lawless desires.[17]

Therefore, a king who failed to perform these actions must be considered guilty of *adharma*. Working out of a lawless desire for the Pāṇḍava property, Duryodhana thus committed such a sin, which needed to be punished:

> When one cruelly covets the land of another
> And, angering destiny, seizes power
> Then this shall be a cause of war among the kings;
>
> Where a thief steals property without witness,
> Whether another steals it by force and in public,

They both are guilty of crime:
What sets Dhṛtarāṣṭra's sons apart?[18]

Then he reminded Saṃjaya of the humiliation of Draupadī.[19] The entire speech gives us a clear idea of the philosophy Kṛṣṇa was propagating. He believed in action. It was the proper performance of one's own duty—which we can call *svadharma*—that sustained the Cosmic Order. The king's duty was in assuring that everybody could perform his own duties. Moreover, the king had his duties as well. A king who failed to do that, coveted the wealth of the others, and was driven by desire was no better than a thief. Only the thief stole secretly, while the powerful seized what he wanted openly. The nature of the crimes was the same. A king who was guilty of a crime was to be punished.

Based on this ideology, Kṛṣṇa ripped apart Dhṛtarāṣṭra's empty peace proposal that advised the Pāṇḍavas about the evils of war without promising anything for avoiding war. Duryodhana was guilty of theft, but there was no promise to rectify that. Draupadī was publicly humiliated. No punishment or apology was promised for that. In such a scenario, it became the kingly duty of the Pāṇḍavas to punish the sinners. However, Kṛṣṇa did not deny the essence of the message that war was evil. Therefore, he took the most crucial decision upon himself by going to the Kuru court for a final attempt at peace. But that peace was possible only when both parties were ready to do their duties to avoid war.

Kṛṣṇa knew that he would fail. Still, he decided to undertake the role of an unsuccessful envoy. There lay the secret of Kṛṣṇa's philosophy—performing a duty for duty's sake, not desiring success, not thinking of the end result. The war was inevitable. Kṛṣṇa knew it. But it was his duty to try his best to stop a war, and that he had to do. When suggested later that his coming as an envoy was unwise, futile, and risky, Kṛṣṇa would again expound the same philosophy:

> Even if a man, while trying to the best of his ability, cannot accomplish a task of Law, he still—and I have no doubt of that—gains the merit of the Law . . . . So I too shall attempt to make peace without dissembling, Steward, to stop a war between the Kurus and Sṛñjayas, who are doomed to perish.

> The wise know that he who does not run to the rescue of a friend who is plagued by troubles and does not try to help him as far as he can is guilty of cruelty. Go as far as grabbing him by the hair to keep a friend from committing a crime, and no one can blame you, for you tried your best.

> No, I have come to help the cause of both parties, and having made the attempt I shall be without blame before all men.[20]

With this decision to go as an envoy to the Kuru court, Kṛṣṇa found himself center stage in the debate between war and peace. And the debate was intense. As we can see, there were two polar opposites at work. On one hand was Yudhiṣṭhira, an ardent pacifist who wanted to avoid war at any cost. On the other hand, Duryodhana, with staunch belief in his *kṣatriya* virtue, valued military victory over everything.

Making the situation more complex, the mothers of the two protagonists propagated doctrines quite opposite to what their sons believed. Gāndhārī, mother of Duryodhana, consistently advised her son to follow the eternal *dharma* for the greater good, while Kuntī fiercely urged her son Yudhiṣṭhira to leave his obsession with peace and perform the duty expected from a *kṣatriya* warrior. Kṛṣṇa stood in the middle. He had made his stand clear that he preferred peace but not at the cost of tolerating criminal offenses. As an envoy, he had the task of persuading the haughty Duryodhana to accept peace. On the other hand, the ambassador of peace had to keep the peace-loving Pāṇḍavas prepared for the war that he knew as inevitable.

Duryodhana believed in the classical Later Vedic *varṇa* order where the hereditary *varṇa* duty was to be followed like a ritual, and the aim was the desire for heaven. That ideology explained a *kṣatriya*'s task as fighting heroically. In military capability lay a *kṣatriya*'s worth and importance. Therefore, Yudhiṣṭhira's pacifism was unrighteous in Duryodhana's eyes, as his love for fighting was in the eyes of Yudhiṣṭhira. Just as the Pāṇḍavas tried hard to make Duryodhana abide by the ethics they followed, so did Duryodhana try to turn his cousins into "true" *kṣatriyas*. The sufferings of the Pāṇḍavas, to him, were the punishment for failing to perform their *svadharma*:

> I called you barren sesame seeds, and rightly so! For in the city of Virāṭa the Pārtha wore a braid and Bhīmasena served as a cook in Virāṭa's kitchen. That was my doing! That is the way *kṣatriyas* punish a *kṣatriya* who runs from a battle: they condemn him to a gambler's row, to the kitchen, to the braid![21]

Therefore, on the verge of war, after all attempts at peace failed, Duryodhana's message to the Pāṇḍavas would be:

> Be a man, remember your banishment from the kingdom, your hardships, your forest exile, the molestation of Draupadī, Pāṇḍava![22]

War was the purpose for which, Duryodhana thought, a *kṣatriya* lady gave birth. Surprisingly, the same thought was shared by the lady who actually gave birth to the pacifist Yudhiṣṭhira, Kuntī:

> Come, heed the Law that was created by the Self-existent; the *kṣatriya* was created from his chest, to live by the strength of his arms, to act always mercilessly for the protection of his subjects.[23]

Yudhiṣṭhira's deviation from the *kṣātradharma* was an irritant to Kuntī, as it was to Duryodhana:

> Look to the kingly Laws that befits your heritage, for the conduct by which you wish to stand was not that of the royal seers. A king infected by cowardice, who does not act ruthlessly, does not win the reward that results from the protection of his subjects. Neither Pāṇḍu nor I nor Grandfather have ever prayed that you be blessed with the wisdom you live by; the blessings I asked were sacrifice, generosity, austerity, heroism, offspring, greatness of spirit, and the enjoyment of strength forever.

Whether it be Law or not, you are born to it by the very fact of birth . . . you are a *ksatriya*, the savior from wounds, living by the strength of your arms.[24]

To inspire Yudhiṣṭhira to the code of conduct of a *ksatriya*, Kuntī told him the story of the lady named Vidurā who had forcibly sent her reluctant son Saṃjaya to a war. Through the mouth of Vidurā, Kuntī sends Yudhiṣṭhira her message:

Where did you come from?. . . . .Too cowardly for anger, barely hanging on to a low branch, you are a man with the tools of a eunuch.[25]

To her, manhood meant truculence and unforgivingness. The meek, forgiving man was neither man nor woman. Contentment, compassion, sloth, and fear only killed off good fortune.[26] While Krṣṇa would describe a greedy king's self-aggrandizement as theft, the exact opposite view would come from Vidurā and Kuntī:

A *ksatriya* who clings to life without displaying to the highest degree possible his talent by his feats, him they know for a thief.[27]

Life and death did not matter to a *ksatriya*. It was better for him to flame briefly than to smoke long.[28] Irrespective of victory or defeat, a wise person should go ahead with his task.[29] The heart of *ksatriyahood* (*ksatrahrdaya*), as described by Vidurā and Kuntī, is expressed in terms identical to those used by Duryodhana. Vidurā is quoted as saying:

I indeed know the eternal heart of the ksatriyahood as proclaimed by our forbears and theirs, and our descendents and theirs. No one born a *ksatriya* here, and knowing the law of the *ksatriyas*, will either out of fear or hope for a living bow to anyone else. "Hold up your head and do not bow." Standing tall means manhood (*pauruṣa*)—rather break in the middle than bend.[30]

However, irrespective of what his mother thought, Yudhiṣṭhira was equally steadfast in his allegiance to his interpretation of *dharma*. Challenging the rationale of the *varṇa* system time and again, he had hardly any regard for the notion of *ksātradharma*. He clearly stated his disapproval of the idea that a person had to be violent and unforgiving just because he belonged to a certain caste by birth. War to him was evil by all means and so was the *ksātradharma* that endorsed it:

What is pretty in war? It is the evil Law of the *ksatriyas* . . . *ksatriya* kills *ksatriya*, fish lives on fish, dog kills dog.[31]

Therefore, the power struggle of the *ksatriyas* is as abominable to Yudhiṣṭhira as a brute fight between dogs:

The wise have noticed that it is the same as in a mess of dogs. It starts with a wagging of tails, then a bark, a bark in reply, backing off, baring the teeth, loud barking, and then the fight; and the stronger one wins and eats the meat, Krṣṇa—it is the same with people, there is no difference at all. It is always the same thing that the stronger does to the weaker: disregard and aggressiveness—and the weak man surrenders.

Father, king and elder always deserve respect, and therefore Dhṛtarāṣṭra deserves our respect and homage, Janārdana.[32]

Earnestly thinking along these lines, Yudhiṣṭhira provided us with one of the earliest and strongest statements against war and violence, standing in an era when heroism was the most respected manly virtue:

War is evil in any form. What killer is not killed in return? To the killed victory and defeat are the same, Hṛṣikeśa.

The victor too is surely diminished: In the end some others will kill a loved one of his; and behold, when he has lost his strength and no longer sees his sons and brothers a loathing for life will engulf him completely, Kṛṣṇa . . . .There is always remorse after the killing of others, Janārdana.

Victory breeds feuds, for the defeated rest uneasy. But easy sleeps the man who serenely has given up both victory and defeat.[33]

Thus, Yudhiṣṭhira viewed heroism as a "powerful disease that eats up the heart." There were only two ways to end a feud—total eradication (*mūlaghāta*) of the enemy or giving it up. Since the former was a cruel thing, the second was preferable.[34] Yudhiṣṭhira, therefore, would prefer peace by subjugation (*praṇipāta*) than either renouncing the kingdom or ruining the family,[35] and his request to Kṛṣṇa was to ensure peace.[36]

Yudhiṣṭhira's teachings seem to have an impact on his brothers as well, for the usually violent Bhīma also requested Kṛṣṇa to try for peace at any cost. Even he would prefer bowing before Duryodhana than causing a disaster in the Kuru family, and he claimed that Arjuna thought the same.[37] Arjuna himself said nothing conclusive except to assert his desire for peace and his faith in Kṛṣṇa's ability to achieve it,[38] while Nakula hoped for the success of the peace mission.[39]

This entire atmosphere of antiwar sentiment would obviously delight our modern sensibilities. However, in this grand debate about the sharing of the kingdom, the issue of Draupadī's humiliation was almost lost. Only the youngest of the Pāṇḍavas, Sahadeva, spoke in a different voice:

What the king has said is the sempiternal Law, but see to it that there be war, enemy-tamer! Even if the Kurus should want peace with the Pāṇḍavas, you should still provoke war with them, Daśārha! How could my rage with Suyodhana subside after seeing the Princess of Pañcāla manhandled in the hall? If Bhīma, Arjuna and King Dharma stick with the Law, I want to fight him in battle, and begone with the law.[40]

It is for this reason precisely that Kuntī urged her sons to go to war:

Not the rape of the kingdom, not the defeat at dice, not the banishment of my sons to the forest grieves me, as it grieves me that that great dark woman, weeping in the hall, had to listen to insults.[41]

Above all, there was Draupadī herself, itching for a war that would avenge her humiliation:

> A curse on Bhīmasena's strength, a curse on the Pārtha's bowmanship, if Duryodhana stays alive for another hour, Kṛṣṇa! If you find favour in me, if you have pity on me, direct your entire fury at the Dhārtarāṣṭras, Kṛṣṇa.
>
> This hair was pulled by Duḥśāsana's hands, lotus-eyed Lord; remember it at all times when you seek peace with the enemies! If Bhīma and Arjuna pitifully hanker after peace, my ancient father will fight, and his warrior sons, Kṛṣṇa! My five valiant sons will, led by Abhimanyu, fight with the Kurus, Madhusūdana! What peace will my heart know unless I see Duḥśāsana's swarthy arm cut off and covered with dust! Thirteen years have gone by while I waited, hiding my rage in my heart like a blazing fire. Pierced by the thorn of Bhīma's words, my heart is rent asunder, for now that strong-armed man has eyes for the Law only.[42]

Again, in seeking this revenge, Draupadī put stress on the *kṣātradharma*, which Yudhiṣṭhira disregarded and Duryodhana held in high esteem:

> For a *kṣatriya*, if he follows his own Law, should kill a *kṣatriya* who has become greedy, and a non-*kṣatriya* too . . . Those who know the Law know that just as it is sin to kill one who does not deserve it, so a sin is found in not killing one who does deserve it. So see to it, Kṛṣṇa, that this sin does not touch you, the Pāṇḍavas, and the Sṛñjayas with their troops, Dāśārha.[43]

In such a heated environment, Kṛṣṇa had to perform his duty of an envoy. His very decision to go as a messenger of peace was an acceptance of Yudhiṣṭhira's pacifism. However, he was almost sure of the failure of his mission. Therefore, he had to make his stand clear about the subsequent action. Thus, he also quoted the clichéd terms of *kṣātradharma* to persuade Yudhiṣṭhira:

> Mendicancy is not a *kṣatriya*'s business, lord of the people. All those who observe the life stages have said what a *kṣatriya* should beg: victory, or death on the battlefield, as the Placer has ordained for eternity. That is the *kṣatriya*'s law, and cowardice is not extolled. For livelihood is impossible by giving in to cowardice, Yudhiṣṭhira. Stride wide, strong-armed king! Kill the foe, enemy-tamer![44]

As a response to Yudhiṣṭhira's hesitation to kill the kinsmen, Kṛṣṇa argued that Duryodhana had already been killed by his sins. However, interestingly, after the stereotypical exposition of *kṣātradharma*, Kṛṣṇa accepted that Yudhiṣṭhira's understanding of the *dharma* was what actually pleased him.[45]

Kṛṣṇa treated Bhīma's pacifism in a totally different manner. If he had respectful admiration for Yudhiṣṭhira's righteousness, he knew that pacifism was not what suited Bhīma. Therefore, he provoked Bhīma to bring out his real nature, by wondering whether he was panic-stricken.[46] The provocation had the desired result, as Bhīma's anger flared up. But it would be wrong to assume Kṛṣṇa as a champion of the *kṣātradharma* on the basis of his advice to Yudhiṣṭhira and Bhīma. Kṛṣṇa, rather, appeared in a totally different light in his trip to Hastināpura.

Kṛṣṇa's message to Duryodhana had nothing to do with the latter's favorite *kṣatradharma*. Rather, it placed the eternal *dharma* over any pursuit for material benefit around which a *kṣatriya*'s life was expected to revolve:

> The undertakings of the wise are consistent with the Three Pursuits, Bharata bull, but when all three are impossible to carry out at the same time, men follow Law and Profit. If those two cannot be reconciled, a sagacious person follows the Law, a middling person prefers Profit, a fool the Pleasure of discord. If a man, driven by his senses, abandons Law out of greed, and strives after Profit and Pleasure by foul means, he perishes. Even if he strives for Profit and Pleasure he should still practice the Law from the start, for neither Profit nor Pleasure ever part company with Law.[47]

Kṛṣṇa's message was accompanied by a long speech by Gāndhārī, who tried to persuade her son to the path of the eternal *dharma* that depended on control over senses, particularly lust, anger, and greed.[48] However, the speeches on *dharma* hardly had any effect on Duryodhana, who decided to bank on his power and keep Kṛṣṇa as a prisoner.[49] The plan failed. Kṛṣṇa left the court as an angry unsuccessful envoy.

We may notice an interesting aspect of Kṛṣṇa's teaching in the entire episode. To Yudhiṣṭhira and Bhīma, he valorized war and *kṣatradharma*. To the warmonger Duryodhana, he spoke of the eternal ethics and peace. What was Kṛṣṇa's own stand then? To understand the matter, we have to go back to Kṛṣṇa's exposition of his ideas to Saṃjaya. He placed action above all. A man chose his own *svadharma*. What Kṛṣṇa did was to persuade everyone to the performance of his own *svadharma* after offering them several alternatives to choose from. The terrible Bhīma, a hardcore warrior, could not be a pacifist. So, he instigated Bhīma to his *svadharma* of an unflinching warrior. He knew that Duryodhana's *svadharma* was *kṣatradharma*, and he ultimately let him have the war he wanted, but only after an exposition of the other faces of *dharma* in front of him. Yudhiṣṭhira was given his choice as well. Kṛṣṇa extolled the *kṣatradharma* in front of him, but could hardly move him. At the end, he happily went off as Yudhiṣṭhira's messenger of peace. Why did Kṛṣṇa decide on this balancing act? There lay his own *svadharma*, the *dharma* of performing his duties irrespective of the results and without any attachment. He had to try his best for peace, though in vain. He had to keep Yudhiṣṭhira ready for war, equally in vain.

What Vāsudeva Kṛṣṇa demonstrates in the "Udyogaparvan" is a politics of balance between pacifism and justice, a balance that the present world greatly needs. In a world where the language of populist politics is becoming increasingly militant, we need to listen more carefully to the voice of Kṛṣṇa, not the deified all-knowing Kṛṣṇa of the *Bhagavad Gītā* but the human Kṛṣṇa of the "Udyogaparvan" who constantly reminds us of the necessity of a resolution that is beneficial to all and offers himself to be a messenger of peace even when a war is imminent because, irrespective of success or failure, one cannot but perform the duty of trying every possible means to ensure peace.

2

Before exploring the *Mahābhārata*'s treatment of the issue of just war further, let us see if these various ancient Indian standpoints can be compared with the philosophical standpoints regarding the same in ancient China, especially within the Confucian tradition. Prof. Daniel Bell, in chapter 10 of this volume, shows how Mencius preferred the resolution of crisis through the awakening of the natural goodness of individuals and detested the use of force. However, there were different positions regarding war among the Confucian thinkers as well.

Mencius's attitude, even within the Confucian tradition, can possibly be contrasted with that of the pragmatist Xunzi, who stood on the frontier of Confucianism and Legalism. As Mencius had a tendency toward dialectics, he contrasted two kinds of power: humane authority and hegemony. While the first was entrenched in justice and benevolence, the second spoke of benevolence but depended on force. Mencius strongly advocated humane authority and considered hegemony undesirable. He was thoroughly against the use of force in politics, and would rather support a small state, depending on moral authority, than political expansion based on force. However, Mencius thought that proper adherence to the principles of justice and benevolence, the core of humane authority, made other rulers willingly accept the leadership of the humane king. Hegemony, based on force and false promises of benevolence, was bound to be short-lived. Xunzi, on the other hand, agreed with Mencius about the supremacy of humane authority, but did not discard hegemony altogether. He thought of three, rather than two, varieties of international power. Therefore, he considered hegemony a value placed between the best, humane authority, and the worst, tyranny. Hegemony, to him, was not just a political system speaking of benevolence but was dependent on force. It also needed to have the quality of reliability. The hegemon must be reliable to his subjects internally and reliable to his allies in international politics, which meant that he needed to adhere to his promises. Moreover, Xunzi thought that conflict was natural and hard power was important except in the ideal but rare state of humane authority. Mencius, on the other hand, pointed out that human nature was not good from birth, but "potentially" good. Therefore, baser instincts had to be curbed and good instincts cultivated to avoid conflict. He had a belief in ultimate human goodness triumphing over narrow desire.[50]

Mencius knew, however, that he inhabited a nonideal world where war was a reality. Therefore, questions need to be asked about Mencius's perception of war. Bell points out that Mencius accepted the possibility of "just war" in two cases. The first was war in self-defense, in which case there was the support of the people. The other was punitive action against unlawful rulers. However, the latter proposition was limited to situations where people's life and subsistence were at stake. Thus, Mencius would not approve of military intervention in case of the violation of freedom of speech or religious rights. Moreover, it is said that the forceful liberation of people from unlawful rule is justified only when the people welcome the force. If the force is unwelcome, they should leave. Thus, Mencius would probably not approve of the *Mahābhārata* war as a "just war," if avenging the molestation of a woman were the sole reason. However, if it was a war in self-defense, to recover the Pāṇḍava share in the kingdom that was taken away from them, it would have been justified as long as the Pāṇḍavas enjoyed popular support.

Moreover, Mencius, arguably, was handicapped by his view that human nature was good, and it was just a matter of getting people to follow their naturally good instincts. He doesn't seem to allow for the possibility that some people can be born bad and are impossible to change, and that the people as a whole can be misguided and in favor of war to the point of being bloodthirsty and fundamentally immoral. In contrast, Kṛṣṇa did not always appeal to the good sense of warmarkers, and he tried to argue against their natural inclinations. The *Mahābhārata* points to large numbers of people, from warmongering mothers to members of the *kṣatriya varṇa*, who favored war. For Mencius, it was important for rulers to gain the hearts of the people because the assumption seemed to be that the people's hearts were fundamentally in the right place. The *Mahābhārata* does not have any such conviction about people being necessarily good. Rather, it is a text that highlights and even celebrates the multiplicity of human nature, and, therefore, acknowledges the need of acting against the immoral, who may enjoy the support of a section of the people. If we think of support in Germany for the Nazis and in Japan for imperial aggression in China, it's hard to agree with Mencius that the people are always in the right side. The *Mahābhārata* reminds one further that, in most cases, there may not be an absolutely right side. Conflict, therefore, is an unavoidable eventuality. But, what the *Mahābhārata* in general, and Kṛṣṇa in particular, points out is that war has to be the last resort, after all alternatives have been tried. It is not something which can be desired or valorized. War cannot be "just" unless all possible efforts to avoid war have been made.

But what about good conduct in war? Is it acceptable to kill civilians even if the war had been indeed the last option? What does the text say about the obligations of the victor to the conquered peoples after the war has been fought? Is *dharma-yuddha* (just war) a question of means or of end? Let us revisit the Bhārata War, the central event of the *Mahābhārata*, to understand the ethics of warfare in the text.

3

To understand the *Mahābhārata* war better, we need to read the text in its original Later Vedic context. War and aggression were part and parcel of the Ṛgvedic world (ca. 1500–1000 BCE), and hardly needed any justification. Prayers for victory and material benefits were routinely uttered without shame, and destruction and devastation of the enemy was celebrated without embarrassment. The use of poisoned arrows or any other weapon was not prohibited. The occasional justification for warfare was always sectarian, as in the case of the clashes against the

Dāsas, Dasyus or phallus-worshippers. Even in the Later Vedic texts (ca. 1000–600 BCE), turning prisoners of wars into slaves was quite usual. Though the idea of contracts and treaties existed, Indra retained his position despite deceitfully killing his friend Namuci.[51] But the Later Vedic sensibilities show a gradual development in moral consciousness that culminated in the Upaniṣads, where nonviolence appeared as a great virtue. The glorification of violence finally gave way to the teachings of the Buddha and Mahāvīra, who passionately pleaded for nonviolence and peace.

The morality of warfare in the *Mahābhārata* lies between these two attitudes. The ethos of a heroic age was still vibrant, but unrighteous conquest was discouraged. The evils of war were pointed out repeatedly to Duryodhana, the champion of the heroic virtue of the *kṣatriyas*. When war could not be averted, a lofty moral standard was set where only equals should fight equals, one should fight one on one, noncombatants should remain unharmed, and the fatigued and frightened should be spared. Ambassadors and *brāhmaṇas* were declared unslayable, so were the spectators.[52]

The reality of war was much different from the ideas of the time. Therefore, when fighting started, many of these promises were forgotten by both parties. Great heroes slaughtered ordinary soldiers, charioteers were mercilessly killed.[53] But that the rules were conceived, a good deal of them were followed, and the aberrations were criticized and debated indicate an age of transition from a period of unrestrained violence to the period when nonviolence would be valued. Kaushik Roy has analyzed the peculiarity of the military ethics of the *Mahābhārata* (*dharmayuddha*) in contrast with the *realpolitik* (*kūṭayuddha*) advocated in the *Arthaśāstra* composed in later times.[54]

M. A. Mehendale attempted to understand why the Bhārata War has been called a *dharmayuddha*—war in the cause of righteousness. He thinks that it means that the war was fought either for righteous ends or by righteous means. In the latter case, the war at issue does not deserve the tag. He enlists the several codes of ethical warfare from the epic and shows that while certain rules were observed by both sides, many other rules were violated. Thus, no side could claim the war to be a *dharmayuddha*.[55] The message that the *Mahābhārata* eventually leaves is, probably, that just war is an impossibility. Circumstances may make war unavoidable. One may have to engage in warfare when all possible alternatives fail. One must also try to limit the casualties or suffering of the civilians to the greatest possible extent. Yet there is something inherently problematic in warfare that can make it only a necessary and unavoidable evil at best. *Dharmayuddha*, war for righteousness, is an absurdity either in terms of the means or in terms of the end. This, perhaps, is one of the reasons why several schools of classical Indian philosophy, especially Jainism and Buddhism, had celebrated *ahiṃsā* (nonviolence) as the highest ideal, which left a lasting legacy in Gandhi's political philosophy.

4

What message do these classical philosophical ideas (both Indian and Chinese) leave for the modern world? Before answering this question, we must remind ourselves that classical normative texts are products of their own time and place. Using ideas from these texts out of their context to analyze modern political phenomena can be, at times, misleading. For instance, the United States, like Xunzi's hegemon, no doubt tries to maintain reliability externally and internally. It also undoubtedly speaks of benevolence but depends on force, as the latest wars in Iraq and Afghanistan prove. However, does it still match the political model of Xunzi? The importance of social and familial norms is crucial in the thoughts of any Confucian thinker. Are these things essential in American politics? Prof. Yan Xuetong has been repeatedly advocating a policy of "moral realism," following Xunzi, to be adopted by China, in which reliability to allies is given high importance. However, can morality be perceived only in terms of reliability? American intervention in the Vietnam War no doubt showed its reliability as an ally of France, but didn't it also expose the American propaganda of democratic benevolence, as Mencius suggested? In the case of China, it has mostly depended on profit-oriented hard power in asserting its rise as a global superpower, something of which Mencius would strongly disapprove. Until now, there has been little in Chinese foreign policy that would make other countries accept China's leadership on moral grounds, without any consideration for hard power. However, such scenario is not impossible even in the modern world. We may think of the Non-alignment Movement led by the Indian prime minister Jawaharlal Nehru and a few other world leaders, during the Cold War, in which newly decolonized third world countries voluntarily came together to combat the hegemony of the two global superpowers, the US and the USSR.

A greater problem in creating a parallelism between ancient texts and modern politics is the difference in context. For instance, both Mencius and Xunzi placed the individual at the center of the polity because both of them lived when monarchy was the established political system. Such individual-oriented theories may still be used for countries ruled by a single individual/party, as in the case of China, but will not be able to capture the political scenario of a democracy, such as in India.

Also, as Bell has discussed, one of the few situations in which Mencius considers warfare "just" is punitive action against unlawful rulers. However, the proposition is limited to situations where people's life and subsistence are at stake. Thus, Mencius would not approve of military intervention in a case of the violation of freedom of speech or religious rights. The question is whether this limit, framed more than two thousand years ago, needs to be accepted verbatim in the post-Enlightenment era when there is greater consciousness about human rights, civic liberty, social justice, gender justice, and minority rights.

Similar issues can be raised about using classical Indian texts to understand modern political issues. After all, just like the classical Chinese texts, the *Mahābhārata* also addressed kings or clan-chiefs. All these texts were composed in a political situation where war and conquest were part and parcel of the expansion of royal power. The situation was additionally complicated in Brahmanical and Brahmanized texts, since duty was often perceived in terms of *varṇa* or *jāti* (together known as caste). Martial valor, for a *kṣatriya* king or warrior, was not only a political necessity but a social ritual obligation. A peace-loving figure like Yudhiṣṭhira could have thus been caught up between two extreme choices: following the stipulated duty that included war and violence, or nonviolent renunciation as prescribed by the heterodox religions. Neither suits the needs and sensibilities of the modern world.

Yet the classical texts address certain issues that have relevance and moral-political lessons transcending the specificities of space and time. Mencius's proposition that the validity of rulership depended upon the support of the people, combined with his idea that the king's duty was to ensure food and education for all, speaks of values which are equally relevant to modern democratic countries. If China were to follow Mencius's political model, availability of food and education will have to be prioritized and the right to dissent will have to be acknowledged. Thus, Mencius can still provide relevant political models. Similarly, Mencius says that the forceful liberation of people from unlawful rule is justified only when the people welcome the force. When the force is unwelcome, they should leave. Thus, India's military intervention in liberating Bangladesh would have been justified according to Mencius. But the same cannot be said about the presence of American forces in Iraq. Mencius would raise controversial but relevant questions about the Chinese control over Tibet or India's handling of Kashmir.

The *Mahābhārata* also offers philosophical middle-grounds opening up possibilities of going beyond the Brahmanical caste framework even without resorting to the heterodox way of renunciation or pursuing the seemingly impossible political utopia of absolute nonviolence. This is a choice that the *Mahābhārata* often celebrates as the highest *dharma* epitomized by the character who represents the ideal rule of *dharma*, the Dharmarāja Yudhiṣṭhira.

Yudhiṣṭhira, despite being the principal hero, is one of the most enigmatic characters of the *Mahābhārata*. Standing against Duryodhana's militant support for the hereditary *kṣātradharma*, the violent *varṇa* duty of the *kṣatriya*, Yudhiṣṭhira emerged as the most vigorous critic of the *varṇa* orthodoxy in the text. Yudhiṣṭhira asserted that *varṇa* should be determined by observance of task, and, hence, a *brāhmaṇa* (the supreme *varṇa*) was one in whom cultured conduct was postulated.[56] Yudhiṣṭhira, thus, was a complete contrast to Duryodhana. As I have shown elsewhere, the new idea of *dharma* that Yudhiṣṭhira espoused was marked by the word *ānṛśaṃsya*, which is a philosophy of noncruelty and considerate empathy for all beings. Following this model, Yudhiṣṭhira chose Nakula (out of consideration for his deceased stepmother Mādrī) over his uterine and heroic brothers Bhīma and Arjuna when faced with the option of keeping only one of them alive, cared for not only the destitute and war widows but also the parents of his deceased enemies with sympathy and respect after victory, and refused entry into heaven at the cost of leaving alone a dog that followed him throughout his final journey. It is a value, to be practiced by the capable, that undergoes multiple tests in life and beyond, and does not have anything to do with the *varna* assigned by birth. Hence, it is stated that *ānṛśaṃsya* can be found among the people of all *varnas*. Moreover, while most of the other conceptions of *dharma* were directed at the afterlife—either the attainment of heaven after death (the goal of the Brahmanical *kṣātradharma*) or the liberation from the cycle of birth and death (the goal of the Śramaṇic religions like Buddhism and Jainism)—*ānṛśaṃsya* seems to be an end in itself. It is an idea suitable even for a completely "disenchanted" universe, for neither divine grace nor a happy afterlife is supposed to be the reward of its performance. Rather, Yudhiṣṭhira would choose *ānṛśaṃsya* over heaven and continue its practice even in his afterlife. Yudhiṣṭhira's *ānṛśaṃsya* was an alternative to the ideal of martial heroism, which celebrated violence and cruelty of a *kṣatriya* clan society, rather than a critique of heterodox nonviolence. The opposition to the ideal was located not in the heterodox religions but in his surroundings, particularly in his cousin Duryodhana, his mother, Kuntī, and—most vocally—in his wife, Draupadī.[57]

If we reflect upon the unstable world order we are living in, where the practice of complete nonviolence seems desirable but impracticable, we must also need to ponder if militant aggression is necessarily the only alternative. At a time when violent aggressive nationalism, ruthless authoritarianism, majoritarianism, and jingoism are becoming dangerously popular all over the world, it is essential to remember the *Mahābhārata* notion of *ānṛśaṃsya* which, despite accepting the occasions of necessary violence in politics and practical life, speaks of the cardinal principle of considerate empathy toward all beings, the ally and the opposition, friend and foe, fellow creatures and the natural environment. In a world now challenged with a pandemic of unheard-of scale, what we need above all is probably the likes of Yudhiṣṭhira, who would remind us, amidst populist, bloodthirsty, jingoistic hatred, of the need for compassionate empathy: "*ānṛśaṃsya* is the highest *dharma*."

NOTES

1. Michel Witzel, "Early Sanskritization: Origin and Development of the Kuru State," in *The State, Law and Administration in Classical India*, ed. B. Kolver (Munich: R. Oldenbourg, Munich, 1997), 27–52.

2. R. S. Sharma, *Material Culture and Social Formations in Ancient India* (Delhi: McMillan, 1983), 135–52; Romila Thapar, "The Historian and the Epic," in *Cultural Pasts* (New Delhi: Oxford University Press, 2008), 613–29.

3. Simon Brodbeck and Brian Black, "Introduction," in *Gender and Narrative in the Mahābhārata*, ed. Simon Brodbeck and Brian Black (London: Routledge, 2007), 3.

4. Vyāsa, I.89.17–20. All references to Vyāsa's *Mahābhārata* are from the multivolume Critical Edition prepared under the general editorship of V. S. Sukthankar, published from the Bhandarkar Oriental Research Institute, Poona. The translations that have been followed are Vyāsa, *The Mahābhārata* (Vol. I), trans. J. A. B. van Buitenen (Chicago: University of Chicago Press, 1973) (for the "Ādiparvan"); Vyāsa, *The Mahābhārata* (Vol. II), trans. J. A. B. van Buitenen (Chicago: University of Chicago Press, 1975) (for the "Sabhāparvan" and the "Āraṇyakaparvan"); Vyāsa, *The Mahābhārata* (Vol. III), trans. J. A. B. van Buitenen (Chicago: University of Chicago Press, 1978) (for the "Virāṭaparvan" and "Udyogaparvan"); Vyāsa, *The Mahābhārata* (Book Six): Bhishma (Vols. 1 and 2), trans. Alex Cherniak (New York: New York University Press, 2008) (for the "Bhīṣmparvan"); Vyāsa, *Mahābhārata* (Book Nine): Shalya (Vols. 1 and 2), trans. Justin Meiland (New York: New York University Press, 2007) (for the "Śalyaparvan"), and Vyāsa, *The Mahābhārata* (Vol. VII), trans. James Fitzgerald (Chicago: University of Chicago Press, 2004) (for the "Strīparvan" and "Śāntiparvan" 1–167). For the rest of the text, the translations are mine unless otherwise specified.

5. Vyāsa, I.89.53, I.90.47.

6. Ibid., I.94.

7. Ibid., I.95–96.

8. Yudhiṣṭhira was known as the son of Dharma, righteousness personified, as well as King Dharma, a king who was righteousness personified.

9. Vyāsa, V.1.13–14.

10. Ibid., V.1.23–24.

11. Ibid., V.25.7.

12. Ibid, V.25.9.

13. Ibid., V.27.2.

14. Ibid., V.28.8.

15. Ibid., V.29.1–2.

16. Ibid., V.29.6–14.

17. Ibid., V.29.25.

18. Ibid., V.29.27–28.

19. Ibid., V.29.31–40.

20. Ibid., V.91.5–20.

21. Ibid., V.158.31–33 (translation slightly modified).

22. Ibid., V.158.9 (translation slightly modified).

23. Ibid., V.130.7 (translation slightly modified).

24. Ibid., V.130.19–29 (translation slightly modified).

25. Ibid., V.131.5.

26. Ibid., V.131.30–32.

27. Ibid., V.132.2.

28. Ibid., V.131.13.

29. Ibid., V.131.15.

30. Ibid., V.132.36–38 (translation slightly modified).

31. Ibid., V.7046–49 (translation modified).

32. Ibid., V.70.70–74.

33. Ibid., V.70.53–59.

34. Ibid. V.70.65–69.

35. Ibid., V.70.68.

36. Ibid., V.70.42–45.

37. Ibid., V.72.1–23.

38. Ibid., V.76; V.81.1–4.

39. Ibid., V.78.

40. Ibid., V.79.1–4.

41. Ibid., V.135.16–17.

42. Ibid., V.80.31–41.

43. Ibid, V.80.16–19 (translation slightly modified).

44. Ibid., V.71.3–5 (translation slightly modified).

45. Ibid., V.71.21–24.

46. Ibid., V.73.15–23 (translation slightly modified).

47. Ibid., V.122.32–35.

48. Ibid., V.127.20–34.

49. Ibid., V.128.1–9.

50. I am grateful to Prof. Xu Jin for the insight on Xunzi.

51. *Maitrāyaṇī Saṃhitā*, ed. F. A. Brockhaus (Leipzig, 1886), IV.3.4; *Taittirīya Brāhmaṇa*, I.7.1.6; ŚB, XII.7.1.1–10, XII.7.3.1.

52. Vyāsa, VI.1.26–32.

53. Sarva Daman Singh, *Ancient Indian Warfare with Special Reference to the Vedic Period* (Leiden: E. J. Brill, 1965), 153–67.

54. Kaushik Roy, *Hinduism and the Ethics of Warfare in South Asia* (New Delhi: Cambridge University Press, 2012); Torkel Brekke, "Breaking the Thigh and the Warrior Code," in *Warfare, Religion and Society in Indian History*, ed. Raziuddin Aquil and Kaushik Roy (Delhi: Manohar, 2012).

55. M. A. Mehendale, *Reflections on the Mahābhārata War* (Shimla: Indian Institute of Advanced Study, 1995).

56. Ibid., III.177.30–35.

57. Kanad Sinha, "Redefining *Dharma* in a Time of Transition: *Ānṛśaṃsya* in the *Mahābhārata* as an Alternative End of Human Life," *Studies in History* 35, no. 2 (2019): 147–61.

Mencius on Just War

A Comparison with Political Thought in Ancient India

Daniel A. Bell

The most basic normative question in international relations, arguably, is the following: When, if ever, should the state engage in warfare? The Confucian tradition has long debated the question of just war and it still informs Chinese thinking on the morally justified use of state violence. Such thinking may hold valuable insights for the modern world. In this essay, I will discuss Mencius's influential ideas on morally justified warfare and I will argue that lessons from ancient political thinking in India can help to remedy the defects of a Mencian-inspired theory of just war.

WAR FOR PEACE[1]

In the early days of the US-led invasion of Iraq, the Chinese-language internet was filled with references to ancient Confucian thinkers. Ming Yongqian's contribution is typical:

> Mencius said, "A true king uses virtue and humanity, a hegemon uses force under the pretext of humanity and compassion." Let us first consider the idea of the hegemon. According to Mencius's saying, a hegemon uses force to attack others in the name of benevolent justice. This kind of war is an unjust war . . . . In ancient times as well as today, most rulers are very clear regarding political realities, they won't lightly abandon the cover of virtue to launch such wars . . . . The best contemporary example is Bush's war of invasion against Iraq! He used the excuses of weapons of mass destruction and terrorism in order to obtain oil resources and to consolidate his strategic position in the Middle East. This is the best example of "using force under the pretext of humanity and compassion." Bush is today's hegemonic king.[2]

The distinction between the aggressive "hegemon" and the peace-loving "true king" was first articulated by Mencius over two thousand years ago and it still informs the moral language that Chinese intellectuals often use to evaluate foreign policy, especially regarding morally justified warfare (in contemporary parlance, "just war"). But what exactly did Mencius say about war and peace? And does it make sense to invoke his ideas in today's vastly different political world? Why not simply stick to the language of human rights? And how can ideas from the *Mahabharata* help to remedy the defects of Mencius's theory? Let us turn to these questions.

In the ideal world of *Tianxia*, an era of global peace without any territorial boundaries and ruled by one sage king, there would be no wars and pacifism would be the only justifiable moral stance. If no one is fighting for territory, then, as Mencius put it, "What need is there for war?" (7B.4). But Mencius was writing at the time of the Warring States period (ca. 500–221 BCE), a time of ruthless competition for territorial advantage between small walled states, and it shouldn't be too surprising that he also provided practical, morally informed guidance for this context.[3] Mencius argued that rulers have an obligation to promote the peaceful unification of the world (1A.6, 2B12). Ideally, the ruler should rely on noncoercive means to do so: "There is a way to gain the whole world. It is to gain the people, and having gained them one gains the whole world. There is a way to gain the people. Gain their hearts and minds, and then you gain them" (4A.10). As a consequence, he was critical of rulers who launched bloody wars of conquest simply in order to increase their territory and engage in economic plunder. Seemingly fearless, Mencius goes to see King Hui of Liang and scolds him for being "overly fond of war" (1A.3). Mencius suggests that wars of conquest cannot even lead to short-term victories, and that they are disastrous for all parties concerned, including the conqueror's loved ones:

> Mencius said, "King Hui of Liang is the antithesis of humanity and compassion. The man of humanity and compassion brings upon the things he does not love the things he loves. But the man who is not humane and compassionate brings upon the things he loves, the things he does not love." Gongsun Chou said, "What does that mean?" Mencius said, "King Hui of Liang ravished his own people for the sake of territory and went to war. When defeated, he tried again and fearing that he might not succeed he drove the son he loved to fight and his son was sacrificed. That is what I meant by 'bringing upon the things he loves, the things he does not love.'" (7B.1; see also 1.A.7)

An unjust war, in short, is a war that is launched for purposes other than peace and humanity. The problem, however, is the world is filled with ruthless men, including some who gained states (7B.13) and won't be moved by moral concerns. Faced with cruel rulers of this sort, what are the morally informed practical responses? Mencius does not counsel nonviolent resistance against tyrants who only respond to the language of force. In domestic policy, Mencius is famous for sanctioning the killing of despotic rulers (1B.8). To prevent attacks from foreign tyrants and secure the peace at home, Mencius suggests that state boundaries can be fortified: "The setting up of border posts in antiquity was to prevent violence. Today they are set up for the purpose of engaging in violence" (7B.8, see also 6B.9). So the first kind of just war approximates the modern idea of self-defense. For example, if a small territory is ruled by a capable and virtuous ruler who seeks to promote peace and humanity, and if that territory is attacked by an unjust would-be hegemon, then the ruler of that territory can justifiably mobilize the people for military action:

> Duke Wen of Teng asked, "Teng is a small state, wedged between Qi and Chu. Should I be subservient to Qi or should I be subservient to Chu?" "This is a question that is beyond me," answered Mencius. "If you insist, there is only one course of action I can suggest. Dig deeper moats and build higher walls and defend them shoulder to shoulder with the people. If they would rather die than desert you, then all is not lost" (1B.13).

This passage suggests that the people's support is crucial for successful warfare (see also 2B.1). It also suggests the people can only be mobilized to fight if they are willing to fight, with the implication that conscription of a reluctant populace would not be effective (or morally desirable).

The second kind of just war approximates the modern idea of humanitarian intervention—Mencius labels these wars "punitive expeditions" (征), and they are meant to bring about global peace and humane government. Certain conditions, however, must be in place. First, the "conquerors" must try to liberate people who are being oppressed by tyrants: "Now the prince of Yen cruelly mistreated his own people and Your Majesty set out on a punitive expedition. Yen's people thought you were saving them from 'flood and fire' [i.e., from tyranny]" (1B.11). Mencius suggests that wicked rulers are not likely to go down without a fight and that liberation of the people may require murdering the tyrant: "He killed the ruler and comforted the people, like the fall of timely rain, and the people greatly rejoiced" (1B.11). Second, the people must demonstrate, in concrete ways, the fact that they welcome their conquerors (7B.4, 1B.10, 1B.11, 3B.5). However, the welcome must be long-lasting, not just immediate. The real challenge is to maintain support for the invading forces after the initial enthusiasm: "The people welcomed your army [which had just carried out a punitive expedition] with baskets of rice and bottles of drink. If you [then] kill the old, bind the young, destroy the ancestral temples, and appropriate the ancestral vessels, how can you expect the people's approval?" (1B.11). Third, punitive expeditions must be launched by rulers who are at least potentially virtuous. One can assume that Mencius bothered to talk to some flawed rulers only because he believed they contained the seeds of virtue within them, or at least that they had sufficient good sense to respond to practical, morally informed advice. Fourth, the leader of justified punitive expeditions must have some moral claim to have the world's support: "The Book of History says, 'In his punitive expeditions Tang began with Ge.' The whole world was in sympathy with his cause. When he marched on the east, the western tribes complained. When he marched to the south, the northern tribes complained. They said, 'Why does he not come to us first?'" (1B.11).

Needless to say, this ancient world is far removed from our own, and one has to be careful about drawing implications for contemporary societies. But Ni Lexiong argues that the Warring States period shares five common characteristics with the contemporary international state system: (1) there is no real social authority higher than the state; (2) the higher social authorities exist in form rather than substance (the Zhou Son of Heaven in the Warring States period, the United Nations today); (3) national/state interest is the highest principle that trumps other considerations in cases of conflict; (4) the dominant principle in international relations is the "law of the jungle"; and (5) universal moral principles are invoked as pretexts for realizing state interests.[4] Thus it should not be entirely surprising if at least some Confucian prescriptions on just and unjust war are held to be relevant for the contemporary world of sovereign states in an "anarchical" global system.

MENCIUS FOR THE MODERN WORLD

This is not just a theoretical point. As mentioned, Mencius's views serve as a normative reference point for contemporary Chinese social critics opposed to wars of conquest. They also serve to underpin judgments regarding just wars. For example, Gong Gang appeals to the distinction between wars of conquest and justified punitive expeditions to differentiate between recent wars in the Persian Gulf:

> One can say that the First Gulf War is a just war authorized by the United Nations, similar to "a guilty duke corrected [punished] by the Son of Heaven" .... In this war [the 2003 invasion of Iraq], the United States says it is using force to exercise humanity and compassion, that it is acting as both a true king and a hegemon. But the Second Gulf War is not the same, because without the authorization of the United Nations ... the United States is using force under the pretext of humanity and compassion, and it is also maintaining its geopolitical, national security, and economic interests in the name of promoting democracy in the Middle East; it is obviously acting as a global hegemon.[5]

Still, one may ask, why not use the modern language of human rights to make such judgments? Michael Walzer, the most influential Western theorist of just and unjust war, explicitly argues that human rights are at the foundation of wartime morality: "individual rights to (life and liberty) underlie the most important judgments we make about war."[6] The obvious response is that "we" does not typically include Chinese intellectuals and policymakers.

In the Chinese context, the language of human rights, when it has been deployed to justify military intervention abroad, has been tainted by its misuses in the international arena. Given the history of colonial subjugation by Western powers, as well as the ongoing conflicts over economic resources and geopolitical interests, the language of human rights is often seen as an ideology designed to rationalize policies of exploitation and regime change. Even where military intervention in the name of human rights may have been justified—as, arguably, in the case of NATO's war on behalf of the Kosovo Albanians—it is difficult, if not impossible, to overcome Chinese skepticism regarding the real motives underlying intervention.

This provides a practical reason for invoking Mencius's theory of just and unjust war in the Chinese context. What ultimately matters is the practice rather than the theory of human rights. So long as people are protected from torture, genocide, starvation, and other such obvious harms, there is no need to worry about the particular political and philosophical justifications. That is, states and other collective agencies should do their best to respect our basic humanity, but whether such practices are backed by human rights morality is secondary. And if Mencius's theory leads to the same judgments regarding the justice of particular wars as theories of wartime morality founded on human rights, then why not deploy his theory in the Chinese context? Having said that, Mencius's theory will not always lead to the same judgments as theories founded on human rights—but this may speak in favor of Mencius's theory. For Mencius, the government cannot secure the peace if its people are not well fed (1A.7). Hence, the first obligation of government is to secure the basic means of subsistence of the people. By extension, the worst thing a government can do—in contemporary parlance, the most serious violation of human rights—would be to deliberately deprive the people of the means of subsistence (by killing them, not feeding them, not dealing with a plague, etc.). A ruler who engages in such acts, for the Confucian, would non-controversially be viewed as an oppressive tyrant, and punitive expeditions against such rulers would be justified (assuming the other conditions for punitive expeditions have also been met). In contrast, the sorts of violations of civil and political rights that might be viewed as constituting tyranny by contemporary Western defenders of human rights, such as systematic denials of the right to free speech or the heavy-handed treatment of political dissidents in the name of social order, would not be viewed as violations sufficiently serious to justify humanitarian intervention by foreign powers.

Such differences in emphasis may influence judgments of just and unjust warfare in the contemporary world. For Western defenders of human rights, Saddam Hussein was non-controversially regarded as an oppressive tyrant because he engaged in the systematic violation of civil and political rights: liberal defenders of humanitarian intervention such as Michael Ignatieff and Thomas Friedman supported the invasion of Iraq largely on those grounds. The invasion of Iraq, in their view, could democratize that country and set a political model for the rest of the Middle East (after Iraq became synonymous with hell on earth, such dreams were set aside). For Confucians, however, so long as the Iraqi people were not being deliberately deprived of the means of subsistence, the intervention could not be justified.

In other cases, however, Confucians may be more likely to support humanitarian interventions compared to liberal defenders of humanitarian intervention. In cases of deliberately engineered famines, such as the Afghanistan government's total road blockade on Kabul in 1996, the Confucian just war theorist would argue for foreign intervention (assuming, as always, that the other conditions for foreign intervention have been met). In contrast, liberal human rights groups such as Amnesty International denounced the shooting and torture of a few victims as human rights violations and treated the manufactured starvation of thousands as background.[7] Similarly, if it is true that the North Korean government deliberately promoted policies that resulted in the starvation of millions of people, the Confucian would have emphasized the need for foreign intervention in North Korea rather than such countries as Iraq.[8] It is worth asking how much of this matters in practice. Even if Confucian views inform the judgments of critical intellectuals in China, do these judgments really affect the political practices of the Chinese state? Confucian theorists of just war may prove to be just as ineffective as moralizing theorists of human rights in the American context (perhaps even more so, if the society lacks a free press and other public forums for communicating criticisms; Chinese Confucian critics tend to reserve their criticisms for foreign hegemons). It is obvious, for example, that war against Taiwan if it declares formal independence would not meet the Confucian criteria for justifiable punitive expeditions: so long as the Taiwanese government does not kill or starve its people, only moral power could be justifiably employed to bring Taiwan back into the Chinese orbit.[9] But it seems just as obvious that Confucian objections are not likely to cause the Chinese government to hold back in such an eventuality. So what exactly is the point of Confucian theorizing on just warfare?

A historical perspective may provide some insight. One feature of imperial China was that it did not expand in ways comparable to Western imperial powers, even when it may have had the technical ability to do so. Instead, it established the tributary system, with the "Middle Kingdom" at the center and "peripheral" states on the outside. In this system, the tributary ruler or his representative had to go to China to pay homage in ritual acknowledgment of his vassal status. In return, China guaranteed security and provided economic benefits, while using moral power to spread Confucian norms and allowing traditional ways of life to flourish. Needless to say, the system often took different forms and the practice often deviated from the ideal.[10] Still, the Confucian-Mencian discourse did help to stabilize the tributary system and curb the excesses of bloodthirsty warriors and greedy merchants.[11] There may be lessons for the future. As China once again establishes itself as an important global power, with the economic and military means to become a regional (or even global) hegemon, it will need to be constrained by more than realpolitik. More than any other discourse, Confucian theorizing on just and unjust war has the potential to play the role of constraining China's imperial ventures abroad, just as it did in the past. Confucian morality would cause the leaders to think twice about collaborating with governments implicated in the mass killings of civilians. Put more positively, China would also have the power and the responsibility to carry out punitive expeditions in neighboring states (e.g., if an East Asian state began to carry out a Rwanda-style massacre of its population). Confucian discourse could provide moral guidance in such cases and the Chinese government wouldn't simply be reacting to international pressure.

Confucian theorizing can also have an impact below the highest levers of the state, particularly once the war is already under way. The torture of prisoners at Abu Ghraib in Iraq is a reminder that evil deeds in warfare are committed "unofficially," by soldiers acting without the explicit authority of the top commanders. Nonetheless, these soldiers took implicit cues from the top, which set the tone for the cavalier approach to the protection of prisoners' well-being. Here the Confucian emphasis on the moral quality of political and military leaders may be particularly relevant. In Imperial China, the idea that those carrying out the war should be humane and compassionate informed the practice of appointing generals who were held to be exemplary persons with both moral character and military expertise. One important reason for emphasizing the moral quality of commanders is that they set the moral example for other ordinary soldiers, and their moral power radiates down to lower levels: as Confucius put it, "under the wind, the grass must bend" (12.19). If the aim is to sensitize soldiers to moral considerations, the leaders should not, as in Clausewitz's idea of the general, simply be concerned with the practical skills required for victory.

There are, in short, two main reasons for invoking Mencius's theory of just war. The first reason is psychological. If there is rough agreement on the aims of a theory of just war—that it should prohibit wars of conquest and justify certain kinds of wars of self-defense and humanitarian intervention—then one should invoke the theory that is most psychologically compelling to the people being addressed. In the Chinese context, the theory of Mencius is most likely to have causal power. The comparison here is not just theories of human rights, but with other Chinese thinkers such as Mozi who have also put forward theories functionally similar to modern theories of just war. Mencius is typically viewed as a "good guy" by contemporary Chinese, so there is no need to qualify or apologize for aspects of his theory.

The second reason is philosophical, and it speaks to the normative validity of Mencius's theory. Compared to alternative theories, Mencius's theory has several advantages, such as the focus on material well-being and the lack of emphasis on religion or ethnicity as justifications for going to war. Mencius's theory can and should be taught in military academies, both in China and elsewhere. And critical intellectuals should draw upon Mencius's views to evaluate the justice of wars in the contemporary world.

Can Mencius's theory come to be seen as part of China's soft power by the rest of the world? For that to happen, the theory has to come alive. Confucian social critics should also direct their critical ammunition at the Chinese state (not just the United States), where such criticisms are more likely to be taken seriously. And the theory should be seen as influencing the foreign policy of the Chinese state.[12] Once the Chinese state acts morally abroad, then it can articulate and promote its theory to the rest of the world. Otherwise nobody will really listen. Confucian moral values should also be seen as influencing domestic policy. Harsh Legalist-style measures that lead to the incarceration of hundreds of thousands of Uighurs undermine China's soft power abroad, even if they help to reduce incidents of terrorism at home.

Even then, however, there is no guarantee that China's foreign policy will come to express Confucian moral values. Much depends on the rest of the world's actions. The United States bears special responsibility. So long as the US maintains global military dominance—with military bases in China's neighboring countries and claims to exclusive rights in what should be common areas, such as outer space—China is not likely to depend solely (or even mainly) on soft power in the international arena. In this context, China's rise may not be entirely peaceful. A more balanced world—with no country having the military capacity to exert its will in the face of global opinion—renders more likely the expression of Confucian moral values. It is also a matter of attitude. So long as Chinese influence is regarded as inherently malevolent and competitive unless it conforms to American values and practices, it will be hard for China to respond with anything but power politics. Yes, China's political opening will make its model more attractive to Americans and forces that seek to demonize the country may not be as successful. But there is no reason to expect that China will—or should—have the same set of moral and political priorities when it engages with other countries. There are areas of justifiable moral difference that need to be tolerated, if not respected.

LIMITATIONS OF MENCIUS'S THEORY OF JUST WAR: LESSONS FROM ANCIENT INDIA

Whatever the merits of Mencius's theory of just war, I do not want to imply that the theory is without faults. Professor Sinha's essay (chapter 9, this volume) shows that insights from ancient Indian theorizing about just war can help to address those worries. At first glance, ancient Indian theorizing may not seem appropriate for supplementing a Mencius-inspired theory of just war meant to be morally persuasive and politically realistic in the contemporary age. For one thing, the characters in the *Mahabharata* often flip-flop between the divine and human worlds, which seems odd in a modern secular age. In contrast, the Confucian tradition, no matter how rich and diverse, is resolutely this-worldly with hardly any discussion of the afterlife. More importantly, perhaps, Krishna's views are juxtaposed against two extreme views that do not exist in Mencius's thought—or Chinese thought as a whole. On the one hand, Krsna has to argue against pacifists who are opposed to war and violence in principle. But Mencius is not against war in principle.[13] On the other hand, Krishna also has to argue against those who celebrate war and heroism in war. Here too, there is an almost complete absence of a tradition in China of thinkers who "valorize militant aggression as heroism and war as a manly effort," as opposed to an unfortunate necessity in terrible times. Even Legalists who affirm the importance of war deny that war is good for the people involved. So while Krsna has to defend a middle way between these two extremes, those extremes do not exist in Chinese thought.

But what about the substance of the "philosophical middle grounds"? What can we learn from ancient Indian thought that can allow us to enrich Mencius's theory? I do not wholeheartedly agree with Professor Sinha's view that Mencius's views about just cause for war are too restrictive (along with the implicit view that ancient Indian theories can provide more expansive justifications for going to war). Sinha criticizes Mencius's views on punitive expeditions because they are justified only when "people's life and subsistence are at stake. Thus, Mencius would not approve of military intervention in case of the violation of freedom of speech or religious rights" and he notes that "Mengzi would raise controversial but relevant questions about Chinese control over Tibet or India's handling of Kashmir." But I think Mencius is right to restrict invasion of another country only if foreign rulers engage in systematic and purposeful killing that deprives large groups of people of the right to life. Let us assume that China and India place restrictions on forms of speech and religious worship in Tibet and Kashmir. Would other countries be justified in invading China and India to liberate oppressed minorities? Mencius would answer quite clearly: punitive expeditions would not be justified in the absence of systemic killing (or genocide, to use modern language). If ancient Indian theories, or any other theories of just war, allow for invasion of countries simply on the grounds that those countries restrict the freedoms of speech and worship, those theories should be rejected. That's not to say the freedoms of speech and religious worship are not important—of course they are—but now, unlike, say, the time of the crusades, we no longer think we should go to war for those reasons. War involves killing and it is justified only to prevent more killing. Put differently: the right to life is the mother of all rights and should trump other rights in cases of conflict.

So why should be turn to ancient Indian theories of morally justified warfare? The key reason, perhaps, is that both theories were developed in times of constant warfare—the Warring States period in China, and in ancient India, war and aggression were part and parcel of the Rgvedic world (ca. 1500–1000 BCE)—and thinkers similarly tried to develop views that allowed for morally informed thinking about violence in terrible, war-filled eras of this sort. But Mencius, arguably, is handicapped by his view that human nature tends to goodness and it's just a matter of getting people to follow their naturally good instincts. He doesn't seem to allow for the possibility that some people can be born bad and are impossible to change, and that the people as a whole can be misguided and in favor of war, to the point of being bloodthirsty and fundamentally immoral. In contrast, Krishna doesn't always appeal to the good sense of warmakers and he tries to argue against their natural inclinations. And the text points to large numbers of people, from warmongering mothers to members of the *ksatriya* class, who favor war. For Mencius, it's important for rulers to gain the hearts of the people because the assumption seems to be that the people's hearts are fundamentally in the right place (or orientation). In the *Mahabharata*, by contrast, it seems the people themselves can be, at times, wrong and immoral, so moral rulers sometimes need to go against the immoral people. If we think of support in Germany for the Nazis and in Japan for imperial aggression in China, it's hard to take Mencius's side that the people are always right. It's a sad fact of human nature that otherwise good people can become fundamentally immoral and bloodthirsty in times of war and there is no shortage of political leaders who are prepared to demonize opponents so as to allow this horrible part of human nature to manifest itself.

The contrast is perhaps most glaring with respect to views about just conduct in war. Besides arguing against the large-scale slaughter of civilians (7B.3), Mencius does not offer any detailed prescriptions for *jus in bello*. Perhaps Mencius thought that war is so distasteful and so incompatible with his view that human nature is fundamentally good that he was unwilling to think through in great detail the implications of going to war (not surprisingly, Xunzi, with his more pessimistic account of human nature, spelled out more detailed prescriptions for just conduct in war). In contrast, Sinha shows that the *Mahabharata* put forward detailed prescriptions for morality in warfare: "Only equals should fight equals, one should fight one on one, non-combatants should remain unharmed, and the fatigued and frightened should be spared. Ambassadors and *brahmanas* were declared unslayable, so were the spectators." The reality of warfare often differed from the ideal, but a good deal of the norms "were followed, and the aberrations were criticized and debated indicating an age of transition from a period of unrestrained violence to the period when non-violence would be valued." In the face of horrible violence, rather than bury one's head in the sand *à la* Mencius, it is sometimes best to devise rules of combat designed to minimize the amount of suffering and cruelty, with the hope that such rules can also help to bring about a more humane age. Some of the rules in the *Mahabharata* seem out of date in our high-tech age (e.g., the rule that soldiers should fight one on one), but others, such as the rule against killing noncombatants and ambassadors, seem eminently sensible today as well.

The more tragic view of human nature in the *Mahabharata* can also help to avoid self-deception. How many wars in the contemporary era are fought by leaders who think they are doing good/God's work? Mencius's positive view of human nature more easily lends itself to misuses and justifications for horrible deeds committed by otherwise compassionate rulers. But there are no such whitewashes in the *Mahabharata*. As Sinha explains, "The message that the *Mahabharata* eventually leaves is, probably, that just war is impossible. Circumstances may make war unavoidable. One may have to engage in warfare when all possible alternatives fail. One must also try to limit the casualties or suffering of the civilians to the greatest possible extent. Yet, there is something problematic in warfare which can make it only a necessary and avoidable evil at best." In other words, war is an unconditional evil, even when it's necessary to stop even worse evil. The language of "just war" is problematic because it seems to imply that war can be good and such views easily lend themselves to justifying horrible acts all in the name of good intentions. At best, war is necessary. Perhaps we can replace the debate about "just war" with the debate about "necessary war," which doesn't lend itself so readily to self-deception about the horrible nature of war.

That's not to deny morality has a place in war. Here the *Mahabharata* puts forward the value of non-cruelty (*Anrishamsya*) which, once again, seems superior to Mencian language of "humanity and compassion" (仁) that lends itself so easily to gross misuses in times of war. The ideal was put forward by the soldier Yudhisthira, who "never accepted that violence could ever be righteous, though he could be persuaded to fight a war for the safe of his rightful claim when all attempts at peace failed."[14] The idea that necessary war involves minimizing cruelty rather than promoting humanity and compassion is perhaps the least problematic way to think about justifications for killing people. Does this turn of language really matter in practice? It may. The idea that morally justified war should still be viewed as an evil deed meant to prevent even greater cruelty helps us to draw the moral line between "necessary war" and "unjust war" in relatively clear ways. On the one hand, the value of minimizing cruelty reduces the risk that Mencian-style language of "humanity and compassion" can justify horrible acts all in the name of good intentions: think of the Vietnam War, or what the Vietnamese call the "American War," which killed an estimated two million Vietnamese civilians all in the name of an anti-communist moral crusade. It's highly unlikely that a modernized Yudhisthira could fall into such traps. On the other hand, the value of minimizing cruelty may indeed help to minimize cruelty in ways that would be difficult, if not impossible, within a Mencian moral framework. Consider the dropping of the atomic bomb on Hiroshima that helped to bring about the end of World War II. For Mencius, this act would be impossible to justify because it killed hundreds of thousands of civilians and American soldiers were not (initially) regarded as liberators. But the value of minimizing cruelty might help to justify this horrible act if it indeed prevented even worse killing, though without any attempt to minimize that fact that use of an atomic weapon is an evil act.[15]

In short, Mencius's theory of just war can and should help us think about morally justified war in a modern context, but it should be complemented, and in some parts replaced, by insights from the *Mahabharata*. Most important, the *Mahabharata* reminds us that war, no matter what kind of war, is always evil. At the very least, we can start by replacing the language of "just war" with the more sober and tragic reminder that war can never be more than a necessary evil.

NOTES

1. This essay draws on my book *China's New Confucianism* (Princeton, NJ: Princeton University Press, 2008), 28–37. I am grateful to Princeton University Press for permission to do so.

2. Ming Yongquan, "Youmeiyou zhengyi de zhanzheng? Yilun Rujia (wang ba zhi bian)" [Are there just wars? A Confucian debate on true kings and hegemons], http:www.arts.cuhk.hk/~hkshp, accessed October 11, 2003; site has been discontinued.

3. Mencius did say that a sage-king, who would conquer the world by means of moral power, was long overdue, but he noted that sage-kings come in five-hundred-year cycles and rarely last more than a generation or two (2B.13, 5A.5). According to Mencius's own theory, the nonideal world of competing states delimited by territorial boundaries is the reality for roughly 90 percent of the time.

4. Ni Lexiong, "Zhongguo gudai junshi wenhua guannian dui shijie heping de yiyi" [The implications of ancient Chinese *Military Culture for World Peace*], *Junshi lishi yanjiu* [*Military History Research*], vol. 2 (2001). An English translation of this article appears in *Confucian Political Ethics*, ed. Daniel A. Bell (Princeton, NJ: Princeton University Press, 2008), chap. 10.

5. Gong Gang, "Shei shi quanqiu lunli de daidao shiwei" [Who is the armed guard of global Ethics?], *Nanfang chuang*, September 2003, http://www.nfcmag.com/news/newsdisp.php3?NewsId = 296&mod =, accessed November 10, 2001; site has been discontinued.

6. Michael Walzer, *Just and Unjust Wars: A Moral Argument with Historical Illustrations*, 5th ed. (New York: Basic Books, 2015), 54.

7. In response to such cases of apparently misguided priorities, Amnesty has expanded its mission to include economic and social rights (see my *Beyond Liberal Democracy* [Princeton, NJ: Princeton University Press, 2007], 94).

8. Given the likely civilian casualties, however, Confucian critics would likely emphasize other means of opposition, such as remonstrance or targeted killing of the North Korean leaders responsible for the famine.

9. But would Taiwan be justified in defending itself if attacked by the mainland? For the Confucian, the judgment would depend partly on the moral character of the Taiwanese ruler, the degree of popular support in Taiwan for that leader, and the likely consequences of other options such as surrender (not so bad if the Chinese army withdraws soon after invasion and the Chinese government restores the *status quo ante*) or exile (Mencius holds that the humane ruler faced with certain defeat will leave his kingdom rather than expose his people to harm, and he will eventually be followed by his people [IB.15]).

10. It may be more historically accurate to refer to different tributary systems that worked differently in different times and places and even to question its reality in certain contexts: see the discussion in my book (co-authored with Wang Pei), *Just Hierarchy: Why Social Hierarchies Matter in China and the Rest of the World* (Princeton, NJ: Princeton University Press, 2020), 126–29.

11. See David C. Kang, *East Asia before the West: Five Centuries of Trade and Tribute* (New York: Columbia University Press, 2012).

12. China has become a consistent advocate of the Responsibility to Protect (R2P), endorsing its application in many countries while urging a constrained, multilateral use of force (see https://www .usip.org/publications/2016/06/china-and-responsibility-protect-opposition-advocacy). The R2P is comparable to Mengzi's idea of punitive expeditions, although as far as I know, the Chinese government has not invoked Mengzi in contemporary discussions of R2P.

13. Edmund Ryden, *Just War and Pacifism: Chinese and Christian Perspectives in Dialogue* (Taipei: Taipei Ricci Institute, 2001), 46.

14. It is worth noting that Yudhisthira was strongly influenced by his mother and his wife: in Mencius, and the Confucian tradition more generally, female voices are almost totally absent in the debates on peace and warfare.

15. Use of the second atomic bomb in Nagasaki would be much harder to justify if the aim was to end the war and thus even worse levels of cruelty. If there is any reason to believe that use of the first atomic bomb in Hiroshima was sufficient for this purpose, then use of the second bomb should be seen as a criminal, unjustifiable act of cruelty that murdered tens of thousands of civilians.

Diplomacy

11

India's Diplomacy *in Absentia*

Violence, Defense, Offense[1]

Deep K. Datta-Ray

INTRODUCTION

The rare occasions when diplomacy does not constitute international politics arise from the presumption there are no other actors or diplomacy's supplementation. An instance of the former was the Chinese diplomat's report which led to the first mention of the Roman Empire in Chinese records, thereby expanding awareness and setting the scene for diplomacy with the empire.[2] As for the latter, it is war.[3] Diplomacy therefore expands awareness, and so its field, and continues alongside war and inevitably replaces it. All three, diplomacy, its presumed absence, and supplementation, are *International Relations'* (IR) subjects. Diplomacy's centrality to IR is what makes it vital to *Political Science*, for IR's domain of interstate relations is at a minimum related to the intrastate relations studied by the latter.[4] This is now recognized by IR, and so it accounts for interstate relations by referring to the intrastate. What this affirms is the inextricable intermixing of intrastate and interstate politics, and so reiterates the role of diplomacy in animating all politics and why diplomats merit study. Yet when they are studied, imposed categories occlude them and nowhere is this more apparent than in the study of Indian diplomacy. When not riddled with factual errors, conceptual imposition makes for incoherent, emaciated, or morally suspect analysis.[5] For instance, *Realist* authors use their theory of rationalism, i.e., *Realism*, to account for Indians and Pakistanis, yet claim both have different rationalities, and all while attenuating actors to materialism and so denying them their culture and history. Meanwhile, *Postcolonial* authors reduce actors to alien concepts of status at the expense of the material. Underscoring both schools is their infantilizing Indians as learning to do diplomacy from *Liberals* and then *Realists*, both understood as past masters, of diplomacy by virtue of being European.[6] Out-of-court at inception then is equality,

223

and so of diplomacy being investigated in terms of its non-Western producers. The price is that their intellectual categories are lost, and so our understanding of international politics enervated. In short, requisite is an intellectual history of diplomacy in producer's terms rather than that of those who study them.

Doing so is to understand coherently, fully, and morally.[7] All three begin with noting discrepancies between the expected and practice, an instance of which is that Indian diplomats make sense of their practice not via European, much less North American, symbols or texts, but through the epic *Mahabharata*. An example from the fieldwork within India's Ministry of External Affairs (MEA) is illustrative. The top diplomat—the Foreign Secretary—after decades in the bureaucracy and aware that new diplomats had no idea of their job, asked if they knew what their job was. His audience said they did not, so the Foreign Secretary explained their job in terms of what is familiar to them, as their murmurs and bobbing heads confirmed—the epic. That the *Mahabharata* is the reference for the MEA was reiterated during my teaching two of its batches. It was impossible to miss that everyone, regardless of caste or religion, knew the ins-and-outs of the epic, perhaps because they were totally removed from the West's semantic fields relating to diplomacy. Symptomatic was a new Hindu diplomat, who said early one morning—while exchanging Mughal couplets with another Hindu diplomat—in a freezing train in Rajasthan: "No matter how English speaking we are, this [the *Mahabharata*] remains our basic." Furthermore, in conversation with nearly six percent of Indian diplomats, not one contradicted the Foreign Secretary's view. Essentially, what he did was retrieve a tool from an intellectual kit already known to new diplomats so they could make sense of their job.[8] This familiarity with the *Mahabharata* at the level of individuals conducting diplomacy is suggestive of the epic playing a role in the very production of diplomacy. Any other suggestion, such as of Western concepts influencing Indian diplomacy, is inexplicable, for it makes for an unfathomable chasm between policy and those who make it. Moreover, such a suggestion contradicts the representativeness of democracy which, regardless of its flaws, defines Indian bureaucratic politics.[9]

That is why the first section of this essay theorizes how the *Mahabharata* produces diplomacy but not in terms of the epic, nor analysts. Rather, the *Mahabharata* is made sense of in terms of its utilization by India's most successful and influential diplomat, Mahatma Gandhi, who understood the myth as a reading on *violence*. To view the myth in, as will be shown, the ever-influential Gandhi's terms, is not an exercise in nativism, but to recognise the epic's lived-quality. An aspect of this is the epic's transmission into the Indian state's corridors of power by Gandhi, as the managing of *violence*. In other words, the *Mahabharata* is utilized to account for diplomacy today not for sentimentality nor for novelty, but to reveal that "which Western observers normally miss or misunderstand," and as it happens, as a "corrective to the allegedly universalistic theories of interest that dominate political analysis."[10] To do both cannot miss that the roots of the production of diplomacy lie in Gandhi's theorizing violence and his invention of *satyagraha*, which absorbed offense instead of replicating it, so as to curtail it. Moreover, *satyagraha*'s formal nationalization to become India's diplomacy was because Gandhi's foremost pupil was also India's first prime minister, Jawaharlal Nehru, and his legacy shapes the diplomacy of the currently ruling Bharatiya Janata Party (BJP).

Before explicating how Indian diplomacy from Nehru to the BJP utilized the *Mahabharata* as presented by the Mahatma, elaborated is how he understood the myth. He had long engaged the epic and reproduced two lessons from it. Between 1905 and 1947 he directly referred to or quoted it nearly three hundred times, patiently studied it, translated entire sections of it, and encouraged its study.[11] The first lesson he took wholesale was the *Mahabharata*'s *dharma*-complex or contextual action. In fact, the word *dharma* in the sense it is used in the epic suffuses his writings, appearing more than three thousand times. The second was the epic's concern with managing offense, defensively, that is, curtailing offense without replicating it. The *Mahabharata*, though professing *ahimsa* or nonviolence, was for Gandhi unable to resolve the quandary of defense without offense. Gandhi solved this by replacing interest with disinterest, applied contextually. This is because interest permits equivalences—that is, contracts between interested parties— to make for politics both between and within nations; but paradoxically, it is to safeguard interests that the parties resort to offense. In contrast, *satyagraha* is defensive and so calls not for interest but for disinterest, extending to a willingness to sacrifice one's own life. No doubt this requires courage, but it also allowed parties to extricate themselves from the dependency and contingency inherent in contracts. Testimony to the effectiveness of disinterest was *satyagraha* terminating British colonialism by absorbing its offenses while not replicating them. But Gandhi had no dictum for what a defense was, apart from that it was always contextual. That Gandhi's *satyagraha* is what India chose is why its diplomacy is *in absentia*, for the very disinterestedness of diplomacy continues to animate practitioners.

The next two sections demonstrate how this intellectual setting arising from Gandhi's *Mahabharata* actually animates diplomatic practice. This begins to emerge in what underscores diplomacy, and that is the *Mahabharata*'s calculations of contextual defense. This is discernible in two diplomatic practices: the instant that India deployed nuclear-capable strategic airpower diplomatically against Balakot, a target in Pakistan, in 2019, and the perpetuity extending beyond the nation-state's history that is Indian nuclear diplomacy, culminating with the adoption of No First Use (NFU) and Credible Minimum Deterrence (CMD). To excavate both in terms of diplomats, rather than analysts, discloses the term for calculation was defense. Noteworthy, too, is that relative to offense, defense improves systemic security, stems sovereignty's fragmentation, and retains control over the future. This is because offense finds security in exceeding opponent's offensiveness, which naturally intensifies competition and so perpetually degrades global security. In addition, sovereignty is fragmented by security being dependent on the opponent's choice to exceed or not, one's own offensiveness. Moreover, offense constantly hands over control to opponents because it is their actions that actors must counter, since security lies in exceeding everyone else's offensiveness. However, the superiority of defense over offense tactically, strategically, and morally, has a cost. Defense is contingent on not matching offense and so necessitates sacrifice, which calls for an uncommon courage. Undoubtedly, offense is courageous, but this is immeasurably intensified in defense because sacrifice requires absorbing offense while not replicating it. Nowhere was this more apparent than in India's nuclear diplomacy as invented by Nehru and now practiced by the BJP. In short, what this shows is that there is no constant to Indian diplomacy in practice except that it is a defense applied contextually.

The preoccupation with context and defense is ironically most apparent in the BJP's attempts to refute it, so as to be able to claim a new intellectual history at a remove from the Mahatma's. For instance, at Balakot the BJP wanted to be shot of the courage defense demands, and so sought to change diplomacy from contextual defense to contextual offense. The desire to be done with being courageous is calculable in the price the BJP's leadership paid. It began with equating India with Pakistan to calculate the offense, and fragmenting India's sovereignty for security became dependent on how Pakistan responded. Moreover, control was handed to Islamabad because it could now legitimately escalate to safeguard itself from an offensive neighbor. That the price was paid to secure freedom from having to be courageous is obvious in what occurred prior to Balakot. Then, New Delhi did muster the courage to contextually sacrifice itself, overwhelmingly in the borderlands, to deaden the offense of terrorism by denying any meaning to Islamabad's provocations. Moreover, defense in the context of China had also denied its provocations meaning, if only until the adoption of NFU between 1998 and 2003. Till then, New Delhi enhanced systemic security, maintained sovereignty, and control, by not responding offensively to Pakistani and Chinese offenses. Doing so, however, meant choosing to live in the shadow of terror as well as nuclear annihilation and this sacrifice called for an uncommon courage. It ensured defense, but that was undone by NFU's adoption because, if only for the bureaucrat who formulated the policy, it was a stop-gap measure until India could be offensive. In short, India was contextually offensive at Balakot but remains defensive in its nuclear diplomacy despite officialdom. Additionally, while Balakot was a shift from defense to relieve the BJP of having to be courageous, NFU was defense but in service of offense.

What attests to the *Mahabharata*'s centrality then is not that it is utilized but that its abrogation consumes diplomatic policy makers even as they seek interest with results disastrous for the globe. How, therefore, interest infiltrates disinterest, requires gauging, and this is done in the conclusion via a calculus of disinterested diplomacy with offensive diplomacy, which exposes its foundations as interest and, inevitably, contracts, because of its Abrahamic origins. Extending the calculus to China makes visible the anti-interest "brightness" (明). Recommended for implementation ritualistically, it not only provides a means to manage the infiltration of interest but also divulges that what is truly at stake is not only the fate of nations but freedom itself.

VIOLENCE

What makes the *Mahabharata* seminal is that it engaged Gandhi, whose most significant follower was Nehru. Looking back on his prime ministerial work in his later years, Nehru said, "The policies and philosophy we implement are taught by Gandhiji . . . His solutions helped us cover the chasm between the Industrial Revolution and the Nuclear Era. After all, the only answer to the Atom Bomb is nonviolence." Nehru elaborated, "Gandhiji organised a practical philosophy of action which we inherited . . . the most practical substitute for violence by bringing about a mighty revolution with the bloodless weapon of passive resistance." Asked if passive resistance, that is, defense, suggested "Gandhiji broke and emasculated your earlier faith in scientific Socialism with his spiritual solutions," Nehru answered: "It is wrong to say that he broke or emasculated anybody. Any such thing would be against his way. The most important thing he insisted upon was the importance of means: ends were shaped by the means, and therefore the means had to be truthful. That is what we learnt from him and it is well we did."[12] As for Gandhi, he never doubted Nehru: "You cannot divide water by striking it with a stick. Jawaharlal will be my successor. He does what I want. When I am gone he will do what I am doing. Then he will speak my language too."[13]

That this language conveys a theory is obvious in Gandhi's abstracting the concerns and elements of the globalized international system to violence and nonviolence, and from it, forging a theory of action. In doing so he forwarded an intellectual stream he had long engaged, most tangibly, in the *Mahabharata*. Its contribution to Gandhi was twofold. The first arises from its very narrativization, which is the moral of contextuality which is also presented contextually. For instance, example after example is made to demonstrate the point of contextuality. This is significant and, following the text, is termed *dharma* or contextual action. There is an interrelated category within the text: highest-*dharma* or the super-moral. Their relationship is complicated by, for instance, *ahimsa* and *anrasamsya* (nonviolence and noncruelty) being amongst highest-*dharma*, which suggests that contextual action cannot be the moral. Indeed, of the fifty-four instances in the text of highest-*dharma*, there are more than twenty-five categories and numerous subcategories, including individual *dharma*s. In other words, if *dharma* is context-dependent action, then highest-*dharma* is knowing that this is the way to act in whatever situation one is in, and recognizing that situation within an ontology that admits virtually endless variation and deferral in matters of formulating and approaching *the highest*. In other words, the text's moral—that is, the highest-truth—is that all contexts generate their own truth. In short, *dharma* is a metaphysic that enables highest-*dharma*.

In putting them forward in combination, what is constructed is the *dharma*-complex, and it accounts for Indian diplomacy's consistent concern with calibrating defense contextually—or its failed abrogation by the BJP now.[14] The second contribution the text made was in its grappling with the problem of defensively managing offense, and even curtailing it without reproducing it. The epic, though preaching the sanctity of all contexts which logically disallows any offense to any context, was unable to manage offense. Hence the epic's story of the killing of a blind beast by the hunter Balaka, who is nonetheless transported to heaven because the beast had vowed to kill all creatures. The issue of what is usually wrong becoming right and its reverse is managed by the *dharma*-complex, but its logic demands nonviolence; so how can Balaka's violence be permissible, much less rewarded? This is what Gandhi resolved by categorizing actions as offensive and defensive, which allowed him to develop the practice of *satyagraha*, and which Nehru made into diplomacy, and the BJP continues to follow, if only, in trying to undo it.[15]

It began with Gandhi recognizing life is violent and so nonviolence is an unrealizable ideal, but that this did not "vitiate the principle itself." Noting the "difference between one action and another lies only in the degree of violence involved," Gandhi classified actions into two classes: offense and defense. The latter is a form of offense since it defends, but it is also ontologically different from offense for absorbing the former and doing so in one's own terms rather than with any reference to the former. This is *satyagraha*, and its success is contingent on its practitioner entirely giving up any interest in themselves, laying themselves open to offense, and in absorbing it, converting it.[16] That accounts for the ferocity of Gandhi's battle-cry. "Fight violence with non-violence if you can and if you can't do that, fight violence by any means, even if it means your utter extinction," he said, knowing full well it was inevitable in the face of offense.[17] Facing it called for the courage unique to defense, and so Gandhi sought in an SS—Schutzstaffel—officer of the Third Reich, for it was one of the most formidable fighting forces of his day, the "art of throwing away my life for a noble cause."[18] This raises the question of what is the *noble cause* and whether resisting to the point of extinction is in keeping with the cause or defense. Taking them in turns, the cause for Gandhi was the epic's *dharma*-complex, which was the *truth*, because of how he placed it in relation to other matters. He wrote: "While the end is truth, non-violence is the means of attaining it. In such matters, the means cannot be separated from the end. Hence I have written that truth and non-violence are the two sides of the same coin."[19] As for truth being synonymous with the *dharma*-complex, this was apparent in his writings, of which he wrote:

> At the time of writing . . . my aim is not to be consistent with previous statements on a question, but to be consistent with truth as it may present itself to me at a given moment. . . . But friends who observe inconsistency will do well to . . . try to see if there is not an underlying and abiding consistency between the two seeming inconsistencies.[20]

Truth *is* the same duality as the *dharma*-complex. Truth is certain within the practitioner's immediate context, and this very momentariness of truth makes for an abiding truth: the truth of contextual truth. If every situation is truthful then its protection had to also be truthful in that it did not destroy any context, including the offensive. That is why only *satyagraha* could do because it internalized, rather than generated, violence. Gandhi relies on converting the offender's violence to nonviolence by the spectacle of the former's effect on the latter—which also reiterates the abiding nature of truth. It is this that brings to the fore the question: Does defense merit death? Clearly, there can be no conversion if the defender perishes. Additionally, there is the momentariness of truth which mandates that it can only be the practitioner in context who can judge what the acuity of the defense ought to be. The combination means that while defending to the point of suicide is acceptable, such a finality must be judged in the moment for whether it maintains truth or converts the offensive. If it does then death can be entertained, but not otherwise because that undermines truth. In practice this translates into tolerance for sacrifice, so long as the truth is not eliminated, and offense is converted. Death is undoubtedly a barbarity and intolerable, but only if it extinguishes truth.

What this was, was a radical departure from the world's conceptualization—note the United Nation's *Universal Declaration of Human Rights* foremost declaration being the *Right to Life*—and underpinning it was the ejection of interest. *Satyagraha's* basis cannot be interest because it relies on disinterest in the most meaningful of senses—to sacrifice one's own life. Gandhi therefore pursued disinterest as the foundation for *satyagraha*. It is, in addition to not seeking life, a disinterested response because it also cannot be contractually engaged by offense since despite its threats or more, it cannot find any interest to offend. Moreover, not only is any offense rendered meaningless by disinterested actors, they are also the means to convert offense. Conversion occurs when offense realizes its "evil," as the British did with the opium trade. Its death knell was sounded, after all, not in China, or because of Chinese actions, or their wars with the British, but at the center of the drug trade, London, because of British regret. It was forged from the realization that they, the British, conducted "the most long-continued and systematic international crime of modern times."[21] In other words, the British realized their ways were offensive and thus evil and so they ceased.

This combination of disinterest and context is not unique to India and indeed long predated the nation-state. By its birth, it was also apparent that the combination was applicable to the realm of international politics. That Gandhi recognized both is apparent in his noting *satyagraha* in at least two instances. The first *satyagraha* was Polish resistance to Nazi Germany, which continued after Warsaw had capitulated. Gandhi's commentary on the resistance is telling. "Supposing a mouse in fighting a cat tried to resist the cat with his sharp teeth, would you call that mouse violent? . . . In the same way, for the Poles to stand valiantly against the German hordes vastly superior in numbers, military equipment and strength, was almost non-violence. . . . You must give its full value to the word 'almost,'" said Gandhi. The second instance of *satyagraha* was created by Pakistan invading Kashmir in 1947, of which Gandhi said: "Pakistan invaded Kashmir. Units of the Indian army have gone to Kashmir . . . on the express invitation of the Maharaja and Sheikh Abdullah . . . the real Maharaja of Kashmir. Muslims in their thousands are devoted to him." For Gandhi and India, Pakistan's violence was an offense against the people epitomized by Sheikh Abdullah, and therefore worthy of resistance which, though by an army, was different enough from Pakistan's offense to be nonviolent since it was not contingent on the former, and sought not to extinguish it by contract, but rather, convert it by sacrifice. "I do not agree that the armed force our Government has dispatched to Kashmir has committed aggression there," said Gandhi, for the troops were conducting a defense. Yet defense was violence, which is why he found it "barbarous," but it had to be done, for as he had said, the end was not nonviolence. It was only the means to truth, which is the lesson he learned from the *Mahabharata*—its *dharma*-complex.[22]

The novelty of Gandhi's philosophy and its practicality as *satyagraha* both within and without nation-states is only apparent if contextualized in diplomacy as it is generally understood. In the Western tradition, the diplomat incorporates only after the grounds have been prepared by crafting everything into interests by academics. In other words, the relatively recent Westphalian system's way of conceptualizing in terms of interests must first be disseminated globally before it can be utilized. Though this conceptualization is new in global terms, it is European and so has a history in states crumbling from a church, splintering out of the papacy. This history of fragmentation was the reproduction of interest into other realms. After all, interest's constitution today in material terms is just a secularization of interest as real and ideal, understood as man and God and which was to be mediated by the contractor, the papacy. The locking together in contract is not new either, just a replay of Christ as mediator trying to unify man with God. Of interest is Christ's purpose because it arises from man's expulsion from the Garden of Eden, and that is doubly significant: for being an Old Testament story, and because it marks the birth of interest as the splitting of the world into components which then must contract, to unify. Indeed, contracting to unify is the entire purpose of this intellectual stream, which, because of where it originates, organizes everything descended from Abrahamic religion. Its most noteworthy contribution is interest not only for its ubiquity but also for highlighting Gandhi's ingenuity as well as the technical finesse of a handful of Indian diplomats in applying it to international politics.

DEFENSE

That the *Mahabharata* became India's diplomacy, via Gandhi, is nowhere more apparent than in nuclear diplomacy. That it was directly drawn from the *Mahabharata*'s lessons on contextual defense is because the formulator for nuclear diplomacy was Gandhi's pupil, Nehru. He limited the atom to research with the 1948 Atomic Energy Act. Moreover, to curtail any slippage to offense, and always aware of context, India proposed in 1954 a Standstill Agreement to suspend nuclear testing. China's announcing it would develop a bomb, the war with China, and its nuclear test in 1964, could not divert India's nuclear research away from research. However, parliament was not as steadfast in defense and more prone to India's deteriorating context, which is why fear of China led to calls for weaponization.[23] Nehru was unaffected, but following his death, democratic pressure made Prime Minister Lal Bahadur Shastri initiate the Subterranean Nuclear Explosion Project (SNEP) in 1965, which upon completion would have put India three months from a test.[24] Even if SNEP was not scrapped within months by Prime Minister Indira Gandhi, it would have maintained India's posture of being less capable by design, and so less offensive, than its nuclear rivals—starting with China and extending to other nuclear powers.

Mrs. Gandhi's policies by being her father's, maintained Gandhi's philosophy. Hence, she pressed for the curtailment of nuclear weapons and proposed at the UN a non-proliferation treaty, a full five years, before the Non-Proliferation Treaty.[25] Despite its efforts, India failed to secure a nuclear guarantee. The unbearable burden of obliteration prompted a test in 1974, but it was not followed by militarization because the logic of defense continued: India remained in an indisputably weaker position *vis-à-vis* adversaries. The next steps were also contextually defensive despite involving weaponization under Indira's son, Prime Minister Rajiv Gandhi, and its revelation in 1998. The context for weaponization was Rajiv's Six Nation Five Continent Appeal for nuclear disarmament at a summit meeting in 1985, which garnered little interest. Meanwhile, undeterred by India's test, China expanded its nuclear weapons program and supplied one to Pakistan. "Beijing has consistently regarded a nuclear-armed Pakistan as a crucial ally and vital counterweight to India's capabilities," testified the CIA's director in 1993.[26] Despite all, India maintained its posture of weakness relative to all including Pakistan, which achieved weapon's capacity some eight years before New Delhi.[27] Its capacity was prompted, in addition to Pakistan, by contradictions in China's NFU policy from the 1980s. "Very often one finds strategists arguing abstractly in favour of first strikes in conventional and nuclear war, even while claiming that China is committed to a second strike posture," commented an analyst.[28] It was in this matrix of nuclear instability, escalation, dissemination, illegality, and deception that India became a nuclear weapons state, disclosed it promptly, and continued its posture of weakness—at least in practice—with NFU and CMD. This was done because at the core of policy change was the abiding concern with defending without offense.

That practice was motivated by contextual defense is confirmed by what was said about it by those who did it. In other words, how practice was made sense of. At a broad level, survey results showed that until the 1990s there was a "remarkable picture of restraint in the face of grave provocation," as nearly half the members of the strategic elite did not consider nuclear retaliation necessary even in response to a minor nuclear attack. It was in this milieu that Rajiv operated, and he reproduced it. His scientific advisor said Rajiv "was genuinely against the bomb," implying he had been forced to weaponize. The sentiment arose from the purpose inherited from his mother, grandfather, and his *guru*, Mahatma Gandhi. A Foreign Secretary who served Rajiv reminisced that he "envisions a world without hate, fear and confrontation . . . This, in Rajiv Gandhi's own phrase, is 'India's millennial concept of the world as a family. This vision of a new world order is a spiritual vision, not unlike Jawaharlal Nehru's but closer, it seems, to Mahatma Gandhi's.'"[29] In noting this, all that is being restated is that defense was policy and that it was an inheritance from India's freedom struggle.

That was also evident in what was said of Mrs. Gandhi, which will have to suffice in the absence of any official records of the decision to test. A secret cable from American ambassador Chester Bowles and about a private conversation between the Canadian high commissioner and Mrs. Gandhi noted: "With China at her [Mrs. Gandhi's] back, and Pakistan lurking on the sidelines, she foresaw no alternative but to keep open her option on the production of nuclear weapons."[30] As for the actual decision, the Indian Foreign Secretary at the time wrote: "There were no policy papers nor had there been any discussion on this crucial matter in the External Affairs Ministry." The official had suggested drawing up background papers and Mrs. Gandhi had agreed, but on the day, she glowered and asked who had authorized their preparation. The official continues: "I tried to refresh her memory, but she would have none of it. She said something about a 'national decision', but we were not aware of any national decision or even debate in Parliament on the sensitive issue. At least three of us [the Secretaries in charge of the Defence, Finance, and Foreign, ministries] were greatly puzzled at our summary and inexplicable rebuff for carrying out what we conceived to be our assigned duty."[31] This firsthand report of the decision-making behind the test reinforces the contention that nuclear decisions rise from inherited beliefs, and that this was so for Mrs. Gandhi was clear to another American ambassador, Daniel Moynihan, who reported it to Washington in January 1974.[32] What is significant here though, is that on both sides of the watershed that was the test, India operated in terms of calculations to defend, as opposed to exceed, at a minimum, Pakistan's offensive capacities.

Mrs. Gandhi's clarity of thought on nuclear policy was an inheritance from her father. He too tried to calculate defense from before India came into existence, but unlike his daughter, spoke of it. For instance, in a lecture prior to independence on "defense and national development," Nehru laid out defense without offense: "India will . . . not prepare for or think in terms of any aggression or dominion over any other country. Defence thus becomes purely defence against external aggression or internal disorder."[33] Inaugurating India's first reactor a few years later, Nehru further detailed the policy: "No man can prophesy the future. But

I should like to say on behalf of any future Government of India that whatever might happen, whatever the circumstances, we shall never use atomic energy for evil purposes. There is no condition to this assurance, because once a condition is attached, the value of an assurance does not go very far."[34]

While it is significant that Nehru denounced nuclear weapons, what is note-worthy is his overt articulation of unconditionality because anything else would be "evil." Its spiritual rather than political connotations convey the issue was not developing or using nuclear weapons but their offensiveness. That is why he wrote in 1964 in the margins of a note to the country's foremost nuclear scientist, Homi Bhabha: "Apart from building power stations and developing electricity, there is always a built-in advantage of defense use if the need should arise."[35] Yet divert-ing the program to military purposes was an abomination, but one dependent on context. That is why Nehru also said that if nothing were done to check weapon-ization then "it may become almost impossible to control the situation."[36] To lose control was ultimately not to weaponize, or even use, but to do so offensively. That is why Nehru sought to placate the offensive amongst his electorate by noting that there was a built defensive capacity to nuclear research. However, the temptation to offense was too great, which is why bombs should never be built, though he was aware of the compunctions of a contextual defense which might necessitate them. Hence, he wrote, at the end of his days: "We are determined not to use weapons for war purposes. We do not make atom bombs. I do not think we will."[37]

What is remarkable is not that India was forced into making bombs but that doing so was in line with the *Mahabharata*'s lessons on *ahimsa*, *dharma*, and the *dharma*-complex. These, however, persist despite bureaucratic elements trying to undercut the *Mahabharata*'s lessons. The most significant instance of this was K. Subrahmanyam, the bureaucrat who drafted the policy of NFU and CMD. His purpose was not to eschew nuclear bombs but to always remain inferior to offen-sive parties who are so by virtue of having more tools, in this case bombs, to be offensive. Hence, India keeps to the epic's lessons, and so continues to make the sacrifice of living in the shadow of being unable to deter annihilation via the logics of Mutually Assured Destruction (MAD). However, the bureaucrat was unable to fully comprehend the logic-stream beginning with the *Mahabharata* that he was engaging, and so undercut the defense he planned, while maintaining contextual-ity. Committed to a contextual nuclear defense, the official repeatedly voiced his case in Gandhian terms. For instance, he wrote a "future strategy has to be based on a vision of non-violence" and also that "non-violence as a resistance strategy had to be on a case-by-case basis: it cannot be treated as universally applicable against all aggression in the world," and indeed the only reason for India's non-violence was that nuclear weapons meant "the globe has shrunk to a small space station."[38] This final conditionality to defense is what negated this very Gandhian thinking, and illustrates Subrahmanyam's limits. That is because the sacrifice implicit in defense neutralizes the offense to meaninglessness and perhaps might even convert it—if the offender realizes the pointlessness of its exertions. However, and in contradistinction to Nehru, the bureaucrat made defense conditional, and mandated the possibility of offense. That undermined India's pledge to only defend and converted it into no more than a stop-gap measure to the day when enough arms could be stockpiled to permit offense. In short, until India achieved first-strike capacity. This also undid defense because a preemptive strike against India was now no longer unjustified because its defense was just a means to play catch-up to being offensive. Nevertheless, and despite the official's long-term intentions, India continues to maintain inferiority to all the nuclear powers that threaten it, which attests to the continuity of the *Mahabharata* despite, in turns, Subrahman-yam's limitations and incompetence.

OFFENSE

A more recent attempt to undo the *Mahabharata*'s lesson only reiterates its organizing significance. This begins to emerge in India describing its airstrike by nuclear-capable Mirage-2000 fighter-bombers against Jaish-e-Mohammad (JEM) terrorist camps in Pakistan's Balakot region on 26 February 2019 as a "non-military" action.[39] The dissonance between the act and its description is not easily resolved. Nevertheless, what is certain is that for India this was a diplomatic rather than a military act because it was designated so and because it was presented by the top diplomat, the Foreign Secretary. That other pronouncements following the strike were overwhelmed by hyperbole and are riddled with inconsistencies, but more importantly bear no relevance to the state's understanding of its actions because they were unofficial. In any case, even before India could unveil its airstrike, Pakistan announced an "effective response" made its enemy bomb in "haste while escaping."[40] Just hours later, *Reuters* journalists visited the bombed location, took photographs, conducted interviews, and concluded India's bombs had indeed missed their target—which in any case was inactive.[41] The Indian leadership's embarrassment teetered on mortification the next day when an Indian MIG-21 fighter jet was destroyed by enemy fire. Humiliation was guaranteed by satellite imagery and third-party sources confirming Pakistan's narrative.[42] India's current BJP leadership which proclaims its *jumla*, or sophistry, turned to it.[43] At an election rally the Home Affairs Minister announced "300 mobile phones were active" in the bombing zone prior to the mission.[44] Proving 300 phones belonged to terrorists, not noncombatants, suggests excellent signals intelligence and human intelligence, despite the complication of there just being 150 recruits present. The implication was that India tracked millions of noncombatants in the expectation that some may become terrorists. This is all very unlikely since it is beyond intelligence agencies with superior budgets, technology, and training at integrating multiple sources of intelligence, noted an Australian military officer.[45]

The only way to understand the strike then is to return to the official pronouncement and read it in the terms of its writers. In addition to it being a diplomatic action, what becomes apparent if Indians are listened to, is a context of change from defense to offense. So said the bureaucrat who announced Balakot, and it was so obvious that even the Chinese "clearly see strategic culture is changing under the current government. India is willing to take risks. Use of force is no longer ruled out."[46] The change arose from the airstrike's architect—the National Security Advisor (NSA), whose role as coordinator for all diplomatic matters was reinforced in the wake of the strike by his elevation to Cabinet rank.[47] What reiterates that the NSA manages diplomacy—rather than the Foreign Minister—is his continuing to be the Prime Minister's special envoy to critical neighbors despite the loss of territory to China at Doklam in 2020 and Balakot, selecting his own people for key assignments such as brokering negotiations with Nepal, and participating in all key diplomatic meetings in India. Indeed, the NSA is the "go-to man in Indian diplomacy . . . the foreign minister . . . a superior clerk," noted India's leading newspaper.[48] The only time the NSA's explanation of his strategic approach, which makes for the means to read the strike, was recorded for general consumption was a lecture instructive precisely because despite notes, it is littered with irregularities and spliced with disfluencies and fillers, common to Indian-English, or *Hinglish*.[49] The content is not a regurgitation of received knowledge, but a lived sense of strategy garnered from background and career.

The NSA said the talk's title—"India's Strategic Response to Terrorism"—equates terrorism to other strategic threats including nuclear war, and so requires a strategic response, that is, behavior applicable to all situations in the long-term. In the nearly hour-long lecture, the NSA said whatever is done must ensure that India's "civilizational values and culture remain intact" and that "we engage the enemy in three modes." They are "defensive mode . . . if somebody comes here we will prevent him, we will defend this . . . defensive-offense, to defend ourselves we will go to the place from where the offense is coming from . . . third is the offensive mode where you go outright." In this context, what was also of consequence was his saying the "nuclear threshold is a difficulty in the offensive mode but not in the defensive-offense" because "you (Pakistan) may do one Mumbai, you will lose Balochistan . . . there is no nuclear war involved in that . . . there is no engagement of troops . . . if you know the tricks, we know the tricks better than you."[50]

Contextual defense was therefore the NSA's term for calculation, but in addition the airstrike was also an offense for being a contextual retaliation intending to kill many times more than the lives claimed by JEM's acts of cross-border terror. The shift to offense then was thought out, but what was its purpose? The answer begins to appear in the price the BJP paid to be offensive. The cost began with the BJP equating, for the first time, India with Pakistan, which had to be done to calculate a more offensive response to Pakistani offensiveness. The very fact that the BJP chose to respond offensively was to also surrender India's sovereignty to Pakistan because it dictated what India did. India's offense also meant that control was handed to Islamabad and that the future was now up to it—for the first time vis-à-vis India. That Pakistan chose not to escalate despite no longer being denied the opportunity to do so by India's defense, for India was no longer defensive, testifies to Islamabad's ability to control itself in a manner impossible for the BJP. Indeed, Islamabad exercised a self-restraint almost equal to what New Delhi had practiced prior to Balakot, and this history provides the rest of the answer to what the BJP sought in its offense. Until February 2019, India had never granted equality to Pakistan. Indeed, equality was impossible because India unconditionally sacrificed itself and so maintained life whereas Pakistan's offense destroyed life. India managed offense by deadening it with sacrifice. There was therefore no equating of Pakistan's offense by India and so no proportionate or disproportionate response. This was so when Pakistanis occupied the heights of Kargil and even for the 2001 terror attack on India's parliament. Kargil was contained because India simply sacrificed itself to take back what it regarded as its own. Noteworthy about 2001 is that courage of an up-to-then uncalled-for intensity was required, and found over several months, to manage a provocation symbolically unprecedented, and so prevent escalation. India's capacity for courage ensured that there could be no escalation, much less to nuclear war, and this was a service to humanity. In other words, the courage to routinely sacrifice a few lives at the border, and even the homeland proper, meant India always retained control of what happened next. Indeed, so intent was India in sacrificing itself to retain control that the will to do so was driven home to Pakistan every so often with cross-border raids.[51] The price the BJP paid to shift to offense then suggests that what the BJP's leadership sought was to be relieved of the courage required in continuing the sacrifices that rendered Pakistani terrorist offenses meaningless. Nevertheless, the shifting of India's diplomacy reiterated the abiding influence of the *Mahabharata's* notion of context, which Mahatma Gandhi brought to light and Nehru made diplomacy, as well as that the starting point for any change was another concept developed by Gandhi and Nehru, defence. Its primacy is highlighted particularly by the attempt at undoing it—no matter how bumbling the attempt.

CONCLUSIONS

The discrepancies that litter analyses of India, if not the entire non-Western world, inexorably and relentlessly coalesce into a requirement to conduct work coherently, fully, and morally. To do so inevitably makes for only one conclusion, that India's diplomacy is conducted *in absentia* for being driven by the lack of interests. This is so because diplomacy's root is *satyagraha*, which became possible because Gandhi theorized ahimsa, *dharma*, and the *dharma*-complex from the *Mahabharata* while solving its problem of engaging offense without replicating it. Doing so requires not interest, but disinterest. Yet it remains, even in India, a rarity, as is attested to by the failures of the bureaucrats shaping nuclear as well as anti-terrorism policy—Subrahmanyam for missing Gandhi's nuance and Doval for miscalculating that offense does not risk troops engaging.

These bureaucratic failures are why disinterest's Chinese covalent is useful. The equivalent to Indian disinterest are the instances of "brightness" in China's intellectual tradition dating to the pre-Christian era's *Zuo Zhuan*, which also struggled with interest.[52] This is of interest because of the means suggested to regularize disinterest and so reap its benefits. The *Zuo Zhuan*'s struggles with disinterest are apparent in, for instance, the section on exchanging hostages to build trust and which is overshadowed by the insufficiencies of reciprocity. The text states: "Even with princes as hostages, there might not be sincere trust. If states dealt with others with brightness, and regulated their behaviour according to ritual, the trust would be solid even without hostages."[53] "Brightness" (明) is the means of overcoming contract's contradictions, which is why it merits interrogation in authorial terms. In the first instance brightness presented as a moral requirement for virtuosity and men with it possessed the virtue of brightness [明主 or 明君]. Virtuosity, in turn, has been understood variously, and including honesty and harmonizing with good rules. Virtuosity leads to rewards, sound government, good diplomacy, and even hegemony of "All Under Heaven" (Tianxia). Moreover, brightness for being moral is untarnished by tricks. "If a state deceives, the people will reciprocate in kind, friendly states will be alienated, and rivals will not be deterred."[54] Such a reading makes brightness procedural and legalistic, thereby reproducing interest and contract—for instance, use brightness to become virtuous to get rewards. Nor can such a reading contain brightness's incommensurability, which is precisely why the concept is proposed to overcome contract's shortcomings in politics and its concepts. Nevertheless, brightness is virtuous, which permits viewing the former as desirable but also as capable of standing on its own, as an alternative with significance. Indeed, that is why 明 was used rather than 明主 or 明君. Brightness is a solution perhaps unutterable in the context of Chinese writings, legalistic, practical, and so interest-bound, as they are—but it was. Inevitably, disinterest, and calculations of defense without offense, follow.

The call to make brightness international politics via ritualization is a uniquely Chinese claim, and in stark contrast to Gandhi's inheritors, who never even contemplated the idea. That is why India's MEA is largely disinterested in disinterest. Fieldwork within the MEA suggests that most diplomats become so to further their interests, often reprehensible for their narcissism, racism, or illegality.[55] That accounts for why there is no transmission of disinterest generationally, formally, or textually, let alone ritually.[56] However, ritual's inheritance, convention, conformity, and integration of life evidently contrasts with the creativity of constructing interest and its contracting. This divergence discloses a concern with a fundamentally philosophical concern: freedom. That freedom is the antithesis of ritual is a commonplace understanding, but it is a false one for being no more than an artifact of interest's claims to offer freedom. These offers are undermined by interest because it limits freedom to contracting and proscribes all else by not even permitting its contemplation. The unexpected result of this realization is that ritual *is* freedom for not curtailing traditions of human action beyond contract. Indeed, any curtailment terminates life, for life is ritual and so everything else must be a sickness. As the Mahatma put it: "The winking of the eyelids does not need to be willed, there must be some disease if it is otherwise."[57]

NOTES

1. The author is indebted to Faisal Devji for commenting on a draft.

2. D. D. Leslie and K. H. J. Gardiner, *The Roman Empire in Chinese Sources* (Rome: Bardi, 1996).

3. Carl von Clausewitz, *On War*, trans. and ed. Michael Howard and Peter Paret (New York: Everyman's Library, 1993).

4. On the centrality of diplomacy see Deep K. Datta-Ray, *The Making of Indian Diplomacy* (New York: Oxford University Press, 2015), 1–26. See also Deep K. Datta-Ray, "Violence, Hermeneutics and Postcolonial Diplomacy," in *Routledge Handbook of Postcolonial Politics*, ed. Olivia U. Rutazibwa and Robbie Shilliam (Abingdon: Routledge, 2018), 140–56.

5. Krishnan Srinivasan, "Special Bond," *The Telegraph*, 31 January 2014, https://www.telegraphindia .com/1140131/jsp/opinion/story_17876883.jsp#.WJCH4onavIU

6. Deep K. Datta-Ray, "The Analysis of the Practice of Indian Diplomacy," in *India Engages the World*, ed. Navnita Chadha Behera (New Delhi: Oxford University Press, 2013), 234–69.

7. Deep K. Datta-Ray, "Diplomacy beyond History: Analytic-Violence, Producer-Centred Research, India," *India Quarterly* 77, no. 1 (2021): 9–24; Deep K. Datta-Ray, "The Interactions of International Relations: Racism, Colonialism, Producer-Centred Research," *All Azimuth* 10, no. 2, (2021): 231–53.

8. Datta-Ray, *Making of Indian Diplomacy*, 71, 110–16.

9. Deep K. Datta-Ray, "India Proves Democracy Is No Longer Fit for Purpose, While China's Model Shows the Way," *South China Morning Post*, 29 May 2018, https://www.scmp.com/comment /insight-opinion/article/2148249/india-proves-democracy-no-longer-fit-purpose-while-chinas

10. See cover endorsement by Faisal Devji and Sir Stephen Chan in Datta-Ray, *Making of Indian Diplomacy.*

11. Datta-Ray, *Making of Indian Diplomacy*, 195–200.

12. Quoted in Datta-Ray, *Making of Indian Diplomacy*, 211–14.

13. M. K. Gandhi, "Speech at AICC Meeting," *Harijan*, 25 January 1942, in *Collected Works of Mohandas Gandhi*, eBook (CWMG-EB), vol. 81, pp. 432–33.

14. Datta-Ray, *Making of Indian Diplomacy*, 119–29.

15. Datta-Ray, *Making of Indian Diplomacy*, 109–36.

16. M. K. Gandhi, "Problem of Non-violence," *Navjivan*, 6 June 1926, CWMG-EB, vol. 35, pp. 323–24; M. K. Gandhi, "Letter to Ambalal Sarabhai," 11 July 1926, CWMG-EB, vol. 36, p. 30. He talks about how a nonviolent polity ought to deal with invasion in M. K. Gandhi, "Triumph of Non-violence," *Navajivan*, 21 November 1920, CWMG-EB, vol. 21, p. 515.

17. M. K. Gandhi, "Speech at Goalundo," 6 November 1946, CWMG-EB, vol. 92, pp. 455–56.

18. M. K. Gandhi, "Interview to Capt. Strunk," *Harijan*, 3 July 1937, CWMG-EB, vol. 71, p. 405.

19. M. K. Gandhi, "What Is One's Dharma?," *Navajivan*, 21 July 1929, CWMG-EB, vol. 46, p. 296.

20. M. K. Gandhi, "Conundrums," *Harijan*, 30 September, 1939, CWMG-EB, vol. 76, p. 356.

21. John K. Fairbank, "The Creation of the Treaty System," in *The Cambridge History of China*, ed. Denis Twitchett and John K. Fairbank (Cambridge: Cambridge University Press, 1978), vol. 10, part 1, p. 213.

22. Quoted in Datta-Ray, *Making of Indian Diplomacy*, 200–206.

23. *Lok Sabha Debates*, vol. 15, 3rd Series (New Delhi: Lok Sabha Secretariat, 23 March 1963), col. 5780–83.

24. Datta-Ray, *Making of Indian Diplomacy*, 248–51.

25. "Resolution 2028 (XX)," in *Disarmament: India's Initiatives* (New Delhi: External Publicity Division: MEA, Government of India, 1988), 29–34.

26. Quoted in Sunanda K. Datta-Ray, *Waiting for America: India and the US in the New Millennium* (New Delhi: HarperCollins, 2002), 41.

27. "Interview with Abdul Qadeer Khan," *The News* (Islamabad), 30 May 1998, https://nuclear weaponarchive.org/Pakistan/KhanInterview.html; Kargil Review Committee, *From Surprise to Reckoning: The Kargil Review Committee Report* (New Delhi: Sage, 2000), 205.

28. Quoted in Datta-Ray, *Making of Indian Diplomacy*, 247.

29. Quoted in Datta-Ray, *Making of Indian Diplomacy*, 245–46.

30. US Embassy India cable A-540 to State Department, *Canadians Warn GOI on NPT*, 1 December 1967, https://nsarchive2.gwu.edu/nukevault/ebb253/doc07.pdf

31. Rajeshwar Dayal, *A Life of Our Times* (New Delhi: Orient Longman, 1998), 588–89.

32. US Embassy India cable 0943 to State Department, *India's Nuclear Intentions*, 18 January 1974, https://nsarchive2.gwu.edu/nukevault/ebb367/docs/1–19–74.pdf

33. Jawaharlal Nehru, "Defence Policy and National Development," 3 February 1947, in *Selected Works of Jawaharlal Nehru, Second Series*, ed. Sarvepalli Gopal, Ravinder Kumar, H. Y. Sharada Prasad, A. K. Damodaran, and Mushirul Hasan (New Delhi: Jawaharlal Nehru Memorial Fund, 1984), vol. 2, p. 364.

34. Jawaharlal Nehru, *Significance of the Atomic Revolution*, 20 January 1957, http://www.dae.gov.in/node/sites/default/files/nideco8.pdf

35. Quoted in Datta-Ray, *Making of Indian Diplomacy*, 238.

36. Jawaharlal Nehru, no title, in *India's Foreign Policy: Selected Speeches, September 1946–April 1961* (New Delhi: Ministry of Information and Broadcasting, 1961), 235.

37. Quoted in Datta-Ray, *Making of Indian Diplomacy*, 239.

38. Quoted in Datta-Ray, *Making of Indian Diplomacy*, 248–51.

39. "Statement by Foreign Secretary on 26 February 2019 on the Strike on JeM Training Camp at Balakot," 26 February 2019, https://mea.gov.in/Speeches-Statements.htm?dtl/31089/statement+by +foreign+secretary+on+26+february+2019+on+the+strike+on+jem+training+camp+at+balakot

40. DG ISPR, 26 February 2019, 9:36 a.m., Tweet, https://twitter.com/OfficialDGISPR/status /1100207947022565377

41. Abu Arqam Naqash and Asif Shahzad, "Pakistani Villagers Shaken Awake as Indian Warplanes Drop Bombs Near Madrasa," *Reuters*, 26 February 2019, https://www.reuters.com/article/us-india -kashmir-pakistan-scene/pakistani-villagers-shaken-awake-as-indian-warplanes-drop-bombs-near -madrasa-idUSKCN1QF13U

42. Reuters Graphics, 2 March 2019, 3:41 p.m., Tweet, https://twitter.com/ReutersGraphics/status /1101749416564682752

43. Amit Shah, Prime Minister Narendra Modi's closest aide and Home Minister, in an interview, said the BJP's resorts to *jumla*, which is recognized by the electorate: "Modiji's Statement on Rs 15 Lakh Returning Was Just a Political 'Jumla': Amit Shah to ABP News," YouTube, 5 February 2015, https:// www.youtube.com/watch?v = Wo9EN-dlZns

44. Krishna Das, "India Cites 'Active Mobile Phones' to Back Air Strike Casualty Claim," *Reuters*, 6 March 2019, https://www.reuters.com/article/us-india-kashmir-airstrike/india-cites-active-mobile -phones-to-back-air-strike-casualty-claim-idUSKCN1QM1EZ

45. Martin White, "A Natural Partner? Intelligence Cooperation with India and Australia's Regional Interests," *Security Challenges*, special issue, Plan B for Australian Defence, 16, no. 2 (2020): 88–105.

46. Maharashtra Education Society, Pune, "3. Seminar on India-China Relations in the 21st Century—Challenges & Opportunities," YouTube, 9 July 2020, https://www.youtube.com/watch?v = H28ByIl9EKI

47. Vappala Balachandran, "Balakot: The Risks of Leaving All Decision-Making to Intelligence Officials," *The Wire*, 8 March 2019, https://thewire.in/security/balakot-ajit-doval-decision-making

48. Paran Balakrishnan, "Vaccine Talks: For Modi, Biden No Cakewalk as with Trump," *The Telegraph Online*, 1 June 2021, https://www.telegraphindia.com/india/vaccine-talks-for-modi-biden-no-cakewalk-as-with-trump/cid/1813839

49. Deep K. Datta-Ray, "Tryst With Modernity," *The Times of India*, 18 August 2010, https://timesofindia.indiatimes.com/edit-page/tryst-with-modernity/articleshow/6326006.cms

50. Daily Mail, "Ajit Doval's Speech at SASTRA University," *dailymotion*, 23 April 2015, https://www.dailymotion.com/video/x2njwui

51. "'6 Surgical Strikes' in UPA Tenure: Cong. Backs Manmohan Singh with Dates," *Hindustan Times*, 2 May 2019, https://www.hindustantimes.com/india-news/6-surgical-strikes-in-upa-tenure-congress-leader-provides-dates/story-VhiGIV6WcSB1oEkBTRMXxH.html; Conversation with Indian Army Officer.

52. I am indebted to Zhao Yujia for her commentary on "brightness" in an email correspondence, following the "Classical Indian and Chinese World Views on Global Order: A Comparison" conference at Tsinghua University in Beijing, 5–6 July 2019.

53. Zuo Zhuan Xunzi, "Hostage Exchange between Zhou & Zheng, Year Three of Yingong" 左传·周郑交质隐公三年》, http://www2.iath.virginia.edu/saxon/servlet/SaxonServlet?source = xwomen/texts/chunqiu.xml&style = xwomen/xsl/dynaxml.xsl&chunk.id = d2.7&toc.depth = 1&toc.id = 0&doc.lang = bilingual

54. *Li Ji* 42 Da Xue. 《礼记·大学》. Mencius 2 Gongsun Chou A4. 《孟子·公孙丑上》. *Xunzi* 9 Humane Governance. 《荀子·王制》. *Xunzi* 18 Correcting: A Discussion. 《荀子·正论》. Correspondence with Zhao Yujia.

55. Ian Hall, "*The Making of Indian Diplomacy*: A Critique of Eurocentrism, by Deep K. Datta-Ray (Book Reviews)," *Asian Studies Review* 42, no. 2 (2018): 378–79.

56. Datta-Ray, *Making of Indian Diplomacy*, 259–69.

57. M. K. Gandhi, "Discourses on the Gita," 4 April 1926, CWMG-EB, vol. 37, p. 118.

From Ancient Silk Road to Modern Belt and Road Initiative

A Signaling Approach to Trust-Building across Narratives

Zhao Yujia

INTRODUCTION

Narratives help people in making sense of the world (Somers 1994: 606), and in interpreting and understanding the surrounding political realities (Patterson and Monroe 1998: 321). These narratives give people reasons to act (Franzosi 1998), but at the same time act as a ruling tool. From a postcolonial perspective, Datta-Ray (2015) demonstrates how the dominant Western diplomatic narratives suppress and marginalize India in important international affairs, and he thus claims the need for India-oriented (non-Western) narratives in diplomacy. Although China's contemporary foreign policies are not usually interpreted in terms of postcolonial narratives, China faces a similar problem in diplomacy, and thus there is a similar demand for Chinese-oriented narratives.

The problems China faces can be illustrated by attitudes surrounding the Belt and Road Initiative (BRI). Launched by President Xi in 2013, the BRI is a building block of China's "going out" global strategy (Zhang and Liu 2019).[1] The BRI consists of the Silk Road Economic Belt (SREB), connecting China, Central Asia, and Europe by land, and the 21st Century Maritime Silk Road Initiative (MSRI), linking China with Southeast Asia, Africa, and Europe by sea. Within three years of its launch, China's outward direct investment (ODI) reached USD170.11 billion in 7,961 overseas enterprises in 164 countries and regions: an increase of 44.1 percent year to year by 2016 (UNDP 2017: 2). China's ODI flow to the 65 BRI countries was $14.4 billion in 2017 (Huang and Xia 2018: 2). A specific example includes a pledge from President Xi on April 2015 of $46 billion as part of an investment and cooperation agreement during a visit to Pakistan (Andam et al. 2017).

From the Chinese perspective, the BRI will enable China to engage with other fast-emerging Asian markets through bilateral infrastructure, trade, and investment cooperation and allow these Asian countries to tap into China's huge domestic market. The export of "Made in China" goods to these BRI countries will help China export many of its manufactured goods, thus addressing domestic production overcapacity and stimulating domestic economic growth through the upgrading of its industries (Irshad et al. 2016). At the same time, by initiating new economic corridors such as the China-Pakistan Economic Corridor (CPEC) in the Maritime Silk Road Initiative (MSRI), China has managed to enhance not only economic cooperation but also diplomatic and tactical partnerships between China and the participating countries (Arshad et al. 2016). These Chinese projects could be instrumental to the development of host countries of the BRI region.

However, criticisms about the intention and possible impacts of BRI projects have emerged in host countries and the rest of the world. A report in the *Financial Times* suggests that there are at least 234 BRI projects suffering setbacks because of low social acceptance (Kygne 2018a). For instance, the railway project in Thailand has been put on hold several times due to social protests from Thai citizens. The West also heavily criticizes the BRI for creating a debt burden for developing countries, and some termed BRI as "debt-trap diplomacy" (Johnson 2019). China, however, regards the BRI as a global public good, believing it will bring huge development to the BRI regions. This divergence between how the Chinese and the rest of the world perceive the BRI is worth investigating.

While many scholars have attributed the low social acceptance of BRI to technical issues, other scholars point to the collision between the Chinese and Western narratives as the underlying problem. Failures or slow progress in project management in international investments are not rare in the era of globalization, and do not inevitably have political consequences (Russel and Berger 2019; Yean 2018; Hurley and Portelance 2019; Zhang and Liu 2019; Hafner et al. 2018; Lu et al. 2018; Liu and Lim 2019; Baltensperger and Dadush 2019). Therefore, lack of understanding the signals has been posited as the problem. Nordin and Weissmann (2018: 232) use the term "imaginaries" to define the BRI because it represents possible worlds that are different from the actual world, and the BRI projects are tied to changing the world. Other scholars indicate that BRI's legitimacy, in conjunction with a series of political and economic narratives, and the collision between the Chinese narrative and others', result in the divergence in perceptions of BRI (Blanchard 2018; Callahan 2016; Sidaway and Woon 2017). Yahuda (2013) argues the main challenges for BRI acceptance is that the Chinese government viewed US power as descending and Chinese power as ascending after the financial crisis and saw an opportunity for a stronger presence at the global stage. President Xi's speech at the 19th Party Congress about "moving closer to the center stage" was interpreted as signaling China's growing ambition, and thus attracted much criticism (for example, see Kynge 2018b; Juan 2018). However, as will be illustrated later, some strategic signals sent via BRI have been better accepted than others via the same channel.

This paper aims to address the question of how trust can be bridged across narratives in International Relations (IR) by linking the notion of strategic signaling with the Chinese concept of "Brightness." Specifically, what factors condition the success of strategic signals for trust-building? It argues that trust in strategic cooperation is the result of a series of signaling and knowledge-building where the signal sender's honesty regarding self-interests and intentions acts as the conditional factor.

Following this introduction, the first section discusses the notions of trust and how the strategic signaling process contributes to trust-building. The next section tests this framework with two case studies. One is the construction of the ancient Silk Road in around 139–114 BCE, when Zhang Qian of the Han Dynasty connected China and Central Asia for the first time. The other is the modern BRI launched in the 2010s. Both cases are regarded as initiatives by China to change the regional order, and both encounter problems originating from different narrative backgrounds. The concluding section explains how the theories of strategic signaling and the notion of brightness could help build trust between China and the rest of the world regarding the BRI project.

SIGNALING AND TRUST-BUILDING

Trust between two parties can be defined as a psychological state comprising the intention to accept vulnerability to the actions of another party, based upon the credibility that the other will perform a particular action that is important to you (Mayer et al. 1995; Rousseau et al. 1998). Trust is an important concept in the field of International Relations, especially in terms of conflict resolution and peace-building processes between countries. It is sometimes regarded as a part of rational decision-making preferences in relation to the external environment (Hollis 1998: 14). Hoffman (2002: 366) defines trust between states as a willingness to take risks on the behavior of others, based on the belief that potential trustees will "do what is right."

Trust-building across narratives is difficult due to the divergence in perception between the senders and the receivers, and to the complexity of decision-making with regard to the interpersonal nature of trust relationships (Booth and Wheeler 2008; Wheeler 2012; Rathbun 2011, 2012). It is an incomplete information game (Kydd 2000), and thus cannot be explained with reference to available information and specific reciprocity alone (Rathbun 2011, 2012). However, trust-building is not impossible between states. Jervis (1976) argues that although misperception occurs far more frequently than is normally realized, the actors can try to minimize it by trying to see the world the way the other sees it, or by examining the world from varied perspectives.

How is trust built? Signaling theory views trust development as a signaling process. Kydd states that "trust can be established and fostered by small, unilateral cooperative gestures that initiate chains of mutually rewarding behaviour" (2000: 333). These gestures are signals. This theory helps to describe the behaviors of two nations in interactions (Breslin 2018).

Not all signaling processes can generate trust, however. Received signals might lead to incorrect inferences. Senders may be able to deceive receivers by the skillful use of signals; and contextual, reputational beliefs may differ in the extent to which they reflect the true intentions and abilities of senders (Jervis 1976). Decision-makers tend to evaluate to what extent a signal reflects the true intention of the signal senders (Glaser 2010).

Scholars, therefore, place a strong emphasis on the significance of costly signals in broadcasting sincerity in cooperation (Glaser 2010; Larson 1997; Pu 2017, 2019). Costly signals are gestures that involve high cost in a reassurance game. In contrast to cheap signals that can be pulled back easily, players would not send (or at least would hesitate to send) costly signals if they are not sincere in their cooperation (Kydd 2000). Consequently, costly signals modify the expectation of the counterparties and thus enable cooperation (Kydd 2005: 187). For instance, the restrictive membership accession procedures of international institutions follow the logic of costly signaling, as these accession procedures serve as filters that enable the candidate to signal their strong interests (Kydd 2001: 821).

Fearon (1997) distinguishes two types of costly signals that states might use for communication purposes. When players try to communicate willingness of cooperation, they can send signals that "tie their hands" and limit room for maneuver. It increases "the costs of backing down if the would-be challenger actually challenges but otherwise entails no cost if no challenge materializes" (Fearon 1997: 70). When state leaders give public statements, they send "hand-tying" signals by creating audience costs among their domestic political audiences. If they do not stay true to their words, they will suffer from domestic pressures (ibid.). The other type of costly signal is the one with sunk costs. Sunk-cost signals are "actions costly for the state to take in the first place but do not affect the relative value of fighting versus acquiescing in a challenge" (ibid.). For instance, signal senders may exhibit their sincerity to their potential cooperators by making unilateral political or financial investments first. It will increase their counterparties' expectation that the signal senders will fulfill their promises, because the previous financial or political investments will be wasted otherwise.

However, there is still no guarantee that signals with high audience costs and sunk costs will always generate trust. BRI is a series of costly signals that involves both high audience costs, considering its important position in China's foreign policy, and high sunk costs with all the infrastructure investments overseas. Yet, the BRI projects still suffer from low social acceptance in neighboring countries. This example illustrates how the current strategic signaling theories fail to explain the puzzle of trust-building.

THE VIRTUE OF "BRIGHTNESS"

The Chinese Pre-Qin masters understood that trust-building between states is difficult. The key to trust-building is to avoid the risk of being deceived. Han Feizi states that for medium-size states, security cooperation with small states may not ensure their own survival, but cooperation with large states risks the chances of being deceived and thereby being controlled (Zhang 2006).[2] In order to reduce the possibility of being deceived and demonstrate their sincerity in cooperation, states in the Spring and Autumn period exchanged their princes (sometimes the crowned princes) as hostages. This kind of action can be regarded as sending costly signals for trust-building. Pre-Qin masters, however, also understood that costly signaling does not always guarantee the success of trust-building.

Zuo Qiumin, the pre-Qin historian who authored *Zuo Zhuan* (左传also known as *Zuo Shi Chun Qiu*左氏春秋), recorded a story that the King of Zhou and the Lord of Zheng exchanged their sons as hostages to enhance their bilateral relation; however, the Lord of Zheng still secretly sent troops to seize Zhou's grain. Zuo Qiumin thus commented that "even with princes as hostages, there might not be sincere trust between states. If states dealt with others with brightness, and regulated their own behavior according to ritual norms, the trust would be solid even without hostages" (Guo 2016: 21).[3]

For the ancient Chinese, brightness (明) was an important quality of noble and virtuous men. The ancient Chinese masters such as Xunzi and Guanzi believed that the best kings are kings with the virtue of brightness [明主 or 明君]. Brightness is also the moral requirement for all virtuous men. *Li Ji* (The Book of Rites) stated that the purpose of "Da Xue" (learning to be a virtuous man; see Hu and Zhang 2017) was to understand the meaning of brightness (ibid.).[4] Zhu Xi (朱熹 also known as Zhuzi, one of the most important Confucian scholars of the Song Dynasty) even valued "understanding the meaning of brightness" as the first and most important step of learning (ibid.).

Brightness originally means the light and everything that the light touches; and as a moral quality it requires rulers and virtuous men to be honest as to their intentions and to act in accordance with clear and transparent rules. Mencius indicates that if rulers can clarify the acting rules of their reign, even large states will not want to be their enemies (Liang 2015).[5] With the virtue of brightness, kings can rule their countries well, establish good relations with other countries, and even rule "All Under Heaven" (*Tianxia*). Xunzi states that "[if kings] clarify the intention of non-annexation and treat friends and enemies with credibility, they will win and dominate *Tianxia* as hegemonies" (Zhang 2012).[6]

The notion of brightness opposes the use of tricks and conspiracy in domestic politics and interstate relations. Xunzi states that "if [a large state] deceives its people for benefits, then the people will not be honest with the ruler; if the state deceives friendly states for self-benefit, it would not be able to deter rival states, or be trusted by the friendly states . . . one can filch a state through tricks and conspiracies, but no one will be able to win 'All Under Heaven' by these means" (Zhang 2012).[7]

For ancient Chinese masters, acting in bright ways was believed as the key to trust-building in strategic cooperation because it could reduce the other partners' fears of being deceived. Using the language of modern IR theorists, honesty in relation to self-interest and intentions could enhance the other parties' confidence in cooperation, because it decreases the uncertainty in the incomplete information game as it is a trust-building process.

This brightness, however, may not be automatically perceived by others. For strategic cooperative purposes, one state's honesty regarding its self-interest and intentions needs to be transformed into the other parties' good understanding of this state's cooperative interests, and this transformation process can be easily disrupted, which is where we find the ancient Chinese masters lacking.

SIGNALING WITH "BRIGHTNESS"

In summary of the literature review above, the consensus among modern IR scholars and ancient Chinese masters is that the key to trust-building is to decrease the uncertainties in this incomplete information game, but their emphases in trust-building diverge. For strategic cooperative purposes, the judgment on whether a state will be trustworthy in a potential cooperation depends on two major factors. One is whether the signal sender may exploit others by backing down from cooperation once the proposal is accepted. It is a problem that costly signals can help deal with. The other factor is the concern whether the signaled proposal reflects the true intention of the signal sender. The counterparties need to know that the signal sender does not have a hidden agenda. It is the problem that the ancient Chinese masters were conscious of.

This paper attempts to integrate these two factors in order to formulate a comprehensive understanding of the trust-building process. The proposed model has two major assumptions. First, the existence of mutual interest determines whether there is a need for strategic cooperation. In other words, both parties have the internal drivers to achieve strategic cooperation. Second, the decision-makers are fully rational. They tend to trust their counterparties when they believe the risk of being deceived or being exploited is low enough. They are also able to independently formulate and update their knowledge based on newly gathered information without bias.

This paper proposes that trust-building is a process of signaling and knowledge-building. Only when the signal sent for strategic cooperation fits the receiver's

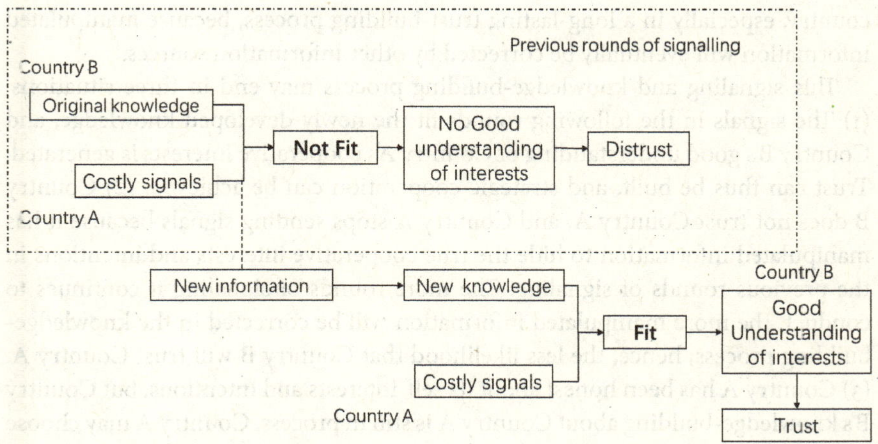

FIGURE 12.1. Trust-building as a process of signaling and knowledge-building.

knowledge about the sender, thus generating a good understanding of the sender's cooperative interests, can the trust-building process end in success. A good understanding of the sender's cooperative interests can be the result of several rounds of signaling, for which the signal sender's honesty regarding self-interest and intention is the necessary condition.

As Figure 12.1 illustrates, Country B would not develop a good understanding of Country A's cooperative interests if A's signal does not fit B's original knowledge about A. This original knowledge could be the product of previous experiences, images, or even stereotypes. If Country B does not have a good understanding of Country A's interests in this proposed strategic cooperation, Country B will not trust Country A and thus decline the proposal. Yet, it may not be the end of the game. Taking the costly signals in this first round as one of the sources of new information, Country B may also gather further information about Country A through various means, such as investigations, negotiations, or personal interactions between state leaders. New information would generate Country B's new knowledge about Country A. If Country A's costly signals fit this newly developed knowledge, Country B would be able to develop good understandings of Country A's interests in cooperation; and the trust can thus be built.

The signal sender's honesty regarding their self-interests and intentions is the necessary condition as to whether the counterparties may generate a good understanding of the sender's cooperative interests. Communication and cognitive theorists point out that people with high cognitive capability can avoid being misguided and make rational choices if they have access to multiple sources of information (Zucker 1977; Zaller 1992; De Vreese and Boogaarden 2005, 2006). This argument suggests that it is difficult to manipulate others' knowledge about a country, especially in a long-lasting trust-building process, because manipulated information will eventually be corrected by other information sources.

This signaling and knowledge-building process may end in three situations. (1) The signals in the following rounds fit the newly developed knowledge, and Country B's good understanding of Country A's cooperative interests is generated. Trust can thus be built, and strategic cooperation can be achieved. (2) Country B does not trust Country A, and Country A stops sending signals because it has manipulated information to hide the true cooperative interests and intentions in the previous rounds of signaling. The more rounds of signaling it continues to conduct, the more manipulated information will be corrected in the knowledge-building process; hence, the less likelihood that Country B will trust Country A. (3) Country A has been honest about its self-interests and intentions, but Country B's knowledge-building about Country A is still in process. Country A may choose to continue with new rounds of signaling, depending on the payoffs of cooperation and the costs of signaling. If the anticipated payoff is larger than the cost of signaling, the signaling process continues; if not, Country A will choose to stop sending signals. This logic supports Kydd's argument that "signals must be costly, but not too costly" (2000: 340).

Good understanding of the signal sender's cooperative interests has three levels of meaning. First, with good understanding of the sender's cooperative interests, the counterparty would have the confidence that the sender does not have a hidden agenda in the proposed strategic cooperation. If Country A proposes to cooperate with Country B and claims that this cooperation is only for the benefit of Country B, Country B may not trust Country A even after many rounds of costly signaling. In fact, the costlier these signals are, the less trustworthy Country A is in the eye of Country B. Country B would worry that Country A seeks hidden benefits resulting in unknown (and possibly dangerous) losses to Country B. However, if both parties' interests from the cooperation are transparent to each other (at least transparent in the eyes of the other party), trust-building may be relatively easy if they feel confident about their understandings of the other party's interests.

Second, with good understanding of Country A's interest, Country B would have the confidence that Country A would not back out of the collaboration, not only because Country A has sent costly signals (audiences cost or sunk cost) but also because Country B understands Country A's opportunity costs in the proposed cooperation. Opportunity cost is an economic concept that expresses the basic relationship between scarcity (of resources) and choices (Buchanan 2017). Unlike audience cost and sunk cost that involve visible inputs, it is mostly unquantifiable (Posnett and Jan 1996). Since resources are scarce relative to needs, decision-makers tend to use resources in ways that can generate beneficial outputs. Opportunity cost is related to future benefits generated by future use of resources including time and labor (Grinols 1991; Bettman et al. 1996). Backing out of a collaboration with high opportunity cost could lead to the loss of potential benefits that might not be achieved from different uses of the same resources.

Third, a good understanding of Country A's cooperative interests means Country B knows that the interests Country A pursues in the cooperation match Country A's capability. Philippe and Durand (2011) argue that trust about the signal sender may include beliefs about its abilities and intentions. Hall and Yarhi-Milo (2012: 3) similarly indicate that the signals of sincerity that are beyond the signal senders' ability to control are not reliable. If the cooperative goal is beyond what Country B knows about Country A's capability, Country B would worry that Country A is attempting to act as a free rider and thus exploiting Country B in this cooperation. The trust-building would thus be difficult, and cooperation may not be achieved.

TWO "SILK ROAD" CASES ON TRUST-BUILDING

The Silk Road has never been a specific name for one road. It is a general notion referring to all routes that connected China, Central Asia, the Middle East, the Mediterranean region, and Europe where people exchanged commercial goods, thoughts, technologies, and culture. Although it has existed for more than two thousand years, the name "Silk Road" was first used in 1877 by the German explorer Baron Ferdinan Von Richthofen (Wood 2002). This section examines two empirical cases where China has attempted to build trust across narratives for a change in regional order. Both cases are related to the name "Silk Road." The first case helps to illustrate how the dynamic signaling process and knowledge-building led to the establishment of trust between states with different narrative backgrounds, and the second case helps to demonstrate the conditions of trust-building in the signaling process.

Case One: Ancient Silk Road in 139–114 BCE

Ancient China's connection with Central Asia (the "Western Region" 西域) started in the Han Dynasty (hereafter "the Han") and its earliest credible record (probably the only direct record) is found in the "Ranked Biographies of the Dayuan" in the *Records of the Grand Historian* (also known in Chinese as *Shiji*) written by the official historiographer Sima Qian (also translated as Ssu-Ma Ch'ien) of the Han. (Note: this paper uses Li Hanwen's annotations to *Shiji* as the texts of analysis; see Li 2016.)

The northern nomads had long been a threat to the Chinese kingdoms (Tong 1946, 2006; Beckwith 2009; Liu 2010). In the early period of the Han, the Xiongnu were in a dominant position in east-central Asia, and the Han emperors had to resort to "He'qin" with the Xiongnu (i.e., marrying off the Han emperors' sisters or daughters to the chiefs of the Xiongnu) in order to make peace on their borders. However, this strategy soon lost efficacy. "He'qin" could no longer effectively stop

TABLE 12.1 The three rounds of interaction between the Han and the Central Asian countries/federacies

Target Country	Mutual Interest	Costly Signal	Good Understanding of the Han's Interests	Consequence
1 Yuezhi	Yes	No	No	Failed
2 Wu Sun and others	Yes	Yes	No	Failed
3 Wu Sun and others	Yes	Yes	Yes	Succeeded

the Xiongnu invasion. Emperor Wu's army might defeat the Xiongnu's troops, but they could not stop the Xiongnu from continually invading (Zhang and Liu 2015).[8]

Against this background, the Han needed allies from Central Asia to help in defending against the Xiongnu. It is worth noting here that, although many researchers reveal the importance of connections between ancient China and Central Asia from economic and cultural perspectives, the original motivations of building this connection were strategic and security concerns. The Han needed allies to balance the threats from the Xiongnu, and this strategic objective remained the top priority of the Han's relationship with the Central Asian countries.

Table 12.1 compares the interaction between the Han and the Central Asian countries/federacies for the establishment of strategic alliances. There are three rounds of interaction that can be identified. In the first round, Zhang Qian and his delegation left the Han territory and went west to find the Yuezhi. The Yuezhi were invaded by the Xiongnu, and the king of the Yuezhi was brutally slaughtered. The son of the king hastily led his people away from their homes and waited for opportunities to retaliate. The Han thus regarded the Yuezhi as a potential ally against Xiongnu. However, Zhang Qian was delayed in his arrival in Yuezhi territory, having been captured and held by the Xiongnu. By the time he arrived in Yuezhi territory, the Yuezhi had conquered the Da Xia (the north bank of the Amu Darya, originally a Greek colony before the Yuezhi arrived; see Liu 2010). The Yuezhi declined Zhang Qian's alliance proposal on the pretext of having no interest in retaliation as their new territory was fertile and secure, far from the Xiongnu and even farther from the Han (Li 2016).[9] However, while it might have been true that the Yuezhi were not interested in retaliation, they still had a shared interest with the Han in defending against the Xiongnu. This view is supported by the fact that they eventually sent envoys and built a relationship with the Han later in the third round of negotiations.

In this first round, although the Han and the Yuezhi shared common interests in defending against the Xiongnu, the Yuezhi knew little, if anything, about either the Han's determination to fight against the Xiongnu or the Han's military capability. Zhang Qian's mission to the Yuezhi might not have successfully sent a costly signal. Even though Zhang Qian could prove his identity as an envoy of the Han, it was impossible for the king of the Yuezhi to know the Han's determination and military capability in fighting the Xiongnu, since Zhang was neither in a formal delegation nor coming with considerable gifts (Li 2016).[10] Therefore, the Yuezhi could not possibly formulate a good understanding of the Han's cooperative interest. It was, therefore, no surprise that the king of the Yuezhi refused to make an alliance with the Han to avoid the risk of being deceived.

In the second round of signaling, the Han altered the targeted cooperative partner from the Yuezhi to the Wu Sun. The Wu Sun was an independent federacy before the Xiongnu's invasion. Kunmo, the king of the Wu Sun, struggled to rebuild the Wu Sun's relative independency, but this independency was fragile. Zhang Qian believed that the Han and the Wu Sun shared common interests in strategic terms, because the Han wanted to further establish deterrence against the Xiongnu, while the Wu Sun desired absolute independence from the Xiongnu's control. He further suggested that once the Han made an alliance with the Wu Sun, the Han could thereby build foreign relations with the Da Xia and other Central Asian countries/federacies (Li 2016).[11]

Zhang Qian subsequently went to Central Asia for the second time. The Han sent costly signals to the Central Asian countries and federacies by presenting a large delegation carrying an enormous amount of valuable gifts. *Shiji* records that the delegation consisted of three hundred delegates with six hundred horses; and they brought tens of thousands of cows and sheep, and hundreds of thousands of precious metals and cloths as gifts (Li 2016).[12] When Zhang Qian arrived in the Wu Sun country he sent his associate envoys to other Central Asia countries and federacies such as the Dawan (modern Ferghana in Uzbekistan; see Liu 2010), the Kangju (or translated as Kangkeu, now Tashkent, plus the Chu, Talas, and middle Jaxartes basins), Yuezhi, Da Xia (Darya), and the Anxi (Persia under the rule of the Parthians).

Regardless of the costly signals that the Han sent with the large delegation and precious gifts, Kunmo, the king of the Wu Sun, declined the Han's proposal because he was not sure whether the Han were powerful enough to protect the Wu Sun from the Xiongnu. The *Shiji* records that as "the Wu Sun were far away from the Han, they did not know the Han's capability; the Wu Sun were close to the Xiongnu and had been its dependency for a long period; the Wu Sun nobles all feared the Xiongnu" (Li 2016).[13]

In other words, even with common interests and costly signals, the Wu Sun had not built knowledge about the Han that fit the Han's cooperative signals, and thus could not generate a good understanding of the Han's strategic interests. Therefore, the second round of signaling failed.

In the third round, the Han repeated the signaling process and further presented the Han's economic and military capability to visiting Wu Sun envoys. The "Ranked Biographies of the Dayuan" records that the Wu Sun's envoys witnessed that the Han had a huge population and the country was rich. When they returned, they reported what they had seen to their king. The Wu Sun thereby took the Han's proposal on strategic cooperation increasingly seriously. In the following year, other Central Asian countries/federacies that Zhang Qian and his delegation had visited all sent envoys to the Han. The Han's foreign relations with these countries/federacies were consequently established in formal ways (Li 2016).[14] Although not by strict definition bilateral military alliances, these foreign relations were of a similar nature. As the "Ranked Biographies of the Dayuan" recorded, the Xiongnu took these actions as betrayal and were furious enough to plan an assault against the Wu Sun (Li 2016).[15] The decisions to establish foreign relations with the Han suggested that the Wu Sun were willing to accept the Han's proposal in changing the regional order in the Central Asia.

The success story of the third round of signaling cannot be separated from the first two rounds. Trust-building is a process of signaling and knowledge-building. If the Han had not sent Zhang Qian to the Yuezhi and the Wu Sun, the Central Asian countries and federacies could not possibly have known about the Han and the Han's cooperative determination, and they would not sent envoys to the Han. Moreover, it was only when the Wu Sun and other Central Asian countries/federacies learned about the Han's economic and military capabilities that they were able to form a good understanding of the Han's strategic interests, and therefore trust-building might succeed.

Case Two: BRI Empowering China as a Global Power

President Xi Jinping first proposed establishing an economic belt across the trans-Eurasian region at Nazarbayev University in Astana, Kazakhstan, on September 7, 2013. Nicknamed "the new silk road," the project would affect three billion people in this region, in areas of conventional energy and mineral resources, and encompass collaboration in technology, investment, finance, and services (*Xinhua News* 2013). This message was quickly followed by a second speech in Indonesia on October 3, 2013, on the launch of the MSRI project. This project would focus on China's ASEAN neighbors for common development and prosperity (Xi 2014: 322). Although beginning as a commercial proposal that enables China to engage with other fast-emerging Asian markets, BRI's scale and extent of investment has attracted enormous attention globally.

There were two main trust-building signals delivered by BRI projects, and they are clearly elaborated in President Xi's three-and-half-hour foreign strategies speech on October 18, 2017, at the 19th National Congress of the People's Republic of China. This speech marks significant differences in Xi's presidency from those of his predecessors in terms of projecting China as a global power. The same message is also apparent in the speeches extracted mainly from *Xi Jinping: The Governance of China* (Xi 2014).

The first signal is economic and political proactiveness largely reflected by the concepts of "striving for achievement" and a "community of shared future for mankind." This rhetoric suggests that China has an increasingly influential role in global economic and political affairs. The BRI project is a continuation of China's "opening up" policy as it supports the expansion of Chinese enterprises abroad to facilitate industrial upgrading at home, paving the way for Chinese outward foreign direct investment (FDI) and trade, and advancing the internationalization of the Chinese currency (Babatunde 2015: 130–31). The importance of the BRI to the Chinese government as a global strategy to take the center stage is undisputed as it was officially enshrined in the 19th National Party Congress (NPC) held in October 2017: the same congress where Xi delivered the above-mentioned speech (Vangeli 2018: 59). The purpose of the BRI is therefore not only to impact the global political economy but also to change the way others relate to and think about the global political economy, their role in it, and their dialogue with China (Vangeli 2018: 59–60). Elizabeth Economy (2010) refers to this foreign policy revolution as a "go out" strategy designed to remake global norms and institutions. This strategy is built on an understanding of the changing nature of authority in the global order, and the way in which alliances can be built to ensure the emergence of a preferred multipolar structure (Breslin 2013).

Another signal that the BRI delivers is military conservativeness, which is mostly reflected by the concepts of a "community of a shared future" and a "new model of international relations." The ancient Silk Road is a symbol of peace among the nations along the road, and China hopes to inherit this symbol in the BRI projects. The notion of "peaceful development" is a cornerstone of China's foreign policies. However, in contrast to Hu Jintao's "peaceful development," Xi's signal of military conservativeness is characterized by a delicate shift from absolute pacifism and the principle of noninterference. Xi's speech at the Central Bureau in 2013 indicates that China advocates dealing with international security issues through dialogue and negotiation, and to solve disputes with mutual trust, mutual understanding, and mutual concession; however, there is a precondition that China's core interests should not be violated (Qian and Liu 2013). Xi's speech at Geneva further suggests that China may undertake interventions in international security crises if necessary. Xi states that "a country cannot have security while others are in turmoil, as threats facing other countries may haunt itself also. When neighbours are in trouble, instead of tightening his own fences, one should extend a helping hand to them . . . All countries should pursue common, comprehensive, cooperative and sustainable security" (Xi 2017a). This shift in international intervention echoes previous criticisms from the West that accuse China of inaction in international peacekeeping and crises settlement.

How have international audiences responded to these two signals? This research examines commentaries on President Xi's speech from all major English news publications in the LexisNexis database, with publishing dates ranging from October 18, 2017 to October 17, 2018 (one year after the speech). There were in total forty-five publications from fourteen countries that present highly relevant comments. This research mainly searches for comments in English, but there were also

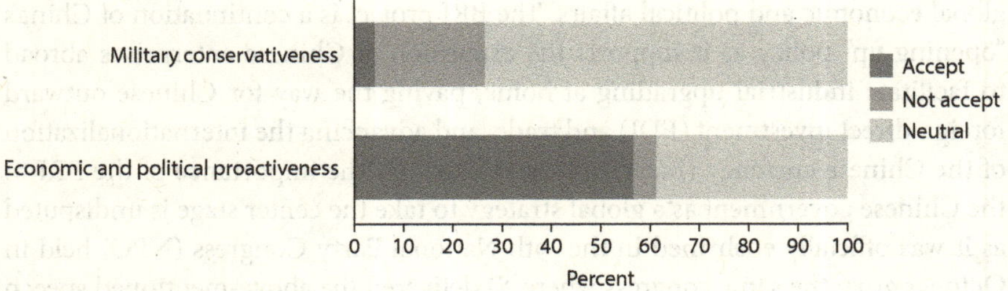

FIGURE 12.2. Audiences' acceptance of the two signals.

a few comments from non-English-speaking countries such as Japan, Thailand, and South Korea included in the analysis. The sampled publications may not fully reflect general public opinion about BRI in these countries, but they help illustrate perceptions and responses to the two signals by global audiences in the given time period.

Figure 12.2 illustrates the acceptance rate of the two signals among the samples. "Accept" here means the signal is accepted as it reflects the true intention of China. The result shows that nearly 60% of the sample agree that China's signal of economic and political proactiveness reflects China's true intention, while only less than 5% do not accept. About 38% of the sample do not show a clear position. In comparison, the signal of military conservativeness is less accepted as reflecting China's true intention. Only less than 5% of the sample accept this signal while more than 20% express a clear stance that they do not believe China will act in accordance with the signal of military conservativeness.

Figure 12.3 shows how the audiences responded differently to the two signals sent by Xi's speech on October 18, 2017. International audiences may accept a signal truly reflecting China's intentions, but some of them may not welcome this changing role of China. Fourteen out of 45 samples welcomed China playing an increasing role in international politics, and some of the views were "very positive." Ten samples express "negative" or "very negative" attitudes. In contrast, international audiences express more negative attitudes toward the signal of "military conservativeness" than that of "economic and political proactiveness." Only 3 out of 45 samples express positive attitudes to China's signal of "military conservativeness" while 21 samples express "negative" or "very negative" attitudes.

Table 12.2 compares the trust-building of the two strategic signals that China sends via the BRI. In terms of mutual interests, both China's "economic proactiveness" and "military conservativeness" fit other countries' interests. The Asian Development Bank estimates the cost of infrastructure needs for development in the Asia-Pacific region at about USD26 trillion through 2030 (OECD 2019). China's huge investment in BRI countries' infrastructure and other projects can substantially contribute to the development of these countries. China also intends to accept more responsibility in global and regional governance, which will also

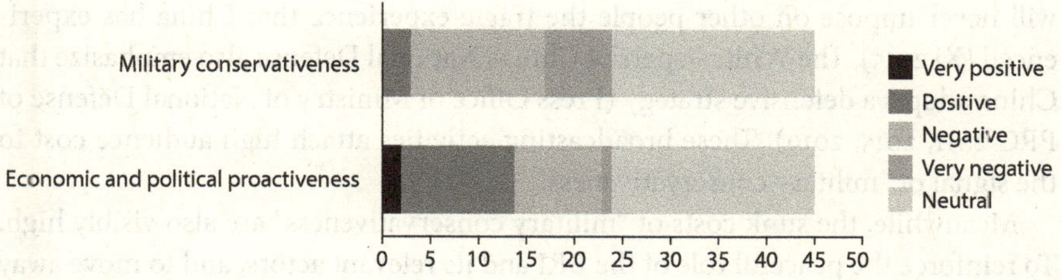

FIGURE 12.3. Audiences' attitudes toward Xi's signals.

TABLE 12.2 Comparing the trust-building of the two signals

	"Economic and political proactiveness"	"Military conservativeness"
Mutual interests	√	√
Costly signals	√	√
Good understanding of interests	Relatively better	Relatively worse
Acceptance (of samples)	Acceptance Rate	Acceptance Rate
Accept	56.8%	4.4%
Neutral rate	38.6%	73.3%
Non-Accept	4.5%	22.2%

benefit BRI countries. China has also stated its intention to remain militarily conservative and has made promises of no military expansion. Xi's speech in 2017 also states that China will provide protection when neighbors are threatened (Xi 2017b). This signal also fits neighboring countries' security interests.

Both "economic and political proactiveness" and "military conservativeness" are costly signals. For the signal of "economic and political proactiveness," Xi Jinping's speech on the 19th Party's Congress of Chinese Communist Party states that "it will be an era that sees China moving closer to centre stage and making greater contributions to mankind" (Xi 2017b). From 2013 to 2018, China has made direct investment for more than $90 billion in BRI partner countries, and the annual growth rate is 5.2% (*Xinhua News* 2019a). These investments also contain the projects that relate to global governance in climate change, poverty, and marine governance (*Xinhua News* 2019b). These investments are the direct sunk cost of China's signal on economic and political proactiveness.

For the signal of military conservativeness, President Xi and other Chinese leaders have repeatedly stated China's determination of military conservativeness in many speeches internationally and domestically. For instance, Xi made a speech on the seventieth anniversary of the victory of the Anti-Fascist War, promising that China will never seek a hegemonic position or expansion of her power; China will never impose on other people the tragic experience that China has experienced (Xi 2015). The White Papers of China's National Defense also emphasize that China adopts a defensive strategy (Press Office of Ministry of National Defense of PRC 2011, 2015, 2019). These broadcasting activities attach high audience cost to the signal of "military conservativeness."

Meanwhile, the sunk costs of "military conservativeness" are also visibly high. To reinforce the peaceful role of the BRI and its relevant actors, and to move away from geopolitical and security concerns, China emphasizes that the deployment of military forces overseas is only to deal with nontraditional security challenges along the BRI route such as maritime search-and-rescue missions, piracy, drug trafficking, and environmental risks (Chen et al. 2018). Deploying such defensive measures attaches high sunk costs to the signal of "military conservativeness."

Despite the high audience and sunk costs, these two signals are not well accepted by international audiences. Examining the samples of this research, there is still much skepticism about China's true intentions behind the signals. The vague interest boundaries of China in BRI projects is the major reason. Those commentaries examined above that are negative toward the BRI express their concerns in terms of China's "secret" motivation, such as intentionally creating "debt traps" in order to interfere in other countries' domestic affairs.

However, international audiences still respond differently to these two signals (see figs. 12.2 and 12.3). This paper argues that the signal "economic and politically proactiveness" is more readily accepted than "military conservativeness" because the former signal better fits international audiences' understanding of China's interests than the latter.

International audiences tend to interpret the signal "economic and political proactiveness" as China's quest for increasing economic and political influence internationally. The decline of US international leadership marked by the US withdrawal from several important international treaties and organizations reveals a vacuum in international leadership that worries the world because many believe in the role of great powers in global governance. China's willingness to take on more responsibilities in international affairs, no matter whether it can fulfill the vacuum left by the US or not, is good news for the world. More importantly, international audiences believe that growing international economic and political influence would largely benefit China's grand strategic goal of the "rejuvenation of the Chinese nation."

In contrast, the signal "military conservativeness" is more confusing to international audiences. China's peaceful rising was of mutual interest to China and the rest of world fifteen years ago, but how does it fit the interests of a powerful China tomorrow, where ideological competition seems to be inevitable given China's different path of development? The skepticism expressed in the comments examined above mainly arise from China's increasing military expenditure (Liu et al. 2019), the development of China's overseas military harbors, and an increasingly muscular stance in the South China Sea, including the denial of international arbitration, the construction of a man-made island, and other new military facilities in this area.

The People's Liberation Army Navy (PLAN) has been focusing on developing "blue water" capabilities to guarantee the security of the BRI (Fanell 2019). The PLAN has also established a broader "security supply chain" with Indian Ocean partners (such as Pakistan and Bangladesh) and Middle Eastern and African countries (Ma 2019), which not only helps improve its operational proficiency but also normalizes its presence in this region (Wuthnow 2017). However, many observe a rapid development of the PLAN along the BRI route, but this increasing role and presence of the PLAN is often intentionally left out of the Chinese official narratives. This lack of transparency increases skepticism about China's motivations.

CONCLUSION

This paper starts from the puzzle of international audiences' mistrust of China's cooperative signal-sending via the BRI, and it attempts to investigate how trust can be built across different narratives. It illustrates that trust-building is a continuing process of signaling and knowledge-building. With the existence of common interests, only when the signals fit counterparties' knowledge about the signal sender can they develop a good understanding of the signal sender's cooperative interests and thus trust the latter. In this process, the signal sender's "brightness"—being honest regarding their self-interest and cooperative intentions—is the necessary condition to whether the signals can fit others' knowledge.

The two case studies help to demonstrate the dynamic nature of trust-building in this one-way signaling process. In the first case, when Zhang Qian and his delegation went to Wu Sun and other Central Asian countries/federacies, they sent costly signals by bringing a huge amount of gifts that could show the Han's determination in strategic cooperation against the Xiongnu, but the Wu Sun and others decided not to trust the Han. The Wu Sun knew the Han's interests in balancing the threat from the Xiongnu, but they were cautious about cooperating because they did not understand the capability of the Han. The Wu Sun's interests might be seriously harmed if the Han were weak and they wanted to deceive the Wu Sun to gain free-riding benefits. The Wu Sun's new knowledge about Han that fit the Han's cooperative signal was developed in the third round of signaling when Wu Sun sent envoys to the Han, which eventually led to an alliance between the Han and the Wu Sun.

In the second case, China has sent costly signals of cooperation by making huge infrastructure investments in BRI partner countries; however, it has not received the expected trust in return. International audiences of the BRI are aware of China's capabilities, but uncertain about its intentions. How and what benefits can China gain from its huge investments in BRI? This is the question that international audiences are concerned about. Therefore, what China needs for trust-building is to further clarify its interests and intentions in the BRI projects and to keep sending cooperative signals in order to help the counterparties develop new knowledge about China and China's cooperative interests. Moreover, China needs to be cautious about the "cost" of its signals. If the cost of signals appears higher than what China stands to gain from its investments, international audiences will likely misunderstand China's cooperative interests, leading to distrust.

This paper illustrates that trust in strategic cooperation is the result of a series of signaling and knowledge-building, where the signal sender's "brightness" acts as a conditional factor. While this trust-building process can decrease the risk for cooperating states in trusting the signal sender, it cannot guarantee this trust will never be betrayed; and this betrayal that undermines the credibility of a state would have its consequences. For instance, Emperor Wu of the Han attempted to reshape the regional order in Central Asia by making alliances with the Wu Sun and other Central Asian countries and federacies. However, this alliance was not well honored by the Han later, possibly because the Xiongnu fell apart and thus were no longer a threat to the Han. However, the Han's untrustworthy behavior toward its allies had serious consequences. The Central Asian countries turned against the Han, and the Han had to wage numerous wars with enormous military expenses to keep their western border secure. Subsequently, the Great Han Empire declined in the late years of Emperor Wu's reign.

It is worth noting that this explanatory framework is only valid for a one-way signaling process where the signal sender and receiver are in an asymmetric power relation. In other words, the signal sender worries little about whether the receiver may exploit their strategic cooperation. This analytical framework is also excessively ideal as it takes states as perfect rational actors with high cognitive capability. Yet, failures in strategic calculation are not rare in diplomacy. Datta-Ray's contribution to this volume (chapter 11) presents the good example of India's diplomatic airstrikes against Pakistan in 2019, illustrating how national leaders may fail to calculate in practicing the notion of "defense without offense." Moreover, even with the wisest leaders or diplomats who are completely rational and cognitively capable, there will never be a perfect signaling process that removes all uncertainties in strategic cooperation. Leaders' wisdom is determinative to the success of practicing diplomacy, as Nehru's to No First Use and Credible Minimum Deterrence, or Mrs. Gandhi's to India's nuclear defense.

NOTES

1. China's "going out" strategy is aimed at encouraging Chinese overseas investment. It began in the early 2000s, when China joined the World Trade Organization. The purpose is to deal with overcapacity in general manufacturing and textile production. After the tax reforms in 2008, the "going out" strategy accelerated. There have since been increasing oversea investments made in manufacturing,

real estate, and information technology, further promoting China's oversea investments. See Zhang and Liu (2019).

2. *Han Feizi* 49, Five Moths. [《韩非子·五蠹》]

3. *Zuo Zhuan*, Hostage Exchange Between Zhou and Zheng, Year Three of Yingong. [《左传· 周郑交质隐公三年》]

4. *Li Ji* 42, Da Xue. [《礼记·大学》]

5. Mencius 2, Gongsun Chou A4. [《孟子·公孙丑上》]

6. *Xunzi* 9, Humane Governance. [《荀子·王制》]

7. *Xunzi* 18, Correcting: A Discussion. [《荀子·正论》]

8. As recorded by *Han Shu* (The History of the Han Dynasty), the Xiongnu invaded the Han's borders twice yearly on average during the early years of Emperor Wu's reign. See *Han Shu* 6, "Records of Emperor Wu."

9. *Shiji* 6, the Ranked Biographies of the Dayuan.

10. The Han delegation to the West was captured by the Xiongnu before they arrived in Yuezhi territory, and Zhang Qian was kept in the Xiongnu's camps for more than ten years before he found an opportunity to escape. He escaped with only two of this retinue, and all the fortune given by the Han Emperor was lost. See *Shiji* 6, the Ranked Biographies of the Dayuan.

11. *Shiji* 6, the Ranked Biographies of the Dayuan.

12. *Shiji* 6, the Ranked Biographies of the Dayuan.

13. *Shiji* 6, the Ranked Biographies of the Dayuan.

14. *Shiji* 6, the Ranked Biographies of the Dayuan.

15. No records, however, exist showing the Xiongnu had implemented any actual assault, probably because of the newly established alliance. See *Shiji* 6, the Ranked Biographies of the Dayuan.

REFERENCES

Andam, F., Shi, G., and Zhang, R. (2017) "Environmental and Social Risk Evaluation of Overseas Investment under the China-Pakistan Economic Corridor." *Environment Monitoring Assessment*. Epub ahead of print, 5 May 2017. DOI: https://doi.org/10.1007/s10661-017-5967-6.

Babatunde, M. A. (2015) "Promoting Connectivity of Infrastructure in the Context of One Belt, One Road Initiatives: Implications for Africa in the Fourth Industrial Revolution." In *Fostering Trade in Africa: Trade Relations, Business Opportunities and Policy Instruments*, edited by Gbadebo O. Odulary, Mena Hassan, and Musibau Adetunji Babatunde, 111–52. Cham, Switz.: Springer Nature.

Baltensperger, M., and Dadush, U. (2019) *The Belt and Road Turns Five*. Policy Contribution (1). Available at https://bruegel.org/wp-content/uploads/2019/01/PC-01_2019_.pdf (accessed 16 August 2019).

Beckwith, C. I. (2009) *Empires of the Silk Road: A History of Central Eurasia from the Bronze Age to the Present*. Princeton, NJ: Princeton University Press.

Bettman, J. R., Luce, M. F., and Payne, J. W. (1996) "When Time Is Money: Decision Behavior under Opportunity-Cost Time Pressure." *Organizational Behavior and Human Decision Processes* 66(2): 131–52.

Blanchard, J. M. F. (2018) "China's Maritime Silk Road Initiative (MSRI) and Southeast Asia: A Chinese 'Pond' not 'Lake' in the Works." *Journal of Contemporary China* 27(111): 329–43.

Booth, K., and Wheeler, N. J. (2008) *The Security Dilemma: Fear, Cooperation and Trust in World Politics*. Houndmills: Palgrave Macmillan.

Breslin, S. (2013) "China and the Global Order: Signalling Threat or Friendship?" *International Affairs (Royal Institute of International Affairs 1944–)* 89(3): 615–34. Available at www.jstor.org/stable/23473846 (accessed 28 April 2020).

Breslin, S. (2018) "The Belt and Road as 'Strategic Signalling.'" Presented at the Understanding the Belt and Road Initiative: Dynamics, Prospects and Implications conference, Beijing, China, 22–23 October 2018.

Buchanan, J. M., ed. (2017) "Opportunity Cost." In *The New Palgrave Dictionary of Economics*, 1–5. London: Palgrave Macmillan.

Callahan, W. A. (2016). "China's 'Asia Dream': The Belt Road Initiative and the New Regional Order." *Asian Journal of Comparative Politics* 1(3): 226–43.

Chen, L., Song, G., and Wei Zheng (2018) "Xin Shidai Renming Haijun 'Zouchuqu' Wenti" [On "go global" strategy in new era]. *Haijun Gongcheng Daxue Xuebao* [Journal of Naval University of Engineering] 15(1): 28–33.

Datta-Ray, D. K. (2015) *The Making of Indian Diplomacy*. New York: Oxford University Press.

De Vreese, C., and Boomgaarden, H. G. (2005) "Projecting EU Referendums: Fear of Immigration and Support for European Integration." *European Union Politics* 6(1): 59–82.

De Vreese, C., and Boomgaarden, H. G. (2006) "Media Effects on Public Opinion about the Enlargement of the European Union." *Journal of Common Market Studies* 44(2): 419–36.

Economy, E. (2010). "The Game Changer: Coping with China's Foreign Policy Revolution." *Foreign Affairs* 89(6): 142–52. Available at www.jstor.org/stable/20788725 (accessed 28 April 2020).

Fanell, J. E. (2019) "Asia Rising: China's Global Naval Strategy and Expanding Force Structure." *Naval War College Review* 72(1). Available at https://digital-commons.usnwc.edu/cgi/viewcontent.cgi?article = 7871&context = nwc-review (accessed 28 April 2020).

Fearon, J. (1997) "Signaling Foreign Policy Interest: Tying Hands versus Sinking Costs." *Journal of Conflict Resolution* 41(1): 68–90.

Franzosi, R. (1998) "Narrative Analysis—Or Why (And How) Sociologists Should Be Interested in Narrative." *Annual Review of Sociology* 24: 517–54. Available at www.jstor.org/stable/223492 (accessed 22 January 2020).

Glaser, C. L. (2010) *Rational Theory of International Politics: The Logic of Competition and Cooperation*. Princeton, NJ: Princeton University Press.

Grinols, E. L. (1991) "Unemployment and Foreign Capital: The Relative Opportunity Costs of Domestic Labour and Welfare." *Economica* 58(229): 107–21.

Guo, D. (2016) *Interpreting Zuo Zhuan: Chinese Classic Book*. Hong Kong: Zhonghua Shuju.

Hafner, M., Knack, A., Lu, H., and Rohr, C. (2018) *China Belt and Road Initiative: Measuring the Impact of Improving Transport Connectivity on International Trade in the Region—A Proof-of-Concept Study*. Rand Europe. Available at https://www.rand.org/content/dam/rand/pubs/research_reports/RR2600/RR2625/RAND_RR2625.pdf (accessed on 16 August 2019).

Hall, T., and Yarhi-Milo, Keren. (2012) "The Personal Touch: Leaders' Impressions, Costly Signaling, and Assessments of Sincerity in International Affairs." *International Studies Quarterly* 56(3): 1–15.

Hoffman, A. M. (2002) "A Conceptualization of Trust in International Relations." *European Journal of International Relations* 8(3): 375–401.

Hollis, M. (1998) *Trust with Reason*. Cambridge: Cambridge University Press.

Hu, P. S., and Zhang, M. Y. (2017) *Li Ji (Annotation)*. Beijing: Zhonghua Shuju.

Huang, B., and Xia, L. (2018) "China: ODI from the Middle Kingdom: What Is Next after the Big Turnaround?" *BBvA Research (China Economic Watch)*, Epub 13 February 2018. Available at https://www.bbvaresearch.com/en/publicaciones/china-odi-from-the-middle-kingdom-whats-next-after-the-big-turnaround/ (accessed 16 August 2019).

Hurley, J. M. S., and Portelance, G. (2019). "Examining the Debt Implications of the Belt and Road Initiative from a Policy Perspective." *Journal of Infrastructure, Policy and Development* 3(1): 139–75.

Irshad, M. S., Qi Xin, Li, X., and Arshad, H. (2016) "Deltoid Analysis of Pakistan-ASEAN-China Free Trade Agreements and Opportunities for Pakistan." *Asian Economic and Financial Review* 6(5): 228–37. Available at SSRN: https://ssrn.com/abstract = 2769335 (accessed 21 April 2020).

Jervis, R. (1976). *Perception and Misperception in International Politics* (rev. ed., 2017). Princeton, NJ: Princeton University Press.

Johnson, K. (2019) "China Gets a British Bedfellow: Left Vulnerable by Brexit, the U.K. Looks Eager to Sign onto Beijing's Giant Belt and Road Program." *Foreign Policy*, 26 April. Available at https://foreignpolicy.com/2019/04/26/china-gets-a-british-bedfellow-belt-and-road-hammond-xi/ (accessed 17 August 2019).

Juan, J. (2018) "As China Takes 'Center Stage,' Europe Stands at a Crossroads." *DW*, 15 February 2018. Available at https://www.dw.com/en/as-china-takes-center-stage-europe-stands-at-a-crossroads/a-42590805 (accessed 12 July 2020).

Kydd, A. H. (2000) "Trust, Reassurance, and Cooperation." *International Organization* 54(2): 325–57.

Kydd, A. H. (2001) "Trust-Building, Trust Breaking: The Dilemma of NATO Enlargement." *International Organization* 55(4): 801–28. Available at www.jstor.org/stable/3078616 (accessed 23 January 2020).

Kydd, A. H. (2005) *Trust and Mistrust in International Relations*. Princeton, NJ: Princeton University Press.

Kynge, J. (2018a) "China's Belt and Road Difficulties Are Proliferating across the World." *Financial Times*, 9 July. Available at https://www.ft.com/content/fa3ca8ce-835c-11e8-a29d-73e3d454535d (accessed 11 February 2020).

Kynge, J. (2018b) "Chinese Contractors Grab Lion's Share of Silk Road Projects." *Financial Times*, 24 January. Available at https://www.ft.com/content/76b1be0c-0113–11e8–9650–9c0ad2d7c5b5 (accessed 21 April 2020).

Larson, D. W. (1997) *Anatomy of Mistrust: US-Soviet Relations*. Ithaca, NY: Cornell University Press.

Li, D. (2015). "Jiedu Zhongguo Junfei Kaizhi" [Interpreting China's military expenditure], *Zhongguo Jingmao Daokan* [Journal of Chinese Economics and Trade], 6: 75–77.

Liu, H., and Lim, G. (2019) "The Political Economy of a Rising China in Southeast Asia: Malaysia's Response to the Belt and Road Initiative." *Journal of Contemporary China* 28(116): 216–31.

Liu, H., Xiao, C., and Zhang, C. (2019) "Spatial Big Data Analysis of Political Risks along the Belt and Road." *Sustainability* 11(2216). Available at doi:10.3390/su11082216 (accessed 16 August 2019).

Liu, X. R. (2010) *The Silk Road in World History*. Oxford: Oxford University Press.

Ma, D. (2019). "Zhongguo junfei zhichu zheshe d zhengce quxiang" [The policy orientation reflected by China's military expenses], *Minister of National Defense of the People's Republic of China*, 20 March. Available at http://www.mod.gov.cn/jmsd/2019–03/20/content_4837902.htm (accessed 21 April 2020).

Mayer, R. C., Davis, J. H., and Schoorman, F. D. (1995) "An Integrative Model of Organizational Trust." *Academy of Management Review* 20(3): 709–34.

Nordin, A. H. M., and Weissmann, M. (2018) "Will Trump Make China Great Again? The Belt and Road Initiative and International Order." *International Affairs* 94(2): 231–49.

OECD (Organisation for Economic Co-operation and Development) (2019). *Infrastructure Connectivity*. Japan G20 Development Working Group, January 2019. Available at https://www.oecd.org/g20/summits/osaka/G20-DWG-Background-Paper-Infrastructure-Connectivity.pdf (accessed 11 April 2020).

Patterson, M., and Monroe, K. R. (1998) "Narrative in Political Science." *Annual Review of Political Science* 1(1): 315–31.

Philippe, D., and Durand, R. (2011) "The Impact of Norm-Conforming Behaviors on Firm Reputation." *Strategic Management Journal* 32: 969–93.

Posnett, J., and Jan, S. (1996) "Indirect Cost in Economic Evaluation: The Opportunity Cost of Unpaid Inputs." *Health Economics* 5(1): 13–23.

Press Office of Ministry of National Defense of the PRC. (2011). "2010 Nian De Zhongguo Guofang" [China's national defense 2010]. Ministry of National Defense of the PRC, 31 March. Available at: http://www.mod.gov.cn/regulatory/2011–03/31/content_4617810.htm (accessed 21 April 2020).

Press Office of Ministry of National Defense of the PRC. (2015) "Zhongguo De Junshi Zhanlue" [China's military strategy]. Ministry of National Defense of the PRC, 26 May. Available at http://www.mod.gov.cn/regulatory/2015–05/26/content_4617812.htm (accessed 21 April 2020).

Press Office of Ministry of National Defense of the PRC. (2019) "Xin Shidai De Zhongguo Guofang" [China's national defense in the new ear]. Ministry of National Defense of the PRC, 24 July. Available at http://www.mod.gov.cn/regulatory/2019–07/24/content_4846424.htm (accessed 21 April 2020).

Pu, X. Y. (2017) "Ambivalent Accommodation: Status Signalling of a Rising India and China's Response." *International Affairs* 93(1): 147–63.

Pu, X. Y. (2019) *Rebranding China: Contested Status Signaling in the Changing Global Order*. Stanford, CA: Stanford University Press.

Qian, T., and Liu, H. (2013) "Xinhua Shipping: Yao Heping Fazhan Ye Jue Bu Xisheng Hexin Liyi" [Xinhua commentary: Advocating for peaceful development without scarifying core interests]. *People.cn*, 1 February. Available at http://opinion.people.com.cn/n/2013/0201/c1003–20399428.html (accessed 12 April 2020).

Rathbun, B. C. (2011) "Before Hegemony: Generalized Trust and the Creation and Design of International Security Organizations." *International Organization* 65(2): 243–73.

Rathbun, B. C. (2012) *Trust in International Cooperation: International Security Institutions, Domestic Politics and American Multilateralism*. Cambridge: Cambridge University Press.

Rousseau, D. M., Sitkin, S. B., and Burt, R. S. (1998) "Not So Different after All: A Cross-Discipline View of Trust." *Academy of Management Review* 23(3): 393–404.

Russel, D., and Berger, B. (2019) *Navigating the Belt and Road Initiative*. Asia Society Policy Institute. Available at https://asiasociety.org/sites/default/files/2019–06/Navigating %20the%20Belt%20and%20Road%20Initiative_2.pdf (accessed 11 April 2020).

Sidaway, J. D., and Woon, C. Y. (2017) "Chinese Narratives on 'One Belt, One Road' in Geopolitical and Imperial Contexts." *Professional Geographer* 69(4): 591–603.

Silk Road Seattle, Walter Chapin Simpson Center for the Humanities, University of Washington. Available at https://depts.washington.edu/silkroad/texts/hantxt1.html (accessed 11 April 2020).

Somers, M. R. (1994). "The Narrative Constitution of Identity: A Relational and Network Approach." *Theory and Society* 23(5): 605–49.

Tong, S. Y. (1946, 2006) *Chun Qiu Shi* [The history of the Spring and Autumn Period]. Re-edited by Tong Jiaoying. Hong Kong: Zhong Hua Shu Ju.

UNDP (United National Development Programme). (2017). "Beyond Business—Chinese Enterprises Overseas, Sustainable Development and the Belt and Road Initiative." *UNDP China*. Available at https://www.cn.undp.org/content/china/en/home/presscenter /pressreleases/2017/05/15/beyond-business-chinese-enterprises-overseas-sustainable -development-and-the-belt-and-road-initiative.html (accessed 11 April 2020).

Vangeli, A. (2018). *The Normative Foundations of the Belt and Road Initiative*. New York: Springer.

Wheeler, N. J. (2012) "Trust-Building in International Relations: Peace Prints." *South Asian Journal of Peacebuilding* 4(2): 1–14. Available athttps://pdfs.semanticscholar.org/8cod /8cff72824466e303902f1f6ca17d7d5d3a9d.pdf (accessed 11 April 2020).

Wood, F. (2002) *The Silk Road: Two Thousand Years in the Heart of Asia*. Los Angeles: University of California Press.

Wuthnow, J. (2017). *Chinese Perspectives on the Belt and Road Initiatives: Strategic Ratio-nales, Risks, and Implications*. Institute for National Strategic Studies: China Strategic Perspectives, no. 12. Washington, DC: National Defense University Press. Available at https://inss.ndu.edu/Portals/68/Documents/stratperspective/china/ChinaPerspec tives-12.pdf (accessed 28 April 2020).

Xi, J. (2014) *Xi Jinping Tan Zhiguo Lizheng* [Xi Jinping: The governance of China]. Beijing: Waiwen Chubanshe [Foreign Language Press].

Xi, J. (2015) Speech on the 70th Anniversary of the Victory of the Anti-Fascist War, Beijing, 3 September 2015. Available at http://news.cnr.cn/special/ybzb/list/20150903 /t20150903_519757913.shtml (accessed 14 April 2020).

Xi, J. (2017a) "Work Together to Build a Community of Shared Future of Mankind." Speech at the United Nations Office at Geneva, 18 January 2017.Available at http://www.xinhua net.com/world/2017–01/19/c_1120340081.htm (accessed 14 April 2020).

Xi, J. (2017b) Speech on the 19th Party's Congress of Chinese Communist Party, Beijing, 18 October 2017. Available at http://cpc.people.com.cn/n1/2017/1028/c64094–29613660 .html (accessed 14 April 2020).

Xinhua News. (2013) "Xi Jinping Fabiao Zhongyao Yanjiang Huyu Gongjian 'Sichou Zhi Lu Jingji Dai'" [Xi Jinping gave an important speech calling on building up Silk Road Economic Belt]. *Xinhua net*, 7 September. Available at http://www.xinhuanet.com /politics/2013–09/07/c_117272280.htm (accessed 11 April 2020).

Xinhua News. (2019a) "Woguo dui 'Yi Dai Yi Lu' yanxian guojia zhijie touzi chao 900 yi mei-yuan" [China makes over 90 billion USD direct investment in BRI partner countries].

Xinhua Net, 18 April. Available at http://www.xinhuanet.com/fortune/2019–04/18/c _1124386214.htm (accessed 11 April 2020).

Xinhua News. (2019b) "Zhongguo tuidong wanshan quanqiu zhili duo you xin zuowei" [China's multiple efforts in driving and perfecting global governance]. *Xinhua Net*, 26 June. Available at http://www.xinhuanet.com/2019–06/26/c_1124670734.htm (accessed 11 April 2020).

Yahuda, M. (2013) "China's New Assertiveness in the South China Sea." *Journal of Contemporary China* 22(81): 446–59.

Yean, T. S. (2018) *Chinese Investment in Malaysia: Five Years into the BRI*. ISEAS Yusof Ishak Institute. Available at http://hdl.handle.net/11540/8046 (accessed 19 August 2019).

Zaller, J. (1992) *The Nature and Origin of Mass Opinion*. New York: Cambridge University Press.

Zhang, J. P., and Liu, H. (2019) "Gaige Kaifang 40 Nian: Yin Jinlai He Zou Chuqu" [Opening up for 40 years: Bringing in and going out]. *Qiushi*, 9 March. Available at http://www .qstheory.cn/llqikan/2019–03/09/c_1124213820.htm (accessed 26 June 2019).

Zucker, L. G. (1977) "The Role of Institutionalization in Cultural Persistence." *American Sociological Review* 42(5): 726–43.

Balancing, Hegemony, and Mandalas

Balancing in Ancient China

Qi Haixia

1. QUESTIONS AND LITERATURE REVIEW

In comparing China's history with that of Europe's, a salient issue emerges: Why did China's Spring and Autumn and Warring States (SAWS) periods conclude with unification under the Qin Dynasty, while for a long period of time Europe remained fragmented? This paper seeks to unravel why, during the rise of the Qin, other states were not able to balance effectively against it, yet were successful in their balancing efforts vis-à-vis the rise of the Wei and Qi kingdoms, which were also major powers. Case studies include balancing directed toward the Wei kingdom—e.g., the "besiege Wei to save Zhao" and the "besiege Wei to save Han" campaigns; balancing directed toward the Qi—e.g., the "six-nation attack on Qi"; and the series of coalitions that arose to balance the Qin kingdom. Statistical analysis is then utilized to discuss and verify the significance of each hypothesis. The paper concludes that the Qin kingdom's success in uniting six nations into one derived not from any ability to avoid other nations' attempts to balance it, but rather due to its striving to avoid catastrophic balancing coalitions directed against it. Through measures that included annexing rather than destroying rivals, its "horizontal alliance" foreign policy, and allying with faraway states while attacking those nearby, the Qin kingdom was able to minimize the degree to which other states perceived it as a threat, making its eventual unification more inexorable.

1.1 Domestic Reform and Unification

Looking back millennia into the past, to the history of pre-Qin China, we will note a phenomenon that distinctly separates its history from that of modern European international relations: the emergence of a unified Qin state following centuries of SAWS warfare, and China's entrance into a period of overall unity. Although Europe's history has seen attempts at unification by a number of powerful countries—most notably Napoleonic France and WW2-era Germany—all eventually fell short. Chinese history notably diverges from that of the West in this regard, and this divergence has been the subject of much scrutiny.[1]

Victoria Hui has posited "reform from strength" and "reform from weakness" as the primary factor behind the differences in East and West.[2] This being so, we should first ask: What, logically speaking, do the two terms mean? We can see that, in Hui's view, the Qin kingdom's unification of China at the close of the SAWS exemplifies "reform from strength," while Napoleonic France's failure to do so in Europe was "reform from weakness." This logic, however, seems to confuse cause and effect; or, rather, it offers different reasons to explain diverging results. Hui's distinction between the two kinds of reform has been criticized by Dingxin Zhao, who states: "Obviously, the measures taken by feudal kingdoms in their struggles for supremacy during the early Spring and Autumn period were archetypically self-defeating."[3] "But who are we to say that the 'self-defeating' road taken in Europe reduced its nations' power in any way?"[4]

Jorgren Moller also analyzed this issue from the perspective of domestic politics. Based on comparing the failure of the Habsburg dynasty in Europe and the success of Qin's unification of China, Moller found that interest groups played a key role here. The strong privileged class in European states directly led to the powerful restriction of governmental power. However, the lack of a middle class led to strong governments in the Warring States and at last the unification of Qin.[5]

It is apparent that the "reform from strength"/"reform from weakness" or "strong government"/"weak government" dichotomy is not sufficient to explain Qin Dynasty unification versus European fragmentation. We can find many differences between ancient China and the Habsburg dynasty in domestic political fields. However, it is not sufficient to say these differences are the real cause. In reality, although both periods saw efforts to balance against would-be hegemons, this chapter asserts that the key difference between Qin unification and long-term European conflict lies in the unifying strategies used by the Qin kingdom.

1.2 Balance of Power

The balance of power is one of the classic, traditional theories of international relations. Kenneth Waltz has pointed out that in anarchy, should one state's strength rapidly increase, other major states would seek to balance this rising state, either solely or together with other countries, so as to bring the broken balance of power back into alignment. Thus, in the international system, we repeatedly observe states confronted with the choice of balancing or bandwagoning.[6]

Stephen Walt's "balance of threat" hypothesis represented an adjustment of the classic balance of power theory. Walt pointed out that in an anarchic system, countries choose balancing not only for the sake of power but also from the perception of threat.[7] Walt went on to point out that "threats" emerge from four factors: aggregate strength, geographical proximity, offensive capabilities, and offensive intentions.[8]

Randall Schweller has further pointed out that there exist two kinds of countries: status-quo powers and revisionist powers. Status-quo powers are, simply put, those countries who are satisfied with the existing order, while revisionist powers are those who are dissatisfied with the existing order and wish to tear it down.[9] Where motives are concerned, balancing is done in search of security, while bandwagoning is done to maximize a country's interests. Revisionist powers dissatisfied with the status quo therefore seek to bandwagon with larger revisionist powers, whereas only status-quo states seek to balance.[10]

The Warring States period did see efforts by other powerful nations to unite in an effort to balance the hegemon—the Qi state's campaign to "besiege Wei and save Zhao" during the reign of King Hui of Wei, the campaign to "besiege Wei and save Han," and coalitions directed at the Qin kingdom were all examples—but the issue lies in the diverging results of this balancing. This paper seeks to unravel why, during the rise of the Qin, other states were not able to balance effectively against it, yet were successful in their balancing efforts vis-à-vis the rise of the Wei and Qi kingdoms. This in turns breaks down into three subsidiary questions: Why did other states seek to balance the Wei kingdom? Likewise, why did balancing efforts directed at the Qi emerge? And why were efforts to balance the Qin kingdom unsuccessful in preventing its drive to unification? To answer these questions requires thoroughgoing analysis of the specific balancing, bandwagoning, and influences that emerged.

2. INTRODUCTION OF BALANCING AND HEGEMONY IN ANCIENT CHINA

From the Spring and Autumn period to the Warring States period, the interaction between the princes became increasingly disordered, diplomatic etiquette was gradually abandoned, and the system culture turned to tyranny. The profound change from "respecting courtesy and respecting trust" in the Spring and Autumn period to "combining deception and falsehood" in the Warring States period has been recognized generally by historians.[11]

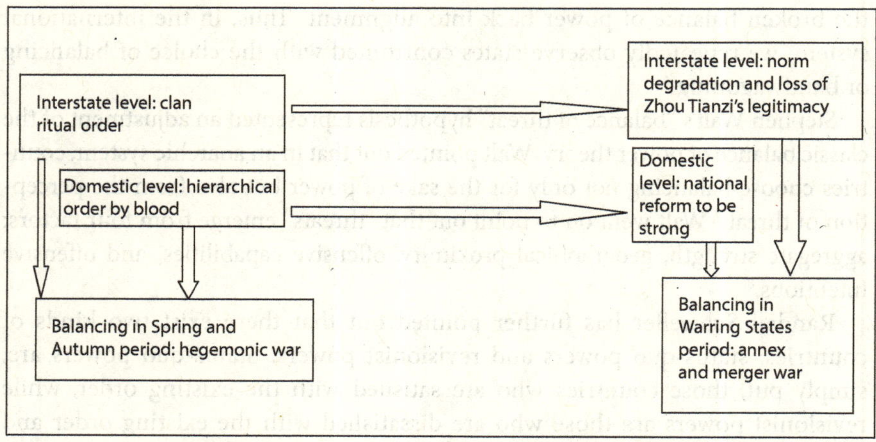

FIGURE 13.1. Transition from the Spring and Autumn period to the Warring States period.

2.1 Interstate Level: Norm Degradation and the Loss of Zhou Tianzi's Legitimacy

In the process of international social degeneration from the Spring and Autumn period to the Warring States period, the patriarchal clan ritual order left over from the Western Zhou Dynasty, with the core of "relatives-respect," gradually collapsed. This is the key to the deterioration of the international community in the Spring and Autumn period and to the more disorderly Warring States period. The collapse of the patriarchal clan system eventually led to the collapse of the international community in the Spring and Autumn period.

The Zhou Dynasty had built a feudal network by blood and marriage ties. There were two backbones to support the order of the world in the Zhou Dynasty: feudalism and the patriarchal clan system. The princes, who mainly bore the obligation of paying tribute to the royal family and helping Zhou Tianzi to expel barbarians and to relieve suffering, were not only political entities established by the Zhou Dynasty but also strategic partners for Zhou. According to the patriarchal clan system of the Western Zhou Dynasty, Zhou Tianzi (周天子) was the majority of the world and the supreme patriarch of the aristocracy with the same surname. The son of Zhou Tianzi was divided into princes (诸侯). The sons of the princes were feudalized as Qing (卿大夫), minor princes to the princes, and major presences in their families.[12] Hence feudalism and the patriarchal clan system were intertwined, with the feudal princes governing their feudal lands by serving their people and paying tribute to Zhou Tianzi.

The system of separation inevitably led to the continuous decentralization of political power and the downward shift of social power. This process is closely related to the development of production and the change of power caused by the feudal system.[13] Over the centuries, with the development of production, technological innovation, and population multiplication, the society greatly expanded. The competition for resources and power among states became increasingly prominent. However, the patriarchal hierarchy, based on the fixed criteria of kinship and consanguinity, had difficulty accommodating and regulating these changes. As the result, increasingly fierce competition and an unbalanced power structure gradually bred attempts to break through the original arrangement and identity order.

2.2 Features at the Unit Level: National Reform

In the Western Zhou Dynasty, the patriarchal clan principle was established. The patriarchal head was also the political leader of different ranks. Tianzi was the majority of the world, the princes were the majority of a country, and the Qing Doctor (卿大夫) was the bulk of a family. Dazong (大宗) had the responsibility to safeguard Xiaozong (小宗), and Xiaozong had the obligation to support Dazong. The patriarchal and monarchal unification was integrated through patriarchal power and each of the regimes supported the other.

The legitimacy of the patriarchal clan system was based on the spiritual appeal of ancestor worship, which was no less important than compulsory means. Blood relationship was the natural social cohesion, and the kinship relationship marked by surname became the basic social cohesion and organizational mode. Thus the rights and obligations of the ruling classes were inseparable from their identities in the patriarchal network. The patriarchal blood relationship was inferred to different surnames, hence patriarchal feudalism was not only applied to the same family name of the Zhou Dynasty but also to the different family names of the princes. With patriarchal consanguinity and marriage as a link, Zhou Tianzi established a social network of common interests with various states. Zhou Tianzi was not only the patriarch of Dazong（大宗）but also the common owner of the world. The patriarchal feudal order with Zhou Tianzi as the core and different kinship states competing to defend each other was formed in the Cathaysian system.[14]

Interstate norms and clan norms were inseparable, and the legitimacy of power depended on these norms. Family network and patriarchal clan rules constructed the common identity, interests, and values. Supported by the belief and emotion of "respecting ancestors and ancestors" and based on "relatives and respecting ancestors," a series of etiquette norms restraining political elites were derived, which strengthened, maintained, and ornamented political order through ritual and music rituals such as sacrificial feasts. There were two prominent features of Zhou rites: first, emphasizing kinship; and second, emphasizing hierarchical superiority and inferiority. A series of rules of etiquette and custom supported and embodied the patriarchal spirit. During this period, patriarchal clan ideas and the rules of etiquette, and the order derived therefrom, were deeply rooted in the hearts of the people and shared by all the states in China. They were established and declared through proclamation and oath, and constructed the "civilization standard" of the pre-Qin Chinese system.[15]

However, with the expanding population, the extension of intergenerational lineage, and the alienation of later subordinates, the consciousness of kinship community tended to be indifferent. As a result, the bond of clan identity was loosening day by day.[16] The practice of hegemony, which called for the maintenance of the old order, exacerbated the disorder. Competition for power, conflict of interests, and emotional resentment that led to tension and conflict between clans were often manifested by destroying the existing order. The accumulation of discontent and resentment further depleted the emotional ties of "relatives" and gave rise to a vicious cycle.[17]

The dissipation of patriarchal clan system rules and the disintegration of the international community created a complex dynamic. In the process of repeated wars, the states who took the lead in efficiency-oriented change had an advantage in war, a case in point being the Qin state that won many wars after the Shang Yang's reform.[18] With the transition from feudal system to county system, patriarchal clan rules also collapsed at the unit level. The social ties, legitimacy, and value consensus among countries were also broken. Finally, the original order foundation was destroyed.

In the Spring and Autumn period, due to the restrictions of social development, it was difficult for governments to legitimately monopolize the use of violence and to achieve effective control over their own people.[19] Compared with the large-scale wars in the Warring States period, the war mobilization ability of noble regimes in the Spring and Autumn period was limited because of the characteristics of aristocracy. Repeated war promoted a tendency toward political centralization, a case in point being the emergence of the county system. While the aristocratic feudal system survived, the county system appeared in some countries in the Spring and Autumn period. At the same time, some countries adopted a series of land rent and tax policies and military levy measures. Such tax policies represented the collapse of the old feudal system. In addition, with the innovation of war technology,[20] the old military service system that relied mainly on clan armed forces was abandoned and the universal military service system began to be implemented. Countries that adopted military reform greatly enhanced their war capabilities.

This series of changes impacted the patriarchal order. At first, under the original order, the political legitimacy of nobles at all levels, such as Zhou Tianzi, princes, and Dafu (大夫), was closely bound up with the patriarchal principle and mutually supportive common interests. With the increasingly centralized power of the princes, authority and political legitimacy were increasingly divorced from the old political principles based on patriarchal clan law. The common interests and value ties based on legitimacy were also ineffective.[21]

Secondly, in order to win the war of hegemony, the rulers of all countries recruited talent and promoted the disintegration of traditional hereditary official system based on blood relationships. A group of people from humble backgrounds stepped onto the political stage, relying on their talents. Driven by this, social mobility intensified, family networks were destroyed, and kinship levels gradually collapsed. The rise of new social relations, values, and moral concepts further broke the patriarchal hierarchical order within the princes. Emerging strata strove for success and profit, and the ruling elites were increasingly alienated. With the disappearance of the aristocratic community, social intimacy and communication ethics, which had been used to maintain order, could no longer restrain diplomatic behavior as they had done before.

At last, the emergence of continued implementation of feudalization and efficiency-oriented reform resulted in crises at the state level. Under the pressure of war, the monarch increasingly handed over the general power and diplomatic leadership to the officials. Ultimately, the complete subversion of the old domestic order and the nature of the feudal units of the Cathaysian system occurred. In many states, the ruling ranks of government officials gradually controlled the power of the state and then coveted the regime. By the middle and late Spring and Autumn period, with the fierce struggle inside the state between officials and monarch, the international disputes were also triggered and the patriarchal hierarchical order was destroyed.[22] Just as Mencius said, "Today's ministers are the sinners of today's princes."[23]

2.3 Features in Balancing Strategy: From Hegemony War to Annex War

2.3.1 Spring and Autumn Period: Hegemony War. After the establishment of the Western Zhou Dynasty, the government designed a complicated feudal system to protect the status of the Zhou Dynasty. The stability of this system was based on the leadership of Zhou Tianzi. To secure the status of Zhou Tianzi, the hierarchical order of rites were strictly emphasized. At the same time, Zhou Tianzi ensured the dominant position by militarily mobilizing local forces to fight against common enemies such as "barbarians" and "savages" who were not civilized. Within the vision of "the world" as a common body and under the interrelatedness of blood ties, each state was connected with the other rather than being isolated. "Prosperity and extinction followed by extinction" ("兴灭继绝") was the concrete embodiment of this principle.[24]

However, once the Zhou king failed in military expeditions, the dominant status of Zhou Tianzi was weakened. As a result, the prestige of the Zhou fell into decline. At last, the ritual system was facing a serious challenge. The declining of Zhou Tianzi's control over states resulted into repeated wars. In the Spring and Autumn period, the system of hegemony gradually developed as a result. To protect themselves from invasive war by the barbarians, the most powerful and influential state become the hegemon in the system. On the one hand, the hegemon state respected the leadership of Zhou Tianzi and gained legitimacy from Zhou Tianzi. On the other hand, the hegemon state provided the public goods for all member states in the system to aid in resisting foreign enemies, sustaining the order and rules in states, and avoiding civil wars in states. Due to the hegemon state's inferior strength and moral appeal, the system was relatively stable.

In the Spring and Autumn period, hegemony war was the predominant form of war. The hegemony states were expected to declare the safeguarding of Zhou Tianzi and etiquette. But in the Warring States period, Zhou Tianzi had completely lost the co-dominant position and the so-called "etiquette" had long been abandoned. The princes cared only about their own interests and the new predominant form of war was merger war.

From the Spring and Autumn period to the Warring States period, the deterioration of order was not only confined to the frequency and scale of wars but also to the norms of war, especially the transition from "justicial and benevolent war" to "treacherous and victory-oriented war." The spirit of military etiquette in the Spring and Autumn period of the Western Zhou Dynasty was mainly manifested in the following aspects: first, upholding the legitimate reasons for the war and emphasizing "invigorating armored troops to fight against injustice"; second, requiring courtesy and benevolence in the process of war; and third, the cessation of fighting once the goal was achieved. Before the middle of the Spring and Autumn period, there was still the restraint of worshipping etiquette and benevolence even in hot-blooded fighting. In the late Spring and Autumn period, military etiquette gradually declined. The custom of advocating deceit and utilitarianism replaced the tradition of respecting rituals and trust. In order to win, ignoring rules became the "only rule."

In the Spring and Autumn period, military ritual norms were still valid. War was an aristocratic affair and the importance of justice was stressed, not swindling.[25] Although many states collapsed in this period, the wars took place mainly between the states in Zhou and barbarians. Common interests and values still existed among states. Hence the question facing each of the strong states in the Spring and Autumn period became, how can I gain legitimacy? One of the ways to gain legitimacy was by respecting Zhou Tianzi and providing public goods such as fighting against the barbarians.

Coinciding with the weakening of Zhou Tianzi's power, the central government of Zhou could neither protect itself nor protect the member states. This power vacuum called for new leaders. The process of seeking hegemony also required that the major states respect Zhou Tianzi, who was still the nominal co-owner of the world. So in the process of power transition, major powers tried to rebuild the political and social rules to strengthen political principles, ethics rules, and the basic institutional status of order and legitimacy.

The leading hegemonic states in the Spring and Autumn period were often expected to meet the following requirements. First, the hegemonic state must have superior national strength. States that were not strong enough could not lead the system's member states to fight against common enemies. Second, the hegemonic state must be legitimized and able to provide institutional arrangements for the interstate system. Third, hegemonic states should not annex other states in the system casually. The hegemonic state should maintain the basic system of Zhou and protect other states from foreign aggression.

At the same time, although the hegemony states in the Spring and Autumn Period put forward slogans such as "respecting Zhou Tianzi and banishing the barbarians," they indeed weakened Zhou Tianzi's authority. There existed the competition for authority between Zhou Tianzi and the hegemony. Most of the member states respected the hegemony states more than they respected Zhou Tianzi. When legitimate strategies such as "respecting Zhou Tianzi" became gradually ineffective, states tended to compete according to the principle of utilitarianism. The great powers then frequently conspired against each other and bullied the smaller powers. International society was getting worse and worse.

According to its rising pattern, the hegemony war period in the Spring and Autumn period can be divided into three stages. The first stage was mainly the Qi Huangong (齐桓公) and Jin Wengong(晋文公) periods. Their ascendant strategies were basically the same. In the Spring and Autumn period, the power transition from Qi(齐) to Jin(晋) did not directly symbolize war. Zheng Zhuanggong (郑庄公), who had defeated Zhou Tianzi, did not become the hegemon because the challenge to Zhou Tianzi's authority could not be accepted by states then. On the contrary, the humiliation of Zhou Tianzi weakened the hegemonic foundation of Zheng Zhuanggong. In fact, different from Zheng Zhuanggong(郑庄公), Qi Huangong's hegemony was based on the protection of Zhou Tianzi's legitimacy and safeguarding member states against the barbarians.

The second stage was mainly represented by Qin Mugong (秦穆公). In this stage, although the legitimacy of Zhou Tianzi still played a role, its effectiveness decreased because the power transition depended less on Zhou's legitimacy and more on the ascendant state's defeat of the former hegemony. The symbol of Qin Mugong's hegemony was the success in war with Jin (晋). At the same time, Qin expanded to the West and dominated Xirong (西戎), which was hailed by Zhou Tianzi.

The third stage was Chu's hegemony. In this stage, Zhou Tianzi's legitimacy was also neglected. After military victory, Chu Zhuangwang (楚庄王) even challenged Zhou Tianzi's authority by asking the weight of nine great tripods (九鼎), which is the symbol of the Zhou Dynasty. Hence Chu Zhuangwang's inquiry here was regarded as the signal of challenging Zhou Tianzi's legitimacy. It is clear that Chu Zhuangwang's hegemony was different from the previous leading states. While challenging the legitimacy of Zhou Tianzi, Chu sought to appease the other states to gain more international support. Unlike previous hegemonies, Chu Zhuangwang did not annex other states after military success. A case in point was the experience of Chen (陈), who had been defeated by Chu and then recovered with the help of Chu. Therefore, in the third stage, Zhou Tianzi's legitimacy had obviously declined and the main source of hegemony legality was the recognition of other states.

It is clear that in the Spring and Autumn period, there were not many great wars in the power transition process. To achieve hegemony, a rising power needed to fulfill at least one of three requirements: victory in the hegemonic war; the supply of public goods such as security to all states; and/or legitimacy through Zhou Tianzi's recognition.

2.3.2 Warring States Period: Annex War. European states had organized six anti-Napoleonic alliances, in which Great Britain played a mainstay role by reducing the probability of defeat of European countries and funding European states who dared to take risks to join the alliance. Great Britain's behavior eventually contributed to the success of the anti-Napoleonic alliance. There is little doubt that without the consistency of Great Britain's balancing, France would have become the hegemon of Europe in the eighteenth or nineteenth century, and Germany would have become the leader of Europe in the contemporary era.[26]

However, closer analysis reveals that none of the Chinese states discussed above played as central and dominant a role as the United Kingdom played in Europe. Far from remaining passive in the face of the Qin drive to unification, the six-kingdom coalition made multiple attempts to balance. Why did these fail?

During the Warring States period, Qin, Qi, and Chu were three major powers of similar strength. Although Chu was active in organizing balancing against Qin, Qi rarely balanced Qin with Chu. From the perspective of strength, geography, and historical influence, Qi was more similar to Britain: a first-class power in strength, geographically on the edge of the mainland, and with the glory of hegemony in its history. Historically, in the early Warring States period, when the state of Wei tried to seek hegemony, the two wars of Qi besieging Wei to save Zhao and Han were classical balancing wars that successfully prevented the rise of Wei. However, in the later stage of the Warring States period, Qi was absent until finally the other five major states were destroyed by Qin.[27] Viewing the anti-Napoleonic alliance, we can see the importance of Britain in maintaining the balance of power. Hence the key to the failure of the Warring States cooperation lay in the lack of a firm counterbalance.[28]

The Qi kingdom's behavior in these coalitions was somewhat anomalous. Under kings Xuan and Min, the Qi state was aggressive in seeking to balance rising hegemons, as in the "besiege Wei to save Zhao" and "besiege Wei to save Han" campaigns, as well as its two coalitions of 298–296 BC and 287 BC. However, during the successive coalitions of the late Warring States period we find no trace of Qi. We can see that Qi state elites were not strongly threatened by the Qin process of unification. Indeed, it consistently adopted what we might term "anti-balancing" strategies. Our question therefore is, Why didn't Qi decision makers agree to balance during the last four decades of the Qin campaign to unite the six kingdoms?

(1) The Five Kingdoms' Assaults on Qi and the Qi "Anti-balancing" Strategy: As described in the preceding analysis, we find that under the rules of the Min and Jun kings, Qi state policy underwent an enormous transformation, moving from a preference for aggressive balancing to a policy of passive neutrality. This shift is of enormous importance to the final destruction of the six kingdoms; the reasons behind it therefore merit further investigation.

If we examine closely the major events in the Qi state, from the reign of the Min king to the late reign of the Jun sovereign, one event—the most significant since the Qi state's founding—stands out: the five kingdoms' assaults on Qi. Qi was defeated by a joint force assembled by the five kingdoms (Qin, Han, Zhao, Wei, and Yan) in 284 BC and nearly destroyed. Although the Qi state managed to reconstitute itself in 279 BC, its strength was greatly compromised. It is reasonable to assume that this event formed the historical background against which the Qi adopted its policy of rigorous neutrality.

We can see, therefore, that the efforts of the six kingdoms' coalition to balancing the Qin ran aground not because the kingdoms did not attempt to balance, but because in choosing the target of their balancing, they often focused on the obvious revisionist powers, i.e., the Wei and Qi in the early Warring States period. After their strength was sapped by conflict, the Qin—their true potential threat—broke up their balancing coalition. Despite their desire to unite their strength to balance the Qin, it was no longer in their power to do so. This is the key reason why the Warring States' balancing strategy failed. Why was it, then, that in the presence of multiple rising or challenging powers, and punitive attacks on other nations by the Wei, Qi, and Qin states, that other states only exerted themselves in attempting to balancing thoroughly to Wei and Qi, but not Qin? The author believes this is due to the significant differences in the strategies and signals adopted by the Qin state during its rise, and those of Wei and Qi.

(2) Examination of Other States' Rationale for Balancing the Qin State: The Qin state rose quickly after Qi's victory over Wei; by 288 BC Qin and Qi were referred to as the "Two Lords of East and West." In reality, other states' efforts to balance Qi were contemporaneous with their balancing of Qin. Anti-Qin balancing coalitions had emerged even before efforts to balance Qi. It is readily apparent, however, that the balancing directed at Qi was backed by a good deal more force; of all the participants, the one whose attitude was most unyielding was the northern kingdom of Yan, who was seeking revenge for Qi interference in Yan internal strife. Other states seeking to balance the Qi were driven by Qi's prior behavior as well. The Qi state's Min king had continually sought to expand Qi territory, creating fear on the part of its neighboring states.

TABLE 13.1 Strategic choices by the seven warring states

Grouping Name	Date	Major Participating Powers	Major Powers Not Participating	Target of Balancing	Did Target of Balancing Violently Annex Large State?	Was Balancing Successful?
Besiege Wei Save Zhao	B.C. 353	Qi, Chu, Qin, Zhao	Han, Yan	Wei	Yes	Successful
Besiege Wei Save Han	B.C. 342	Qi, Han, Zhao, Qin	Chu, Yan	Wei	Yes	Successful
First Coalition	B.C. 318	Wei, Han, Zhao, Yan, Chu (latter two, Yan and Chu, did not contribute troops)	Qi	Qin	No	Unsuccessful
Second Coalition	B.C. 298–296	Qi, Han, Wei	Zhao, Chu, Yan	Qin	No	Successful
Third Coalition	B.C. 294–286	Han, Wei	Qi, Zhao, Chu, Yan	Qin	No	Unsuccessful
Fourth Coalition	B.C. 287	Qi, Han, Zhao, Wei, Yan	Chu	Qin	No	Successful
'Balance Qi' Coalition	B.C. 284	Qin, Han, Zhao, Wei, Yan	Chu	Qi	Yes	Successful
Fifth Coalition	B.C. 274	Qi, Wei	Han, Zhao, Yan, Chu	Qin	Yes	Unsuccessful
Sixth Coalition	B.C. 259–257	Chu, Wei, Zhao	Han, Yan, Qi	Qin	Yes	Successful
Seventh Coalition	B.C. 247	Wei, Chu, Han, Yan, Zhao	Qi	Qin	No	Successful
Eight Coalition	B.C. 241	Chu, Zhao, Wei, Han, Yan	Qi	Qin	No	Unsuccessful

Through empirical testing, the author has determined that the "balance of threat" theory can explain the emergence of balancing behavior, but cannot account for its success or failure. Perceptions of threat are subjective, and can correspond to the threat sensed by the balancer or the balancee. States must choose not only whether or not they wish to balance, but the strength of their balancing efforts as well. Whether the balancing directed toward the rising state is a mere slap on the wrist or a fierce assault derives from the balancing state's determination of the rising state's ambitions, a determination which itself is tied to contemporary international norms. If a rising power is violating fundamental international norms, the balancing efforts will be correspondingly powerful. If the rising power is circumspect in its handling of said norms, the efforts to balance will be relatively weak.

In the Warring States period, violent annexation of a major power was a violation of fundamental international norms. The deep-rooted reason for the difference between tough balancing against Wei and Qi and the relatively weak balancing against Qin lies in the baseline of international norms at that time. During the Warring States period, the international system was in Hobbes's anarchy state. Instead of seeking hegemony, countries tried to gain more territory and even eliminate other countries. Whether the goal of war was to fight for hegemony or to annex became an important feature to distinguish the Spring and Autumn period and the Warring States period.[29] The total number of states declined from hundreds in the Spring and Autumn period to seven major states and several medium-sized states in the Warring States period. The annexing of major states meant the thorough destruction of the power balance, which easily induced system collapse. Hence in the Warring States period, the taboo of international norms was that the annex war of major powers was forbidden, but the annex war of medium-sized states and the cession of cities in major powers were permitted.

The Qin state's success in uniting the six kingdoms laid not in its avoidance of balancing by other states, but rather in its strenuous efforts to avoid catastrophic balancing coalitions directed against it. In the early Warring States period, the Qin state avoided rash efforts to annex other major powers, and through its "horizontal alliance" foreign policy was able to reduce other states' perceptions of it as a threat. As the Qin state's power grew, the Wei and Qi states were both subject to successive, successful balancing efforts by other states. When the Qin state's strength had grown far beyond that of other kingdoms, it maintained an intelligent policy of allying with faraway states while attacking those nearby, reducing the readiness of the relatively distant states of Qi and Chu, and making its eventual unification of the six kingdoms a foregone conclusion.

Although Qin had experienced many instances of balancing by other major states, it retained a proper strategy of not annexing the major powers at one stroke. What's more, by using wedge strategies (lianhen "连横"), Qin also effectively prevented enemy coalitions named "合纵" (Hezhong). Additionally, to reduce the resistance, Qin chose a new strategy named "allying distant states and attacking nearby states" (Yuanjiao Jingong远交近攻). All of the other major powers mistakenly judged the ambition of Qin. Therefore, they chose to check and balance Qi, which gave Qin a favorable opportunity to unify China at last. After Qi has been defeated completely, Qin naturally became the strongest power and began to show its ambition.[30]

The result is that in 221 BC Qin unified China. It is clear that the reason why the other six states could not resist Qin firmly was that they did not realize the threat of Qin. In the period of Qin's strength accumulation, Qin only sought cession of territory from the defeated, which did not break through the psychological bottom line of each state because Qin at that time did not choose to seek annexation of all major powers. At last, when Qin's strength was supreme to all of the other states, it adopted the new strategy of "allying distant states and attacking nearby states" (Yuanjiao Jingong远交近攻), which also reduced the threat perception of major states who were farther away. In the end, the unification process went smoothly.

3. CONCLUSIONS AND IMPLICATIONS FOR THE CONTEMPORARY WORLD

This study has sought to determine the deep-rooted reasons for China's long-lasting wars in the SAWS periods and the unification under the Qin Dynasty when compared to the long-term divisions of Europe. Through historical analysis, we can explain the peculiarity of ancient China from three perspectives. First, at the interstate level, the norm degradation and the loss of Zhou Tianzi's legitimacy can explain the tangled warfare in this period and the unification by Qin, which was the strongest state then and defeated all the other strong powers. Second, at the unit level, national reform resulted into a Hobbesian anarchy in which every state fought with other states. Third, the diplomatic and military strategy of each state from hegemony war to annex war triggered fierce struggles, and only the winner can survive in such a system.

The empirical study of ancient China provides new findings that the balancing theory from threat perception can explain part of the reason for the occurrence of balances, but cannot explain the success or failure of the balances. Whether the balancing states choose to punish the rising state slightly or fiercely depends largely on their judgment of the rising country's ambition, which is based on the degree to which the rising state violated the then-current international norms. The rising state who challenged the bottom line of international norms would face severe punishment. However, those who acted cautiously within the international norms would face lighter punishment. Compared with other rising states such as Wei and Qi in the Warring States period, the success of Qin's unification of China lies not in Qin's avoidance of containment but its escape of fatal balancing by other major powers.

The roots of success, however, also contained within them the beginnings of failure. Qin's success relied heavily on strategy, by reducing the other major powers' perception of fear. But the end of the Qin Dynasty was attributed to its overemphasis on strategy and relative neglect of morality. Strategy and intelligence helped Qin defeat its enemies, but the lack of morality did not help Qin win the support of the people, so it soon lost the world.

The end of the six other major states was not due to Qin but to themselves. The key reason lay in the degradation of international norms and their abandonment of benevolent rule in domestic governance. In the Warring States period, the princes overlooked the importance of morality and tried their best to expand territory. Therefore, the key reason why the six states could not unite was that they competed against each other for land. After relinquishing land to Qin, they often had to make up for it by taking land from other states, and the weaker states defeated by Qin also could become the targets of other major powers. For example, in 251 BC, after Zhao fought with Qin in the Changping (长平) War and the defensive war of Handan (邯郸), Yan also attacked Zhao to acquire territory. The reason why the six states could not unite with each other, and instead were eager to seek advantage through fraud, lay deep in the degeneration of international norms and the collapse of rites. Without moral restraint, states competed against each other and sought to conquer each other.

Although the events of the SAWS periods took place in the distant past, we can learn from the history. The traditional Western international relations theories, although sometimes using cases from Asian history, most often concentrated on European and American histories. In recent years, the rise of China and the rapid development of India should arouse widespread reflection among scholars that the rediscovery of Eastern Asian history may challenge current Western IR theory.[31] For example, in Chinese history, in addition to the end of the Warring States period and the unification of the Qin Dynasty, there was also a long Confucian peace during the tributary system. What's more, India also has political thoughts and philosophies that are quite different from Western thoughts and will provide us new insights into solving problems in today's world. According to the analysis of the pre-Qin period, we can see the importance of international norms and morality. Therefore, in order to maintain world peace, major powers should not overemphasize tactics and power, but should stress the importance of morality. Benevolent government is required of leaders not only due to domestic demand, but it is the sine qua non for an international society.

NOTES

1. Victoria Tin-bor Hui, *Zhanzheng yu guojia xingcheng: Chunqiu zhanguo yu jindai zaoqi ouzhou zhi bijiao* [War and state formation: A comparison of the Spring-Autumn Warring States Period and Early Modern Europe], 1.

2. Hui points out: "In a policy of 'reform from strength', destroying one's enemies in detail and deploying underhanded stratagems hugely amplifies coercive strength and reduces the costs of war. If a hegemon can increase its military and economic strength and endeavour to face its adversaries singly, while ensuring victory on the battlefield and using the spoils of war to sustain its military machine, then the results of opportunistic expansion may come to resemble a snowball, growing ever larger until unification is achieved. Conversely, if a hegemon employs 'reform from weakness', failing to use all the means at its disposal to support a strategy of divide and conquer, and failing to be sufficiently Machiavellian in its tactics, then its invasions will become more difficult to sustain, and the system may endure." Victoria Tin-bor Hui, *Zhanzheng yu guojia xingcheng: Chunqiu zhanguo yu jindai zaoqi ouzhou zhi bijiao* [War and state formation: A comparison of the Spring-Autumn Warring States Period and Early Modern Europe], 25–26.

3. Dingxiang Zhao, *Dongzhou zhanzheng yu rufa guojia de yansheng* [The wars of the Eastern Zhou and the birth of the Confucian state], 190.

4. Ibid., 195–96.

5. Jorgren Moller, "Why Europe Avoided Hegemony: A Historical Perspective on the Balance of Power," *International Studies Quarterly* 58 (2014): 660–70.

6. Kenneth N. Waltz, *Theory of International Politics* (New York: McGraw-Hill, 1979), 123–28.

7. Stephen M. Walt, *The Origins of Alliances* (Ithaca, NY: Cornell University Press, 1987), 8, 29–33, 148–52.

8. Ibid., 22–24; see also Stephen M. Walt, "Alliance Formation and the Balance of Power," *International Security* 9, no. 4 (Spring 1985): 9–12.

9. Randall L. Schweller, "Bandwagoning for Profit: Bringing the Revisionist State Back In," *International Security* 19, no.1 (Summer 1994), 87–88; Schweller, *Deadly Imbalances: Tripolarity and Hitler's Strategy of World Conquest* (New York: Columbia University Press, 1998), chap. 1.

10. Schweller, *Deadly Imbalances*.

11. Si Maguang has said that since the destruction of the king's legitimacy, the states were entrapped in prolonged wars with each other; see Si Maguang, *zizhi tongjian*, "zhouji yi". 司马光说道：“呜呼！君臣之礼既坏矣，则天下以智力相雄长，遂使圣贤之后为诸侯者，社稷无不泯绝，生民之类糜灭几尽，岂不哀哉！”，司马光：《资治通鉴·周纪一》。

12. Zuo Qiuming, *Zuo Zhuan*, "Huanggong Ernian" "故天子建国，诸侯立家，卿置侧室，大夫有贰宗，士有隶子弟，庶人、工、商，各有分亲，皆有等衰。”（左丘明：《左传》"桓公二年"）。

13. Guan Donggui, *Cong zongfa fengjianzhi dao huangdi junxianzhi de yanbian: Yi xueyuan jieniu wei mailuo* (Beijing: zhonghua shuju, 2010), 34. 管东贵：《从宗法封建制到皇帝郡县制的演变——以血缘解纽为脉络》，北京：中华书局，2010年，第34页。

14. Yaqing Qin, "Rule, Rules, and Relations: Towards a Synthetic Approach to Governance," *Chinese Journal of International Politics* 4, no. 2 (2011): 117–45. Yongjin Zhang, "System, Empire and State in Chinese International Relations," in *Empires, Systems and States: Great Transformations in International Politics*, ed. Michael Cox et al. (Cambridge: Cambridge University Press, 2001), 43–63; David C. Kang, *East Asia before the West: Five Centuries of Trade and Tribute* (Cambridge: Columbia University Press, 2010); Yuan-Kang Wang, *Harmony and War: Confucian Culture and Chinese Power Politics* (Cambridge: Columbia University Press, 2011); Yongjin Zhang and Barry Buzan, "The Tributary System as International Society in Theory and Practice," *Chinese Journal of International Politics* 5, no. 1 (2012): 3–36.

15. Chen zhen, "Chunqiu huaxia zhixu wajie yu guoji shehui tuihua jizhi," *Shijie jingji yu zhengzhi* 2 (2015): 41–64. 陈拯：《春秋华夏秩序瓦解与国际社会退化机制》，《世界经济与政治》，2015年第2期。第41–64页。

16. Gu Yanwu, *rizhilu*, "zhoumo fengshu". 顾亭林指出：“春秋时犹严祭祀，重聘享，而七国则无其事矣！春秋时犹论宗姓氏族，而七国则无一言及之矣！邦无完交，士无完主，此皆变于一百三十三年之间，史之阙文，而后人可以意推者也，不得始皇之并天下，而文武之道尽矣。”，参见顾炎武：《日知录》卷十三《周末风俗》。

17. Han Feizi, "Wu du" 韩非子指出："上古竞於道德，中世逐於智谋，当今争於气力。"《韩非子·五蠹》。

18. Si Maqian, *Shiji* "qin benji". 司马迁：《史记·秦本纪》。

19. *The Analects of Confucius*, "Ji Shi Pian" 孔子曰："天下有道，则礼乐征伐自天子出；天下无道，则礼乐征伐自诸侯出。《论语》"季氏篇"。

20. Stephen van Evera, "Offense, Defense, and the Causes of War," *International Security* 22, no. 4 (Spring 1998): 5–43.

21. *Yijing*, "Wenyan, Kun"《易经·文言传·坤》："臣弑其君，子弑其父，非一朝一夕之故，其所由来者渐矣。由辩之不早辩也。"

22. Zhao dingxin, Dongzhou zhanzheng yurufa guojia de dansheng, Shanghai sanlian shudian (2006), 102–3. 赵鼎新：《东周战争与儒法国家的诞生》，上海，华东师范大学出版社，上海三联书店，2006年，第102–103页。

23. 孟子曰："今之大夫，今之诸侯之罪人也"，《孟子》"告子章句下"。

24. *Lunyu* "yaoyue", *zhongyong* "zhangju", "兴灭国，继绝世，举逸民，天下之民归心焉"(《论语·尧曰》)"继绝世，举废国，治乱持危，朝聘以时，厚往而薄来，所以怀诸侯也"(《中庸·章句》)

25. For example, Song Xianggong obeyed the norms of war even when fighting with the Chu state, and did not have regrets even though the result of obeying the norms was failure in the war. Si Maqian, *Shiji* "Song Weizi Shijia"（宋襄）公曰："君子不困人於阨，不鼓不成列。"参见司马迁：《史记·宋微子世家》。

26. Daniel J. Whiteneck, "Long-term Bandwagoning and Short-term Balancing: The Lessons of Coalition Behaviour from 1792 to 1815," *Review of International Studies* 27, no. 2 (2001): 151–68.

27. Gu Zuyu sighed: "I feel sorry for the Tian family of Qi because he tied up his hands and was captured by Qin when the five kingdoms were destroyed." Gu Zuyu, *Summary of Fangyu in History Reading* "preface to Summary of Fangyu in Shandong Province." 顾祖禹：《读史方舆纪要》"山东方舆纪要序"。"吾尝慨夫齐之田氏，席霸国之余业，不能于纵横之日，发愤为雄。及五国既灭，王贲东下，遂束手而臣虏于秦也。"

28. Su Xun pointed out: "The reason why Qi was at last occupied by Qin although Qi did not bribe Qin by cession of territory lies in the fact that Qi has chosen to bandwagon on the side of Qin but not other five states." 苏洵：《六国论》。"齐人未尝赂秦，终继五国迁灭，何哉？与嬴而不助五国也。"

29. Zhao Dingxin, *The War of the Eastern Zhou Dynasty and the Birth of Confucianism and Legalism*, 102–3. 赵鼎新：《东周战争与儒法国家的诞生》，第102–3页。Yang Kuan: *History of the Warring States Period*, 1–2. 杨宽：《战国史》，第1–2页。

30. Yang Kuan, *History of the Warring States Period*, 158. 杨宽：《战国史》，第158页。

31. Yan Xuetong, *Ancient Chinese Thought, Modern Chinese Power* (Princeton, NJ: Princeton University Press, 2011).

14

International Order in Ancient India

Manjeet S. Pardesi

INTRODUCTION

Did ancient India display a propensity towards balance-of-power or hegemony? The balance-of-power versus hegemony debate is one of the core debates in International Relations (IR) theory.[1] Ancient India witnessed a hegemonic international order dominated by a single polity for roughly five-and-a-half decades (~260–205 BCE) under the Magadha-centered Mauryan Empire. Mauryan domination was exceptional but relatively fleeting in the nine centuries from the emergence of the sixteen *mahajanapada*-states (or "great-territorial" states) in 600 BCE until the second phase of hegemony under the Gupta Empire (post-320 CE). However, the absence of hegemony/domination in the pre-Mauryan period and in the five post-Mauryan centuries (~205 BCE–320 CE) was not characterized by a balance-of-power system. Instead, I make the case for a de-centered *mandala* ("circle" or zone of competition) international order in these centuries when ancient India was an "open" region of the larger South-West Eurasian international system.[2] The aim of this chapter is to explain the emergence of Mauryan hegemony/domination, and to elucidate the *mandala* international order that prevailed in the pre-/post-Mauryan period.

I argue that Mauryan domination was the combinatorial outcome of four causal factors: (i) expansionist ideas, (ii) the relatively "closed" South Asian region from 305 to 205 BCE, (iii) inefficient relational balancing (and the absence of systemic balancing), and (iv) the contingency of Magadhan geography.[3] In the absence of Mauryan domination, the *mandala* order prevailed in ancient India. The Indic *mandala* order comprised six interacting zones (or *mandalas*) that were the primary sites of inter-polity competition. Most polities sought to dominate their own respective *mandalas* (with only a few expanding outwards into other *mandalas*). However, the extremely competitive multi-polity system meant that even as many polities rose and fell within individual *mandalas*, only a few were able to dominate their own *mandala*, and no single polity was able to dominate all the Indic *mandalas* during this period (with the exception of Mauryan-Magadha). The presence of multiple *mandalas*, and multiple competing polities within these *mandalas*, gave rise to a truly de-centered international order. This *mandala* order was held together by ideas related to the management of power asymmetry in a region where the "deep structure" was marked by political and cultural heterogeneity.[4]

In other words, contra Waltz, I demonstrate that the "India of Kautilya" (or the period under analysis here) did not practice systemic "balance of power politics."[5] Similarly, contra Wight, I show that despite "common [macro-]culture," the Indic system did not "end" in a "universal empire" (or hegemony/domination).[6] As such, the study of ancient India contributes to "Global IR" as it expands our repertoire of international orders beyond power balances and hegemony.[7] In fact, the *mandala* order is also distinct from the historic Sinocentric orders as it was de-centered power-politically and ideationally.[8]

The rest of this chapter is divided into six sections. The first section provides a brief history of ancient India as part of the larger South-West Eurasian international system. This is followed by a theoretical explanation of the concept of the *mandala*. The third section explains the rise of Mauryan domination (~260–205 BCE). I argue that even as the Mauryas sought political domination only in the Indian subcontinent, the domain of their ideational domination was system-wide (or the South-West Eurasian international system). The subsequent section applies the concept of the *mandala* to the post-Mauryan period for a theoretical analysis of the international history of these centuries. In the fifth section, I demonstrate that the concept of the de-centered *mandala* order can help us understand the emerging order in the contemporary Indo-Pacific. The theoretical generalizations that emerge from India's ancient history can spatially and temporally transcend the domain of their origin, thereby contributing to Global IR. Finally, given the comparative nature of this book project, I conclude with a theoretical and empirical comparison of international order in ancient India and China.

ANCIENT INDIA (AND THE SOUTH-WEST EURASIAN INTERNATIONAL SYSTEM)

Ancient India was an "open" region of the South-West Eurasian "interregional-scale international system."[9] The emergence of the sixteen *mahajanapadas* in sixth century BCE was nearly simultaneous with the domination of northwestern India by the Persian-Achaemenid Empire (until 330 BCE).[10] After the conquest of the Achaemenid Empire by Alexander the Great, northwestern India fell under Hellenistic domination (~327–305 BCE).[11] Although northwestern India came under Mauryan domination for a century (~305 BCE—205 BCE) after the Mauryan-Seleucid Treaty of the Indus, the collapse of the Mauryan Empire (in 181 BCE) saw four centuries (~second century BCE–second century CE) of conquest-migrations in northwestern, north-central, and western India of the Bactrian-Greeks,

Scythians/Shakas, Parthians, and finally the Kushans, whose empire stretched from Central Asia to the Ganges.[12] These interactions are crucial theoretically, and Lieberman has cautioned against treating "India" as an autonomous unit in world history because the Achaemenids and Kushans (among others) politically connected parts of India with the world beyond.[13] At the same time, it should be noted that the sixteen *mahajanapadas* stretched in an arc from Magadha in the eastern Ganges to Gandhara (in contemporary Afghanistan-Pakistan) and Kamboja (in modern Tajikistan).[14]

However, ancient India was home to multiple polities beyond the ones noted above. For example, around the time of Alexander's conquest of northwestern India, there were twenty-eight small states in that part of the subcontinent alone.[15] Similarly, the southern states like the Cholas and Pandyas were not members of the club of "great" states noted above.[16] While the nature of the historical sources mean that we do not have the complete list (or number) of states during these centuries, a broad geopolitical profile can nevertheless be sketched.[17] When Magadha was expanding into Anga around 545 BCE in the eastern Ganges, Gandhara (and other parts of the northwest) fell under Achaemenid sway. Meanwhile, Magadha continued with its relentless expansion and annexed the "great" states of Kosala, the Vajjian Confederacy, Avanti, and most of northern and central India by the time of Alexander's invasion of the northwest (~327–6 BCE). The northwest then became a part of Alexander's Seleucid successors, while the Mauryan dynasty assumed power in the Magadhan Empire under Chandragupta (in 321 BCE).

The Mauryans and the Seleucids had a politico-military encounter that culminated in the so-called Treaty of the Indus in 305 BCE as a result of which the northwestern regions came under Mauryan domination.[18] Later, Chandragupta's grandson Ashoka fought a particularly bloody war with Kalinga (in contemporary Odisha) in 260 BCE, thereby eliminating the only serious challenger to Mauryan domination in the subcontinent. While the Cholas, Pandyas, Satiyaputras, and Keralaputras continued to exist as independent states in the deep south as did Tamraparni (Sri Lanka), the Mauryan Empire stretched from southern Afghanistan to Karnataka, and from Baluchistan to Bengal.

However, Mauryan domination lasted only for a few decades (~260–205 BCE). In 205 BCE, the Seleucids marched towards India again. However, they did not encounter the Mauryas (whose empire had begun to shrink). Instead, the Seleucids met with Subhagasena, who was the ruler of a northwestern state that had heretofore been a part of the Magadhan Empire.[19] In the meantime, the Mauryan dynasty collapsed while the Magadhan Empire continued to shrink to its original core as many erstwhile polities that were annexed by Magadha, such as Kalinga, reappeared.[20]

The Bactrian-Greeks then descended into northwestern India after 181 BCE, and as "Indo-Greeks" reached Malwa in the south and Mathura in the east. They even attacked Pataliputra, the capital of Magadha, from where they were pushed back.[21] In the first century BCE, King Kharavela of Kalinga emerged victorious over the Indo-Greeks in the eastern Ganges while also fighting with the Satavahana rulers of the Deccan and the Tamil polities of the deep south.[22] The Satavahana Empire that had emerged as a major power in the western Deccan defeated Magadha in 28 BCE.[23] In the following century, the Satavahanas found themselves in a rivalry with the Western Shakas, one of three separate groups of Scythians who migrated to India in the last two centuries BCE, and who survived in western India until 415 CE.[24] The Western Shakas with their access to seaports maintained amicable relations with the Kushan Empire (first to third centuries CE) that controlled parts of contemporary Uzbekistan, Tajikistan, Turkmenistan, Xinjiang, Afghanistan, Pakistan, and northern and central India, thus playing a crucial role in the establishment of the Silk Roads.[25] Not surprisingly, the Kushan Empire faced significant external challenges from beyond the subcontinent, and finally collapsed in the mid-third century under Persian-Sassanian assault. Subsequently, a Persia-oriented Kushano-Sassanid dynasty rose to power in north-western India.

In order to decipher the general trends in the complex history of the subcontinent during these nine centuries (~600 BCE—300CE), Schwartzberg divided the Indian subcontinent into five "analytic regions"—the Northwest, North-central, Northeast, West, and South—that were the centers of the major polities.[26] In addition to these five centers, some polities arose in the "Far Northwest" (beyond the subcontinent in West-Central Eurasia) that brought some polities in the Northwest, North-central, and the West under their sway. In these nine centuries, only the Magadhan-Mauryan Empire (~260–205 CE) rose to dominate the entire subcontinent. Furthermore, apart from Magadha, no other power emerged in the subcontinent until 200 BCE that was able to control two or more of these five analytical regions for more than a decade, the occasional military foray notwithstanding. In the subsequent four centuries (~200 BCE–200 CE), there were 140 years without any power being able to dominate more than one of these five regions. When major powers dominating two (or occasionally three) regions did arise during these four centuries, they were centered either in the Northwest (the Shakas or the Kushans) or in the West (the Satavahanas) as opposed to the Northeast (Magadha's home region). Even then, at any given point in time, there were never more than two powers in the subcontinent each of whom simultaneously dominated two (or occasionally three) of these five regions. In other words, ancient India was a zone of multiple polities most of whom competed for power largely in the region of their origin.

However, there are two further observations that are geopolitically salient. First, Fussman has argued that "at times, [the] Southern states were without any contact with the Northernmost ones."[27] For example, we do not know of any direct politico-military interaction between the Kushan Empire and the Cholas of the deep south even as long-distance trade certainly connected them. However, the lack of direct politico-military links cannot be reduced to a lack of interaction capacity, as the campaigns of the Mauryas and Kharavela demonstrate that such capabilities could certainly be generated when needed.

Second, while Indic polities were at the receiving end of the invasions and migrations from West-Central Eurasia, the Bactrian-Greeks, Scythians, Parthians, and Kushans were eventually "Indianized."[28] For example, the Western Shakas were the first rulers in India to use Sanskrit as a language for the expression of political power (as opposed to sacral power).[29] (The Mauryas did not use Sanskrit, as noted subsequently.) Keay has even argued that the tag of "classical" India belongs to these "non-Indian successors" of the Mauryas for their contributions to Indian culture.[30] Notably, the *Arthaśāstra*, the classical Indian text of statecraft, "was probably composed" between 100 BCE and 100 CE "during the decline of Śaka rule or the rise of the Kuśānas," even as the text's exact geographic provenance remains unknown, although it was certainly based on traditions established in the preceding centuries.[31] The *Arthaśāstra* is important for our purposes because of its approach to foreign policy and the idea of the *mandala*.

THE *ARTHAŚĀSTRA* AND THE *MANDALA*

The *Arthaśāstra*, attributed to Kautilya, "approaches interstate relations from the perspective of a small state seeking to empower itself"[32] in a geopolitical environment of multiple large and small polities with "multivalent and heterogeneous traditions of kingship and statecraft."[33] The monarch of the small state seeking power vis-à-vis his rivals in ancient India had to contend with states with different regime-types (monarchies and oligarchies) in an environment where ideas of governance were informed by multiple traditions from within and outside India (Buddhist, Brahmanical, Jain, Persian, Hellenistic, and Central Asian).[34]

Kautilya proposed the *mandala* theory of statecraft (see Figure 14.1).[35] In any given *mandala*, several rival polities (A, B, and C) competed for power as they shared borders with each other. States with common borders were considered "natural enemies," while states on the other side of the natural enemies with whom no common borders were shared were considered "natural allies." Kautilya also identified "intermediate states" (P and Q) that were located between two enemies who could help any of the rival polities (A, B, or C). Finally, there was the "distant state" (X) that was outside the *mandala*, but it was powerful enough to help any rival polity or choose to remain neutral.

The goal of statecraft for an ambitious monarch was to dominate/neutralize rivals in the *mandala*, and to acquire wealth (including territory).[36] In theory, the monarch was advised to conquer the world "to its four directions"[37] as it would achieve all of these goals. However, it was recognized that war was "unpredictable" and "expensive."[38] Therefore, international politics was driven by a search for strategies "to outmaneuver and outwit the opponent."[39] Consequently, Kautilya advocated six foreign policy strategies: initiating hostilities (war), entering into peace pacts, remaining quiet (hiding), threatening others (distracting), seeking (temporary) refuge as a subordinate of a powerful monarch, and pursuing a "dual strategy" of making (temporary) peace with one rival while fighting another.[40] In other words, these foreign policy strategies aimed at outfoxing the opponent in order to dominate him or to seek temporary truce/subordination (while searching for the opportunity to dominate the opponent). As such, the quest for interstate peace was not the dominant goal in international politics. Instead, the aim was the pursuit of political gain vis-à-vis the rival when the opportunity arose.

While Kautilya advocated the ruthless pursuit of power, his text is not without important ideational features. There were two important ideas guiding the international relations of ancient Indian monarchs in this period. First, the expanding monarch sought the status of a *cakravartin* ("paramount") ruler.[41] The concept of the *cakravartin* ruler is a multivalent idea. There is a tendency to equate the realm of the *cakravartin* ruler with the Indian subcontinent as the *Arthaśāstra* refers to the region between "the Himalayas and the sea" as the *cakravartin*'s strategic domain.[42] However, this title was not used by Ashoka to refer to himself even as his empire dominated the subcontinent.[43] By contrast, the rulers of the small(er) post-Mauryan kingdoms, most of whom remained confined to their own analytic regions, did refer to themselves as *cakravartins*.[44] As such, the idea of the *cakravartin* simply meant that the monarchs sought to expand and control translocal domains (as opposed to seeking domination over the Indian subcontinent).

Second, *dharma-vijayin* ("righteous conquest") represented the "ideal" conquest in ancient India.[45] As per the norm of *dharma-vijayin*, the conquering monarch was expected to be magnanimous in victory, seeking political submission of the vanquished (through tribute, troops, and symbols) instead of formally/institutionally incorporating the territory of the vanquished. In fact, the victor was expected to reinstate the ruler of the losing side, albeit as a subordinate monarch. Only the *asura-vijayin* ("demonic victor") seized the territory of the vanquished (at least in theory), thereby eliminating the losing state and its ruler. The incorporation of the vanquished through *dharma-vijayin* led to a form of empire-building that was obviously prone to fragmentation (when the opportunity arose). However, many *cakravartins* did formally incorporate the territories of the vanquished in practice, especially in regions close to the imperial center.

Finally, it should be noted that multiple *mandalas* of states existed in ancient India (Figure 14.2). Since the domain of strategic competition for most polities was limited only to their own "analytic region," as demonstrated by Schwartzberg, we can hypothesize the presence of five *mandalas* in ancient India (with a sixth *mandala* to the northwest of the subcontinent that directly influenced the developments in some of the other five). In other words, a *mandala* was a zone of amity and enmity over which paramountcy was sought. In theory, there were four factors that delimited the frontiers of any given *mandala*. First, the "righteous conquest" of subordinates that left them intact delimited the military reach of the domination-seeker as it became difficult to radially project power beyond the subordinates. It is well known in International Relations scholarship that a state's ability to project military power declines with distance.[46] This issue was amplified for ancient Indian polities that sought to build empires through the norm of *dharma-vijayin*.

Second, the presence or absence of physical infrastructure such as roads and riverine networks circumscribed the frontiers of a *mandala*. Notably, paramount rulers such as Ashoka paid particular attention to the creation and maintenance of such networks of connectivity.[47] Third, political relationships as prescribed by the *Arthaśāstra* (such as seeking allies on the other side of the enemies) and "marriage alliances"[48] also bounded these *mandalas*. Political factors at the level of the individual (such as Ashoka's innovative leadership discussed subsequently) could also redefine the frontiers of a *mandala*.[49] Finally, it should be noted that these factors varied over time, and therefore the limits of the Indic *mandalas* were inherently fluid.

Ancient India can then be considered as "a patchwork of overlapping *mandalas*" with continuities into Western-Central Eurasia that could "expand and contract" vis-à-vis other *mandalas* after a powerful monarch dominated his own *mandala* (which then ceased to exist) while this expanding state became a part of the neighboring *mandala*.[50] Each of the *mandalas* also contained a number of subordinate states "some of whom could repudiate their vassal status when the opportunity arose and try to build up their own networks of vassals."[51] The following two sections will respectively discuss how Mauryan domination arose out of such geopolitical dynamism, and how the *mandala* order maintained itself in the absence of hegemony/domination.

MAURYAN DOMINATION

Political Domination

Mauryan domination resulted from a combination of four causal factors. First, the onset of the idea of the transregional *cakravartin* made territorial expansion and political domination the goals of warfare in ancient India in mid-sixth century BCE. Ancient Indian states had two dominant regime types: monarchic (where decisions were made by the king) and oligarchic (where decisions were made by many in large deliberative assemblies). All ancient Indian polities began their political careers as oligarchies that only fought over status, booty, and border territory.[52] However, domestic institutions influence (and are influenced by) wars and expansion.[53] Magadha and Kosala were the first oligarchies to transition into monarchies. This regime change corresponded with their respective territorial annexation of Anga and Kasi (~550 BCE) that transformed the goal of warfare in ancient India.[54] It is very likely that the Achaemenids provided the inspiration of this "empire-model" of a "transregional" polity through territorial annexation and/or political domination.[55] After all, the Achaemenids brought all of the Northwest under their control during this period, and there was no pre-Achaemenid indigenous model of empire in India.

Second, the presence of multiple (five-to-six) *mandalas* (including some that partially overlapped and others that did not) along with the presence of multiple domination-seeking monarchies made systemic balancing difficult (at the pan-Indian level). Balancing strategies were only pursued against "local" rivals (within the same *mandala*) and not against powerful expanding monarchies in different *mandalas*. The English School has argued that the balance-of-power (as an order/systemic goal) obtains only when it is an intersubjectively held value among the system's major powers.[56] However, this understanding of the balance-of-power did not exist in ancient India where the intersubjectively held goal among the monarchs was to emerge as *cakravartin* rulers with extensive transregional domains. Notably, Kautilya's list of six strategies of dealing with other states discussed above does not include systemic power balancing (even as it allowed for temporary local/relational balancing through his idea of "natural enemies/allies").

Although it is a later text, "the *Arthaśāstra*'s principal thought of concentric, interacting polities is one that fits both the pre- and post-Mauryan times, that of the originally 'sixteen polities' of northern India and that of the re-emerging tribes and states of post-Mauryan times."[57] For example, when Magadha was expanding against Kosala and the Vajjian Confederacy in the Northeastern *mandala*, Avanti was engaged in warfare for supremacy with Vatsa in the North-central *mandala*, while Gandhara in the Northwestern *mandala* was oriented westward due to Achaemenid domination.[58] While Magadha's domination of the Northeastern *mandala* brought its rivalry with Avanti to the fore as the Northeastern *mandala* expanded and merged with the North-central *mandala*, it took Magadha "about a hundred years to subjugate" Avanti.[59] What is noteworthy here is that Avanti did not enter into an alliance with Kosala and the Vajjian Confederacy when the two had earlier allied in the face of Magadhan expansion, as the chief threat to Avanti then came from Vatsa.

In other words, while polities in ancient India did engage in external balancing strategies (e.g., the Kosala-Vajjian alliance), this happened mostly within the same *mandala*. Indian polities also engaged in other types of countervailing strategies, including co-binding and wedge strategies.[60] The Vajjian Confederacy practiced co-binding as it was a "compound republic" of several oligarchies (including Lichchhavi and Videha) that had banded together in the face of Magadhan expansionism.[61] However, Magadha sought political opportunities in the form of wedge strategies for expansion (in addition to open warfare), and eventually annexed Vajjian "not due to military defeat, but due to an effort to undermine the unity of the league."[62]

The presence of oligarchies (with their different war aims that eschewed territorial annexation or political domination) made external balancing even more difficult in a geopolitical environment of multiple *mandalas* with multiple expanding monarchies. The monarchies enjoyed a distinct advantage over oligarchies in warfare in the long run for three reasons: (i) they had a centralized decision-making process; (ii) they maintained standing armies (paid for by the state) instead of relying on armed militia or mercenaries as in oligarchies; and (iii) they maintained an efficient fiscal-administrative system (managed by state bureaucracies) instead of relying on tax farming as in the oligarchies.[63]

Third, the collapse of the Achaemenid Empire and the Treaty of the Indus between the Mauryas and the Seleucids meant that ancient India became a "closed" region of the South-West Eurasian international system after 305 BCE. As a result of this politico-military encounter, the Seleucids ceded their domains in the Northwestern Indic *mandala*—Gandhara, southern Afghanistan, and Baluchistan—to the Magadhan-Mauryan Empire.[64] Most importantly, peace was maintained along their common frontier in the northwest over the next century (until the next Seleucid encounter with Subhagasena in 205 BCE).[65] Relative peace around this frontier for almost one century is noteworthy because this had been the zone of expansion from the sixth "Far Northwestern" *mandala* into the subcontinent before the Treaty of the Indus (~550–305 BCE), and because this was also the pathway for the post-Mauryan expansion of the Bactrian-Greeks, Scythians, Parthians, and Kushans (~200 BCE–200 CE).

The "closing" of this frontier for a century (~305–205 BCE) is significant because the Mauryans emerged as the dominant power in the subcontinent during this period (~260–205 BCE). It is widely believed in IR scholarship that "open" regions tend towards balances (or system fragmentation), while hegemonies are possible in "closed" regions.[66] While there are multiple mechanisms through which external powers in "open" regions cause balancing (or system fragmentation)—from the creation of new polities to financing local alliances against expanding powers—the "closing" of this frontier and the relative peacefulness of this Seleucid-Mauryan frontier is noteworthy because the Seleucids and the Mauryas fought many wars along their other frontiers in the following decades. Arguably, the maintenance of relative peace along this frontier—the foundations for which were laid down by a politico-military encounter while the relationship was subsequently maintained through diplomacy (e.g., Megasthenes was the Seleucid envoy to the Mauryas)—allowed the Mauryas to expend their military resources towards dominating the subcontinent as opposed to fighting costly wars against other powerful extra-regional adversaries trying to make inroads into the subcontinent.

Fourth and finally, given its geographical location, Magadha enjoyed a number of strategic advantages even as no other state in ancient India had access to *all* of them—fertile alluvial soil along the northern trade route, natural/geographical defenses for its capital city, and access to iron ores and war elephants.[67] Not surprisingly, Ashoka fought the most important (and perhaps the most destructive) ancient Indian war in 260 BCE with Kalinga, a powerful regional kingdom in the peninsula that had access to war elephants and was connected with Southeast

Asia through maritime trade (although it lacked Magadha's advantages in agriculture). According to Ashoka's inscriptions, the Kalinga War killed 100,000 people while displacing another 150,000 (although these figures are certainly exaggerated).[68] The Mauryans established their domination in the subcontinent after the Kalinga War.

I choose to characterize the Mauryan regional order in the subcontinent as "domination" instead of empire, hegemony, or leadership.[69] While subordinate states cease to exist as independent actors in international politics in imperial orders, small polities continued to exist in the deep south of the peninsula and in Sri Lanka after 260 BCE as noted above. In other words, even as the Mauryan Empire was organized as an empire, it did not "have" an empire in the south.[70] Similarly, while the subordinate states pursue the goals of the superordinate actor in international affairs in a hegemonic system, this was not true for subordinate actors in ancient India where Kautilya's prescription saw subordination as temporary and advised the subordinates to pursue "dual strategies." Finally, unlike those systems where the leadership of the superordinate is recognized as socially legitimate, the subordinate states in ancient India made the decision to accept this lesser status based on considerations of relative power (as opposed to social/ideational factors). The subordinate states submitted due to the exigency of power politics as they sought to "buy time" to improve their relative position. After all, the ultimate goal for all actors, including those that were (temporarily) subordinate, was to emerge as dominant actors themselves.

Mauryan domination resulted out of the interaction of expansionist ideas, the absence of systemic balancing, the strategic "closing" of India (~305–205 BCE), and Magadhan geography. Notably, neither of these four factors was capable of producing domination alone. Despite the presence of expansionist ideas in the post-Mauryan period, a second period of domination took five centuries to emerge under the Guptas. Importantly, Gupta domination emerged in an "open" international system with the Kushano-Sassanids (and later, the Huns) in the northwest of the subcontinent, thus showing that "open" international systems are also capable of producing hegemonies/domination.[71] Similarly, systemic balancing did not emerge in the Maurya-Gupta interlude due to the presence of multiple *mandalas* and different regime types (and is discussed subsequently). Finally, post-Mauryan Magadha continued to enjoy its geographical advantages. However, neither of these four factors automatically led to (Magadhan) domination.

Ideational Domination

There were two dominant axes of Mauryan (Ashokan) domination—political and ideational. However, the limited IR scholarship on Mauryan domination has ignored the ideational dimension as it treats India as an "autonomous" international system while ignoring the connections with West-Central Eurasia.[72] Ashoka sent diplomatic envoys to the Seleucids (to the immediate northwest of his empire) and to other Hellenistic monarchs in Egypt, Macedon, Cyrene (in contemporary Libya), and Epirus/Corinth (in contemporary Albania/Greece).[73] While seeking political domination only over the Indian subcontinent, Ashoka sought system-wide ideational domination throughout the known world (in South-West Eurasia).

The Treaty of the Indus between Ashoka's grandfather Chandragupta and the Seleucids was a pact between "equals"[74] as the Seleucids ceded territory to the Mauryas (in the Northwest) in exchange for five hundred war elephants, while the two sides also entered into a marriage pact. The subsequent exchange of envoys between the Hellenistic world and the Mauryas created a world of "peer polities" in South-Western Eurasia.[75] The treaty also formally "bounded and thereby ter-ritorialized" the limits of both the Seleucids and the Mauryas for the first time.[76] Thus, the Mauryas established a finite limit to their political domination that was limited to the Indian subcontinent. Pollock has termed the Mauryan idea of "world conquest" limited politically to the subcontinent as "finite universalism"[77] because the Mauryas were not only aware of but were also in close contact with other territorially large bureaucratic polities that were literate, wealthy, and cultur-ally sophisticated.

Unlike their "finite" political universalism, the Mauryan quest for ideational hegemony was boundless and truly universal. We know that states in a system of peer polities compete over status.[78] Analogous to the Mauryan claim to finite political universality in the Indian subcontinent, the post-Alexandrian Hellenis-tic polities were also competing for finite "universal lordship" in the Hellenistic world.[79] Since the Mauryans had given five hundred war elephants to the Seleucids and the two sides maintained close diplomatic relations, it is reasonable to assume that the Mauryans were aware of the Seleucid claims in the Hellenistic world. In fact, we know that Ptolemaic Egypt also sent a diplomatic representative to the Mauryas who "acted against Seleucid interests."[80] In such a peer polity system of mutually recognized political equality (and mutually agreed territorial limits), Ashoka resorted to "social creativity" by "finding a new dimension" in which he believed he was "superior" in order to claim higher status.[81]

Consequently, Ashoka, as an "innovator,"[82] turned to the ideational policy of propagating *dhamma* ("ethics") in the known world (and beyond). Asoka's *dhamma* was a complex policy of statecraft (not to be confused with the norm of *dharma-vijayin* discussed earlier) through which he seemingly renounced war, abjured violence, promoted the socioeconomic welfare of his subjects (and even animals), and encouraged sociopolitical tolerance between different ethnic groups, thereby calling for the moral transformation of the monarch, state, and society.[83] Importantly, in his edicts that were written in four languages (Prakrit, Gandhari, Aramaic, and Greek) and scripts (Brahmi, Kharosthi, Aramaic, and Greek) that were scattered through his empire, Ashoka proclaimed victory through *dhamma* in the entire known world. In his bilingual Greek-Aramaic inscription, Ashoka referred to himself as "the ruler of all things over the whole earth,"[84] and otherwise claimed that "even where the king's envoys do not go, people have heard of dhamma and are conforming to it."[85]

In other words, Ashoka sought superior status vis-à-vis his Hellenistic contemporaries through his political ideas in a peer polity system as the domain of his ideational hegemony was system-wide (and even included those areas that were beyond direct contact). My interpretation of Ashoka's *dhamma* policy as a consequence of the geopolitics of status is distinct from the existing interpretations in the historical literature.[86] However, the geopolitics of status through which Ashoka competed with his Hellenistic contemporaries needs further consideration because it has recently been argued that their cultural competition extended into multiple domains, including script/writing and philosophical exchanges.[87] Notably, Ashoka was aware that his own rule extended over Greek and Persian peoples (where he left his edicts in Greek and Aramaic). Not surprisingly, Ashoka was convinced of his superiority over his Hellenistic contemporaries, and Basham has argued that "Asoka was the most powerful ruler of his time, and he seems to have been well aware of the fact."[88] In fact, at the peak of Ashoka's reign, the Mauryan Empire was the largest polity in the world.[89] While it may be overreaching to assert that Ashoka achieved system-wide ideational domination, I am simply arguing that unlike "finite" political domination limited to the subcontinent, the realm of Ashoka's ideational domination was truly universal.[90]

POST-MAURYAN *MANDALA* ORDER (~200 BCE–300 CE)

Magadhan-Mauryan domination was short-lived and ended by 205 BCE. India once again became an "open" region of the South-West Eurasian international system that saw new waves of conquest-migrants. The collapse of the Mauryan Empire meant that many erstwhile monarchies reappeared, perhaps due to the Mauryan form of empire-building that was informed by the norm of *dharmavijayin*. At the same time, many oligarchies formed (or reappeared), especially in the Northwest and the western Deccan.[91] These centuries also witnessed the rise of new polities in the western Deccan (the Satavahanas), while the polities in the deep south (like the Cholas and the Pandyas) flourished through maritime trade.

In other words, the five *mandalas* or "analytic regions" of the subcontinent that were the domains of strategic competition for most states (along with the sixth *mandala* in the "Far Northwest") reappeared. While most post-Mauryan states were small and had limited reach (e.g., we know of forty-two Bactrian-/Indo-Greek kings, most of whom ruled over small kingdoms in the Northwest over two centuries),[92] others occasionally forayed across the *mandalas*. For example, the Satavahanas in the West defeated Magadha (although this did not result in their political control of the Northeast), while the Kushans eventually came to control not just the Far Northwest but the Northwest and North-central *mandalas* too in addition to leading military expeditions into Magadha in the Northeast.

However, we know very little about the "international order" during this period as it has not been studied by IR scholars, although Watson dismissed it as a "patchwork quilt of independent and warring states."[93] According to Thapar, the leading historian of ancient India, even as "there appears to have been no connecting theme in the post-Mauryan period" at first glance, "there was a theme, even as it was less immediately apparent in political events."[94] Thapar highlights the spread of Buddhism, commercial dynamism, and cultural efflorescence during these centuries. It should also be noted that the *Arthaśāstra* itself says nothing about international order in this zone of multiple *mandalas* as "[w]e read nothing of how a network of such polities might be fitted into larger political frameworks,"[95] because the text ultimately deals with the foreign policy choices of a small state seeking power. Nevertheless, we can derive the broad features of the *mandala* "international order" from the discussion above by approaching international order in an explanatory sense as "partly descriptive, [and] partly normative," as noted by Aron.[96]

There were four dominant attributes of the *mandala* international order in ancient India. First, ancient India was an "open" region of the South-West Eurasian international system that enabled the injection of extra-regional (human) resources along with their ideologies of statecraft and kingship. This "opening" also promoted trade and cultural exchange between Indic polities and the world beyond. Second, during this period (~200 BCE–300 CE), ancient India was a de-centered region in terms of power politics. Unlike the period of Mauryan domination which was Magadha-centered, the post-Mauryan period did not witness the emergence of hegemony/domination. While multiple powers periodically emerged dominant within different *mandalas* during this period, it did not lead to the creation of systemic (multipolar) balances either for reasons related to different threat perceptions and regime-types as discussed previously. Notably, the intersubjectively held goal among the monarchies in the system was the quest for *cakravartin* status with extensive transregional domains (as opposed to the creation of power balances).

Although the Kushans or the Satavahanas may have risen to prominence in two or occasionally three *mandalas*, most post-Mauryan states competed for paramountcy only within their own analytic regions. Even at the peak of Satavahana, Western Shaka, and Kushan power, the system was not multipolar/polycentric because these powers did not interact directly, let alone coordinate to "run" the system.[97] Given that the geopolitical environment had polities informed by multiple traditions of governance that drew upon ideas from within and outside India, no single state (or "analytic region") emerged as the center for political ideas that radiated throughout India. In other words, ancient India was de-centered not only in terms of power politics, but also ideationally because no single state surfaced as the ideational center that provided ideas of governance that were emulated by all of the others. In the words of Pollock, India of this period represented a "geobody . . . whose center was everywhere and periphery nowhere."[98]

Third, despite this diversity, the *mandala* international order was normatively held together by ideas related to the management of power asymmetry.[99] While the subcontinent was incredibly diverse politically (and in terms of languages, religions, and ethnicities), a degree of sameness emerged in the geopolitical sphere and at the level of macro-culture. For example, the Kushan adoption of Buddhism did not require them "to give up" their own "indigenous" traditions or the patronage of other religions even as the Kushan emperor Kanishka came to be regarded as "a second Ashoka."[100] Kushan ruling ideology and imperial titles (along with the empire's languages and scripts) continued to draw upon Indic, Hellenistic, Persian, and Central Asian traditions.[101] In other words, the deep macro-cultural substratum of ancient India was supportive of political and cultural heterogeneity. Simultaneously, a degree of sameness emerged in the realm of power politics due to a multitude of factors: the threefold interaction of Buddhist institutions; long-distance trade networks, and their patronage by monarchs in addition to the spread of literacy after Ashoka; the historical memory of his rule; and the "Indianization" of the conquest-migrants.[102]

Informed by the norm of *dharma-vijayin* and the belief that wars were expensive and unpredictable, the domination-seeker sought political domination in international relations through the pursuit of various stratagems advocated by Kautilya (only one of which was war) as opposed to the elimination and incorporation of the vanquished, while the subordinate ruler thought of subordination as temporary. The aim of the subordinate ruler was to wait to seek advantage when the opportunity arose in order to become the domination-seeker (and eventually the *cakravartin* ruler). In such a system, the hierarchy between the dominant and subordinate state was linked to material power disparity and political opportunity. This hierarchy was not maintained ideationally or through formal institutions, and was quickly overthrown (or even reversed) when the opportunity arose as evidenced in the intense rivalry between the Western Shakas and the Satavahanas.[103] Fourth and finally, there were several *mandalas* in the system, some that partially overlapped and others that did not directly interact (see Figure 14.2). So local hierarchy in a given *mandala* was of no strategic importance to distant *mandalas*. However, the ideas related to the management of power asymmetry were common to all of them.

In other words, the *mandala* order represented dynamic geopolitical equilibrium where change was constant as polities frequently rose and fell within *mandalas* (and where the *mandalas* occasionally expanded and contracted). However, this change was not system-destroying because the new dominant and subordinate states were informed by the same ideas related to the management of power asymmetry (and because multiple *mandalas* continued to exist in a system supportive of political and cultural heterogeneity). Although "change" certainly existed in this system in the form of new waves of conquest-migrants, with the emergence of new polities, and due to changing patterns of trade, this was representative of change within recognizable patterns that had historical precedents even as war and conflict was endemic. At the same time, this geopolitical order was neither imposed from "above" (by the dominant state) nor was it built from "below" (by the subordinate state). Instead, it was mutually constitutive of the dominant-subordinate relationship, and emerged out of the interaction of material power, political opportunity, and ideas related to the management of power asymmetry. This dynamic order pointed towards a deep plurality of polities and cultures.

The *mandala* order should thus be conceived as self-regulating behavior that can emerge in a geopolitical environment even in the absence of a grand design or system-maker in a region with multiple large and small polities informed by heterogeneous traditions (even in the absence of a central authority over and above them). This self-regulating behavior was the outcome of the (selfish) self-interest of the dominant and subordinate states. As such, it represents a distinct type of international order compared to the better-known hegemonic, balance-of-power, and (Sino)centric systems. This order made ancient India into an open region of multiple *mandalas* (only some of which partially overlapped). The *mandala* international order was politically and normatively de-centered but was held together by ideas related to the management of power asymmetry. As in its better-known counterparts, the threat of conflict was ever-present in the *mandala* order as well. Nevertheless, the post-Mauryan *mandala* order was very durable and lasted for almost five hundred years (even as dozens of polities rose and fell and several *mandalas* expanded and contracted). The frequent conflicts notwithstanding, ancient India was economically vibrant and culturally dynamic as argued by Thapar, and in aggregate terms represented the largest economic center in the world according to Maddison.[104]

A DE-CENTERED *MANDALA* ORDER IN THE INDO-PACIFIC

One of the aims of Global IR is to develop concepts and theories from Asia's past, and have them temporally and spatially transcend the sites of their origins to provide insights into contemporary geopolitics. This is because contemporary IR has emerged out of Western historical experiences. For example, Gilpin has argued that "Thucydides' theory of hegemonic war constitutes one of the central organizing ideas for the study of international relations."[105] More recently, this idea has been repackaged as the "Thucydides's trap" to understand the emerging conflict dynamic as a result of the so-called "power transition" between the United States and a rising China.[106] While this Greek idea portends a looming conflict in the transition from American hegemony to Chinese hegemony, the *mandala* order provides us with an alternative view of contemporary dynamics.

Using the *mandala* framework, we can conceptualize the Indo-Pacific region—the primary region of the US-China strategic competition—as four (partially) overlapping *mandalas* (or subregions): South Asia, Southeast Asia, Northeast Asia, and Oceania. These four regions interact directly and indirectly to varying degrees across military, economic, and cultural dimensions. In South Asia, China and India are the domination-seekers, while the United States is trying to prevent Chinese hegemony. In Southeast Asia, China and the United States are the domination-seekers, while the region itself is trying to prevent domination by any power through the various mechanisms related to the framework of the Association of Southeast Asian Nations (ASEAN). Japan and India are also trying to prevent Chinese hegemony in Southeast Asia. In Northeast Asia, China and the United States are competing for domination, while Japan is seeking to forestall Chinese hegemony. Although Oceania has not seen such great power rivalries in recent decades, Australia and New Zealand aim to remain the region's primary powers even as the United States, China, France, and others are beginning to compete for influence. In other words, the boundaries between these four *mandalas* are fluid and variable (and may further fluctuate over time). The degree of interaction across these four *mandalas* will depend on military factors (such as wars, military bases, and logistics agreements), economic factors (such are free trade agreements and investment patterns), and political relationships (such as alliances and clientage).

Notably, the *mandala* framework prognosticates a very different regional order in contrast to the Thucydidean power transition. While there are important differences between the contemporary Indo-Pacific and ancient India (such as the presence of nationalism as a major force in world politics today even as it was absent in ancient India), the *mandala* framework is representative of isomorphism across time and space (and should not be taken literally).[107] After all, significant differences also exist between Thucydides's world and ours.

The most significant parallel between ancient India and the contemporary Indo-Pacific has to do with the nature of imperial formations. The norm of *dharma-vijayin* meant that the domination-seeker did not extinguish the vanquished polity in ancient India; instead, its subordination was the main goal. In other words, a *mandala* needs both dominant and subordinate states by definition. Similarly, in the contemporary world, the norm of territorial integrity means that "state death" has become an exception (even as border conflicts continue).[108] However, this has not stopped the domination-seekers from pursuing "informal empires" through military means (such as occupation and bases), economic coercion, and through other forms of clientelist relationships.[109] As such, contemporary domination-seekers wish to cultivate subordinate states analogous to their ancient Indian counterparts. Not surprisingly, Cooper has argued that just because "we no longer live in a world of empires, in the conventional sense, does not mean" the "demise" of empires nor "of the possibilities of turning empire into new forms of political organization."[110]

Consequently, a few characteristics of the Indo-Pacific *mandala* order are worth highlighting. First, the Indo-Pacific is an "open" region as it includes external powers such as the United States that is present in the region through alliances, forward military deployments, commerce, and culture. In this sense, the United States can be thought of as the Kushan Empire of ancient India with its genesis outside of the Indian subcontinent in the "Far Northwest" (even as it eventually expanded into the Northwest and the North-central regions, while making military forays into the Northeast).

Second, the Indo-Pacific is a de-centered region, both power-politically and ideationally. In the Northeast Asian *mandala*, the US and China are the most important power-political centers. However, Japan's strategic options preclude the characterization of Northeast Asia as a bipolar *mandala*.[111] By contrast, Southeast Asia has built a layered hierarchical order through the omni-enmeshment of all of the major powers of the Indo-Pacific: the United States, China, Japan, India, and Australia.[112] In the South Asian *mandala*, China and India are vying for geopolitical influence while the United States seems to be promoting Indian primacy.[113] In Oceania, China is in the process of emerging as an important strategic player in addition to the region's primary powers, Australia and New Zealand. At the same time, the United States, Japan, France, Indonesia, and India are paying renewed strategic attention to Oceania.[114] In other words, contrary to the belief in an incipient bipolarization of the Indo-Pacific due to the US-China competition,[115] there are multiple power centers within and across the four *mandalas* with variable reach and interests.

Similarly, the Indo-Pacific is ideationally de-centered too. In terms of domestic political models, China's authoritarian-meritocratic system is emerging as a distinct alternative to America's liberal-democratic system.[116] At the same time, consolidated "hybrid" regimes continue to exist in this region.[117] Likewise, in terms of politico-economic governance, there are at least four competing models in the Indo-Pacific: America's liberal-democratic capitalism, Japan and India's social-democratic capitalism, Southeast Asia's competitive authoritarian capitalism, and China's state-bureaucratic capitalism.[118] In other words, the region is not ideationally bipolar, nor is it America-centric. Furthermore, the Indo-Pacific is not moving towards Sinocentrism even as China will soon emerge as the largest economy in the world and the closest trading partner of almost all of the regional players. As such, political and cultural heterogeneity will remain a central regional trait.

Third, the management of power asymmetry is at the core of the emerging order in the Indo-Pacific. While the subordinate states of ancient India thought of subordination as temporary (and hoped to reverse it), the secondary states of the contemporary Indo-Pacific wish to maintain autonomy in their strategic decision-making while expanding their choices and options. According to Tellis, "many countries or regions attempting to avoid being penalized by the U.S.-China competition, seek to exploit it for their own ends, or hope to enmesh both rivals in order to promote their own interests."[119] Arguably, these ideas related to the management of power asymmetry in contemporary Indo-Pacific have emerged out of the region's historical experience with colonialism and the Cold War, and may even be embedded in the regional institutions led by ASEAN.

Fourth and finally, the Indo-Pacific is neither hegemonic nor is the region practicing systemic balance-of-power politics. The Indo-Pacific is a region with multiple domination-seekers: the United States (the declining superpower that is trying to arrest and reverse its relative decline), China (the foremost rising power), Japan (a former great power that is trying to re-emerge as a "normal" great power), and India (another rising power). As these powers joust for influence, the region's secondary states are determined to prevent the domination of any single great power by giving all of them varying stakes in regional and national affairs. Even as relational balancing exists in the region (with India balancing against China in the South Asian *mandala* and with Japan doing the same in the Northeast Asian *mandala*), no systemic balances exist in the Indo-Pacific as the "Quad" forum of the United States, Japan, India, and Australia is not a multilateral security alliance. Nevertheless, the threat of conflict is real in the Indo-Pacific and is not simply about the rise of China (as multiple states seek power and strategic advantage). In other words, a dynamic de-centered order is organically emerging in the Indo-Pacific (that is neither top-down nor bottom-up) as the domination-seekers and the subordinate states pursue their own self-interested policies.

Despite this jostling for influence, the Indo-Pacific remains economically dynamic and culturally vibrant. In fact, it is possible that this state of affairs may continue for a few decades even as the intensity of interactions across the various subregional *mandalas* changes over time, while the region avoids hegemony, systemic balances, and the emergence of a single "centric" power. It is possible that a de-centered *mandala* order is the future of this region. Whether or not things pan out this way, the larger point is that IR theoretical generalizations drawn from the ancient Indian experience can provide us with new ways of looking at contemporary geopolitics (and for explaining actual state behavior). Global IR needs to pay more attention to such de-centered orders as many leading scholars are already arguing that the post-American world order will be de-centered.[120]

ANCIENT INDIA AND CHINA

In contrast to ancient India, where Mauryan domination gave way to a de-centered *mandala* order, the ancient Chinese multi-polity system that transformed into a system-wide empire in 221 BCE was relatively long-lasting (and survived until 220 CE under the Han dynasty). There are at least three important reasons behind the different geopolitical trajectories in ancient India and China. First, the concept of "peace" was understood differently in these two civilizations. Although the quest for political peace is absent in ancient Indian textual tradition (and is missing from the *Arthaśāstra*),[121] Olivelle has argued that Ashoka sought "universal peace" in practice through *dhamma*. According to him, Ashoka's *dhamma* is analogous to the "democratic-peace" hypothesis of contemporary IR because Ashoka believed that universal peace would prevail if all polities adhered to his *dhamma*.[122] By contrast, China's multiple philosophical traditions had debated the concept of geopolitical peace centuries before the emergence of the Qin Empire in 221 BCE, and they all agreed that only such "unification" of the "civilized world" or *tiānxià* could guarantee it.[123] While a comparative study of the idea of peace in ancient India and China is warranted, it should be noted that Ashoka's idea of universal peace only emerged after his empire established its dominance although the Chinese idea of peace had been internalized over the centuries before the emergence of an all-encompassing empire.

Second, the Mauryan Empire was short-lived because the mode of empire-building was informed by the norm of *dharma-vijayin* that was prone to fragmentation as it left the vanquished rulers, states, and their traditions intact. In other words, ancient Indian empires and the *Arthaśāstra* lacked the idea of Weberian bureaucracies to govern the state.[124] By contrast, a meritocratic "recommendation system," the "forerunner of the more discerning civil-service examination system," was already in place under the Han.[125] Furthermore, empire-building in China not only included the bureaucratic incorporation of the vanquished kingdoms but also an empire-wide standardization of the "soft-technologies" of governance such as script. Meanwhile, the Mauryas used multiple scripts and languages, thereby maintaining regional differentiation. These differences are especially significant because even as "a discernable consciousness of being Chinese (called *Huaxia*)" had emerged by the time of the Warring States,[126] the "peoples" of ancient India "were never geographicized-and-politicized,"[127] and that sociopolitical equivalents of terms such as "India/Indian" did not even exist.

Third, ancient India was an "open" region of South-Western Eurasia that had been in close contact with other large, culturally sophisticated, and literate empires centuries before the emergence of Mauryan domination. By contrast, "China corresponded to the entire civilized world" after the Qin unification, and that "in its early centuries, the Chinese empire really did not confront any comparably organized governments or literate and economically productive cultures anywhere nearby," as "Rome and India were far away."[128] This made China not only "'a' civilization but the essence of civilization itself," and "[w]ithin the Chinese mental universe, there could only be a binary choice: Chinese or barbarian."[129]

A combination of the above three factors ensured the longevity of the imperial state in China and its subsequent political trajectory. The "strategic terrain" of the Chinese *tiānxià* corresponded with the "cultural core that originated with the ancient Huaxia (華夏) people," and to those who were "acculturated" through contact with them through invasions and migrations.[130] Not surprisingly, these core areas of Sinic culture have remained well-defined since ancient times even as they have gradually expanded. Consequently, "[i]nvasions from outside . . . had to be heroically resisted in defense of tianxia,"[131] although the Chinese tradition was flexible enough to accommodate the cultural outsiders who adapted and adopted the civilization of this region. By contrast, no such association between state and civilization existed in ancient India, while the Chinese (Hua) geographical *imaginaire* (to borrow a term from Echoes?). [...] the imperial genesis of the centralized ruler was mellowed [...] along [...] the idea of the *mandala* began to spread to Southeast Asia especially [...] the CE. Subsequently, India remained "open," not just in the Northwest, but also toward Southeast Asia over the following millennium.

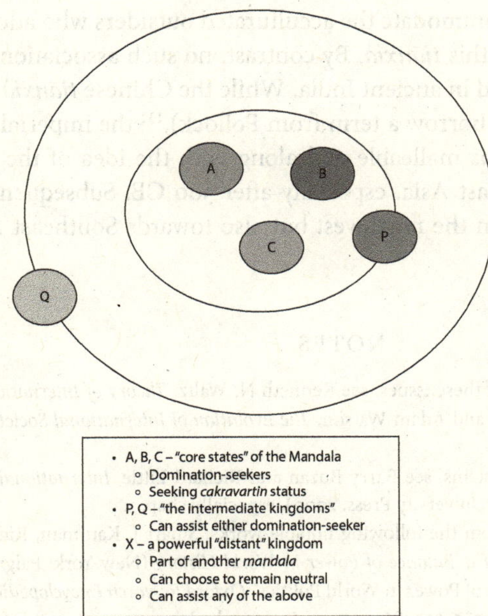

FIGURE 14.1. The Kautilyan *mandala*.

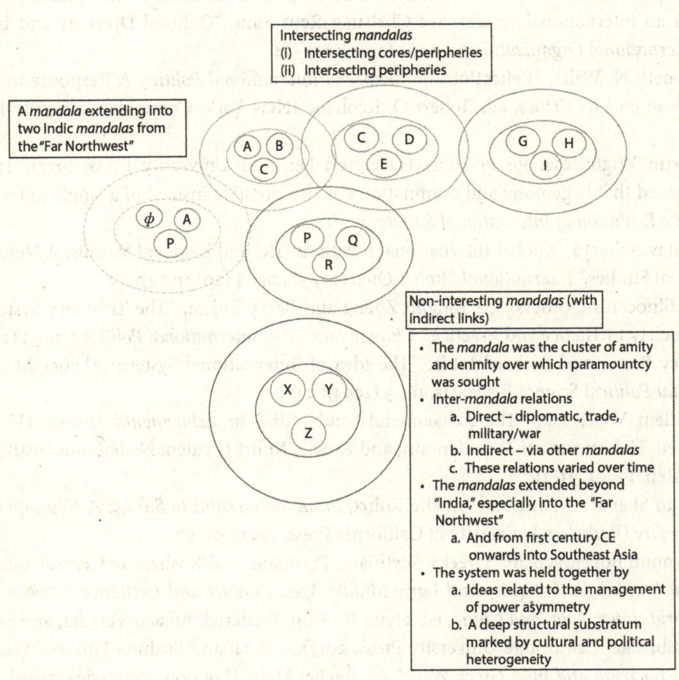

FIGURE 14.2. The *mandala* international order.

was flexible enough to accommodate the acculturated outsiders who adopted and adapted the civilization of this *tiānxià*. By contrast, no such association between state and civilization existed in ancient India. While the Chinese *tiānxià* was geographically "emplaced" (to borrow a term from Pollock),[132] the imperial geobody of the *cakravartin* ruler was malleable and along with the idea of the *mandala* began to spread to Southeast Asia, especially after 300 CE. Subsequently, India remained "open" not just in the northwest but also towards Southeast Asia over the following millennium.

NOTES

1. For the classic treatment of these issues, see Kenneth N. Waltz, *Theory of International Politics* (Reading: Addison-Wesley, 1979); and Adam Watson, *The Evolution of International Society* (London: Routledge, 1992).

2. On "open" and "closed" systems, see Barry Buzan and Richard Little, *International Systems in World History* (New York: Oxford University Press, 2000), especially chap. 3.

3. These factors are drawn from the following notable works: Stuart J. Kaufman, Richard Little, and William C. Wohlforth, eds., *The Balance of Power in World History* (New York: Palgrave, 2007); Randall L. Schweller, "The Balance of Power in World Politics" *Oxford Research Encyclopedia of Politics*, May 2016, DOI: 10.1093/acrefore/9780190228637.013.119 (accessed 9 January 2019); and Dani K. Nedal and Daniel H. Nexon, "Anarchy and Authority: International Structure, the Balance of Power, and Hierarchy," *Journal of Global Security Studies* 4, no. 2 (2019): 169–89.

4. "Deep structure" refers to the shared macro-cultural substrate or the primary "social institutions" of an international system. See Christian Reus-Smit, "Cultural Diversity and International Order," *International Organization* 71, no. 4 (2017): 873–74.

5. Kenneth N. Waltz, "Reflections on *Theory of International Politics*: A Response to My Critics," in *Neorealism and Its Critics*, ed. Robert O. Keohane (New York: Columbia University Press, 1986), 328, 341.

6. Martin Wight, *Systems of States* (Leicester: Leicester University Press, 1977), 43, 46. Later, Watson argued that hegemony and domination are also possible instead of a single universal empire. Watson, *The Evolution of International Society*, 15.

7. Amitav Acharya, "Global International Relations (IR) and Regional Worlds: A New Agenda for International Studies," *International Studies Quarterly* 58, no. 4 (2014): 647–59.

8. On Sinocentric orders, see Yongjin Zhang and Barry Buzan, "The Tributary System as International Society in Theory and Practice," *Chinese Journal of International Politics* 5, no. 1 (2012): 3–36.

9. Barry Buzan and Richard Little, "The Idea of 'International System': Theory Meets History," *International Political Science Review* 15, no. 3 (1994): 240.

10. Willem Vogelsang, "The Achaemenids and India", in *Achaemenid History IV: Centre and Periphery*, ed. Heleen Sancisi-Weerdenburg and Amelie Kuhrt (Leiden: Nederlands Instituut voor het Nabije Oosten, 1990), 93–110.

11. Susan Sherwin-White and Amélie Kuhrt, *From Samarkand to Sardis: A New Approach to the Seleucid Empire* (Berkeley: University of California Press, 1993), 91–97.

12. Osmund Bopearachchi, "Greeks, Scythians, Parthians, and Kushans in Central Asia and India," in *Eurasian Empires in Antiquity and Early Middle Ages: Contact and Exchange between the Graeco-Roman World, Inner Asia, and China*, ed. Hyun Jin Kim, Frederick Juliaan Vervaet, and Selim Ferruh Adali (Cambridge: Cambridge University Press, 2017), 251–74; and Sushma Jansari, "South Asia," in *The Graeco-Bactrian and Indo-Greek World*, ed. Rachel Mairs (London: Routledge, 2020), available at https://doi.org/10.4324/9781315108513.

13. Victor Lieberman, *Strange Parallels: Southeast Asia in Global Context, c. 800–1830, Volume 2* (Cambridge: Cambridge University Press, 2009), 656.

14. R. S. Sharma, *India's Ancient Past* (New Delhi: Oxford University Press, 2005), 147.

15. Dilip K. Chakrabarti, "Mahajanapada States of Early Historic India," in *A Comparative Study of Thirty City-State Cultures*, ed. Mogens Herman Hansen (Copenhagen: Reitzels, 2000), 382.

16. Noboru Karashima, "Beginnings of South India History," in *A Concise History of South India*, ed. Noboru Karashima (New Delhi: Oxford University Press, 2014), 30.

17. Upinder Singh, *A History of Ancient and Early Medieval India* (Delhi: Pearson, 2009), 256–471.

18. Paul J. Kosmin, *The Land of the Elephant Kings: Space, Territory, and Ideology in the Seleucid Empire* (Cambridge, MA: Harvard University Press, 2014), 31–58.

19. Kosmin, *The Land of the Elephant Kings*, 35–36.

20. Hermann Kulke and Dietmar Rothermund, *A History of India*, 4th ed. (London: Routledge, 2004), 73.

21. Kulke and Rothermund, *A History of India*, 74–76.

22. John Keay, *India: A History*, revised and expanded edition (New York: Grove, 2010), Kindle location 2597.

23. Kulke and Rothermund, *A History of India*, 74.

24. Jason Neelis, *Early Buddhist Transmission and Trade Networks* (Leiden: Brill, 2011), 113, 126, 127.

25. Craig Benjamin, *Empires of Ancient Eurasia: The First Silk Roads, 100 BCE–250 CE* (Cambridge: Cambridge University Press, 2018), 176–203.

26. Joseph Schwartzberg, "A Geopolitical Synopsis: The Evolution of Regional Power Configurations in the Indian Subcontinent," in Joseph Schwartzberg, *A Historical Atlas of South Asia*, 2nd impression (New York: Oxford University Press, 1992), 254–61. This paragraph draws from Schwartzberg's analysis.

27. Gérard Fussman, "Revising the History of Ancient India: The Need for a New Vision," Seventeenth Gonda Lecture, Royal Netherlands Academy of Arts and Sciences, Amsterdam, 20 November 2009, available at https://www.knaw.nl/en/news/publications/revisiting-the-history-of-ancient-india-the-need-for-a-new-vision (accessed 10 May 2019), 18.

28. Sharma, *India's Ancient Past*, 197.

29. Sheldon Pollock, *The Language of the Gods in the World of Men: Sanskrit, Culture, and Power in Premodern India* (Berkeley: University of California Press, 2006), 67.

30. Keay, *India*, Kindle location 2518.

31. Mark McClish and Patrick Olivelle, eds., *The Arthaśāstra: Selections from the Classic Indian Work on Statecraft* (Indianapolis: Hackett, 2012), xxxi–xxxii.

32. McClish and Olivelle, *The Arthaśāstra*, xxxii.

33. Mark McClish, *The History of the Arthaśāstra: Sovereignty and Sacred Law in Ancient India* (Cambridge: Cambridge University Press, 2019), 163.

34. On different regime-types in ancient India, see Thomas R. Trautmann, *Arthashastra: The Science of Wealth* (New Delhi: Allen Lane, 2012), 28–49.

35. Patrick Olivelle, trans. and ed., *King, Governance, and Law in Ancient India: Kautilya's Arthaśāstra* (New York: Oxford University Press, 2013), 46–51.

36. McClish, *The History of the Arthaśāstra*, 165; and Olivelle, *King, Governance, and Law*, 43.

37. McClish and Olivelle, *The Arthaśāstra*, lxxi.

38. Olivelle, *King, Governance, and Law*, 49.

39. Olivelle, *King, Governance, and Law*, 50.

40. McClish and Olivelle, *The Arthaśāstra*, 122–23.

41. Upinder Singh, *Political Violence in Ancient India* (Cambridge, MA: Harvard University Press, 2017), 31–33, 486.

42. Olivelle, *King, Governance, and Law*, 350.

43. A. L. Basham, "Asoka and Buddhism—A Reexamination," *Journal of the International Association of Buddhist Studies* 5, no. 1 (1982): 135.

44. Sheldon Pollock, "Empire and Imitation" in *Lessons of Empire: Imperial Histories and American Power*, ed. Craig Calhoun, Frederick Cooper, and Kevin W. Moore (New York: New Press, 2006), 184.

45. Singh, *Political Violence*, 318.

46. Kenneth Boulding, *Conflict and Defense* (New York: Harper, 1962), 262.

47. Jason Neelis, "Overland Shortcuts for the Transmission of Buddhism," in *Highways, Byways, and Road Systems in the Pre-Modern World*, ed. Susan E. Alcock, John Bodel, and Richard J. A. Talbert (Malden, MA: Wiley-Blackwell, 2012), 12–32.

48. Singh, *A History of Ancient and Early Medieval India*, 261. Such marriages also played a crucial role in the international relations of early modern Europe. See Daniel H. Nexon, *The Struggle for Power in Early Modern Europe: Religious Conflict, Dynastic Empires, and International Change* (Princeton, NJ: Princeton University Press, 2009).

49. For a general discussion of leadership factors in international relations, see Daniel L. Byman and Kenneth M. Pollack, "Let Us Now Praise Great Men: Bringing the Statesman Back In," *International Security* 25, no. 4 (2001): 104–46.

50. These ideas are borrowed from Wolters's scholarship on Southeast Asian *mandalas*. O. W. Wolters, *History, Culture, and Region in Southeast Asian Perspectives*, rev. ed. (Ithaca, NY: Cornell University Press, 1999), 27. Kulke has specifically called for the cross-fertilization of ideas in South and Southeast Asian history, especially the concept of the *mandala*. While the *mandala* designates "a regional kingdom" in medieval Southeast Asian historiography, it refers to a "states system" in the *Arthaśāstra*. Hermann Kulke, "State Formation and Social Integration in Pre-Islamic South and Southeast Asia: A Reconsideration of Historiographic Concepts and Archaeological Discoveries," in *State Formation and Social Integration in Pre-modern South and Southeast Asia*, ed. Karashima Noboru and Hirosue Masashi (Tokyo: Toyo Bunko, 2017), 317, 327.

51. Wolters, *History, Culture, and Region*, 28.

52. Michael Witzel, "Early Sanskritization: Origins and Development of the Kuru State," *Electronic Journal of Vedic Studies* 1, no. 4 (1995): 17; and Schwartzberg, *A Historical Atlas*, 163.

53. Stuart J. Kaufman, Richard Little, and William C. Wohlforth, "Conclusion: Theoretical Insights from the Study of World History," in Kaufman, Little, and Wohlforth, *The Balance of Power in World History*, 242.

54. Romila Thapar, "The Evolution of the State in the Ganga Valley in the Mid-First Millennium BC," in Romila Thapar, *Cultural Pasts: Essays in Early Indian History* (New Delhi: Oxford University Press, 2003), 391–92.

55. Sheldon Pollock, "Axialism and Empire," in *Axial Civilizations and World History*, ed. Johann P. Arnason, S. N. Eisenstadt, and Björn Wittrock (Leiden: Brill, 2005), 399.

56. Richard Little, *The Balance of Power in International Relations: Metaphors, Myths, and Models* (Cambridge: Cambridge University Press, 2007).

57. Michael Witzel, "Brahmanical Reactions to Foreign Influences and to Social and Religious Change," in *Between the Empires: Society in India 300 BCE to 400 CE*, ed. Patrick Olivelle (New York: Oxford University Press, 2006), 488n121.

58. Hemchandra Raychaudhuri, *Political History of Ancient India* (Calcutta: Calcutta University, 1923), 109.

59. Sharma, *India's Ancient Past*, 150.

60. On co-binding, see Daniel H. Deudney, *Bounding Power: Republican Security Theory from the Polis to the Global Age* (Princeton, NJ: Princeton University Press, 2007), 55–58. On the wedge strategy, see Timothy W. Crawford, "Preventing Enemy Coalitions: How Wedge Strategies Shape Power Politics," *International Security* 35, no. 4 (2011): 155–89.

61. William J. Brenner, "The Forest and the King of Beasts: Hierarchy and Opposition in Ancient India (c. 600—232 BCE)," in Kaufman, Little, and Wohlforth, *The Balance of Power in World History*, 99–121.

62. Brenner, "The Forest and the King of Beasts," 113.

63. Singh, *A History of Ancient and Early Medieval India*, 265–69.

64. Kosmin, *The Land of the Elephant Kings*, 33.

65. Sherwin-White and Kuhrt, *From Samarkand to Sardis*, 96–97.

66. Kaufman, Little, and Wohlforth, *The Balance of Power in World History* (especially "Introduction" and "Conclusion").

67. Sharma, *India's Ancient Past*, 149–52.

68. Romila Thapar, *Early India: From the Origins to AD 1300* (New Delhi: Penguin, 2002), 181.

69. For the classic treatment of these concepts, see Hedley Bull, *The Anarchical Society: A Study of Order in World Politics*, 3rd ed. (New York: Palgrave, 2002). There is a vast literature on these concepts, and some of the more notable contributions include Robert Gilpin, *War and Change in World Politics* (New York: Cambridge University Press, 1981); Adam Watson, *The Evolution of International Societies: A Comparative Historical Analysis* (London: Routledge, 1992); Michael W. Doyle, *Empires* (Ithaca, NY: Cornell University Press, 1986); G. John Ikenberry, *After Victory: Institutions, Strategic Restraint, and Rebuilding of Order after Major Wars* (Princeton, NJ: Princeton University Press, 2001); David A. Lake, *Hierarchy in International Relations* (Ithaca, NY: Cornell University Press, 2011); and Ayse Zarakol, ed., *Hierarchies in World Politics* (Cambridge: Cambridge University Press, 2017).

70. On the distinction between "being" an empire and "having" one, see Charles S. Maier, *Among Empires: American Ascendancy and Its Predecessors* (Cambridge, MA: Harvard University Press, 2006), 66.

71. While the emergence of Gupta domination remains to be answered in International Relations scholarship, it should be noted that the mode of extra-regional resource injection is of causal significance, and can lead to hegemonies in "open" regions. Manjeet S. Pardesi, "Mughal Hegemony and the Emergence of South Asia as a 'Region' for Regional Order-Building," *European Journal of International Relations* 25, no. 1 (2019): 276–301.

72. The ideational dimension of Mauryan hegemony is missing from Watson and Brenner's analyses. Watson, *The Evolution of International Society*, 77–84; and Brenner, "The Forest and the King of Beasts." Also see Modelski's now dated work that is more interested in the textual analysis of the *Arthaśāstra* than in empirically analyzing ancient Indian history for its theoretical insights. He also reduces ancient India to the "Hindu World" despite the prominence of Buddhism and the presence of other religious traditions. George Modelski, "Kautilya: Foreign Policy and International System in the Ancient Hindu World," *American Political Science Review* 58 (1964): 549–60.

73. Klaus Karttunen, "Aśoka, the Buddhist Samgha, and the Graeco-Roman World," *Studia Orientalia* 112 (2012): 35–40.

74. Kosmin, *The Land of the Elephant Kings*, 33.

75. On "peer polity" international systems, see Jack Donnelly, "Beyond Hierarchy," in *Hierarchies in World Politics*, ed. Ayse Zarakol (Cambridge: Cambridge University Press, 2017), 255.

76. Kosmin, *The Land of the Elephant Kings*, 32.

77. Pollock, "Empire and Imitation," 182.

78. T. V. Paul, Deborah Welch Larson, and William C. Wohlforth, eds., *Status in World Politics* (New York: Cambridge University Press, 2014).

79. Peter Fibiger Bang, "Between Aśoka and Antiochus: An Essay in World History on Universal Kingship and Cosmopolitan Culture in the Hellenistic Ecumene," in *Universal Empire: A Comparative Approach to Imperial Culture and Representation in Eurasian History*, ed. Peter Fibiger Bang and Darisuz Kołodziejczyk (Cambridge: Cambridge University Press, 2012), 67.

80. Klaus Karttunen, *India and the Hellenistic World* (Helsinki: Finnish Oriental Society, 1997), 264.

81. On "social creativity," see Deborah Welch Larson and Alexi Shevchenko, "Chinese and Russian Responses to U.S. Primacy," *International Security* 34, no. 4 (2010): 73.

82. On Ashoka's uniqueness in the contemporaneous world of his time, see Singh, *Political Violence in Ancient India*, 272–73.

83. Upinder Singh, "Governing the State and the Self: Political Philosophy and Practice in the Edicts of Aśoka," *South Asian Studies* 28, no. 2 (2012): 131–45.

84. Umberto Scerrato, "An Inscription of Aśoka discovered in Afghanistan: The Bilingual Greek-Aramaic of Kandahar," *East and West* 9, no. 1/2 (1958): 6.

85. Singh, *Political Violence in Ancient India*, 260.

86. These explanations interpret Ashoka's *dhamma* through the lenses of Buddhism, the Kalinga War, or factors "internal" to India. Nevertheless, my interpretation complements the existing explanations and can coexist with them.

87. Harry Falk, "The Creation and Spread of Scripts in Ancient India," in *Literacy in Ancient Everyday Life*, ed. Anne Kolb (Berlin: de Gruyter, 2018), 43–66; and Matthew Canepa, "Cross-Cultural Communication in the Hellenistic Mediterranean and Western and South Asia," in *Mercury's Wings: Exploring Modes of Communication in the Ancient World*, ed. F. S. Naiden and Richard J. A. Talbert (New York: Oxford University Press, 2017), 249–72.

88. Basham, "*Asoka and Buddhism*," 135. Neither Ashoka's India nor China's "Warring States" was aware of the other. Qin "unification" was completed only in 221 BCE, almost a decade after Ashoka's death in 232 BCE.

89. Rein Taagepera, "Size and Duration of Empires: Systematics of Size," *Social Science Research* 7, no. 2 (1978): 116.

90. It is often noted that the Hellenistic sources are silent on Ashoka's envoys. My interpretation based on status offers one possible explanation for this. Since Ashoka ruled over the most powerful empire of his day, silence was a prudent choice for his Hellenistic contemporaries. Acknowledgment of Ashoka's domination would have undermined their own claims of "universal domination," while challenging Ashoka may have resulted in a military showdown with him (and the loss of trade). Hellenistic silence can therefore be explained as a "cognitive" strategy to deal with the paradox of their own universal pretensions and the simultaneous existence of other powerful empires. On such strategies in a different context, see Rolf Strootman, *Courts and Elites in the Hellenistic Empires* (Edinburgh: Edinburgh University Press, 2014), 11.

91. Thapar, *Early India*, 210, 226.

92. Singh, *A History of Ancient and Medieval India*, 374.

93. Watson, *The Evolution of International Society*, 84.

94. Thapar, *Early India*, 209.

95. McClish and Olivelle, *The Arthaśāstra*, lxxi.

96. Raymond Aron quoted in Stanley Hoffmann, "Report of the Conference on Conditions of World Order: June 12–19, 1965, Villa Serbelloni Bellagio, Italy," *Daedalus* 95, no. 2 (1966): 456.

97. While the Western Shakas were in direct contact with the Kushans and the Satavahanas, the latter two interacted indirectly via the former.

98. Pollock, "Axialism and Empire," 431, 434.

99. I am grateful to Robert Ayson for extensive discussions on this issue that helped me clarify my ideas.

100. Neelis, *Early Buddhist Transmission and Trade Networks*, 137, 140.

101. Harry Falk, "Kushan Religion and Politics," *Bulletin of Asia Institute*, New Series, vol. 29 (2019): 1–55.

102. On the emergence of broad cultural commonality amidst heterogeneity, see Thapar, *Early India*, 209–79.

103. On this rivalry, see Neelis, *Early Buddhist Transmission and Trade Networks*, 126–31.

104. Angus Maddison, *The World Economy: A Millennial Perspective* (Paris: OECD, 2001), 261.

105. Robert Gilpin, "The Theory of Hegemonic War," *Journal of Interdisciplinary History* 18, no. 4 (1988): 591.

106. Graham Allison, *Destined for War: Can America and China Escape Thucydides's Trap* (Boston: Houghton Mifflin Harcourt, 2017).

107. The author would like to thank an anonymous reviewer for emphasizing this point.

108. Tanisha M. Fazal, *State Death: The Politics and Geography of Conquest, Occupation, and Annexation* (Princeton, NJ: Princeton University Press, 2007).

109. Alexander Cooley, *Logics of Hierarchy: The Organization of Empires, States, and Military Occupations* (Ithaca, NY: Cornell University Press, 2012); and Atul Kohli, *Imperialism and the Developing World: How Britain and the United States Shaped the Global Periphery* (New York: Oxford University Press, 2020).

110. Frederick Cooper, "Epilogue: Beyond Empire?," in *The Oxford World History of Empires, Volume Two—The History of Empires*, ed. Peter Fibiger Bang, C. A. Bayly, and Walter Scheidel (New York: Oxford University Press, 2021), 1274. Also see Calhoun, Cooper, and Moore, *Lessons of Empire*.

111. Barry Buzan and Evelyn Goh, *Rethinking Sino-Japanese Alienation* (Oxford: Oxford University Press, 2020), especially chap. 7.

112. Evelyn Goh, "Great Powers and Hierarchical Order in Southeast Asia: Analyzing Regional Security Strategies," *International Security* 32, no. 3 (2007/08): 113–57.

113. Frédéric Grare, *India Turns East: International Engagement and US-China Rivalry* (New York: Oxford University Press, 2017).

114. Michael Wesley, "Oceania: Cold War Versus the Blue Pacific," in *Strategic Asia 2020: U.S.-China Competition for Global Influence*, ed. Ashley J. Tellis, Alison Szalwinski, and Michael Wills (Seattle: National Bureau of Asian Research, 2020).

115. Øystein Tunsjø, *The Return of Bipolarity in World Politics* (New York: Columbia University Press, 2018).

116. Eric X. Li, "The Life of the Party: The Post-Democratic Future Begins in China," *Foreign Affairs* 92, no. 1 (2013): 34–46.

117. Thomas Carothers, "The End of the Transition Paradigm," *Journal of Democracy* 13, no. 1 (2002): 5–21.

118. Barry Buzan and George Lawson, "Capitalism and the Emergent World Order," *International Affairs* 90, no. (2014): 71–91.

119. Ashley J. Tellis, "The Return of U.S.-China Strategic Competition," in Tellis, Szalwinski, and Wills, *Strategic Asia 2020*, 32.

120. Barry Buzan, "The Inaugural Kenneth N. Waltz Annual Lecture—A World without Superpowers: Decentered Globalism," *International Relations* 25, no. 1 (2011): 3–25; and Amitav Acharya, *The End of American World Order*, 2nd ed. (Cambridge: Polity, 2018).

121. Richard Salomon, "Ancient India: Peace Within and War Without," in *War and Peace in the Ancient World*, ed. Kurt A. Raaflaub (Malden: Blackwell, 2007), 53–65.

122. Patrick Olivelle, "Aśoka's Inscriptions as Text and Ideology," in *Reimaging Aśoka: Memory and History*, ed. Patrick Olivelle, Janice Leoshko, and Himanshu Prabha Ray (New Delhi: Oxford University Press, 2012), 175.

123. Yuri Pines, *The Everlasting Empire: The Political Culture of Ancient China and Its Imperial Legacy* (Princeton, NJ: Princeton University Press, 2012), 3.

124. A. L. Basham, *The Wonder That Was India: A Survey of the Culture of the Indian Sub-continent before the Coming of the Muslims* (New York: Grove Press, 1959), 123.

125. Dingxin Zhao, *The Confucian-Legalist State: A New Theory of Chinese History* (New York: Oxford University Press, 2015), 289.

126. Charles Holcombe, *A History of East Asia*, 2nd ed. (Cambridge: Cambridge University Press, 2011), 13.

127. Pollock, "Axialism and Empire," 442.

128. Charles Holcombe, *The Genesis of East Asia, 221 B.C.—A.D. 907* (Honolulu: University of Hawai'i Press, 2001), 30.

129. Holcombe, *The Genesis of East Asia*, 41.

130. Wang Gungwu, *Renewal: The Chinese State and New Global History* (Hong Kong: Chinese University of Hong Kong), Kindle location 307.

131. Wang, *Renewal*, Kindle location 2036.

132. Pollock, "Empire and Imitation," 182.

List of Contributors

Amitav Acharya (American University)
Roger T. Ames (Peking University)
Daniel A. Bell (Shandong University)
Rajeev Bhargava (Center for the Study of Developing Societies)
Deep K. Datta-Ray (Nanyang Technological University)
Zhou Fangyin (Guangdong University of Foreign Studies)
Qi Haixia (Tsinghua University)
Xu Jin (Chinese Academy of Social Sciences)
Patrick Olivelle (The University of Texas at Austin)
Manjeet S. Pardesi (Victoria University)
Deepshikha Shahi (O. P. Jindal Global University)
Upinder Singh (Ashoka University)
Kanad Sinha (The Sanskrit College and University)
Yan Xuetong (Tsinghua University)
Zhao Yujia (Shandong University)

Founded in 1893,
UNIVERSITY OF CALIFORNIA PRESS
publishes bold, progressive books and journals
on topics in the arts, humanities, social sciences,
and natural sciences—with a focus on social
justice issues—that inspire thought and action
among readers worldwide.

The UC PRESS FOUNDATION
raises funds to uphold the press's vital role
as an independent, nonprofit publisher, and
receives philanthropic support from a wide
range of individuals and institutions—and from
committed readers like you. To learn more, visit
ucpress.edu/supportus.